THE NATIONAL INSTITUTE OF
ECONOMIC AND SOCIAL RESEARCH

Economic and Social Studies
XVI

CONCENTRATION IN BRITISH INDUSTRY

THE NATIONAL INSTITUTE OF ECONOMIC AND SOCIAL RESEARCH

OFFICERS OF THE INSTITUTE

PRESIDENT

S. P. CHAMBERS, C.B., C.I.E.

COUNCIL OF MANAGEMENT

PROFESSOR E. A. G. ROBINSON (*Chairman*)

PROFESSOR G. C. ALLEN
PROFESSOR R. G. D. ALLEN
DUNCAN BURN
PROFESSOR A. K. CAIRNCROSS
PROFESSOR C. F. CARTER
S. P. CHAMBERS
SIR GEOFFREY CROWTHER
PROFESSOR E. DEVONS
SIR NOEL HALL
SIR ROBERT HALL
PROFESSOR J. R. HICKS
W. A. B. HOPKIN
SIR DONALD MACDOUGALL
SIR JEREMY RAISMAN
W. B. REDDAWAY
THE RT. HON. LORD ROBBINS
PROFESSOR RICHARD STONE
D. TYERMAN
SIR JOHN WOODS
THE BARONESS WOOTTON OF ABINGER

THE DIRECTOR

EXECUTIVE COMMITTEE OF THE COUNCIL OF MANAGEMENT

PROFESSOR E. A. G. ROBINSON (*Chairman*)

PROFESSOR R. G. D. ALLEN
DUNCAN BURN
PROFESSOR C. F. CARTER
S. P. CHAMBERS
PROFESSOR J. R. HICKS
W. A. B. HOPKIN
SIR DONALD MACDOUGALL
SIR JEREMY RAISMAN
W. B. REDDAWAY
D. TYERMAN
SIR JOHN WOODS
THE DIRECTOR

DIRECTOR

C. T. SAUNDERS

SECRETARY

MRS A. K. JACKSON

2 DEAN TRENCH STREET, SMITH SQUARE
LONDON, S.W. I

The National Institute of Economic and Social Research is an independent, non-profit-making body, founded in 1938. It has as its aim the promotion of realistic research, particularly in the field of economics. It conducts research by its own research staff and in co-operation with the universities and other academic bodies. The results of the work done under the Institute's auspices are published in several series, and a list of its publications up to the present time will be found at the end of this volume.

CONCENTRATION IN BRITISH INDUSTRY

AN EMPIRICAL STUDY OF THE STRUCTURE OF INDUSTRIAL PRODUCTION
1935–51

BY
RICHARD EVELY
AND
I. M. D. LITTLE

CAMBRIDGE
AT THE UNIVERSITY PRESS
1960

CAMBRIDGE UNIVERSITY PRESS
Cambridge, New York, Melbourne, Madrid, Cape Town,
Singapore, São Paulo, Delhi, Tokyo, Mexico City

Cambridge University Press
The Edinburgh Building, Cambridge CB2 8RU, UK

Published in the United States of America by Cambridge University Press, New York

www.cambridge.org
Information on this title: www.cambridge.org/9781107601345

© Cambridge University Press 1960

This publication is in copyright. Subject to statutory exception and to the provisions of relevant collective licensing agreements, no reproduction of any part may take place without the written permission of Cambridge University Press.

First published 1960
First paperback edition 2011

A catalogue record for this publication is available from the British Library

ISBN 978-1-107-60134-5 Paperback

Cambridge University Press has no responsibility for the persistence or accuracy of URLs for external or third-party internet websites referred to in this publication, and does not guarantee that any content on such websites is, or will remain, accurate or appropriate.

CONTENTS

List of Tables page x

List of Figures xiii

Preface xv

GENERAL INTRODUCTION AND SUMMARY OF FINDINGS

1 The background and scope of the study 1

2 The value and limitations of concentration data 4

3 Summary of findings 8

PART I

CONCEPTS AND METHODOLOGY

I CONCENTRATION AND THE CENSUS TRADE

1 The concentration concept 25

2 The Census Trade 27

3 The indicators of concentration 32

4 The importance of small firms 34

II CONCENTRATION, INDUSTRY STRUCTURE AND PLANT STRUCTURE

1 Concentration and industry structure 36

2 The size-ratio of business units 37

3 The number-ratio and size-ratio of plants 38

III CONCENTRATION AND MONOPOLY POWER

1 Concentration and monopoly power 41

2 Factors affecting the concentration of output controlled or influenced by the largest business units 42

3 Market factors affecting output concentration as a measure of monopoly power 45

4 Conclusion 47

Part II

CONCENTRATION AND INDUSTRY STRUCTURE IN 1951

IV Concentration in 1951

1 Introduction *page* 49

2 The selection of trades for analysis 49

3 Classification of trades according to level of concentration 50

4 Concentration by broad industry groups, 1951 60

5 The distribution of employment and net output among the 220 trades, 1951 63

V Industry Structure in 1951

1 Introduction 66

2 Industry structure among the high-concentration trades 68

3 Industry structure among the medium-concentration trades 73

4 Industry structure among the low-concentration trades 77

5 Summary 81

VI Plant Structure in 1951

1 Introduction 83

2 Plant structure of trades with large differences in sizes of business units 84

3 Plant structure of trades with small differences in sizes of business units 91

4 Summary 96

VII Statistical Analysis of Factors Relating to Concentration

1 Introduction 100

2 The number- and size-ratio of business units 104

3 The average size of units and trade employment 106

4 Concentration estimated from trade size and unit size 109

5 Concentration, plant size and plants per unit 110

6 Conclusion 113

VIII THE GROWTH OF LEADING FIRMS IN THE HIGH-CONCENTRATION TRADES

1 Introduction *page* 115

2 High-concentration trades with externally expanded leading firms 116

3 High-concentration trades with internally expanded leading firms 124

4 High-concentration trades where leading firms have expanded in differing ways 127

5 Summary and conclusion 129

IX FACTORS CONTRIBUTING TO THE MAINTENANCE OF HIGH CONCENTRATION

1 Introduction 131

2 The state of trade activity 132

3 Production factors restricting entry and hampering growth in the high-concentration trades 133

4 Market factors restricting entry and hampering growth in the high-concentration trades 140

5 Summary and conclusion 143

PART III

CHANGES IN CONCENTRATION, 1935–51

X CHANGES IN CONCENTRATION: SOME PROBLEMS OF METHODOLOGY

1 The concentration-ratio and changes in concentration 144

2 The effects of changes in the definition and comprehensiveness of Census trades 145

3 The selection of trades for the analysis of changes in concentration, 1935–51 148

XI CHANGES IN CONCENTRATION AND FACTORS RELATING TO CONCENTRATION, 1935–51

1 Introduction 151

2 Association analysis 154

3 Regression analysis 160

4 Changes in plant and unit sizes and concentration for thirty-five trades with concentration-changes, and for all factory trades, 1935–51 *page* 166

5 Summary and conclusions 173

XII FACTORS CONTRIBUTING TO CHANGES IN CONCENTRATION, 1935–51

1 Introduction 176

2 The general characteristics of the 1935–51 period 176

3 The effects of World War II 178

4 Technological factors 181

5 State action 183

6 Mergers, acquisitions and joint enterprises 186

7 Other factors 190

8 Concluding comments 192

PART IV

CASE-STUDIES OF TRADES WITH CHANGES IN CONCENTRATION, 1935–51

XIII INTRODUCTION TO INDUSTRY CASE-STUDIES 193

XIV TRADES WITH INCREASED CONCENTRATION, 1935–51

1 Coke ovens and by-products 195

2 Razors and razor blades 198

3 Mineral oil refining 203

4 Watches and clocks 208

5 Metalliferous mines and quarries 213

6 Lead 219

7 Building bricks 224

8 Metal boxes and containers 228

9 Tinplate 233

10 Cinematograph film printing 240

11 Sugar and glucose 243

12 Wrought iron and steel tubes 247

13 Bread and flour confectionery 253

14 Soap 259

XV TRADES WITH DECREASED CONCENTRATION, 1935–51

1 Polishes and canvas dressings *page* 265

2 Wallpaper 269

3 Biscuit 273

4 Linoleum and leathercloth 277

5 Grain milling 281

6 Matches 289

APPENDICES

A. Glossary 293

B. Concentration of output and employment in Census of Production Trades, 1951 296

C. Frequency distribution of 147 Census Trades and 167 Sub-Trades according to degrees of specialisation and exclusiveness, 1951 313

D. Formulae for the estimation of principal product concentration 314

E. Importance of small firms 324

F. The relation between concentration, size-ratio of units and the number- and size-ratios of establishments 325

G. The selection of trades for the analysis of 1951 concentration 327

H. Average size of units and plants, size-ratio of units and number- and size-ratios of plants for 219 trades, 1951 329

I. Regression and correlation coefficients for variables in analysis of Chapter VII 334

J. Degree of comparability, gross output and estimated principal products concentration for 185 trades, 1935 and 1951 335

K. Changes in the number and average sizes of establishments and business units, 1935–51 340

L. Regression and correlation coefficients for variables in analysis of Chapter XI 341

M. Method of estimating average size of business unit for factory trades, 1935 342

General Index 343

Index of Companies 349

Index of Trades 352

LIST OF TABLES

1 Distribution of 220 trades by concentration category, 1951 *page* 51

2 High-concentration trades with employment or net output concentration-ratios of 67 per cent and over, 1951 52

3 Medium-concentration trades with employment or net output concentration-ratios of 34 to 66 per cent, 1951 54

4 Low-concentration trades with employment and net output concentration-ratios of 33 per cent and under, 1951 57

5 Concentration of employment and net output by trade groups, 1951 62

6 Frequency distribution of 220 trades according to degree of employment concentration, 1951 65

7 Distribution of the 220 trades according to degree of concentration, number- and size-ratio of units, 1951 67

8 High-concentration trades with few units and large unit size-ratios by average unit size, 1951 69

9 High-concentration trades with many units and large unit size-ratios by average unit size, 1951 70

10 High-concentration trades with few units and small unit size-ratios by average unit size, 1951 70

11 Medium-concentration trades with many units and large unit size-ratios by average unit size, 1951 72

12 Medium-concentration trades with few units and small unit size-ratios by average unit size, 1951 74

13 Medium-concentration trades with many units and small unit size-ratios by average unit size, 1951 76

14 Low-concentration trades with many units and large unit size-ratios by average unit size, 1951 78

15 Low-concentration trades with many units and small unit size-ratios by average unit size, 1951 79

16 Twenty-eight trades with large unit size-differences, small plant size-ratios and small average plants, by number-ratio of plants and concentration category, 1951 85

17 Eight trades with large unit size-differences, small plant size-ratios and large average plants, by number-ratio of plants and concentration category, 1951 87

18 Eighteen trades with large unit size-ratios and large plant number- and size-ratios, by number-ratio of plants and concentration category, 1951 88

19 Forty-four trades with large unit size-differences, large plant-size ratios and small plant-number ratios, by average plant size and concentration category, 1951 *page* 90

20 Fourteen trades with small unit size-differences, large plant number-ratios and small plant size-ratios, by number-ratio of plants and concentration category, 1951 92

21 Sixty-eight trades with small unit size-differences, small plant number- and size-ratios, by average plant size and concentration category, 1951 93

22 Thirty-nine trades with small unit size-differences, small plant number-ratios and large plant size-ratios, by average plant size and concentration category, 1951 95

23 Distribution of 219 trades by size-ratio of units and the size- and number-ratio of plants, 1951 96

24 Distribution of 219 trades by average plant size and plant size-ratios, 1951 97

25 Distribution of 219 trades by average plant size and plant number-ratios, 1951 98

26 Distribution of 219 trades according to average plant size and the relative importance of the number- and size-ratio of plants, 1951 98

27 Distribution of 219 trades according to concentration category and the relative importance of the number- and size-ratio of plants, 1951 99

28 High-concentration trades with high prevalent plant sizes, 1951 134

29 Changes in principal product concentration for forty-one comparable trades, 1935–51 152

30 Distribution of thirty-five trades according to changes in concentration and number of units, 1935–51 155

31 Distribution of thirty-five trades according to changes in concentration and size-ratio of units, 1935–51 156

32 Distribution of thirty-five trades according to changes in concentration and average size of units, 1935–51 157

33 Distribution of forty-one trades according to their changes in concentration and trade size, 1935–51 158

34 Distribution of forty-one trades according to changes in concentration and average size of plants, 1935–51 159

35 Changes in concentration, plant size and unit size for thirty-five trades, 1935–51 168

36 Changes in average size of establishments and business units for thirty-five trades and all factory trades, 1935–51 171

37 Number of units and concentration-ratios for fourteen case-study trades with increased principal product concentration, 1935–51 *page* 196

38 Capacity of major oil refineries, 1938–53 206

39 Number of units and concentration-ratios for six case-study trades with decreased principal product concentration, 1935–51 265

LIST OF FIGURES

1 Frequency distribution of employment and net output for 200 trades in 1935 and 220 trades in 1951 *page* 64

2 Correlation coefficients between concentration and other variables 104

3 The relation between concentration and employment 108

4 Correlation coefficients for changes in concentration and in other variables 160

5 The relation between changes in concentration and changes in employment 163

PREFACE

This study of concentration in British industry has been conducted at the National Institute of Economic and Social Research with the assistance of a grant made available under the Conditional Aid programme of economic research.

The objects of the project as originally conceived were to measure changes in business concentration and the private collective regulation of British industry in the last half-century, and to identify as far as possible the factors responsible for those changes. As time passed, however, the investigations began to develop along two distinct though related lines. One investigation was concerned with the analysis of changes in concentration in industry as a whole, based on the size-distribution at various dates of companies quoted on the Stock Exchange. The preliminary results of this investigation were presented in a paper to the Royal Statistical Society by Mr P. E. Hart and Dr S. J. Prais in February 1956 (*Journal of the Royal Statistical Society*, Series A, vol. 119, part 2, 1956).

The other investigation, whose results are presented in this study, was based on an analysis of the concentration-ratios indicating the shares of Census of Production Trades controlled by the largest business units in 1951. This was the concept of concentration adopted by Messrs Leak and Maizels in their paper to the Royal Statistical Society (*Journal of the Royal Statistical Society*, vol. 108, parts 1–2, 1945) which described the position in 1935. Indeed, the existence of these earlier data provided an opportunity to examine changes in the concentration of individual trades between 1935 and 1951.

Many persons have been associated with this project at different stages in its development. The conception and design of the project as a whole owe much to Dr J. B. Jefferys, who acted as its director until his departure from the Institute in the autumn of 1955. He was also responsible for the negotiations with the Board of Trade to obtain the basic statistical data for this study. Similarly, Mr P. E. Hart and Mr S. Kessler were, at an early stage in its development, concerned with the preparation of background material on individual industries.

The association of the present authors with this project began in the autumn of 1955, at a time when the statistical material was becoming available from the Board of Trade. Indeed, it is our first pleasure and duty to acknowledge the work of our predecessors, and the indispensable service rendered by the Board of Trade and its Census of Production Office in making available the necessary concentration data. It is obvious that without this statistical material the study could not have been undertaken, but it must equally be emphatically stated that the Board of Trade is responsible neither for the uses to which the data have been put nor for the conclusions drawn from the analysis.

Our thanks are also due to Dr S. J. Prais who, as statistical consultant to the project, has greatly contributed to its shape and content, and to Miss B. M. Swift who was responsible for a number of the industry case-studies and assisted in the preparation of the general material. The large amount of laborious computing has been undertaken by Mrs M. Hill and Miss B. Pye, while secretarial assistance was given first by Miss V. Farries and later by Miss A. Ruston. To them, we express our gratitude and appreciation.

We are indebted to Mr W. A. B. Hopkin, during whose term as Director of the Institute this project was undertaken, for his helpful advice and comments as the inquiry proceeded. Indeed, there are many past and present members of the Institute's staff who have contributed in this way, including Messrs A. Maizels, T. Barna, P. E. Hart and S. Kessler.

We wish also to express our appreciation to Miss Alison Clarke, Librarian and Editorial Assistant at the Institute, for her cheerful acceptance of all our demands and for her work on the proofs, and to Mrs A. K. Jackson, Secretary of the Institute, for her readiness to help at all times.

Finally, we have greatly appreciated the help given by the many organisations, companies and individuals, whom we consulted in the course of the inquiry, for almost without exception they readily responded to our requests for information and assistance.

R. W. E.
I. M. D. L.

NATIONAL INSTITUTE OF ECONOMIC
AND SOCIAL RESEARCH
January 1959

GENERAL INTRODUCTION AND SUMMARY OF FINDINGS

1. THE BACKGROUND AND SCOPE OF THE STUDY

In 1945, H. Leak and A. Maizels read to the Royal Statistical Society a paper entitled *The Structure of British Industry*.[1] This paper attracted much attention at the time, and in the decade that has since passed its contents have been repeatedly quoted. In particular, frequent use has been made of their data on the concentration of output and employment in Census of Production Trades and Sub-Trades in 1935.[2]

The measure of concentration used by Leak and Maizels referred to the share of the total gross output, net output and employment of a Census trade controlled by the three largest units in that trade. By 'unit' was meant a single firm, or aggregate of firms owned or controlled by a single parent company, control being defined as ownership of more than half the capital (or voting power) of each firm.[3] The authors were obliged to make the concentration data apply to the three largest units rather than to a small number since the Census regulations precluded the publication of particulars relating to individual concerns, and three was the minimum number needed to avoid disclosure.

The concentration-ratios produced by Leak and Maizels measured the share of trades controlled by a fixed and specified number of business units, and not the number of firms accounting for a fixed and specified proportion of the various trades. Both types of concentration-ratios have been used in other countries. For example, Dr W. F. Crowder applied the same type of measure as Leak and Maizels to 1,808 products of the United States Census of Manufactures for 1937,[4] while Dr G. Rosenbluth has applied the other measure to a selected number of trades of the Canadian Census of Manufactures for 1948.[5] Concentration-ratios for

[1] H. Leak and A. Maizels, 'The Structure of British Industry', *Journal of the Royal Statistical Society*, vol. 108, parts 1–2, 1945, pp. 142–207.

[2] The term 'Sub-Trade' is applied here to those subdivisions of Census trades described by the Census authorities as 'the specialist producers' of a particular product or group of products. In general, 'Trades' and 'Sub-Trades' are here collectively described as 'trades', retaining the individual terms for use where distinction between them is necessary.

[3] The 'firm' was defined in this instance as the aggregate of establishments under single ownership and operated under the same trading name.

[4] W. F. Crowder, 'The Concentration of Production in Manufacturing' in Temporary National Economic Committee, Monograph no. 27, *The Structure of Industry*, part v (Washington, U.S. Government Printing Office, 1941).

[5] G. Rosenbluth, *Concentration in Canadian Manufacturing Industries*, a study by the National Bureau of Economic Research, New York (no. 61, General Series), Princeton University Press, 1957.

a large number of industries in the United States Census of Manufactures have also been presented by the Department of Commerce[1] and the Federal Trade Commission[2] for 1947 and 1950.

Concentration, industry structure, and monopoly power

It is perhaps significant that the pioneer works in both the United States and the United Kingdom emphasised in their titles and their text the relevance of concentration measures to the analysis of the structure of industry. But concentration data have also been frequently used to establish the existence and extent of monopoly power in individual industries and the economy as a whole.

The connection between concentration, industrial structure and monopoly power has been summed up by Dr Rosenbluth in the following way:

> 'Economic theory suggests that concentration . . . is an important determinant of market behaviour and market results. *Ceteris paribus*, monopolistic practices are more likely where a small number of the leading firms account for the bulk of an industry's output than where even the largest firms are of relatively small importance. Hence, in the explanation of business policy, the characteristics of an industry expressed in the concentration index are likely to play an important part. This relation to the degree of monopoly has motivated most of the empirical studies involving the measurement of concentration.'[3]

The dual purpose to be served by concentration data was also noted by the Committee on the Census of Production and Distribution.[4] It expressed the view, in the first place, that 'Census data presented on the basis of firms or controlling units may be of some help to the Board of Trade in carrying out its duties under the Monopolies and Restrictive Practices Act, 1948'.[5] But this was neither the only nor the main advantage of collecting the information. More important was the contribution it could make to 'providing a more detailed picture of the structure of industry'.

[1] United States Department of Commerce, *Concentration of Industry Report* (Business Information Service, December 1949).

[2] United States Federal Trade Commission, *Changes in Concentration in Manufacturing, 1935 to 1947 and 1950* (Washington, U.S. Government Printing Office, 1954).

[3] G. Rosenbluth, 'Measures of Concentration' in *Business Concentration and Price Policy*, a report of the National Bureau of Economic Research, New York (Special Conference Series, 5), Princeton University Press, 1955, p. 57.

[4] *Report of the Committee on the Censuses of Production and Distribution*, Board of Trade, Cmd. 9276 (H.M.S.O. 1954), par. 95.

[5] Under the 1948 Act, for the conditions of the Act to apply, one-third of the supply of the goods in question has to be controlled by a single firm or two or more firms acting together. By the Restrictive Trade Practices Act, 1956, one-third is retained as the share which makes the single firm liable for investigation by the Monopolies Commission.

The scope and purpose of the present study

The present study is concerned with the structure and concentration of British industry in 1951, as well as with the changes that have occurred in a number of specific trades between 1935 and 1951. The basic material is the concentration data for 147 Trades and 200 Sub-Trades of the Census of Production, 1951,[1] which were provided for this inquiry by the Board of Trade.

It must be emphasised, however, that the responsibility of the Board of Trade ended with the provision of the concentration data. It is not responsible either for the uses to which they have been put, or for the findings and conclusions of this study. In particular, the Board of Trade has properly taken care not to identify the largest or other units in any trade. Where such identification has been attempted in this study, it has been based entirely on published material and general knowledge of the trades in question.

Apart from particular sources noted in the text, the statistical data have been taken mainly from the *Reports on the Census of Production* for various years, while the sources of the descriptive material used in the industry case-studies are described in Chapter XIII.

The main results of this study are to be found in Parts II and III, for Part II is concerned with the analysis of the 1951 concentration data and Part III with the examination of changes in concentration between 1935 and 1951. Thus, in Part II, the trades selected for analysis are first classified according to their level of concentration in 1951 (Chapter IV), and then their industry structure (Chapter V) and plant structure (Chapter VI) are examined. An attempt is next made to analyse statistically the relationships between concentration and various possible determining factors among those trades in 1951 (Chapter VII).

The next two chapters of Part II are more descriptive in character, and relate to the high-concentration trades. In the first place, we are concerned with the historical development of high concentration and the growth of the leading firms in these trades (Chapter VIII), and next with the factors that have contributed to the persistence of high concentration over time (Chapter IX).

Turning to changes in concentration between 1935 and 1951, Part II begins with a discussion of the main methodological problems involved and the basis on which trades are selected for this exercise (Chapter X). Next comes a statistical analysis, analogous to Chapter VII, of some of the relationships that might be expected to hold between concentration-changes and changes in the factors relating to concentration (Chapter

[1] These basic data are presented in Appendix B: for most trades, the concentration-ratios refer to the share of the three largest units, but where there is a risk of disclosure by this measure, the number of units is larger than three.

XI). Since the explanation is incomplete on this basis, a more detailed examination of a selection of trades with concentration-changes was undertaken, and from the resulting series of case-studies (which form Part IV of this study), a number of contributory factors are identified and discussed in the final descriptive chapter of Part II (Chapter XII).

Before proceeding to summarise the main findings of Parts II and III, it is important to discuss some of the general problems attaching to the use of concentration data based on Census of Production trades. These problems are dealt with at some length in Part I, but their nature and consequences can now be briefly stated in the following section.

2. THE VALUE AND LIMITATIONS OF CONCENTRATION DATA

The measurement of concentration, particularly where monopoly power is under investigation, should refer to a group of products which are close substitutes in the market. But the Census trade, to which the concentration data of this and similar studies relate, is primarily defined from the side of supply. That is, the principal products that comprise it are likely to be either of a similar nature or capable of being produced by the same technical processes and facilities. Thus, the extent to which the principal products of a Census trade are in fact close substitutes in use is somewhat fortuitous.

Moreover, the aggregation of establishments to form a Census trade inevitably means that there will be included, in the output of those establishments to which the concentration data refer, products which are classified as characteristic of other Census trades. Similarly, not all the output of the principal products of a Census trade will be produced in the establishments classified to it. As a consequence, the concentration-ratio refers not to the entire output of a group of close substitutes nor yet to the entire output of the principal products characteristic of the Census trade, but to a conglomeration of products, some principal but others subordinate, that happen to be produced in the establishments classified to the trade.

Even where a Census trade approaches the ideal—that is, where the principal products are close substitutes in the market, and the establishments classified to it produce the entire output of those principal products and little else—the concentration-ratio cannot stand alone as an indication of the structure of that industry. Among other things, the number of concerns that comprise it must also form part of any adequate description or analysis of the industry. Fortunately, details of the number of business units are available for Census trades in 1951 though not in general for 1935, so that our description of industrial structure in 1951 is improved to that extent.

Even so, relative sizes of all the concerns in a Census trade cannot be established from the concentration-ratio. In particular, considerable differences may exist in the individual share of the largest units, which may be significant for the structure of the industry, or monopoly power. They may all be of much the same size, two may be much larger than the third, or one of them may be very much larger than the other two. Such variations in size are concealed by a single concentration-ratio.

In addition, the concentration-ratio, even for the ideal Census trade, does not refer to the total supply of a trade's principal products in the home market; for this account must be taken of imports and exports.

Moreover, determination of the degree of concentration of domestic supply is only the first step in any assessment of monopoly power. A high degree of concentration may be offset by factors arising from the demand side of the market, including potential competition from new products or near-substitutes, and elements of countervailing power. On the other hand, geographical segmentation of the market may mean that the concentration-ratio for the national market underestimates the degree of control exercised in particular localities by various concerns. Besides, monopoly power may sometimes be acquired by agreements between independent business units, even in an industry with a relatively low degree of concentration. Looser degrees of association between firm and firm, such as interlocking directorships and exchanges of shares, are also left out of account.

The value of concentration data

Bearing all these qualifications in mind, it may well be asked: why bother with concentration-ratios at all?

The answer is that any practical study of monopoly or competition, or of market behaviour in general, must almost inevitably start with an examination of the relative sizes of firms, or parts of firms, divided into groups in some way or other. But no such group of firms can ever be ideal. If the lines are so drawn that few firms are included in the group, then firms will be excluded which are significantly competitive with at least some of those included. If the net is cast wider, then firms are included in the group which are scarcely competitive at all with some, or even many, others in the group.

At one extreme, it is possible to study the relative sizes of all firms in the economy, or of a very large group drawn regardless of industrial classification. But a group of this kind is clearly too large to be ideal for the purpose of indicating the presence or absence of monopoly power. For instance, although the size-difference of the firms in the group as a whole may have increased, it is possible that if they were arranged into smaller groups according to product-substitutability, then their size-differences would have decreased in most, or even all, cases. At the other extreme, it might be desired to draw a line round a single firm if its product was one for which there was no close substitute.

If the Census of Production were arranged solely for the purposes of assessing the degree of competition or monopoly, it is obvious that fewer reservations would be necessary. But it is important to realise, first, that no possible arrangement would be ideal, and secondly, that some arrangement is essential in order to study problems of competition and market behaviour at all.

There is no doubt that much more narrowly defined trades than those of the Census would often be more appropriate. Studies, such as those of the Monopolies Commission, relating to the supply of a specific group of products may shed more light on monopoly, and on some kinds of market behaviour, but they cannot be undertaken over the whole range of industry.

Moreover, the limitations of the Census classification do not apply with equal strength to all trades. Some concentration-ratios, for trades whose output is very heterogeneous, mean very little. But other Census trades are fairly close to being well defined competing groups of firms. If trades are rejected where too great a proportion of the principal products is produced elsewhere, or the principal products account for too little of the trade output, or where the principal products are not really competing products, analysis of the rest can proceed with more confidence that the results will have some economic significance. Such selection has been practised in this study.

Even so the study of the concentration of Census trades is only a first step towards any full appreciation of the elements of monopoly and competition in our economy. It cannot be expected that any very secure knowledge of these elements can be culled from the few figures relating to the size structure for each trade which have been available for use.

All the same, the concentration-ratios are a useful starting point in any analysis of the structure of individual industries, for they provide a rough-and-ready guide to the potentialities of the market situation: monopolistic practices are more likely to be present, in the absence of cartel agreements, where concentration is high than where it is low.

Further uses of concentration-ratios

Economists have also found other uses for concentration-ratios. Adventurous sorties have been made into the territory of international comparisons of concentration data, both for individual industries and the economy as a whole, and of changes in concentration in a single country over a period of time.

International comparisons of concentration (which are not attempted in this study) are seemingly prompted by a desire to establish whether industries have roughly the same level of concentration in different countries, and whether the factors associated with high concentration are common to all, as well as to determine whether one economy is more or less 'competitive' than another.[1]

Comparisons over time are concerned with trends in concentration, again for individual industries as well as the industrial sector as a whole, both as a check on the effectiveness of anti-monopoly measures[2] and in order to establish the factors contributing to concentration changes.[3]

Both extensions of the use of concentration data involve problems of their own, quite apart from the qualifications attaching to the concentration-ratio itself. International studies demand that the trades to be compared be, in fact, comparable; often, though they are superficially similar in name or description, they differ in their product composition. In addition, it is sometimes necessary to reconcile the concentration-ratios of the two countries: as, for example, when the concentration-ratios for the United States refer to the four largest units and the United Kingdom data to the three largest.[4]

There is a comparability problem too in assessing changes of concentration over time. The definition and composition of Census trades may be different at the two dates, and this severely complicates comparison of concentration-ratios, as will be seen from the discussion of Chapter X. A further difficulty is that whereas a trade's concentration-ratio may be the same at two dates, the identity or rank of its largest units may have altered. It is important that this size-mobility of firms should be known, for changes in rank suggest that conditions in the trade are more dynamic than would otherwise have been supposed from its unchanged concentration-ratio. But since the concentration-ratio does not reveal the identity of the largest units at either date, it is impossible to say by comparing them whether or not the leading concerns have changed.

Only an examination of each trade individually will reveal whether or not the circumstances suggested by the change in the concentration-ratios accord with reality, and also establish the nature of the forces con-

[1] Cf. G. Rosenbluth, 'Measures of Concentration', p. 70: 'It is often said that the British economy is less competitive than that of the United States and it is of interest to see whether there is any basis for such a view in the size structure of business firms.'

[2] See United States Joint Committee on the Economic Report, *Statistical Gaps*, 1948, quoted in Federal Trade Commission, *Changes in Concentration in Manufacturing, 1935 to 1947 and 1950* (Washington, 1954), p. 2; 'Congress, the administrative agencies, and the general public should be supplied with a continuing body of information which would show the level or extent of economic concentration in the various industries, as well as the changes which have occurred and are constantly taking place. Data of this type are essential to formulate and implement policies and programs in this area.'

[3] See Federal Trade Commission, *op. cit.* ch. IV, pp. 50–61.

[4] See G. Rosenbluth, 'Measures of Concentration', pp. 70–7.

tributing to concentration-changes. That is the purpose of the twenty short case-studies in Part IV. Eventually, by more detailed studies, it might be established more clearly to what extent a limited knowledge of the size structure of the trade—such as the concentration-ratio and number of business units provide—is a guide to the kind of market behaviour to be expected or the degree of monopoly power prevalent in the trade.

3. SUMMARY OF FINDINGS

In summarising the main findings of this study, it is convenient to follow the later arrangement and present them under two main headings: first, concentration and industry structure in 1951; and second, changes in concentration between 1935 and 1951.

(a) *Concentration and industry structure in 1951*

Although concentration data are available for 147 Trades and 200 Sub-Trades of the Census of Production, 1951, it is necessary to begin by removing some of them from the analysis. The main purpose of selection is to ensure that the concentration data are reasonably meaningful, and to avoid duplication as between Trade and constituent Sub-Trades. As the result of applying certain rules of selection which are described in Appendix G, we are left with 220 trades (with an aggregated employment of nearly 6,370,000 or just under three-quarters of the total for the 147 Census Trades) on which to base our analysis. Lack of comparable data, however, requires the omission of one of these trades when we come to examine industry and plant structure and, by means of regression analysis, the factors affecting concentration.

(i) *Industry concentration in 1951*

In Chapter IV, the 220 trades are classified, according to their employment or net output concentration-ratios, into three categories of concentration:

1. High concentration (67 per cent and over)
2. Medium concentration (33–66 per cent)
3. Low concentration (33 per cent and under)

On this basis, there are fifty high-concentration trades in 1951, but their combined employment is only one-tenth of the total labour-force in the 220 trades. Some of them are small and comparatively unimportant trades, like Incandescent Mantles which employs only 800 persons. But it is by no means the case that all the most highly concentrated trades are small, for there are eight which combine a labour-force of more than 10,000 with concentration-ratios of more than 80 per cent, namely:

Explosives and Fireworks	Cement
Cotton Thread	Motor Cycles, etc.
Photographic Plates and Films	Valves and Cathode Ray Tubes
	Mineral Oil Refining
Sugar and Glucose	

The high-concentration trades are very varied in their type of activity, and since they are all the more interesting for that reason, their characteristics are later studied in greater detail.

The sixty-nine trades with medium concentration account for less than one-quarter of the total labour-force in the 220 trades, although they represent nearly one-third of the total number. There are, however, large differences in the sizes of these trades. The smallest, in terms of both the number of units and employment, is the Ice trade (where fourteen units employ 600 persons), while the trade with the largest number of units (375) is Textile Machinery and Accessories, and that with the largest labour-force (157,500) is Aircraft Manufacture and Repair.

Finally, there are 101 trades with low concentration and together they account for roughly two-thirds of the total employment. Among them are to be found such large trades as New Building Construction (with 404,000 persons employed), Iron and Steel (Melting and Rolling) and Shipbuilding and Ship Repairing (both with more than 200,000). Even so, while there are ten trades with more than 100,000 employed, there are twenty with less than 10,000.

When the 220 trades are classified according to broad industry groups instead of categories of concentration, it is possible to estimate a concentration-ratio for each industry group. This group concentration-ratio is obtained by weighting the employment (or net output) concentration-ratio for each trade by that trade's employment or net output. While too much importance must not be attached to these group concentration-ratios because of the large arbitrary element embodied in their calculation, it is found that the industry groups with the highest and lowest employment concentration are:

Highest	*Per cent*	*Lowest*	*Per cent*
Chemicals and Allied Trades	51	Building, Contracting and Civil Engineering	12
Electrical Engineering and Electrical Goods	48	Clothing and Footwear	14
Vehicles	41	Woollen and Worsted	18

Although its significance is limited, an overall degree of concentration is also calculated for the 220 trades taken together. This weighted average is 29 per cent in terms of employment and 33 per cent in terms of net output in 1951. A similar overall employment concentration-ratio of 26 per cent was given by Messrs Leak and Maizels for 1935. It does not follow, however, that concentration over industry as a whole rose by the 3 per cent difference between 1935 and 1951, or even rose at all, since the trades are not always individually comparable and some included in 1935 have been excluded in 1951. It is impossible, therefore, to reach any definite or clear-cut conclusion about the change in the level of concentration in British industry between 1935 and 1951.

(ii) Industry structure in 1951

When a trade's degree of concentration is associated with the number of its business units and the relative size of those units, it becomes possible to determine its type of industry structure. The combination, for example, of high concentration, a small number of units and a large size inequality suggests that the trade in question is dominated by one or two large concerns. There are, in fact, twenty trades which possess such strong monopolistic elements, and these are identified in Chapter v. But since they are generally small trades, their combined employment only represents 3 per cent of the total labour-force in the 219 trades.

For another thirty-two trades, the units are few and comparatively equal in size, and since all of them have medium or high concentration, the conditions seem favourable for collusion though active and fierce competition (of an oligopolistic kind) may actually prevail. But again, these trades are small, accounting for only 5 per cent of total employment.

A more typical structure, found in thirty-eight trades with more than 21 per cent of the total labour force, is where there are a few relatively big concerns (reflected in high or medium concentration) and a large number of smaller units. Tacit collusion, or price leadership, is likely to be a common form of market behaviour in such circumstances.

The structure of the other twenty-nine trades with medium concentration is possibly more competitive (since there are many units without great size-differences between them), but it is still conceivable, particularly in a collectively organised trade, that the largest units will have considerable influence. But, because they are relatively small, these trades account for only 6 per cent of the total labour-force.

While low concentration makes competition more probable, it is unlikely to be perfect competition in the economist's sense if some concerns are absolutely as well as relatively large. Given that an average employment per largest unit of more than 2,500 indicates their presence, giant concerns are to be found in twenty-two (out of forty) trades where the unit size-differences are large, and in four (of the sixty) trades where size-differences are small. These twenty-six trades account for nearly 38 per cent of total employment.

Conditions in the remaining seventy-four trades (with some 25 per cent of total employment) are probably close to those of perfect competition, provided that there is no collective regulation.

All in all, therefore, it appears that while there are only comparatively few trades with very strong monopolistic elements in their structure, it is also true that something approaching the perfectly competitive type of structure is only found in trades with about one-quarter of the total employment. By far the largest proportion of total employment is represented by the trades where conditions are suitable or even favourable for tacit or open collusion, or where the largest units have, by virtue of their absolute size, considerable influence.

Finally, despite the fact that the average size of units is small (that is, less than 250 persons per unit) in more than three-fifths of the 219 trades the largest units are frequently not only relatively much larger than the others, but also very large in absolute terms. Thus, giant concerns (as defined above) are to be found in twenty-seven of the 138 trades with small average unit size, and in seventy-three out of the total number of trades. Moreover, employment per largest unit was more than 10,000 persons in ten trades, and between 5,000 and 10,000 in another twenty-one.

(*iii*) *Plant structure in 1951*

In Chapter VI, we are concerned with examining the plant structure of the 219 trades in 1951 in order to try to answer two important questions. First, to what extent are the size-differences between the units due to technological, commercial and other factors which affect the number and size of plants operated by different business units? Second, what is the ease or difficulty of entry into the various trades?

There are ninety-eight trades where large differences, by our definition, exist between the average size of the three largest units and the average size of the rest, compared with 121 where such differences are small.

Among the ninety-eight trades where the units differ greatly in size, there are thirty-six in which the difference in the size of plants operated by the largest three units and the rest is nevertheless small. The absence of substantial technological economies of scale, whether due to a demand for a variety of products or other reasons, combined with high transport costs or other locational factors, would appear to limit the size of plant in twenty-eight of these thirty-six trades. Multi-plant operations (in order to achieve managerial or commercial economies) are a condition of growth for individual firms in such trades, and for all but four of them there are large differences in the number of plants operated by the largest and the other units. But in eight trades where concentration is medium or high, amalgamations probably aimed mainly at controlling a large share of the trade have also increased the number of plants operated by the largest units. For the remaining eight of the thirty-six trades with small plant-size differences, the average plant size is large. In such cases, where all or most of the plants in a trade tend to be large, it is probable that technological economies are of considerable importance in determining plant size. Moreover, where the largest units also have a large number of plants in such trades, amalgamations for the sake of controlling the market, important commercial economies, or vertical integration probably constitute the main explanation.

For the majority of the trades with large differences in unit size, there are also large differences in the size of plants. This large plant-size disparity accounts almost entirely for the difference in unit size in forty-four of these sixty-two trades. Yet in thirty-two of these cases the average plant size is small, so that while the largest units employ mass-production techniques, the small plants, serving more specialised or limited territorial markets, still predominate. For the other twelve trades where the average plant size is large, the technical economies of scale are no doubt even more marked in the plants of the largest units, and it is probable that the small plants are mostly on the periphery of a rather heterogeneous trade. In the remaining eighteen trades, the large differences in unit size are due to the fact that the largest units operate both considerably more plants and considerably larger plants than the rest. Product heterogeneity probably again accounts to a great extent for the differences in plant size, while differences in the number of plants operated may be attributed to differences in product-range or commercial economies between firms.

Among the 121 trades with only small differences in the sizes of the business units, there are nevertheless fourteen in which the largest units have a relatively large number of plants, and thirty-nine others in which the relative size of their plants is large. Among the fourteen trades multi-plant operation is again a condition of growth (as in the case of twelve trades where average plant size is small), or commercial economies or merger activity are important. But multi-plant operation is evidently at a discount for the thirty-nine trades, in all but five of which the average plant size is also small, so that despite the plant size-difference entry is likely to be easy. In the remaining sixty-eight trades, the relative size of the largest units, and the relative size and number of the plants they operate, are all small. For fifty-two of the sixty-eight trades the average plant size is also small, so that technical and commercial economies of size are not likely to be important in their case. On the other hand, technical economies are probably very important, and constitute a substantial obstacle to entry, in most of the remaining sixteen trades where the average plant size is large, while for some, commercial economies may also be substantial.

By way of summary it may be stated that there are only small differences in the relative size and number of plants of the largest units compared with the rest in seventy-four (or one-third) of the 219 trades, while both differences are large in only eighteen cases. The largest units have much larger plants, but not many more plants, in eighty-three trades, while the reverse holds for forty-four trades.

There does not appear to be any association between the more important of the two factors and the average size of plants in either case. But there would appear to be some slight association between the relative importance and concentration; concentration tending to be higher when the relative size of plants is the more important, than when the relative number of plants predominates.

Technical economies of scale may be a factor governing the size of plant and conditioning entry in twenty-six trades, while locational, transport and demand factors which limit the size of plant, and keep entry easy, operate in ninety-two trades. While the largest plants enjoy technical economies of scale in another twenty-four trades, small plants, perhaps reflecting the product-heterogeneity of these trades, can still exist. For the other seventy-seven trades, while there are substantial variations in the scale of production between plants, entry will be even easier.

Multi-plant operation is an important factor in the activities of the largest units in sixty-two trades, and may be regarded as a condition of growth for most of the forty-seven trades where average plant size is small, and as evidence of commercial economies or combination for control in the other fifteen. Finally, we must note that the apparent precision of the above figures should not be taken too seriously, since they result from drawing arbitrary lines, whereas, in reality, all the distinctions we make shade into each other.

(iv) *Statistical analysis of factors affecting concentration*

So far the concentration data have been used, in conjunction with Census of Production material, to analyse the structure, in terms of units and plants, of the 219 trades in 1951. But the same two sets of data can also be used to explore the relationships that may exist between concentration on the one hand, and the various factors, like the number and average size of units or plants, which may possibly determine concentration on the other. Although regression analysis, conducted in terms of the logarithms of the variables, establishes strong associations between concentration and certain variables *among* the trades in 1951, it is necessary to be cautious (as always) in drawing causal inferences from these cross-sectional relationships. Moreover, the variables are all affected by Census practice; and in view of the fact that certain mathematical relationships exist between them, care must be taken to avoid tautologies in discussing the results of the regression analysis.

The first relationships examined are between concentration, the number of business units, and the size-ratio of business units, the latter variable being now defined, for the purpose of this analysis, as the average employment of the three largest units divided by the average employment of *all* the units. It is found, in common with comparable investigations in other countries, that there is a strong negative correlation (−0·83) between concentration and the number of units, and that, on the average, a trade with 10 per cent fewer units than another will have 5 per cent lower concentration. There is also a moderately strong negative correlation (−0·40) between concentration and unit size-ratios, but since the number and size-ratios of units are themselves highly correlated (+0·84), it is impossible to say which is the more important in accounting for the variations in concentration.

Moreover, the number of units and the size-ratio are not only definitionally related to concentration, but they are also variables whose values cannot be any better explained in economic or technological terms than can concentration itself. The same is not true of unit size or trade size, for these are undoubtedly influenced by technology, market conditions, and demand. This makes the manner in which they are related to concentration more interesting. Similar considerations also apply to plant size and the number of plants per unit.

There is a good positive correlation (+0·63) of average unit size with concentration. If the average size of units is regarded as an independent variable, it may act on concentration either through the number of units or the size-ratio of units, with both of which it is negatively correlated. But again the high correlation between unit numbers and size-ratios precludes any distribution of its influence.

Trade employment is also negatively correlated with concentration (−0·42), and it may reasonably be assumed that any causal relation between the two works from employment to concentration. The explanation of this correlation would appear to be that the tendency for larger trades to have more units (+0·66), and thereby less concentration, outweighs the tendency for them also to have larger units (+0·24) and thereby more concentration. Thus, the negative correlation between employment and concentration results mainly from the fact that the number of units rises in greater proportion than the size of units as employment increases.

Taking both trade size and unit size as possible causal factors in concentration, multiple regression analysis yields the result that a 10 per cent increase in unit size (keeping trade size constant) is associated with a 6 per cent increase in concentration; and a 10 per cent increase in trade size (keeping unit size constant) with a 4 per cent decrease in concentration. Moreover, these two variables together explain (in the statistical sense of the word) 72 per cent of the variation in concentration.

The average size of units in a trade is, however, the same as the average size of plants multiplied by the number of plants per unit for the trade. If average plant size is taken to reflect technological factors, and plants per unit, transport costs, commercial economies, as well as concentration for the sake of control, it is obviously important to examine their respective associations with average unit size and concentration.

In the first place, it is discovered that unit sizes vary more than plant sizes *between* trades; indeed, the size of plants is positively correlated with the number of plants per unit (+0·34). The latter association suggests that the initiating cause of an increase in concentration is often a fall in the number of units (due to merger or acquisition) which is followed by reorganisation and the rationalisation of production in larger plants, and this hypothesis is supported by the experience of several trades. At the same time, it is plant size rather than plants per unit that is the more important factor affecting unit size, for a 10 per cent increase in unit size consists, on the average, of a 8·6 per cent increase in plant size and a 1·4 per cent increase in plants per unit. Moreover, since the plants-per-unit factor varies only slightly about its average value for all trades, it can be dismissed as an unimportant part of any explanation of concentration.

Average plant size is, on the other hand, fairly highly correlated (+0·60) with concentration. Indeed, it alone explains 36 per cent of the variation in concentration (compared with the 40 per cent by unit size), and, together with employment, the proportion explained is 67 per cent. This proportion remains the same even when the size-ratio of plants—defined here as the average size of the plants of the three largest units divided by the average size of all plants—is also taken into account. But when the number of plants operated by the three largest units is substituted for the plant size-ratios, the proportion rises to 76·5 per cent, so that the further contribution of this factor—which may reflect transport factors and commercial economies as well as concentration for concentration's sake—amounts to about 9 per cent.

To sum up, it can be stated that among the 219 trades in 1951, concentration is negatively correlated with trade size and the number and size-ratio of units, and positively correlated with the average size of units or plants. Both plant size and unit size account for 35–40 per cent of the variance in concentration, and when coupled with trade size, the former accounts for 67 per cent and the latter 72 per cent. The proportion of concentration variations explained is, however, raised to three-quarters by combining plant size, the number of plants of the three largest units, and trade employment. Finally, the effect on concentration of a given percentage change in one of these three factors, independently of changes in the other two, is greatest in the case of plant size; a 10 per cent increase in plant size resulting in a 7 per cent rise in concentration, compared with a 5 per cent fall or a 3 per cent rise in concentration from the same percentage increase in trade size or the plants of the largest units respectively.

(v) The high-concentration trades

We have already noted that trades with high concentration are in a minority and that they account for only one-tenth of the total labour-force in the trades surveyed. By this token, they are relatively less important than trades with lower concentration, but since the strongest elements of monopoly are likely to be found among the high-concentration trades, it is interesting to examine them in some detail.

There are a number of questions that immediately spring to mind. How did high concentration develop in these trades, when did it emerge, and what factors were responsible? Again, why and how has high concentration been maintained since it emerged?

The first set of questions is considered in Chapter VIII, where the high-concentration trades are examined from two points of view: first, according to the growth pattern of the leading firms (whether they have grown by internal or external expansion, or a combination of both); and second, whether the number of firms in those trades was once large or has always been relatively small.

All the trades where the leading firms have grown principally by external expansion were once much more heavily populated than they are today. But it is possible to distinguish three main ways in which the leading firms have grown and the number of concerns has been reduced. In the first place, there have been amalgamations, involving a large number of firms, which were prompted by severe price competition in trades with surplus capacity, such as wallpaper, salt, and cement. Secondly, there have been mergers between firms which were already relatively large, either because combination was preferred to competition (as for matches and transmission chains), or because the actual or potential contraction of the trade made combination desirable (as for explosives, incandescent mantles, tin and zinc). Thirdly, there has been the more protracted process of piecemeal acquisition by one or more firms until they attained a position of dominance in their trade. Spirit distilling, scales, and soap are examples where one firm has initially been largely responsible for concentrating the trade, while for fertilisers, wrought iron and steel tubes, motor cycles, linoleum, and tinplate, concentration has been associated with the growth of more than one concern.

Turning next to the high-concentration trades where the leading firms have grown primarily by internal expansion, it is usually the case that the number of concerns in such trades has always been small. Where the number of firms once was (or still is) large, the largest firms usually owe their size to the exploitation of new techniques or new products which gives them a distinct advantage over the other concerns: razors and ice cream are cases in point. For the rest, the relatively small number of firms through the trade's history may be explained by the fact that they are relatively new industries, or that entry has always been difficult. Either way, the leading producers have grown with the trade or entered it on a large scale, with the result that it has always been highly concentrated; examples are rubber tyres, rayon, mineral oil refining, and asbestos cement goods.

Finally, there are the trades where the leading firms have grown in different ways: some by acquisition and merger, some by internal expansion. Once again, the number of firms may once have been large (as in the case of starch, photographic plates and films, bicycles, and seed crushing) or have always been small (as in the case of cinematograph film printing, and valves and cathode ray tubes).

For the majority of high-concentration trades in 1951, the leading firms have grown primarily by external expansion. Moreover, although the tendency for firms to grow by merger and acquisition has not been confined to any one period of time, amalgamations appear to have been most frequent fifty to sixty years ago, and again in the 1920's, when surplus capacity plagued many industries. Thus, high concentration dates back several decades for many of the trades which still enjoyed that distinction in 1951.

The tendency for high concentration to persist, combined with the fact that once a firm has become one of the leaders in a high-concentration trade it is not easily displaced, clearly calls for some explanation. When a trade has ceased to expand or even begun to contract, the leading firms will be able to maintain their share of the trade (and thereby concentration) by keeping their own output stable or reducing it proportionately with the trade as a whole. There will be little, in such circumstances, to attract newcomers to the trade; the existing firms, on the other hand, may try to rationalise production by amalgamation and acquisition. Thus, the fact that the trades are *not* expanding constitutes part of the explanation of continuing high concentration for some of the fifty trades.

For the great majority of the high-concentration trades, however, long-term demand has been rising, not falling. It follows, therefore, that the leading firms must expand at least at the same rate as the trade as a whole if concentration is to be maintained. In theory, such a rate of growth might seem difficult to achieve in the face of competition from new entrants as well as established firms. But, in fact, high concentration is usually maintained in expanding trades, so that there would appear to be factors operating which frustrate the development of new competition.

The factors which make it difficult for newcomers to enter a highly concentrated trade or, even if entry is relatively easy, hamper the rate of growth of the new or established concerns, fall naturally into two groups. In the first place, there are the factors which operate from the side of production, including the economies of large-scale operation, capital requirements, patents and technical know-how, access to raw materials, restrictive arrangements, and State regulation. In the second place, there are the factors which operate from the side of the market, such as advertising and sales promotion, distribution methods and service facilities, and restrictive practices in distribution.

The greater part of Chapter IX is concerned with the presence of these factors among the fifty high-concentration trades. Although it is difficult to assess their relative importance in the same trade or between trades, their incidence appears marked and their cumulative effect very considerable in sixteen of the fifty trades. Thus, even though the obstacles to new entry and growth are not always insuperable, the fact that they are generally formidable can be held to contribute substantially to the maintenance of high concentration.

(*b*) *Changes in concentration, 1935–51*

The comparison of concentration over time is, as already mentioned above, complicated by a number of factors. In particular it is necessary to look beyond the ratios for the trade, and establish what has happened to concentration in terms of its principal products. To this end, formulae have been devised which, by taking account of changes in the definition, specialisation, and exclusiveness of a trade, yield concentration-ratios, in terms of principal products, for 185 trades in both 1935 and 1951. Since the principal product concentration-ratio is usually expressed as a range in both years, there are only sixty-one trades for which a change in concentration can be claimed. Moreover, there are Trades as well as constituent Sub-Trades among these sixty-one trades, while in other cases, trades must be rejected from the analysis because their specialisation, exclusiveness or comparability are so low. As a result of these and other considerations, we are left with only forty-one trades on which to base an analysis of changes in concentration between 1935 and 1951.

(*i*) *Changes in concentration and factors relating to concentration, 1935–51*

Principal product concentration rose for twenty-seven, and fell for fourteen, of these forty-one trades between 1935 and 1951, and in Chapter XI an attempt is made to examine the relationships between these changes and changes in other Census variables. The approach is analagous to that of Chapter VII, and the regression analysis is again conducted in terms of the logarithms of the variables. The difference is that we are now concerned with comparing concentration in the same trade at different dates, rather than between trades at the same date.

For various reasons (stated in Chapter XI), it was decided to start with an 'association' analysis, which takes account only of the *direction* of changes in the variables, before proceeding to a regression analysis (along the lines of Chapter VII) for which the magnitude of the concentration-changes must be determined arbitrarily in view of the range of principal product concentration in both years.

Taking the results of the association analysis, it is found that the distribution of trades by changes in concentration and changes in the number of units is such that the expected tendency for concentration to rise when numbers fall (and vice versa) cannot be confirmed or, for that matter, denied. There is, on the other hand, a positive and significant association between changes in concentration and the size-ratio of units, which corresponds to the correlation between them among the 1951 trades. The positive correlation between average unit size (and also average plant size) and concentration among the 1951 trades is also confirmed by the association between the changes in the same variables between 1935 and 1951. But the association analysis neither confirms nor denies the negative correlation between concentration and trade size observed among the 1951 trades, and thus neither supports nor contradicts the *a priori* case that concentration will fall in an expanding, and rise in a declining, trade. Thus, it is concluded that among the trades in the 1935–51 analysis, any tendency for an increase in trade size to imply more units (and thereby lower concentration) has been offset by a tendency for the average size of units and the size-differences between them to increase.

Turning now to the regression analysis, we find only a weak and scarcely significant correlation (—0·27) between changes in concentration and the number of units, which confirms the results of the association analysis. But it differs from the relation between the same variables (—0·83) among the 1951 trades, although the difference may be explained by sampling errors and the fact that concentration-changes are here measured in terms of principal products rather than employment.

There is, on the other hand, a good positive correlation (0·63) between changes in concentration and in the size-ratio of units (confirming the association analysis, although the size-ratio used there was different from here), whereas the analogous relation among the 1951 trades was negative (—0·40). But this change of sign is no more than a by-product of the fact that the positive correlation between changes in unit size-ratio and unit numbers (0·57) on the one hand, and the negative correlation between unit numbers and concentration (−0·27) on the other, are both much weaker than the corresponding relationships among the 1951 trades.

Turning now to changes in unit size and trade size (measured in terms of employment), we find that changes in concentration and in unit size are positively correlated (0·44), and since there is no significant direct correlation between changes in unit size and in the size-ratio of units, it can be presumed that an increase in unit size tends to increase concentration through reducing the number of units. As for changes in trade size, they are positively correlated with both unit numbers (0·47) and average unit size (0·49), while there is also a small positive correlation (0·17) between them and concentration-changes. Although the latter relationship is the reverse of the comparable relationship (−0·42) among the 1951 trades, there is a large standard error in the 1935–51 result so that the difference could be due to chance, though this is rather unlikely.

Compared with the results among the 1951 trades, an increase in trade size in the 1935–51 sample tends to come about more by an increase in average unit size and less by an increase in unit numbers which, together with the much weaker association between changes in unit numbers and concentration, explains the positive correlation between changes in trade size and concentration. It can also be shown, by multiple regression analysis, that changes in both trade size and unit size explain about 20 per cent of the variations in concentration-changes between 1935 and 1951. But a change in unit size is almost as good an indicator of a change in concentration as any combination of unit size and trade size, since it alone explains 19 per cent of variations in concentration-changes.

When attention is concentrated on plant size and plants per unit rather than unit size, it is found that there is no correlation between changes in average plant size and in plants per unit, whereas there was a positive correlation between these two factors among the 1951 trades. But the absence of any correlation between the two variables during the 1935–51 period does not conflict with the theory (postulated on the basis of their positive correlation among the 1951 trades) that higher concentration was often associated first with a fall in the number of units through combination and then with an increase in the average size of plants through a process of rationalisation.

Changes in the average number of plants per unit between 1935 and 1951 were far larger than differences in plants per unit among trades in 1951, but they do not help to explain changes in concentration. Thus, changes in plant size alone explain 27 per cent of the variation in concentration-changes, while changes in plant size and in plants per unit explain 28 per cent. Nor does trade size significantly increase the explanation afforded by plant size alone, for the portion explained by trade size and plant size is also only 28 per cent. It should be noted that plant size and trade size together, as also unit size and trade size together, explain very much less of the variation in concentration over time than of the variation in concentration among the 1951 trades.

Examining in detail the changes in concentration, in plant size, and in unit size, for the trades in the 1935–51 sample, we find that there are fourteen trades (out of thirty-five) where all three variables rose. The increase in unit size was greater than in plant size for seven of them; in other words, plants per unit also rose, often as the result of mergers and combination. But in the other seven trades, plants per unit fell with the entry of newcomers, though concentration still rose because some firms grew faster than others. There are, on the other hand, five trades where concentration, plant size and unit size all decreased between 1935 and 1951, but for two of them, a rise in plants per unit made the fall in unit size less than the fall in plant size. Out of the other sixteen trades, the change in concentration was the opposite of the change in *both* plant size and unit size for six trades, the same as the change in plant size only for five trades, and the same as the change in unit size only for the remaining five trades.

Taking the thirty-five trades together, it is found that their aggregated number of plants fell by 17 per cent between 1935 and 1951, whereas there was only a negligible fall (assuming that no unit appeared in more than one trade) in their number of units. As a result, average plant size rose by 35 per cent, compared with a 12 per cent increase in average unit size. Similarly, among all factory trades between 1935 and 1951, average plant size rose more than average unit size although the number both of plants and units increased. At first sight, this result might appear contrary to general expectation, but it is possibly explained by the tendency for the concentration of production in larger plants at one end of a trade to be offset by the entry of new concerns with smaller plants at the other. Whether or not concentration rises in such circumstances will then depend on the relative importance of the new entrants as well as on the degree of rationalisation among the older units.

Since relatively (and disappointingly) few of the cross-sectional relationships between the variables are definitely confirmed by the analysis of changes between 1935 and 1951, it is risky to argue from differences between trades as to what may happen even over a considerable period of time. Of course, we have omitted many factors which might be important in explaining concentration by confining our attention to Census data, while it may be that a considerable part of the variations in concentration is inexplicable in terms of measurable economic facts. For these reasons, twenty of the trades with concentration-changes between 1935 and 1951 were selected for more detailed case-studies (presented in

Part IV), and from these studies, a number of the more important contributory factors have been identified.

(*ii*) *Factors contributing to concentration-changes, 1935–51*

The period 1935–51 was full of events which might be expected to affect industry in various ways. During the pre-war years, governments had turned away from *laissez-faire* and towards protection and industrial self-government, while the War itself forced drastic changes upon industry, at least 'for the duration'. There was only a gradual return to more normal conditions in the post-war period, since controls and restrictions were retained in some trades for several years. In addition, the post-war years saw the nationalisation of some basic industries, and a more hostile attitude towards restrictive practices.

It might have been anticipated that the dislocation and disturbance of the war years would have left a permanent mark on the structure of many industries. But this was not so in most cases. Although some manufacturing capacity was destroyed or damaged, the effect on trade concentration was generally slight, an exception being grain milling. Similarly, although statutory concentration schemes, designed to release factory space and labour for war work, were applied to several of the forty-one trades, they had little permanent effect on the structure of those trades, except in the case of tinplate, building bricks, textile finishing, and possibly carpets. The restrictions on the use of scarce raw materials were probably more important, particularly as they persisted long into the post-war period. Paradoxically enough, shortages sometimes encouraged the entry of new firms, provided that they operated on a sufficiently small scale to avoid the need for licences. But in other trades, such as bread and flour confectionery, restrictions tended to reduce the number of firms, or even to encourage mergers and acquisitions in order to obtain additional quotas or allocations of raw materials.

Among the more normal factors affecting concentration, pride of place must go to technological change. In the first place, there are the major technological advances which threaten the survival or lessen the importance of concerns which cling to the older processes. Technological advances of this kind have certainly been a primary influence in increasing concentration in such trades as tinplate, wrought iron and steel tubes, watch and clock, mineral oil refining and cinematograph film printing. Secondly, there are the improvements in technique, which though less spectacular than the major advances, give some firms an advantage over others and enable them to increase their share of the trade as a result. Examples of trades where such considerations appear to apply are razors, metal boxes and containers, bread and flour confectionery, cement, and china and porcelain.

State action has also played a significant part in affecting concentration in a number of trades. It may have taken the form of protective tariffs and import quotas, when its effect has often been to encourage foreign (mainly American) firms to establish manufacturing plants in this country, as in the case of razors, watches and clocks, soap, toilet preparations, and drugs and pharmaceuticals. Or it may be that the State provides subsidies for the domestic producers, and, as in the case of beet-sugar manufacture, makes statutory regulation of the trade a condition. Finally, although the direct effect of nationalisation has been eliminated from this analysis by the omission of the publicly owned industries, it has had an indirect effect on the concentration of trades, like coke ovens and building bricks, in which nationalised undertakings have ancillary interests.

The most commonly quoted cause of increased concentration is combination by merger or acquisition, and although there have been few monster amalgamations in the trades during the period now under consideration, combination on a significant scale has still occurred in a number of trades. We have already noted that surplus capacity has been a major historical reason for amalgamation; and in tinplate, grain milling and building bricks it has also been an important factor during the 1935–51 period. In other trades, mergers, acquisitions and joint enterprises have accompanied technological change: examples are to be found in wrought iron and steel tubes, watches, cinematograph film printing, and china and porcelain. Where quota arrangements for the division of the market or allocation of materials exist, acquisition may be the easiest way for firms to expand their share of the trade, and this appears to have occurred in cement, grain milling and sugar-refining. Merger and acquisition have also been adopted as the most convenient method of expansion by some of the leading concerns in bread-making, biscuits, polishes, drugs and pharmaceuticals, and toilet preparations and perfumery, although it does not always follow that concentration is thereby increased.

Even the most easily recognisable factors contributing to concentration-changes may serve opposing ends in the same trade, and concentration will also be influenced by other factors, such as changes in the pattern of trade demand (as in the case of slate, fish curing, polishes), advertising and sales promotion, and trade association activity, which affect the fortunes of different firms in different ways. Moreover, it is also the case that an apparent change in concentration is sometimes due to some peculiarity in the composition of the Census trade.

For these reasons alone, general conclusions are better avoided. But it must be noted that for the majority of the trades with concentration-changes that have been studied, there were also changes in the identity or ranking of the largest units. In addition, it is probable that events since 1951 may have intensified the established trend of concentration-change between 1935 and 1951 in some trades, but contradicted it in others. Either way, there can be no doubt that changes in concentration are continually proceeding among British trades (although they are not always readily established from concentration data based on Census trades), and that the factors affecting these changes are many and diverse.

PART I

CONCEPTS AND METHODOLOGY

CHAPTER I

CONCENTRATION AND THE CENSUS TRADE

I. THE CONCENTRATION CONCEPT

The practice of indicating the relative importance of individual firms by the share they control of the industries to which they belong is well established. That a high proportion of a trade is in the hands of a particular firm is information valued by students of industrial structure and by governments interested in the growth of giant concerns and the emergence of monopoly power. The Standing Committee on Trusts, for example, attached great importance to the share of an industry's output controlled by a dominant firm or trade association, and its various sub-committees which reported in the years immediately following the First World War frequently gave such data for the trades they investigated.[1]

The Monopolies Commission, moreover, is obliged to take account of the degree of concentration in the supply of the goods under investigation. Under its terms of reference, as amended by the Restrictive Trade Practices Act, 1956, the Commission must establish that a single firm is responsible for at least one-third of the trade, before it can proceed to inquire into the nature and effects of its operations. A similar condition also applied to the activities of trade associations under the Monopolies and Restrictive Practices Act, 1948.

As a consequence, the reports of the Commission include information, generally for more than one year, on the shares of the investigated trades held by single firms or by trade associations. As the result of these and other investigations, both official and unofficial, there exists a considerable body of information about concentration in British industry.

Much of this information is, on the other hand, not comparable between trade and trade, and its value is limited to that extent. The need for a more comprehensive and systematic survey of concentration was recognised by the Census of Production Advisory Committee for 1935, and to that end a voluntary inquiry was made, in conjunction with the

[1] See Ministry of Reconstruction, *Report of the Committee on Trusts* [Cmd. 9236], H.M.S.O. 1919.

1935 Census, on the connections between larger firms in order to establish their relative contribution to national output.

The results yielded by the Census and the voluntary inquiry were not presented until near the end of the Second World War, when Messrs H. Leak and A. Maizels read to the Royal Statistical Society a paper which embodied 'for the first time, comprehensive statistical measurements of the degree of concentration in each of the principal industries of the country'.[1] The Leak and Maizels paper contained much information on the connections between trades and the resultant strands to be observed in the pattern of British industry, but the feature which attracted most interest and comment was the concentration data for the 1935 Census of Production trades.

The present study is in direct line of descent from the Leak and Maizels paper, and the basic data follow the same general pattern. The concept of concentration used in both studies is the percentage share of Census trades —expressed in terms of gross output, net output and employment—controlled by the three largest business units in each trade.

The business unit, as already stated, consists of a single firm or a parent company together with its subsidiaries (that is, firms in which it owns more than 50 per cent of the capital or voting power), and its ranking by size is determined by the number of persons it employs in establishments classified to the trade in question. Once the units have been ranked on this basis, the concentration-ratio for the trade is obtained by expressing the aggregated particulars of the establishments in that trade belonging to the three largest units, as a percentage of the totals for the trade as a whole.

Two points immediately call for comment. First, the ranking of units by employment may mean that the units selected as the largest by that indicator are not necessarily the largest in terms of their output. In general, this is probably not a serious disadvantage, but there is at least one trade where the largest producer (in terms of output) in 1935 was not included among the three largest units, owing to the relative smallness of its labour-force. Second, the concentration-ratios are independent of the total number of business units in the trades. To that extent, it is an easier measure to compute than others, such as the 'concentration curve' used by the Federal Trade Commission,[2] that require data for a larger number of business units.

It is argued in Chapter II that knowledge of the total number of busi-

[1] Leak and Maizels, 'The Structure of British Industry', p. 143.

[2] Federal Trade Commission, *The Concentration of Productive Facilities, 1947* (Washington, U.S. Government Printing Office, 1950). Such a concentration curve is drawn by showing the cumulative share of a trade's employment or output by an increasing number of firms along the ordinate, with the firms arrayed from the largest to the smallest along the abscissa. The concentration-ratio for the three largest units corresponds to one point on this curve.

ness units in each trade is necessary for an appreciation of their structure. Fortunately, the total number of business units in each trade has been provided by the Board of Trade for 1951; unfortunately, comparable data are not available for 1935, except for a limited number of trades. Thus, while it is possible to establish various types of industry structure for 1951, it is not generally possible to do the same for 1935.

2. THE CENSUS TRADE

Since the concentration data presented in this study are based entirely on Census of Production trades, the definition and scope of these trades determine the significance of the concentration-ratios. It is important, therefore, to examine the principles by which Census trades are determined, and how far they constitute economically significant groups.

The Census of Production Trades are usually defined as the 'establishments engaged wholly or mainly' in the production or manufacture of a number of products collectively described as 'the principal products of the Trade'. Thus, the basic definition of Census Trades is in terms of products, but the association of products together to form a Trade is by no means a simple or straightforward process.

In deciding what principal products should be grouped together to form a Trade, the Census authorities take account of many factors, of which technological considerations are probably the most important. Where distinctive products are naturally associated, in that they are the main and the by-products of a particular manufacturing process, it is convenient to regard them as the principal products of one and the same Trade, however much they may differ in use. Thus, it is understandable that the by-products of coal carbonisation are included with coke as the principal products of the Coke Ovens and By-Products Trade, and that the various substances yielded at different stages in the refining and distillation of petroleum and shale oil should together comprise the principal products of the Mineral Oil Refining Trade.

Distinctive products are, however, frequently produced in the same establishment because of a fundamental similarity in the technical processes or raw materials required for their manufacture. Thus, motor cars, commercial vehicles, tractors, motor cycles, bicycles, caravans, as well as a considerable variety of parts and accessories, are all included in the principal products of the Motor Vehicles and Cycles (Manufacturing) Trade.

Mere similarity in the technological processes of manufacture may be sufficient to bring diverse products into a single Trade. Thus, linoleum and leathercloth are neither produced in the same plants nor compete in the market, and for the most part manufacturers of the one are not manufacturers of the other. Yet together they form the bulk of the principal products of the Linoleum, Leathercloth and Allied Trades of the Census of Production. Other groupings of products, such as matches and firelighters to constitute the Match Trade, are probably explained by administrative convenience.

The same product may occasionally make its appearance as a principal product of more than one Trade. Thus, sulphate of ammonia is a principal product of three Trades,[1] and animal and poultry feedingstuffs are common to another three trades.[2] Differences in both the raw materials and the manufacturing processes used to produce essentially the same type of product are reflected in this way.

Technological considerations are obviously the primary factor in the construction of Census Trades, and a comparatively minor role is played by market considerations such as the close substitutability of the products in use.[3] The resultant heterogeneity of some Census Trades is, however, frequently reduced by the practice of distinguishing subdivisions of the Trades; subdivisions which are generally defined as consisting of 'the specialist producers' of a group of 'characteristic products', and which are described in this study as Sub-Trades. Thus, the Census authorities distinguish seven Sub-Trades of the Motor Vehicles and Cycles (Manufacturing) Trade. Yet there still remains an element of heterogeneity in their definitions: for example, included in one Sub-Trade are the specialist producers of commercial vehicles and chassis with engines therefor; tractors; and industrial and works trucks and works tractors. On the other hand, the Floor Coverings Sub-Trade of the Linoleum, Leathercloth and Allied Trades is a much more homogeneous and satisfactory entity than the Trade of which it forms part.

While the fundamental definition of the Census Trade is in terms of products, the basic unit for the collection of information is the establishment, such as a mine, plant, or factory. Where an undertaking has more than one establishment, a return is required from each. Moreover, where two or more distinct trades are carried on in separate departments

[1] Fertiliser, Disinfectant, Insecticide and Allied Trades; Coke Ovens and By-Products; and Gas Supply.

[2] Grain Milling; Seed Crushing and Oil Refining; and Cattle, Dog and Poultry Food.

[3] Cf. M. R. Conklin and H. T. Goldstein, 'Census Principles of Industry and Product Classification, Manufacturing Industries' in *Business Concentration and Price Policy*, National Bureau of Economic Research (N.B.E.R.), 1955, p. 21: 'Physical or technological structure and homogeneity of production are more important considerations in the classification system than close substitutability of demand for products. Although the industry generally represents a group of close competitors, producing close substitute commodities, the different commodities frequently cannot be substituted (lathe and drill press). Further, all close substitute commodities are not in the same industry. For example, tin cans and glass containers are close substitute commodities, but are defined in two different industries because of the differences in materials, process of manufacture, types of machinery, etc., that is, differences in supply characteristics.'

of a single works, the firm is generally required to treat them as separate establishments and to make separate returns.

A distinction is made in the information required from firms according to the size of their labour-force. Firms employing ten or fewer persons need furnish information only about the numbers employed and the nature of the business carried on, although for a small number of trades where the small firms were thought to be responsible for a relatively large proportion of the total output, some particulars of output were also obtained. For the larger establishments (those employing eleven and over), much greater detail on output and employment is required, and it is to the larger establishments only that the concentration data refer. The effect on the level of concentration in individual trades by the inclusion of small firms will be discussed later.

An establishment is classified to a Trade if its production of the principal products of that Trade accounts for a larger proportion of the value of its output than its production of the principal products of any other Trade. But an establishment ranks as a 'specialist producer', thereby classified to a Sub-Trade, only if at least half of its output consists of the specified principal products characteristic of the Sub-Trade.

In the process of aggregating establishments, according to the nature and importance of their principal products, to comprise a particular Trade, the whole of the employment and output of those establishments is credited to that Trade. Included in the Trade's employment will be persons engaged on the production of goods which are principal products of other Trades; and included in the value of the Trade's output will be the value of those goods. The great majority of Census Trades relate, in fact, to establishments producing a mixed assortment of products, most of which are characteristic of the Trade, but some of which are characteristic of other Trades. Few Trades are completely specialised and exclusive entities in that they produce only and all of their principal products.

The Census trade and the ideal industry

The principles followed in the construction of Census trades limit the significance of the concentration data for those trades. The measurement of concentration is often implicitly directed to the study of monopoly power but, for such studies, concentration should relate to a group of products that are substitutes either in production or in the market.

Thus, Professor Stigler has stated

> 'An industry should embrace the maximum geographical area and the maximum variety of productive activities in which there is strong long-run substitution. If buyers can shift on a large scale from product or area B to A, then the two should be combined. . . . Economists usually state this in an alternative form: All products or enterprises with large long-

run cross-elasticities of either supply or demand should be combined into a single industry.'[1]

There are occasions when the most significant concentration data would refer to a single product. Such is the case when there are no close-substitutes for that product and when other manufacturers can embark on its production only with difficulty. But such instances are rare. More often, before conclusions can be reached about the reality of monopoly power, a number of products must be brought together on the basis of close-substitutability either on the demand or the supply side.

The Census definitions of a trade may be too broad or too narrow by this criterion.[2] They are seldom just what one would have wished. But there is no escape from this dilemma. It is not possible to combine the concentration data for Census trades in such a way as to bring close-substitutes, and only close-substitutes, together. The data relate to Census trades, and it is in terms of Census trades that the analysis must proceed.

The comprehensiveness of Census trades

There is, however, a further factor complicating the interpretation of concentration data based on Census trades: namely, that Census trades, for the reasons examined above, are neither confined to the production of their principal products nor account for the entire output of those principal products.

A concentration-ratio of 80 per cent for a hypothetical Pins and Needles Trade would imply, and is frequently assumed to mean, that four-fifths of the total output of pins and needles is controlled by the three largest pins and needles producers. But, in fact, it may mean nothing of the kind. Strictly interpreted, the concentration-ratio only states that four-fifths of the total output (or employment) of the establishments classified to the Pins and Needles Trade is controlled by the three largest units (in terms of labour employed) in that Trade. The output of these establishments may well include products other than pins and needles; some of these other products may be listed as the principal products of the Pins and Needles Trade, the rest being principal products of other Trades. A considerable output of pins and needles (as well as the other principal products of the Pins and Needles Trade) may also be included in the output of other Trades, and it is even conceivable (though hardly likely) that some of the largest pins and needles producers may be found in other Trades. Such factors may mean, therefore, that the proportion of the total output of pins and needles (as well as the other principal products of the

[1] George J. Stigler, 'Introduction' to *Business Concentration and Price Policy*, N.B.E.R., p. 4.

[2] The Census authorities cannot, in fact, give concentration data for individual products if the result would be to disclose particulars of individual firms.

Trade) controlled by the three largest units is substantially different from the four-fifths implied by the concentration-ratio.

The extent to which a Trade concentration-ratio reflects the share of the principal products of the Trade controlled by the three largest units must, therefore, be examined. While it is impossible to distinguish those employed in a Census Trade on the production of its principal products from those engaged on the production of other products, the Census data do permit the distinction to be made in terms of value. Thus, the value of the sales-and-work-done element of the Trade's gross output can be divided into (*a*) the sales of the principal products by establishments classified to that Trade, and (*b*) the sales by establishments in the Trade of other than principal products.

The proportion of the gross output of a Trade consisting of its principal products is termed its *degree of specialisation*.[1] For a Census Sub-Trade, the term refers to the proportion represented by its characteristic products. Similarly, the extent to which establishments in a trade are responsible for the total national output of the appropriate principal products is denoted by its *degree of exclusiveness*.[2] Once again, for Sub-Trades, it is to their characteristic products that the relationship applies.[3]

If the degrees of specialisation and exclusiveness are both 100 per cent, the trade concentration-ratio is equal to the three largest units' combined share of the principal products of the Trade. But the farther the degrees of specialisation and exclusiveness depart from the 100 per cent mark, the less accurately may the trade concentration-ratio reflect their share of the principal products. Fortunately the degrees of specialisation and exclusiveness among Census trades are, on the whole, reasonably high. In Appendix C, the 1951 trades are arranged in frequency distributions according to these two variables. For the 1947 Trades for which specialisation can be determined, nearly three-fifths had degrees of specialisation of 90 per cent and over, and over nine-tenths of 80 per cent and over. Similarly, two-thirds of the Trades had degrees of exclusiveness of 90 per cent and over, and more than nine-tenths of 80 per cent and over.

The degrees of specialisation and exclusiveness are generally lower for Sub-Trades than for Trades. Thus, only one-quarter of the 167 Sub-Trades were more than 90 per cent specialised, though nearly seven-tenths were more than 80 per cent specialised. The results were rather better in terms of exclusiveness; nearly one-third had degrees of ex-

[1] P. Sargant Florence, *Investment, Location and Size of Plant*, National Institute of Economic and Social Research, Economic and Social Studies 7 (Cambridge University Press, 1948), p. 3.

[2] *Ibid.*

[3] The Census reports do not give as detailed an analysis of gross output for Sub-Trades as they do for Trades. But characteristic products can generally be identified with sufficient accuracy to give a good estimate of the degree of exclusiveness.

clusiveness of 90 per cent and over, and nearly two-thirds of 80 per cent and over.

All in all, it appears that the Census authorities are largely successful in their aim of maximising the homogeneity and comprehensiveness of Census trades in terms of the principal products that define their scope. Only in comparatively few instances are the degrees of specialisation and exclusiveness so low that the concentration data are rendered meaningless as a result. By removing such trades from the analysis at the start, the confidence with which the interpretation of the remainder can proceed is increased.[1]

3. THE INDICATORS OF CONCENTRATION

The concentration data supplied by the Board of Trade generally relate to the gross output, net output, employment and number of establishments of the three largest units[2] in each Census trade.[3] There are, as a result, four indicators of the degrees of concentration for each trade, but since each of them has distinct characteristics, their relative virtues and defects as concentration measures must be examined.

The *gross output* concentration-ratio purports to measure the share of the trade's sales handled by the three largest business units in that trade. But some trades are so broadly defined that they include two or more stages of production in the one Census trade—that is, the production of semi-manufactures or parts as well as the finished goods—with the result that the total sales embody a degree of double-counting. Thus, in the Metal Boxes and Containers Trade certain can components are valued twice, once in respect of the establishment where they are produced and again as part of the complete containers. The effect in such cases, where the largest units produce their own semi-finished products in separate establishments, is for the gross output indicator to overstate the degree of concentration for the finished products.

There is a further danger that vertically integrated concerns with establishments in the same or different trades may supply misleading gross output data to the Census authorities and consequently falsify the concentration-ratios. Although the Census lays down that inter-plant transfers of goods must be valued on the basis of 'the charge that would have been made to an independent purchaser buying similar quantities', it may well happen that, as in the United States, some inter-plant transfers are not reported at all while others are reported incorrectly.[4] If the verti-

[1] See Chapter IV, p. 49.

[2] Where there is a risk of disclosure, the number of units is larger than three.

[3] For Census definitions of gross output, net output and employment, see Appendix A.

[4] Federal Trade Commission, *Changes in Concentration in Manufacturing, 1935 to 1947 and 1950*, p. 8. See also Leak and Maizels, p. 154.

cally integrated concerns are the largest units and they fail to make complete returns, the gross output concentration-ratio may be an underestimate. Conversely, if such a large vertically integrated unit is not among the three largest, the gross output concentration-ratio may be an over-estimate.

While the *net output* indicator should not be subject to the double-counting problem, since net output is essentially a value-added concept, it is liable in the same way as gross output to distortions arising from improperly reported inter-plant transfers. For any given year, however, net output is the best available indicator of the relative importance of trades in terms of the resources used, while it is permissible to aggregate net output, but not gross output, for groups of trades.

The *employment* concentration-ratio was chosen by Leak and Maizels as the key indicator of concentration, both because the largest units are ranked in terms of employment and because it is 'the most convenient one to use when comparing concentration in different industries'.[1] At the same time, it is to be supposed that the employment indicator may understate the degree of concentration in physical terms[2] since the largest units might be expected 'to use more capital-using and small firms to employ more labour-using methods of production'.[3]

The *establishments* indicator has less intrinsic value than the three preceding measures, and the number of establishments operated by the three largest units is a more valuable fact than the proportion they represent of the total number of establishments in the trade.[4]

There is, however, a fifth indicator of concentration which has not been supplied by the Board of Trade but which can be estimated, subject to certain assumptions, from the gross output concentration-ratio and other Census data. For those trades where the degrees of specialisation and exclusiveness are both available, it is possible to compute within limits a *principal product* concentration-ratio, that is, the share of the three largest units of the total output of the principal products of each trade. The formulae devised for the estimation of principal product concentration are presented in Appendix D, but it is important to note that they embody an assumption that the three largest units in a trade have no share in the output of that trade's principal products by establishments classified to other trades. This need not be so, for the three largest units

[1] Leak and Maizels, p. 155.

[2] Among the 220 trades in the 1951 analysis, there were twenty-six trades where the concentration-ratio was the same in terms of both employment and net output, 114 trades where net output was higher than employment concentration, and eighty where employment was higher than net output.

[3] T. Scitovsky, 'Economic Theory and the Measurement of Concentration' in *Business Concentration and Price Policy*, N.B.E.R. p. 111.

[4] See Chapter II, section 4 below.

in Trade A may have establishments classified to Trades B and C in which the secondary production consists of Trade A's principal products.

In theory, the principal product concentration-ratio has more significance than the other ratios, since it refers to a specific and self-contained group of products. But in practice, if trades with low degrees of specialisation and exclusiveness are rejected, the other indicators are likely to be fairly close to principal product concentration. In any case, the assumptions on which the principal product formulae are based may be inaccurate in specific instances, while their application results in a range of possible concentration-ratios for most trades. On the other hand, principal product concentration is a necessary concept when examining changes in concentration over time, and its function in that respect will be discussed in Chapter x.

Each of the three main indicators—gross output, net output and employment—has its disadvantages, and in practice the choice of indicator is determined both by what we are seeking to measure and by the information available. For the purpose of estimating principal product concentration, gross output has perforce to be used. For detecting the effect on the degree of concentration of the inclusion of small firms, it is necessary to use the employment indicator since the small firms' data are generally not available in the other measures. Similarly, where it is desirable to aggregate concentration and trade data, the appropriate choice is either employment or net output. In the main, however, the Leak and Maizels practice of using employment as indicative of concentration in each trade has been adopted, supplementing it with the other indicators where necessary or desirable.

4. THE IMPORTANCE OF SMALL FIRMS

It has already been noted that Census data relate only to the larger establishments employing more than ten persons. Where the small firms represent an appreciable proportion of a Trade's activity, the actual degree of concentration will be correspondingly lower than indicated by the Trade concentration-ratio based on the larger establishments.

In general, the relative importance of the small firms' activities is given only in terms of employment, though the Census Reports give the number of returns made by smaller firms.[1] It is reasonable, however, to assume that the number of returns is equivalent to the number of small firms in the Trade, as well as the number of establishments they operate.

From Appendix E, Table 1, it may be seen that the total numbers employed by small firms amounted to more than 1,000 in the case of sixty-

[1] The number of small firms is given by the Census only for Trades, so that their relative importance in Sub-Trades cannot be assessed.

four Trades (or 43 per cent of the total), and to more than 10,000 in eight Trades. At the other end of the scale, there were four Trades—Coke Ovens and By-Products; Blast Furnaces; Steel Sheets; and Tinplate—where there were no small firms in 1951.

The 147 Trades have also been arranged in a second frequency distribution according to the relative numbers of small firms (expressed as a percentage of the total number of business units, including small firms). For 60 per cent of the total number of Trades, the small firms represent 20–60 per cent of the total number of units. Indeed, there were nine Trades where the small firms accounted for more than 80 per cent of the total number of units.[1]

The effects of the inclusion of small firms on the employment concentration-ratios are summarised in Table 2 of Appendix E. For sixty of the 147 Trades, their inclusion made no difference to the employment concentration-ratio, and in another forty-six Trades only a 1 percentage point reduction resulted. Changes in the employment concentration-ratio of 6 percentage points and over occurred for nine Trades.[2]

In general, however, the small firms in Census Trades do not account for much of the total employment, nor do they often affect the concentration-ratio greatly. Even where the effect of their inclusion on the Trade concentration-ratio is large, it may not be significant in relation to the Trade's main activity. Thus, the decrease in the concentration-ratio for the Match Trade does not arise from the presence of a large number of small manufacturers of matches; it reflects instead the number of small firms engaged in the production of firelighters, which are also a principal product of the Match Trade. It is convenient and justifiable, therefore, to ignore the small firms in the general analysis of concentration, particularly since data are not available for Sub-Trades. But their presence must be borne in mind when the circumstances of individual Trades are being examined.

[1] Bread and Flour Confectionery; Ice; Ice Cream; Cattle, Dog and Poultry Food; Match; Carts, Perambulators, etc.; Chain, Nail, Screw and Miscellaneous Forgings; Small Arms; and Building and Contracting.

[2] Ice (17 points); Ice Cream (14 points); Match (10 points); Wallpaper (9 points); Scrap Metal Processing; Fish Curing; Cattle, Dog and Poultry Food; and Vinegar and Other Condiments (7 points); and Watch and Clock (6 points).

CHAPTER II

CONCENTRATION, INDUSTRY STRUCTURE AND PLANT STRUCTURE

I. CONCENTRATION AND INDUSTRY STRUCTURE

The structure of industry is a term capable of several different interpretations, but it refers here to the number and the relative sizes of the business units in an industry. Similarly, plant structure refers to the relative number and size-differences of the establishments belonging to those units.[1]

An industry in this context once again relates to a Census trade; as such, it is subject to the limitations, already examined in Chapter I, arising from the definitions of Census trades. Even so, it is worth while to examine the structure of such loosely defined industries, since the number and relative sizes of the business units that comprise a trade have a direct connection with the likely situation in the market for its products.

The concentration-ratio, however, unless supported by other data, does not always reveal very much about an industry's structure. In the first place, it is not dependent on the number of business units in the trade for its computation. In the second place, it measures only the proportion of the trade's activity carried on by the three largest units, without revealing their individual shares *vis-à-vis* each other and the other units in the trade.

It is demonstrable that two trades with identical concentration-ratios may have very different structures. For the sake of argument, suppose that the three largest units act to all intents and purposes as one concern, X. In an industry where the degree of concentration is, say, 90 per cent, X will occupy a powerful position. Even if there is only one other concern, Y, in the industry, the share of X will be nine times greater than that of Y, and Y will be dominated by X. If there is more than one other firm, X's position will probably be stronger still.

In reality, X comprises three separate firms—A, B and C. Suppose, first of all, that they are all of equal size, each with a 30 per cent share of the trade. No single one of them is, on this supposition, likely to dominate the industry, though each is several times larger than any of the concerns comprising the remainder of the trade. There may, in the absence of any collusion between them, be keen rivalry at the top with each of them eager to improve or at least maintain its relative share of the trade. Com-

[1] It should be noted that where a business unit operates in more than one trade, its size in each trade is given by the employment in its establishments classified to those trades, and not by the total employment in all its establishments.

petition in one form or another may thus typify the behaviour of the industry, even though its concentration-ratio is as high as 90 per cent.

Secondly, suppose that A, B and C are in size of the order of 3 : 2 : 1, so that A's share of the trade is 45 per cent, B's share, 30 per cent, and C's, 15 per cent. Now A has clearly more power than when the firms were of more equal size, while C's share of 15 per cent makes it considerably inferior to both A and B. Even so, A's power is qualified by the importance of B which may, in conditions of market rivalry, be a constant challenge and threat to its position.

Suppose, finally, that A's individual share is still greater at 80 per cent so that B and C together control only the same proportion of the trade as the other concerns in the industry. Clearly, A's power is more than ever established, and probably neither B nor C, independently or together, can threaten its position.

The above circumstances are, of course, extreme in that the trade is assumed to be very highly concentrated. Differentiation between the respective shares of the three largest units is less important when the degree of concentration is low. Thus, when the concentration-ratio is 30 per cent, the relative sizes of A, B and C are less important than the fact that 70 per cent of the trade's activity is distributed between the other units.

Knowledge of the individual shares of the three largest units, even if it were available, would not permit a full appreciation of an industry's structure. It is desirable to know not merely how the three largest units compare in size one with the other, but also whether the three largest are very much larger than the other units in the trade, or only a little larger. Thus, once again, two trades with the same concentration-ratio may have markedly different structures, dependent this time on the total number of units in the trade. Two industries may both have a concentration-ratio of 75 per cent, but in one case the industry may consist of five firms, and in the other, twenty-five firms. In the first trade, the two smaller firms which share the 25 per cent not belonging to the three largest units are still large enough to exert some influence in the market. In the other case, the individual shares of the other twenty-two concerns are too small for any such effect.

2. THE SIZE-RATIO OF BUSINESS UNITS

The data on the total number of business units which have been provided by the Census authorities for each trade in 1951, together with their concentration-ratios, permit the calculation of an indicator which provides a crude measure of the differences in size that exist between the business units that comprise a trade. The indicator is the *size-ratio of units* (W), which measures the average size of the three largest units relative to the average size of the other units in the trade.[1] It measures the minimum degree of inequality in the sizes of the business units.[2] In the example of the two trades with concentration-ratios of 75 per cent, the size-ratio of the units would be 2 in the first case and 22 in the second, indicating that in the first case the five units would be much the same size, whereas large disparities would exist among the twenty-five units of the second trade.

Together with the number of units and the concentration-ratio, the size-ratio of units can be employed to distinguish various types of industry structure. It permits a rough-and-ready division of the highly concentrated trades into those where one or two concerns are overwhelmingly predominant, and those where a limited number of firms are more evenly matched in size. Similarly, among the trades where concentration is low, it can assist in detecting whether or not there are still concerns which, by virtue of their size, can be regarded as occupying a leading position in the trade. The results of the application of these principles of classification to the 1951 Census trades are presented in Chapter v.

3. THE NUMBER-RATIO AND SIZE-RATIO OF PLANTS[3]

Differences in the sizes of the units comprising a trade may reflect differences in the relative number and size of the plants they operate, while the absolute size of the plants may indicate whether or not entry into the trade is easy. If the plant size is generally large, it suggests that newcomers may find it more difficult to enter the trade than where plant sizes are smaller. The measurement of plant size for an industry is not, however, a straightforward matter, since an industry may have a wide range of plant sizes. Thus, Professor Sargant Florence has argued that no simple average of the numbers employed in a trade's establishments—such as the median, mode or arithmetic mean—is a satisfactory summary of the size of plant that is characteristic of that trade. Instead he devised rules for classifying the size of the prevalent plant in different trades, recognising at the same time that in some trades there may be no size of plant that prevails.[4]

Although the concept of prevalent plant sizes is briefly introduced in Chapter IX below, it cannot be generally employed since the necessary

[1] See Appendix F for an algebraic treatment of the relationship between the concentration-ratio, the size-ratio of units and the number- and size-ratio of plants.

[2] For the particular purposes of Chapter VII, an alternative measure of inequality is adopted; see p. 102 below.

[3] The term 'plant' is used here as synonymous with 'establishment' in the Census terminology.

[4] P. Sargant Florence, *Investment, Location, and Size of Plant* (1948), pp. 11–22.

information is available only for Census Trades, and not for Sub-Trades. Thus, the measure of plant size that is generally used in this study is the mean number of persons employed per establishment, in Trades and Sub-Trades alike.

Since the Board of Trade has supplied the number of establishments operated by the three largest units in Census trades for 1951, it has proved possible to proceed further in the analysis of their plant structure. For this purpose, two further concepts must be introduced. The first is the *number-ratio of plants* (R), which is the average number of establishments controlled by each of the three largest business units divided by the average number of establishments controlled by each of the other business units in the trade. The second concept is the *size-ratio of plants* (S), which is the average numbers employed per establishment controlled by the three largest units, divided by the average numbers employed per establishment controlled by the other units.

Since the size-ratio of units (W) is equivalent to the number-ratio of plants (R) multiplied by the size-ratio of plants (S),[1] the size-disparity of units can be analysed for each trade in terms of (i) the disparity in the number of plants, and (ii) the disparity in the size of plants controlled by the three largest units, compared with the rest.

Given these concepts, some useful distinctions can be drawn between trades on the basis of their establishment data. Where the size-ratio of plants is small (that is, the plants of the largest units do not differ greatly in size from the plants of the other units), it would appear that technological or locational factors largely determine the size of plant. If the average size of these plants is large, then the economies of scale are important and entry into the trade may be difficult; if the average size of plants is small, then economies of scale would not appear to be important and entry should be easier. Furthermore, a high degree of concentration in trades with small plants and small size-differences implies the presence of multi-plant concerns among the largest in the trade: an implication which can be tested by reference to the number-ratio data. Similarly, whether the plants be large or small, an increase in concentration in trades with small plant-size differences would seemingly be more likely to result (assuming that technological factors do not require a change in the size of plants) from the largest units acquiring more plants (by new building or through mergers and acquisitions) than from the building of larger plants.

On the other hand, large differences in the size-ratio of plants in a trade suggest that, though there may be technological economies of scale to be exploited, the small establishments can still survive alongside the large plants. The size-disparity of plants can largely account for the concen-

[1] See Appendix F.

tration of the trade, though in some cases the largest units may also operate several plants.

Given the number of business units and the concentration data for a trade (including the number of establishments controlled by the three largest units), the concepts presented in this chapter permit its industry and plant structure to be analysed to a considerable degree. But before presenting such an analysis in Chapters V and VI, it is necessary to consider more fully the relation between concentration and monopoly power.

CHAPTER III

CONCENTRATION AND MONOPOLY POWER

I. CONCENTRATION AND MONOPOLY POWER

The measurement of monopoly power is a difficult problem, not least because monopoly can be defined in many different ways. For present purposes we regard monopoly power as the long-run ability of a firm (or a group of firms) to choose, within a range and without reducing its sales to zero, the price it sets for a product (or, if it sets no price, the ability to influence the market price by varying the amounts it offers for sale). To put it another way, a firm with monopoly power has significant room for manœuvre in its price or output policies, whereas other firms without such power are constrained by forces external to themselves.

A firm may have great monopoly power because it is the sole seller of a product for which there is no good substitute and because other firms are, or can be, prevented from embarking on its manufacture. But a firm may still enjoy monopoly power, even when its competitors are fairly large, if for one reason or another it can dominate them and ensure that they do not adopt selling policies which undermine its own influence in the market.

Where firms act together as a group, they may also possess and exercise monopoly power, even though individually none of them would have had much room for manœuvre. In such cases, it is the monopoly power of the group that matters rather than the influence of the members individually. At the same time, it may well be that one or a few firms are the dominant partners in the group so that they can influence its policies to their own advantage. On the other hand, such monopoly power may be precarious since the group, particularly in times of stress, can easily disintegrate as firms pursue their own interests.

What is the connection between monopoly power, as here outlined rather than precisely defined, and the concentration concept? It is clear that the connection cannot be very close, both because of the inevitable inexactness of the concept of monopoly power, and because of the limited information which, as we have seen, a concentration-ratio conveys. But it is equally obvious that there is some connection between the two concepts which it is important to identify.

In the first place, a firm is unlikely to be the sole seller of a product, for which there are no close-substitutes and little potential competition, unless the concentration-ratio for the relevant trade as a whole is fairly high. Secondly, unless the concentration-ratio is high, the firm is unlikely to be in a position to dominate or overawe any possible competitors. Thirdly, cartel arrangements are difficult to arrange and preserve in trades which combine low concentration and a large number of units.

High concentration does not, on the other hand, prove the existence of monopoly power. Even the largest firm in a trade comprising a few large firms may have very little power if the others are determined to act as rivals. Moreover, the Census trade, as we have seen, may not embrace the right assortment of products for the measurement of monopoly power and may not be comprehensive as far as the output of those products is concerned.

There are, however, additional reasons why the concentration-ratio, even if the Census trade was ideal for the measurement of monopoly power, might still be positively misleading in specific cases. The reasons fall into two classes: (i) reasons why the concentration of production may not reflect (and will generally understate) the true degree of control over the output of a trade (Section 2 below); and (ii) reasons why even a true measure of control over output may not reflect (and will generally overstate) the degree of monopoly power (Section 3 below).

2. FACTORS AFFECTING THE CONCENTRATION OF OUTPUT CONTROLLED OR INFLUENCED BY THE LARGEST BUSINESS UNITS

The concentration-ratio may understate the degree to which output is controlled by the largest units either because of the definitions used, or because of the nature of the Census trade or the organisation of the industry.

Joint subsidiaries and minority interests

Take, first, the definition of the business unit. For one firm to rank as a subsidiary of the other, and the two to be consolidated as a business unit, the parent must own more than 50 per cent of the share-capital or voting-power of the subsidiary. This places the jointly-owned subsidiaries, which are sometimes to be found in British industry, in a peculiar position. Where the ownership of such a concern is divided on a strictly fifty-fifty basis, neither parent company is entitled to claim it as a subsidiary. It must rank, therefore, as a separate business unit in the assessment of concentration.

The share of the Census trade controlled by the three largest units is, therefore, understated if any of them have a 50 per cent interest in another concern in the same trade. The same principle would also apply if one or more of the largest units owned a minority interest (often sufficient to give control) in other firms in the same trade. In fact, however, no account is taken of such degrees of ownership, with the result that the concentration-ratio may represent only the minimum degree of effective concentration in the trade.

The effect of vertical integration

The horizontal stratification of industry, which generally characterises Census trades, cuts across the vertical organisation of many business concerns. An integrated steel concern, for example, may make its appearance in several Census trades—Metalliferous Mines and Quarries; Coke Ovens and By-Products; Blast Furnaces; Iron and Steel (Melting and Rolling); Steel Sheets; Tinplate; and so on—and its share of each trade will determine whether it ranks as one of the three largest units in each separately.

Yet the fact of vertical integration may bestow upon a particular concern a greater power than its share of the trade which constitutes its main line of activity would suggest. Such a situation arises where a concern has been disproportionately integrated,

> 'so that at one or more stages of production or distribution it acts as a supplier or customer for enterprises with which it is in competition at other stages.... If a disproportionately integrated concern is big enough to be important to its competitors, it has the power to squeeze them. As a supplier of raw materials it may adopt a policy of high prices for materials and relatively low mark-ups above these prices in its own sales of products that have been given further processing. Thus it may reduce the operating margins of its customer-competitors by high prices for materials and low prices for finished products. As a purchaser it follows the reverse policy, holding down the prices of raw materials which it both makes and buys, and enhancing the operating margins which it enjoys in subsequent parts of the productive process.'[1]

The reality of this power deriving from vertical integration has been commented upon by the Monopolies Commission in its report on the match industry. Among the factors which have hampered 'the development of competition by independent British match manufacturers' was the practice of the British Match Corporation 'of charging its competitors higher prices for certain materials of which it controls the distribution'.[2]

The concentration-ratio cannot measure the extent of vertical integration, unless the Census Trade itself takes account of it. It measures only the degree of horizontal concentration in horizontally defined

[1] C. D. Edwards, *Maintaining Competition* (New York, McGraw-Hill, 1949), p. 98.

[2] Monopolies and Restrictive Practices Commission, *Report on the Supply and Export of Matches and the Supply of Match-Making Machinery* (London, H.M.S.O. 1953), par. 215.

trades. But the fact remains that the relative power of large concerns in a particular trade may be greater than their share of that trade's output suggests, because of their vertical integration.

Multi-product firms

Similar considerations may also apply in the case of concerns that are active in several different trades. Their relative importance in any trade may be disproportionate to their share of that trade. Thus, Professor Machlup has stated, that 'even if the concern, on the strength of its own share in the markets in which it buys or sells, should have no great influence over prices and other terms, it may acquire such influence as an adjunct of the power generated by sheer bigness'.[1]

The manifestations of such influences have been described by Professor Edwards as follows

> 'If such a concern finds itself matching expenditures or losses, dollar for dollar, with a substantially smaller firm, the length of its purse assures it of victory. In encounters with small enterprises it can buy scarce materials and attractive sites, inventions and facilities; pre-empt the services of the most expensive technicians and executives; and acquire reserves of materials for the future. . . . Moment by moment the big company can outbid, outspend, or outlose the small one; and from a series of such momentary advantages it derives an advantage in attaining its large aggregate results.'[2]

Once again, the trade concentration data cannot convey any sense of the power that springs from the special status of the multi-product firm.[3] Even an enumeration of the number of trades in which a particular concern is among the three largest units can only indicate the scope and scale of their activities.[4] But in the interpretation of concentration-ratios, such factors should properly be taken into account.

Collusion

To the extent that the degree of collusion may be expected to be well correlated with concentration based on business units, the concentration-ratio is not, on this account, invalidated as an indicator of monopoly power. Certainly a high concentration-ratio and a few units are circumstances which suggest that collusion is feasible and not improbable,

[1] F. Machlup, *The Political Economy of Monopoly: Business, Labor and Government Policies* (Baltimore, The Johns Hopkins Press, 1952), p. 112.

[2] C. D. Edwards, 'Conglomerate Bigness as a Source of Power' in *Business Concentration and Price Policy*, N.B.E.R., pp. 334–5.

[3] Professor Edwards has also argued that, apart from advantages in the market, the multi-product firm has special advantages 'in litigation, politics, public relations, and finance'. *Op. cit.* p. 345.

[4] See, for example, Leak and Maizels, pp. 158–9.

whether it be the tacit collusion exemplified by informal price-leadership, or the explicit collusion of cartel arrangements. Even so, collusion may not exist, so that quite different degrees of monopoly power may prevail in trades where the number of units and their relative sizes are identical.

The greater the number of firms and the lower the degree of concentration in the trade, the more difficult it is to arrange and maintain formal or informal agreements. Nevertheless, they may still be found in such trades, and where they exist the significant factor is not unit concentration, but the share of the trade subject to restrictive control.

In general it is true that the largest units may, through their influence in the councils of a trade association or cartel, exercise a degree of power which is greater than that suggested by the concentration-ratios. They may play, for example, a decisive role in the determination of cartel prices. Thus, the Monopolies Commission reported in 1951 that prices of electric lamps 'are first discussed between the two largest producers, General Electric Company and British Thomson-Houston, and when proposals have been agreed between these two companies, and at a later stage Siemens, their representatives table a resolution' in the Council of the Electric Lamp Manufacturers' Association.[1]

3. MARKET FACTORS AFFECTING OUTPUT CONCENTRATION AS A MEASURE OF MONOPOLY POWER

Monopoly power is a concept based on the market, so that any market factors which serve either to intensify or offset the effects of concentration in production are relevant and important. There are three such factors which, in particular, call for comment: the geographical fragmentation of the market; imports and exports; and countervailing buying power.

The geographical fragmentation of the market

The concentration data refer to a trade's output computed on a national basis. But the market may not be national in its scope; it may be subdivided into smaller local markets owing to localisation of production and high transport costs. As a result, the degree of monopoly power enjoyed by various business units in their geographically fragmented markets may be appreciable, despite the fact that the concentration-ratio is low for the trade as a whole.

Imports and exports

Where a trade's products are imported or exported on a considerable scale, the concentration-ratio may again be misleading as an indicator of

[1] Monopolies Commission, *Report on the Supply of Electric Lamps* (London, H.M.S.O. 1951), par. 147.

monopoly power. Domestic supply is simply stated as home production *plus* imports *minus* exports, so that the degree of control in the domestic market cannot be equated with the degree of control in home production unless imports are negligible and the export trade is shared between producers in the same proportion as home production.

The competitive effect of imports on a highly concentrated trade presupposes that the largest units have no responsibility for those imports. This is not always the case. The match trade, for example, is highly concentrated: the British Match Corporation was responsible for 87 per cent of total sales (including exports) of home-produced matches in 1949–50. But large quantities of matches are imported into this country (as well as exported abroad), and in the same year imports accounted for 38 per cent of the total sales of matches in the United Kingdom market. If these imports were marketed independently of the United Kingdom producers, they might be expected to have considerably offset the high degree of concentration in production. In fact, however, the British Match Corporation was very much concerned with match imports—indeed, it was responsible for nearly 89 per cent of imports in 1949–50—so that, far from reducing the Corporation's power in the market, imports served to reinforce it.[1]

The experience of the match industry is an argument in favour of precise examination rather than general observations on the effect of imports on the concentration-ratio as an indicator of monopoly power. But either way, the existence of a large import element in domestic supply is a factor which must be taken into account in interpreting concentration-ratios.

Countervailing buying power

Whether the concentration-ratio measures control over production or control over supply, it is still confined to concentration on one side of the market, whereas for the assessment of monopoly power it is important to determine whether or not there is a corresponding degree of concentration on the other side of the same market.

Professor J. K. Galbraith's concept of 'countervailing power' postulates that concentration in production is not infrequently matched by concentration in buying; his broad proposition is that

> 'The long trend toward concentration of industrial enterprise in the hands of relatively few firms has brought into existence not only strong sellers, as economists have supposed, but also strong buyers as they have failed to see.'[2]

The existence of these strong buyers acts as a severe check on the mono-

[1] Monopolies Commission, *Supply and Export of Matches* (1953), par. 9.
[2] J. K. Galbraith, *American Capitalism* (London, Hamish Hamilton, 1952), p. 118.

poly power of the strong sellers. Indeed, the large buyers 'are often big enough to play one big supplier off against another' and in the last resort, 'they often have the capital and skill to "roll their own" if their suppliers cannot make it worth their while to buy'.[1]

Without going to such lengths, the British Electricity Authority has bought mains cable on the basis that 'in the absence of genuine free competition, the only satisfactory evidence of fair and reasonable prices lies in the full disclosure of costs, and the proper examination of this information by independent accountants'. This was approved by the Monopolies Commission, which recommended that the firms in question should be obliged to submit their costs for investigation by the British Electricity Authority (now the Central Electricity Authority) in order to ensure that the prices charged are reasonable.[2] Similarly, submarine telegraph cable, which is monopolised by a single company, has been costed by the General Post Office since 1947 not only for the G.P.O.'s 'own relatively small contracts but also an increasing amount of the large purchases made by Cable and Wireless'.[3]

Where countervailing power exists and is effective, the monopoly power of the larger seller is clearly modified, if not nullified. On the other hand, the potentialities of countervailing power will be blunted by vertical integration, whereby the largest sellers command their own sales outlets, or pre-empt supplies of raw materials.

4. CONCLUSION

In the preceding sections of this chapter, we have been concerned with identifying the principal factors which prevent the use of the concentration-ratio as a sure and certain measure of monopoly power. To them must be added the difficulties described in Chapter 1, arising from the fact that the Census trade, to which the concentration data refer, is seldom the most suitable entity for the measurement of monopoly in that it fails to include all the close-substitutes in the market, but includes other products which are scarcely competitive at all.

Perhaps it is, as Professor Miller has suggested, 'a sign of the immaturity of the science of economics that the notion should persist that the competitiveness of the economy or of a sector of the economy can ultimately be characterised by some single number or set of numbers'.[4]

[1] A. D. H. Kaplan and A. E. Kahn, 'Big Business in a Competitive Society' (*Fortune*, Section 2, February 1953, p. 4).

[2] Monopolies Commission, *Report on the Supply of Insulated Electric Wires and Cables* (London, H.M.S.O. 1952), pars. 27 and 278.

[3] Monopolies Commission, *Insulated Electric Wires and Cables* (1952), par. 288.

[4] J. P. Miller, '*Measures of Monopoly Power and their Significance*', in *Business Concentration and Price Policy*, N.B.E.R. p. 119.

All the same, it is useful and important to express whatever we can numerically, and since the degree of concentration is amenable to such measurement, it would be wrong to neglect it.

Even so, what does the concentration-ratio tell us? The answer would seem to be that it provides little concrete information. But that does not mean that it is entirely pointless.

A high degree of concentration is certainly incompatible with anything like perfect competition in the economist's sense. If competition exists (with no explicit collusion), it will be oligopolistic in form and rarely extend to active price competition. Even so, the monopoly power of any individual firm, operating in such circumstances, may be very small, and the concentration-ratio cannot distinguish such cases from those where one firm has it all its own way.

It is perhaps advisable to claim no more than this: that if the purpose is to detect monopoly power, then the trades which should be given priority are those with a high degree of concentration. While restrictive agreements are consistent with low concentration-ratios, it is probable that, unless transport costs break up the market to a marked degree, no firm will have very much discretion in its selling or buying policies and each firm will be under pressure from its competitors to be efficient. Thus, most cases of monopoly power, though not all, will be found in trades with high concentration-ratios.

To conclude, the concentration-ratio is little more than a starting-point in the detection of monopoly power, and its interpretation is hedged around with many qualifications. Yet it is at least a starting-point and, with the help of more detailed descriptive material, it can be used both to analyse industrial structure and to provide a first very rough but systematic assessment of market conditions for a large number of trades.

PART II

CONCENTRATION AND INDUSTRY STRUCTURE IN 1951

CHAPTER IV

CONCENTRATION IN 1951

1. INTRODUCTION

The Board of Trade has provided concentration data, presented in Appendix B, for 147 Trades of the 1951 Census of Production, as well as for 200 of their constituent Sub-Trades. Employment in those 147 Trades amounted to more than 8,750,000 in 1951, or some 86 per cent of the total employment in all the Trades covered by the Census of Production.

The Trades include a variety of extractive, manufacturing and processing industries, as well as a few service trades, and represent the bulk of privately owned industry in the United Kingdom. Indeed, the only Trades omitted by the Board of Trade are those where concentration data would have been inapplicable by virtue of the fact that they were either nationalised or government-controlled trades[1] or the province, wholly or in part, of local authorities.[2]

The object of this chapter is to review the 347 trades[3] for which concentration data are available and, after removing a number of trades for various reasons, to classify the remainder according to their level of concentration, and finally to examine how far it is possible to establish concentration-ratios for broader groups of trades and for all the trades together.

2. THE SELECTION OF TRADES FOR ANALYSIS

Before the analysis of concentration in 1951 can proceed, it is necessary to review the 347 Census Trades and Sub-Trades and to establish their suitability for that purpose.

The first principle that guides the selection of the trades for analysis is that the Sub-Trades, as the more specialist entities, are generally to be preferred to the more heterogeneous Trades of which they form part.

[1] Coal Mines, Manufactured Fuel, Gas Supply, Electricity Supply, Wholesale Slaughtering, and Flax Processing.

[2] Local Authorities (Building and Civil Engineering) and Water Supply.

[3] As already explained above 'Trades' and 'Sub-Trades' are collectively described as 'trades', except where distinction between them is necessary.

But in order to avoid duplication, the selection of a Sub-Trade means that the Trade to which it belongs must be omitted from the analysis.

The process of selection must be guided also by the comprehensiveness of the Census trade. For reasons discussed in Chapter 1, the concentration data will not be meaningful if the specialisation or exclusiveness of a Census trade is unsatisfactorily low. Thus, all trades with degrees of specialisation or exclusiveness of 67 per cent and under are omitted from the analysis, while other trades have been rejected because the data are inadequate or unsatisfactory for specific reasons.

The principles governing the selection of trades for analysis, and the reasons why particular Trades or Sub-Trades have been rejected, are described more fully in Appendix G. Altogether 220 Census trades have been selected, and their combined employment of 6,368,700 represents 73 per cent of the total labour-force in the 147 Census Trades covered by the concentration data.

By specifying a minimum level of specialisation and exclusiveness, the trades where the concentration data have little or no meaning are eliminated at the outset. There are, however, distinct shades of meaning which can be attached to the concentration data for trades that satisfy the minimum standards. In particular, it is possible to distinguish those trades where the concentration-ratios correspond closely to the degree of control over the home-produced supply of a particular product (or group of close-substitute products) from those where the product-structure is much more heterogeneous. Such trades must, in the first place, have high degrees of specialisation and exclusiveness (90 per cent and over). Secondly, where the trade consists of more than one principal product, either they must be close-substitutes in the market, or one principal product must account for the overwhelming proportion of the trade. The trades which seem to satisfy these two conditions, and for which the concentration-ratios can consequently be regarded as a close approximation to the degree of control over the production of specific products, are italicised in the tables of this chapter. Between the two extremes fall the bulk of the trades selected for analysis: the concentration-ratios are meaningful but are qualified both by the heterogeneity and comprehensiveness of the trades to which they refer.

3. CLASSIFICATION OF TRADES ACCORDING TO LEVEL OF CONCENTRATION

The degree of concentration in a particular trade depends, to some extent, on the way in which it is defined. In general, the more broadly an industry is defined (that is, the greater the number and range of the principal products that comprise it) the higher will be the number of business units included and the lower will be its concentration-ratio. Thus, concentration-ratios for individual products are frequently higher than the concentration-ratio for the trade of which they form part.[1]

Furthermore, the choice of categories of concentration to which trades may be classified must be somewhat arbitrary. There is no established definition of 'high' or 'low' concentration which can be used. For our purposes, however, it is convenient to distinguish three categories of employment and/or net output concentration by which trades can be classified:

(*a*) High concentration (67 per cent and over)
(*b*) Medium concentration (34–66 per cent)
(*c*) Low concentration (33 per cent and under)

In Table 1, the 220 trades which have been selected for the 1951 analysis are arranged according to these three categories of concentration, and the relative importance of the trades in the three categories is shown by their aggregated employment. Thus, it can be seen that the fifty high-concentration trades (or more than one-fifth of the total number of trades) account for only 10 per cent of the total employment in the 220 trades, while the sixty-nine medium-concentration trades (or just under one-third of the total number) account for another 24 per cent of the total employment. The largest concentration category, both in terms of the number of trades and total employment, comprises the 101 low-concentration trades, representing 46 per cent of all trades and 66 per cent of total employment.

Table 1. *Distribution of 220 trades by concentration category, 1951*

Concentration category (employment or net output)	Trades		Employment	
	Number	Percentage of total	Thousands	Percentage of total
High (67 per cent and over)	50	23	636	10
Medium (34–66 per cent)	69	31	1,545	24
Low (33 per cent and under)	101	46	4,188	66
Total	220	100	6,369	100

High-concentration trades

The fifty trades which, by employment or net output, had concentration-ratios of 67 per cent and over in 1951 are identified in Table 2, which also gives the number of business units and the total employment in each of these trades.

For twenty of these fifty trades, included in Section (*a*) of Table 2, the concentration-ratios supplied by the Board of Trade refer to more than the three largest units. The reason for this departure from general prac-

[1] See, for example, Leak and Maizels, table 12, p. 161. Also Richard Evely, 'Concentration in American Industry', *Cartel*, January 1958, p. 18.

tice is that concentration data for the three largest units would risk disclosure of the absolute importance of individual concerns. But it is unlikely that the concentration-ratio for the three largest units in these trades would be substantially lower than that given.

Table 2. *High-concentration trades with employment or net output concentration-ratios of 67 per cent and over, 1951*

Group and code number	Trades*	Number of business units	Concentration-ratios: Employment (%)	Concentration-ratios: Net output (%)	Trade employment (thousands)
	(a) Trades for which concentration-ratio refers to more than three business units†				
E13	Primary Batteries (8)	8	100	100	9·0
O33	*Incandescent Mantles* (5)	5	100	100	0·8
D20	Transmission Chains (5)	5	100	100	6·1
G4	Razors (excl. Electric) (4)	11	94	99	3·9
H5	Cotton Thread (8)	27	94	91	12·7
B23	Explosives and Fireworks (6)	29	93	91	30·5
A14	Asbestos Cement Goods (4)	9	92	92	7·3
G36	Photographic Plates and Films (4)	14	90	91	10·2
A1	*Cement* (4)	12	87	89	12·3
E14	Accumulators and Parts (4)	20	86	89	7·5
F4	Motor Cycles, etc. (4)	17	86	87	15·0
N6	*Wallpaper* (4)	16	86	86	5·5
B24	*Match* (6)	27	85	86	4·1
D17	Scales and Weighing Machinery (6)	23	85	83	6·0
M8	Spirit Distilling (6)	38	80	73	5·3
L23	Margarine (4)	27	77	85	5·3
C15	Wrought Iron and Steel Tubes (4)	81	77	79	42·4
L26	Vinegar and Other Condiments (4)	21	75	80	1·9
C22	Zinc (5)	42	68	82	8·1
M7	Wholesale Bottling of Wines/Spirits (7)	112	58	74	9·2
	(b) Trades for which concentration-ratio refers to three largest business units				
E10	Valves and Cathode Ray Tubes	9	85	82	14·5
B16	Mineral Oil Refining	8	84	35	12·1
L5	*Sugar and Glucose*	25	84	82	18·8
A5	Salt Mines, etc.	12	83	87	5·6
G27	Precious Metals Refining	13	83	84	5·7

* The trades in italics are those for which the concentration-ratios closely approximate to the degree of control over the production of the specific products; see p. 50.

† The figures in brackets after the names of trades in section (*a*) give the number of business units to which the concentration-ratios refer.

Table 2 (*continued*)

Group and code number	Trades*	Number of business units	Concentration-ratios Employment (%)	Concentration-ratios Net output (%)	Trade employment (thousands)
L18	Starch	11	83	89	2·6
D21	Small Arms	15	82	85	5·2
B17	Seed Crushing and Oil Refining	26	81	79	9·4
D9	Prime Movers: internal combustion	25	77	80	28·3
A18	Abrasive Wheels, etc.	19	76	79	5·4
M9	Spirit Rectifying	10	75	83	1·6
C23	Tin	13	75	80	2·0
O23	Floor Coverings	11	75	76	10·5
P10	Tramway, Trolleybus and Omnibus Undertakings (Civil Engineering)	11	75	74	4·5
O2	Rubber Tyres and Tubes	11	75	73	35·1
D13	Ball and Roller Bearings	15	75	70	21·5
B7	Fertilisers	68	73	75	16·5
J3	Rayon, Nylon C.F. Yarn and Staple Fibre	10	72	82	40·3
B19	Soap and Glycerine	74	72	80	18·8
C14	*Tinplate*	18	71	72	16·9
M12	*Tobacco*	60	70	74	46·0
C10	Cast Iron Stoves and Grates: Other	15	68	69	9·9
D8	Boilers and Boiler-house Plant	40	67	62	26·5
C11	Cast Iron Pipes and Fittings	31	66	68	13·9
N12	Notepaper, Pads, Envelopes	30	66	68	10·1
L22	Ice Cream	65	65	76	6·1
J26	Asbestos Manufactures	31	65	70	13·5
F6	Bicycles and Tricycles	99	64	69	26·4
O35	*Cinematograph Film Printing*	18	61	70	2·4
C21	Lead	40	53	69	3·2

* The trades in italics are those for which the concentration-ratios closely approximate to the degree of control over the production of the specific products; see p. 50.

Three points emerge from an examination of Table 2. First, the number of business units in the great majority of these high-concentration trades is relatively small. Thus, only thirteen of the fifty high-concentration trades have more than thirty units, and among the others are eight where the units are ten or under (including three for which the Board of Trade concentration-ratios are 100 per cent), and twenty-nine with eleven to thirty units.

Secondly, the size of the trades in terms of employment varies considerably, for the smallest has an employment of 800 persons and the largest of 46,000. Yet it is by no means inevitably the case that the high-concentration trades are small trades. Ten of them have a total employment of less than 5,000, but there are twenty-three where it exceeds 10,000.

Thirdly, the high-concentration trades are very varied in their type of activity. They include producer goods trades, such as transmission chains, cement, and wrought iron and steel tubes, as well as such consumer goods trades as razors, wallpaper, margarine and bicycles. Indeed, the high-concentration trades are so important and their characteristics so diverse that they will be later studied in greater detail in Chapters VIII and IX.

Medium-concentration trades

Among the sixty-nine trades with medium concentration-ratios (that is, from 34 to 66 per cent inclusive) in 1951, there are fifteen where the number of business units is thirty or under. For the other fifty-four trades, the number of business units varies greatly, the largest total being recorded for Textile Machinery and Accessories; Dry Cleaning, Valeting, Dyeing etc.; and Chemicals (General).

There is, as may be seen from Table 3, a corresponding variety in the sizes of the trades as measured by employment. The smallest trade is Ice with only 600 employees, and the largest is Aircraft Manufacture and Repair with 157,500. But whereas only three of the fifteen trades with thirty or fewer business units employed more than 10,000 people, thirty-eight of the fifty-four trades with a larger number of units had labour-forces of 10,000 and over.

Table 3. *Medium-concentration trades with employment or net output concentration-ratios of 34 to 66 per cent, 1951*

Group and code number	Trades*	Number of business units	Concentration-ratios: Employment (%)	Concentration-ratios: Net output (%)	Trade employment (thousands)
	(*a*) *Trades for which concentration-ratio refers to more than three business units*†				
G13	Metal Boxes and Containers (4)	83	60	61	26·1
B1	Chemicals (General) (4)	307	49	48	87·3
I8	Blankets, Shawls, Travelling Rugs (5)	52	45	35	3·0
	(*b*) *Trades for which concentration-ratio refers to the three largest business units*				
A6	*Slate Quarries and Mines*	21	65	64	4·8
B5	Coke Ovens and By-Products	24	63	63	18·7

* The trades in italics are those for which the concentration-ratios closely approximate to the degree of control over the production of the specific products; see p. 50.

† The figures in brackets after the names of trades in section (*a*) give the number of business units to which the concentration-ratios refer.

Table 3 (*continued*)

Group and code number	Trades*	Number of business units	Concentration-ratios Employment (%)	Net output (%)	Trade employment (thousands)
F12	Locomotive Manufacturing†	28	61	53	21·3
D16	Gas Meters	20	60	63	7·7
G30	Watch and Clock	61	60	62	11·1
C13	Steel Sheets	21	59	65	19·7
A16	Roofing Felts	13	58	65	1·9
P11	Canal, Dock and Harbour Undertakings (Civil Engineering)	51	58	58	24·8
C17	*Iron Ore and Ironstone*	26	58	55	6·8
L8	Cocoa and Chocolate	85	57	61	44·0
G33	Other Optical Instruments and Appliances	27	57	58	6·1
E11	Electric Lamps	41	55	56	13·0
A23	Electrical Ware	15	54	60	7·0
C9	Cast Iron Stoves and Grates: Solid Fuel	36	54	56	12·3
N16	Magazines and Periodicals	86	54	53	18·5
B4	Plastics Materials	51	53	51	20·4
O32	Office Machinery Requisites	18	52	46	4·4
B21	Polishes and Canvas Dressings	38	52	43	4·6
J11	Woven Cotton, etc. Fabrics—Printing	52	51	50	18·8
C19	Copper and Copper Alloys	104	51	35	32·5
E6	Electric Wires and Cables	46	50	48	50·0
F3	Commercial Vehicles	77	49	51	61·5
E4	Electric Cookers and Heaters	65	49	45	12·6
I9	Mechanical Cloth and Wool Felts	23	48	50	4·5
E2	Electrical Machinery	212	48	46	154·3
L25	Preserved Meat	21	48	32	5·7
D18	Refrigerating Machinery	35	47	55	15·4
A25	Glass Containers	48	47	45	24·9
L27	*Ice*	14	46	57	0·6
A26	Glass (other than containers)	249	46	51	42·2
J14	Textile Packing	42	46	48	2·7
F9	Aircraft Manufacture and Repair	117	46	47	157·5
F5	Motor Bodies, Sidecars, Trailers	244	45	48	58·7
C1	*Blast Furnaces*	35	45	47	27·8
O34	Cinematograph Film Production	54	45	40	6·0
C20	Aluminium and Magnesium	138	44	43	48·7
G35	Photographic and Cinematograph Apparatus	34	44	38	2·8
L14	*Animal Feedingstuffs*	134	43	55	13·6
L29	Tea Blending	76	43	45	7·0
N9	Cartons	64	42	35	16·8

* The trades in italics are those for which the concentration-ratios closely approximate to the degree of control over the production of the specific products; see p. 50.

† Excluding railway locomotive shops.

Table 3 (*continued*)

Group and code number	Trades*	Number of business units	Concentration-ratios Employment (%)	Concentration-ratios Net output (%)	Trade employment (thousands)
	(*b*) *Trades for which concentration-ratio refers to the three largest business units*				
L2	Milled Wheat	164	41	46	23·8
N13	Paper Bags	72	40	51	8·3
B25	Ink	37	40	45	4·2
B22	Glue, Gum, Paste and Allied Trades	53	39	41	5·5
A21	Sanitary Earthenware	19	38	47	4·1
O27	Toys and Games	163	38	42	23·7
J18	Jute	49	38	38	17·5
N10	Fibreboard Packing Cases	29	37	43	7·9
G17	Safes, Locks, Latches, etc.	68	36	40	8·3
D4	Textile Machinery and Accessories	375	36	36	73·5
G9	Anchors and Chains	49	36	35	4·1
G8	Steel Drop Forgings	70	36	35	15·5
B12	Toilet Preparations and Perfumery	77	35	41	10·2
A9	Roofing Tiles of Clay	40	34	39	3·7
G26	Scrap Metal Processing	156	34	37	9·4
J8	Cotton Yarn—Finishing	57	34	36	7·8
O38	Dry Cleaning, Valeting, Dyeing, etc.	310	34	34	34·7
B15	Lubricating Oils and Greases	78	34	32	7·1
L4	*Biscuit*	92	34	31	41·8
D7	Agricultural Machinery	134	32	40	20·2
A20	Glazed Tiles	39	32	37	10·1
O31	Pens, Pencils, Crayons, etc.	57	32	35	7·6
M6	Wholesale Bottling of Beer	220	30	36	17·6
A22	China and Porcelain	44	30	35	13·3
D12	Office Machinery	51	29	34	21·2
J17	Cordage, Cables, Ropes, etc.	86	27	40	12·3

* The trades in italics are those for which the concentration-ratios closely approximate to the degree of control over the production of the specific products; see p. 50.

Low-concentration trades

There remains the group of 101 trades for which both the employment and net output concentration-ratios are 33 per cent or under. These trades are identified in Table 4, from which it may be seen that they vary very greatly in size whether determined by the number of business units or by total employment. Thus, the smallest by both measures is Fellmongery with forty-one business units employing 1,700 persons, and the largest is New Building Construction with 5,312 business units employing 404,000 persons.

Table 4. *Low-concentration trades with employment and net output concentration-ratios of 33 per cent and under, 1951*

Group and code number	Trades*	Number of business units	Concentration-ratios: Employment (%)	Concentration-ratios: Net output (%)	Trade employment (thousands)
	(*a*) *Trades for which concentration-ratio refers to more than three business units*†				
L19	*Fish Curing* (4)	129	30	28	5·7
A4	Clay, Sand, Gravel, Chalk (4)	277	29	26	14·3
G34	Medical, Surgical, Veterinary Instruments (4)	125	29	20	9·0
O20	Leather Goods (4)	315	10	9	17·3
	(*b*) *Trades for which concentration-ratio refers to the three largest business units*				
D14	Mining Machinery	41	33	32	10·9
J10	Woven Cotton Fabrics—Dyeing	79	32	32	18·1
G28	Musical Instruments	92	32	28	6·9
J12	Woven Woollen and Worsted Fabrics—Finishing	76	31	33	6·1
D23	Printing and Bookbinding Machinery	104	31	33	19·1
A8	*Building Bricks*	397	30	32	39·1
K18	Hats, Hoods, etc. of Fur Felt	63	30	32	6·3
N15	Newspapers	351	30	32	74·2
E9	Radio Apparatus and Gramophones	180	30	27	80·2
K17	Hats, Hoods, etc. of Wool Felt	79	30	23	5·1
O15	*Fellmongery*	41	29	26	1·7
O26	Sports Requisites	104	29	26	7·5
K11	Corsets and Brassières	76	29	25	13·7
G37	Scientific, Engineering, Industrial Instruments	171	28	30	29·4
J6	*Carpets, Rugs of Wool*	59	28	26	26·8
G7	Bolts, Nuts, Screws, Rivets	244	28	25	41·3
G2	Edge and Similar Tools	94	27	31	9·7
A10	Refractory Goods	123	27	30	18·0
D2	Marine Engineering	79	27	27	57·0
J15	Linen and Soft Hemp	62	27	27	11·9
H2	Cotton Spinners and Doublers	212	27	25	129·7
B9	Drugs and Pharmaceutical Preparations	232	27	24	50·7
G32	Ophthalmic Instruments and Appliances	147	26	31	12·2
D15	Heating and Ventilating Apparatus	143	26	29	14·2

* The trades in italics are those for which the concentration-ratios closely approximate to the degree of control over the production of the specific products; see p. 50.

† The figures in brackets after the names of trades in section (*a*) give the number of business units to which the concentration-ratios refer.

Table 4 (*continued*)

Group and code number	Trades*	Number of business units	Concentration-ratios: Employment (%)	Concentration-ratios: Net output (%)	Trade employment (thousands)
	(*b*) *Trades for which concentration-ratio refers to the three largest business units* (continued)				
F13	Railway Carriages, Wagons and Trams†	107	25	25	32·5
D1	Shipbuilding and Ship Repairing	513	25	23	207·8
K24	Boot and Shoe Repairs for the Trade	105	24	30	4·0
C2	Iron and Steel (Melting and Rolling)	282	24	25	204·9
K3	Wholesale Tailoring—Men's and Boys'	424	24	20	95·8
L21	Whole Milk (Bottled or Processed)	334	23	22	44·2
D22	Mechanical Handling Equipment	186	23	21	31·5
G12	Domestic Hollow-ware	119	22	31	14·6
I5	Worsted Yarns	199	22	27	54·0
G21	Wire and Wire Manufactures	227	22	23	35·5
M11	Soft Drinks	357	22	23	21·4
G5	Knives	99	22	21	7·2
J13	Hosiery and Knitted Fabrics—Finishing	64	22	20	7·8
J28	Hair, Fibre and Kindred Trades	94	22	20	5·9
K9	Women's and Girls' Nightwear and Underwear	202	21	23	14·8
N1	Paper and Board	193	21	19	73·7
I4	Woollen Yarns	80	21	12	8·7
G19	Needles, Pins, Fish Hooks and Metal Smallwares	145	20	22	23·0
G10	Springs, other than laminated	104	20	20	10·2
B13	*Paint and Varnish*	296	19	20	36·0
G14	Other Hollow-ware	87	19	19	9·5
L15	Bacon Curing and Sausage	320	19	17	23·5
G15	Metal Furniture, other than aseptic hospital furniture	136	18	21	11·2
A15	Lime and Whiting	83	18	17	4·3
I7	Woven Worsted Fabrics	238	18	17	38·0
L10	Preserved Fruit and Vegetables	287	17	21	50·7
O7	Shop and Office Fittings	255	17	15	17·4
D5	Constructional Engineering	363	16	17	62·2
O14	Bedding	181	16	17	12·6
O25	Plastic Goods	252	16	16	23·6
A11	Sanitary Ware	83	16	14	11·1
C12	Iron Engineering Castings	613	15	17	62·4

* The trades in italics are those for which the concentration-ratios closely approximate to the degree of control over the production of the specific products; see p. 50.

† Excluding railway establishments.

Table 4 (*continued*)

Group and code number	Trades*	Number of business units	Concentration-ratios: Employment (%)	Concentration-ratios: Net output (%)	Trade employment (thousands)
L3	Bread and Flour Confectionery	1,512	15	17	132·0
J22	Narrow Fabrics	165	15	16	19·7
K12	Heavy Overalls and Aprons	115	15	13	11·3
K20	Gloves and Mittens	123	15	13	8·4
L9	Sugar Confectionery	225	15	12	26·1
D24	Mechanical Engineering (Repairing)	679	15	11	33·3
K21	Umbrella and Walking Stick	48	14	16	2·5
A24	Other Earthenware and Stoneware	126	14	15	36·0
O21	Fur	187	14	13	7·5
O28	Brushes and Brooms	195	13	18	14·0
A3	Stone	419	13	18	23·0
D3	Machine Tools	590	13	15	87·1
N8	Rigid Boxes	273	13	14	19·7
K7	Proofed Garments	244	13	14	26·2
M1	Brewing and Malting	283	13	11	70·8
O12	Upholstered Furniture	317	12	15	21·4
A13	Pre-cast Concrete Goods	326	12	14	23·8
K4	Wholesale Tailoring—Women's and Girls'	457	12	9	41·4
J20	Lace	179	12	8	12·1
J27	Flock and Rag	170	11	13	8·4
K14	Making-up of Tailored Garments	700	11	9	29·3
O16	Leather (Tanning and Dressing)	393	11	7	33·4
O11	Wooden Furniture	654	10	12	60·4
G29	Jewellery and Plate	333	10	10	19·0
J19	Canvas Goods and Sack	211	10	8	13·8
J1	Hosiery and Knitted Goods	865	8	12	116·8
G25	Brass Manufacture	533	8	10	45·9
P2	New Building Construction	5,312	8	8	404·0
K23	Boots, Shoes, Sandals, Slippers, etc.	649	8	8	113·5
K8	Men's and Boys' Shirts, Underwear, etc.	228	8	7	34·0
I6	Woven Woollen Fabrics	278	8	6	52·5
N17	Printing, Publishing, Bookbinding, Engraving	2,664	7	8	186·9
G18	Specialist Finishers of Metal Goods	363	6	9	14·8
K6	Wholesale Dressmade Garments	700	6	6	45·7
K15	Work Done—Dressmade Garments	370	6	6	11·2
K2	Retail Tailoring and Dressmaking	475	6	6	13·8
O37	*Laundry Work*	1,500	6	6	126·9

* The trades in italics are those for which the concentration-ratios closely approximate to the degree of control over the production of the specific products; see p. 50.

Table 4 (*continued*)

Group and code number	Trades	Number of business units	Concentration-ratios: Employment (%)	Concentration-ratios: Net output (%)	Trade employment (thousands)
	(*b*) *Trades for which concentration-ratio refers to the three largest business units* (continued)				
O5	Saw Mill Products	789	6	5	48·6
O9	Wooden Boxes, Packing Cases, etc.	335	5	5	21·5
H7	Woven Cotton Cloth	539	5	4	103·6
F8	Motor Vehicles and Cycles (Repairing)	726	4	4	71·1

4. CONCENTRATION BY BROAD INDUSTRY GROUPS, 1951

When concentration-ratios are available for over two hundred trades, varying greatly in their individual size and importance, it is clearly desirable that an attempt should be made to summarise them in some way. The obvious basis on which summary may proceed is provided by the classification of trades to broad industry groups, corresponding to the Standard Industrial Classification Orders, by the Census of Production authorities themselves. Indeed, only by this means can answers be even attempted to such pertinent questions as: are some groups of trades more prone to high concentration than others; or what is the level of concentration in industry as a whole?

A broader grouping of Census trades might sometimes be desirable if it brought close-substitutes together. It would then be logical to relate the concentration-ratio to the largest business units in the group of trades as a whole. But this approach is not possible on the basis of the available data. The only kind of concentration-ratios which can be established for a group of trades is a weighted average of the individual trade concentration-ratios. The so-called group concentration-ratio is thus obtained by weighting the employment (or net output) concentration-ratio for each trade by the trade's employment (or net output).

There is, of course, a large arbitrary element in the concentration-ratios for groups of trades computed on this basis. In the main, it springs from the definition of the Census trade, which has complicated the discussion of concentration throughout. If the Census trades were more narrowly defined, then the individual trade concentration-ratios would probably be higher, and the group concentration-ratio would be higher as well. The reverse would apply if business units were aggregated into larger groups.

The significance of a weighted average concentration-ratio for all trades or for groups of trades depends entirely on how far the individual trades can be regarded as mutually exclusive competing entities. Since the trades under consideration include some which are well defined and others badly defined from this point of view, it would be wrong to attach very much significance to the absolute value of such a weighted average.

There is no escape from the fundamental problem of the Census trades: we must accept them as they are. But the concentration-ratios for groups of trades are also affected by the movement of a trade from one group to another. And there is still the element of arbitrariness in the classification of the sixteen Groups of Census trades as they are listed in Appendix B. These Groups, as stated above, are largely determined by Census of Production practice, though certain modifications have been made by sub-dividing some Census Orders and amalgamating others.[1]

In Table 5, the 220 trades selected for the analysis of concentration in 1951 are allocated to their respective Groups which, in turn, are arranged according to their estimated degree of concentration. The Groups with the highest degree of concentration in terms of employment and net output are Chemicals and Allied Trades, Electrical Engineering and Electrical Goods, and Vehicles; those with the lowest are Building, Contracting and Civil Engineering, Clothing and Footwear, and Woollen and Worsted. For ten Groups, net output concentration was higher than employment concentration, the differences being greatest for Other Textiles (9 percentage points), Drink and Tobacco (6 points), Mining and Quarrying and Treatment of Non-Metalliferous Mining Products (6 points) and Food (5 points). For the other six Groups, with the exception of Chemicals and Allied Trades, employment concentration exceeded net output concentration by only a few percentage points.

For the sixteen Groups combined, the degree of concentration in 1951 was 29 per cent on the basis of employment, and 33 per cent in terms of

[1] The principal changes are as follows:

(*a*) Order VI: Engineering, Shipbuilding and Electrical Goods has been divided into: Shipbuilding and Non-Electrical Engineering (Group D); and Electrical Engineering and Electrical Goods (Group E).

(*b*) Order X: Textile has been divided into: Cotton (Group H), Woollen and Worsted (Group I), Other Textiles (Group J).

(*c*) Order VIII: Metal Goods not elsewhere specified; and Order IX: Precision Instruments, Jewellery, etc. have been combined in Other Metal Industries (Group G).

(*d*) Orders XI: Leather, Leather Goods and Fur; XIV: Manufactures of Wood and Cork; and XVI: Other Manufacturing Industries have been combined in Other Manufacturing and Service Trades (Group P).

(*e*) Part of Order II: Mining and Quarrying; and part of Order III: Treatment of Non-Metalliferous Mining Products (other than Coal) have been combined in Mining and Quarrying and Treatment of Non-Metalliferous Mining Products (Group A).

(*f*) Order XIII: Food, Drink and Tobacco has been divided into Food (Group L) and Drink and Tobacco (Group M).

Table 5. *Concentration of employment and net output by trade groups, 1951*

	Trade group	Total group employment (000's)	Selected trades: Total number of trades	Selected trades: Employment: Total (000's)	Selected trades: Employment: Aggregated employment of three largest units in each trade (000's)	Selected trades: Net output: Total (£m.)	Selected trades: Net output: Aggregated net output of three largest units in each trade (£m.)	Group degree of concentration: Employment (%)	Group degree of concentration: Net output (%)
B	Chemicals and Allied Trades	376·7	16	335·8	170·2	319·0	146·8	51	46
E	Electrical Engineering and Electrical Goods	614·3	8	341·1	164·1	207·3	95·3	48	46
F	Vehicles	767·5	8	443·9	181·9	272·1	119·4	41	44
C	Iron and Steel and Non-Ferrous Metals	545·8	15	511·6	199·7	418·4	168·4	39	40
M	Drink and Tobacco	177·1	7	172·0	62·4	209·2	88·5	36	42
A	Mining and Quarrying and Mining Products	347·4	21	312·2	108·5	206·3	84·5	35	41
D	Shipbuilding and Non-Electrical Engineering	1,115·3	20	754·6	235·7	476·1	152·2	31	32
L	Food	495·4	18	453·5	136·4	297·3	104·8	30	35
G	Other Metal Industries	539·6	27	402·5	116·8	268·0	85·2	29	32
J	Other Textiles	510·2	18	360·2	98·8	243·3	88·1	27	36
N	Paper and Printing	466·1	10	421·6	87·8	366·4	86·8	21	24
H	Cotton	290·9	3	246·0	51·6	158·0	29·2	21	18
O	Other Manufacturing and Service Trades	689·0	23	539·2	105·2	285·2	64·9	20	23
I	Woollen and Worsted	192·4	6	164·3	29·8	99·7	18·3	18	18
K	Clothing and Footwear	559·7	17	476·9	65·7	202·2	24·6	14	12
P	Building, Contracting and Civil Engineering	1,066·1	3	433·3	53·8	214·7	24·2	12	11
	Total	8,753·5	220	6,368·7	1,868·4	4,243·2	1,381·2	29	33

net output. As already indicated, however, too much importance must not be attached to these concentration-ratios, since they can only be held to indicate the general level of concentration in 1951 in the most imprecise way.

It may be noted that Leak and Maizels, obtaining an overall degree of employment concentration of 26 per cent in 1935, went on to state that 'about one-quarter of the total number of persons employed in an "average" productive industry in 1935 were employed by the three largest units in that industry'. Yet this concept of an 'average productive industry' is not very clear, while its concentration-ratio does not appear very meaningful.

It does not follow, moreover, because Leak and Maizels obtained an overall degree of employment concentration of 26 per cent in 1935, and our figure is 29 per cent for 1951, that concentration over industry as a whole has risen by the extent of the difference during the 1935–51 period. In the first place, some of the trades included in the 1935 analysis have been excluded from the scope of the present study, because the concentration data either would be inappropriate (for example, Coal Mines), or unsatisfactory in terms of exclusiveness and specialisation.[1] In the second place, as we shall see in Chapter x below, there have been extensive changes in the definitions of trades between 1935 and 1951. These changes, if they had taken place in 1935, would have altered the concentration-ratios of the individual trades in 1935, and the overall degree of concentration for the revised trades might, as a consequence, be higher (or lower) than the original 26 per cent.[2] Thus, for both these reasons, it is impossible to come to any definite and clear-cut conclusion about the change in the level of concentration in British industry between 1935 and 1951, even assuming that such an average level of concentration is accepted as a significant concept.

5. THE DISTRIBUTION OF EMPLOYMENT AND NET OUTPUT AMONG THE 220 TRADES, 1951

An alternative method of summarising concentration data is by a frequency distribution of the trades according to their concentration-ratios. In Table 6, the 220 trades have been arranged according to their em-

[1] When the trades for which 1951 data are not available are removed from the 1935 list, and the principles of selection used for 1951 (see Appendix G) are applied to the remainder of the 1935 trades, the revised overall degree of concentration for the 200 1935 trades is estimated to be 27 per cent in terms of employment, and 32 per cent in terms of net output. Even so, the revised figures cannot be directly compared with their 1951 equivalents because of the changes in the definition of the trades.

[2] It is not, in fact, possible to estimate what the 1935 overall degree of concentration would have been if trades were defined in 1935 in the same way as in 1951.

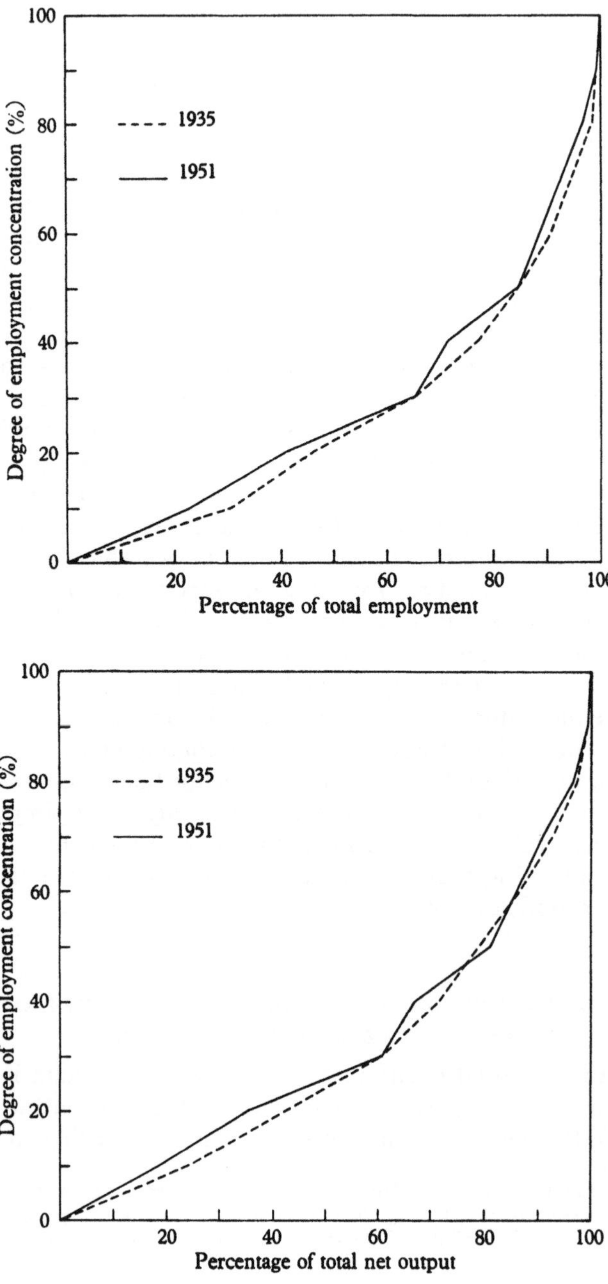

Fig. 1 Frequency distribution of employment and net output for 200 trades in 1935 and 220 trades in 1951

ployment concentration-ratios in 1951, and for each concentration-class, the total employment and net output of the trades therein are given.

It will be seen that around 55 per cent of the 220 trades had employment concentration-ratios higher than the overall degree of concentration of 29 per cent in 1951, but that together they accounted for only 34 per cent of total employment and some 39 per cent of total net output. Similarly, although 17 per cent of the total number of trades had concentration-ratios of 70 per cent and over, they did not account for more than 7 per cent of total employment and 9 per cent of total net output in 1951. Altogether half of all the employment is in trades where employment concentration is less than 24 per cent, while half of the total net output is in trades where employment concentration is less than 26 per cent.

Table 6. *Frequency distribution of 220 trades according to degree of employment concentration, 1951*

Degree of employment concentration	Total number of trades		Total employment		Total net output	
%		%	000's	%	£m.	%
1–10	20	9·1	1,521·5	23·9	797·8	18·8
11–20	37	16·8	1,082·9	17·0	702·6	16·6
21–30	43	19·6	1,586·3	24·9	1,078·8	25·4
31–40	26	11·8	386·3	6·1	258·9	6·1
41–50	23	10·4	831·1	13·0	604·1	14·2
51–60	20	9·1	292·1	4·6	233·5	5·5
61–70	13	5·9	207·7	3·3	187·3	4·4
71–80	18	8·2	267·8	4·2	235·4	5·6
81–90	17	7·7	177·1	2·8	136·1	3·2
91–100	3	1·4	15·9	0·2	8·7	0·2
Total	220	100·0	6,368·7	100·0	4,243·2	100·0

In Fig. 1, the cumulative frequency distribution of employment and net output for the 220 trades of 1951, grouped according to their employment concentration-ratios, are compared with the distributions for the 200 trades of 1935 which are valid for analysis on the basis described above. It will be seen that the curves for the two years are close together and, in the case of net output, they actually cross. On the whole, concentration would appear to be somewhat higher in 1951 than in 1935, though the difference is small. Moreover, the arbitrary element in the definition of Census trades is as relevant to this distribution of trades as it was to the overall concentration-ratio.

In comparing concentration over time it seems better to proceed on a selective rather than a general basis, particularly in order to reduce the effect of changes in the definition of Census trades. To this problem we turn in Part III.

CHAPTER V

INDUSTRY STRUCTURE IN 1951

I. INTRODUCTION

The relevance of concentration data to the analysis of industry structure has already been discussed in Chapter II, and the purpose of the present chapter is to distinguish as far as possible the different types of industry structure among 219 trades in 1951.[1]

In order to determine its structure, a trade's concentration-ratio must be associated not only with the number of business units in the trade but also with the size-ratio of those units (that is, the average employment of the three largest units relative to the average employment of the other larger units).[2] In addition, it is helpful to take into account the average size of units.

The three categories of concentration—high, medium and low—have already been defined in the last chapter, and the distinction has also been made there between trades with 'few' business units (that is, thirty and under) and those with 'many' (thirty-one and over). Similarly, in this chapter we shall make a broad distinction between the trades with a 'large' size-ratio of units (sixteen and over) and those with a 'small' size-ratio (fifteen and under). As for concentration and the number of units, the choice of the demarcation line at sixteen is purely arbitrary, though it appears to conform fairly well with the known characteristics of the trades. Finally, three categories of average size of units—that is, trade employment divided by number of units—are distinguished: 'large', with more than 750 persons per unit; 'medium', with 250–749 persons per unit; and 'small', with less than 250 persons per unit.

The results of classifying the 219 trades according to their concentration, number and size-ratio of units are presented in Table 7, while the relative importance of the trades in the various categories is indicated by the size of their labour-force. In order to interpret Table 7 in terms of the different type of industry structure, as well as to identify the trades belonging to these different types, each of the three main concentration categories is examined separately below.

[1] The trade omitted from the 220 trades of the preceding chapter is New Building Construction, for which certain data are not comparable.

[2] As already stated, some of the concentration-ratios supplied by the Board of Trade refer to the share of the four, five, six, etc. largest units. Estimates have been made of the probable concentration-ratios for the three largest units in such trades, and in the ensuing analysis, the data refer to the three largest units irrespective of the number of units covered by the Board of Trade concentration-ratio.

Table 7. *Distribution of the 220 trades according to degree of concentration, number- and size-ratio of units, 1951*

Concentration category	Large size-ratios of units (16 and over)						Small size-ratios of units (15 and under)						Total		
	Few units (30 and under)			Many units (31 and over)			Few units (30 and under)			Many units (31 and over)					
	Number of trades	Total employment (000's)	%	Number of trades	Total employment (000's)	%	Number of trades	Total employment (000's)	%	Number of trades	Total employment (000's)	%	Number of trades	Total employment (000's)	%
High (67 per cent and over)	20	199	3·3	13	236	4·0	17	201	3·4	—	—	—	50	636	10·7
Medium (34–70 per cent)	—	—	—	25	1,043	17·5	15	121	2·0	29	381	6·4	69	1,545	25·9
Low (33 per cent and under)	—	—	—	40	2,542	42·6	—	—	—	60	1,242	20·8	100	3,784	63·4
Total	20	199	3·3	78	3,821	64·1	32	322	5·4	89	1,623	27·2	219	5,965	100·0

2. INDUSTRY STRUCTURE AMONG THE HIGH-CONCENTRATION TRADES

It will be seen from Table 7 that the fifty high-concentration trades fall into three main groups: (*a*) the twenty trades with few units and large size-ratios; (*b*) the thirteen trades with many units and large size-ratios;[1] and (*c*) the seventeen trades with few units and small size-ratios.

Trades with few units and large size-ratios

Where concentration is high and units are few, and their size-differences large, it is likely that strong elements of monopoly power exist by virtue of the fact that one or two large concerns dominate the trade. There are twenty trades where such considerations apply, and in Table 8 they are identified and arranged according to the average size and size-ratio of their business units.[2] The variation in the size-ratio of units is very great: it ranges from sixteen for Wallpaper to seventy for both Explosives and Fireworks, and Cotton Thread.

The trades also vary considerably in terms of employment, and in the average size of their units. For six of the twenty trades, the average size of units is large, which means that the biggest units are not only relatively but absolutely large. Indeed, the employment per largest unit is more than 2,500 for five of these six trades, the exception being Transmission Chains with just under 2,000 persons per largest unit. On the other hand, there is only one trade, Photographic Plates and Films, among the eleven with medium unit size, where the largest units have an average of more than 2,500 persons. Even so, the average for the others is between 1,000 and 2,500. Moreover, the large size-ratios mean that the largest units still have an average employment of more than 1,000 for two (Margarine and Match) of the three trades where the average unit size is small. The other trade, Incandescent Mantles, is itself so small that the three largest units employ, on the average, between 250 and 300 persons.

Indeed, all these twenty trades tend to be relatively small in terms of employment, so that although they represent 9 per cent of the total number of trades, their combined labour-force accounts for only 3 per cent of the total for the 219 trades.

Trades with many units and large size-ratios

Even where the trades possess a larger number of units, the existence of large unit size-differences in a high-concentration trade means that the

[1] Included in this group is Lead, which has forty units but whose unit size-ratio is fourteen. The low size-ratio is due to the fact that its employment concentration was as low as 53 per cent. Its net output concentration-ratio is, on the other hand, as high as 69 per cent, and since it is classified among the high-concentration trades by this indicator, it is permissible to use the same indicator to determine its unit size-ratio, which thereby becomes large.

[2] The basic data for this and other tables are given in Appendix H.

Table 8. *High-concentration trades with few units and large unit size-ratios by average unit size, 1951**

Size-ratio of units	Average size of units					
	Large		Medium		Small	
16–20	Transmission Chains	*17*	Wallpaper	*16*	Incandescent Mantles	*17*
			Notepaper, Pads, Envelopes	*17*		
			Precious Metals Refining	*17*		
			Abrasive Wheels, etc.	*17*		
			Small Arms	*18*		
21–30	Motor Cycles, etc.	*22*	Photographic Plates and Films	*23*	Margarine	*22*
	Prime Movers: internal combustion	*24*	Razors (excl. Electric)	*24*		
			Accumulators	*26*		
			Scales and Weighing Machinery	*28*		
31–40	Sugar and Glucose	*38*	Seed Crushing and Oil Refining	*34*	Match	*33*
41–50	Primary Batteries	*42*	—	—	—	—
51 and over	Explosives and Fireworks	*70*	Cotton Thread	*70*	—	—

* The figures in italics are the size-ratios of units for each trade.

Table 9. *High-concentration trades with many units and large unit size-ratios by average unit size, 1951**

Size-ratio of units	Average size of units: Large		Medium		Small	
16–20	—	—	Asbestos Manufactures	*17*	—	—
			Cast Iron Pipes and Fittings	*19*		
21–30	—	—	Boilers and Boiler-house Plant	*26*	Zinc	*24*
					Lead†	*28*
31–40	—	—	—		Spirit Distilling	*38*
					Ice Cream	*39*
41–50	Tobacco	*44*	—		Wholesale Bottling of Wines and Spirits	*46*
51 and over	—	—	Bicycles and Tricycles	*58*	Fertilisers	*59*
			Soap and Glycerine	*62*		
			Wrought Iron and Steel Tubes	*74*		

Table 10. *High-concentration trades with few units and small unit size-ratios by average unit size, 1951**

Size-ratio of units	Average size of units: Large		Medium		Small	
6–10	Rayon, Nylon C.F. Yarn and Staple Fibre	*6*	Tramway, Trolleybus and Omnibus Undertakings (Civil Engineering)	*8*	Spirit Rectifying	*7*
	Floor Coverings	*8*	Cast Iron Stoves and Grates: Other	*9*	Cinematograph Film Printing	*8*
	Mineral Oil Refining	*8*			Tin	*10*
	Rubber Tyres and Tubes	*8*				
11–15	Valves and Cathode Ray Tubes	*11*	Salt Mines, etc.	*14*	Starch	*13*
	Tinplate	*12*			Vinegar and Other Condiments	*15*
	Ball and Roller Bearings	*12*				
	Asbestos Cement Goods	*14*				
	Cement	*15*				

* The figures in italics are the size-ratio of units for each trade.

† See p. 68, n. 1.

largest concerns, surrounded by a considerable number of pygmies, may also possess a significant degree of monopoly power. There are thirteen trades which come within this category, and these are shown in Table 9, together with their average size and size-ratios of units.

The range of the unit size-ratios is even greater than for the 'monopolistic' group of high-concentration trades. The smallest exists for Asbestos Manufactures (17) while the largest exists for Wrought Iron and Steel Tubes (74). Among the seven trades where the average unit size is medium or large, the large size-ratio once again indicates the presence of giant concerns.[1] Thus, there are two trades where the largest units have an average employment of more than 10,000 (Tobacco, and Wrought Iron and Steel Tubes), and another two where the average is more than 5,000 (Boilers and Boiler-house Plant, and Bicycles and Tricycles). Although the largest units are generally smaller among the trades where the average unit size is small, the average employment of the largest units is more than 4,000 in the case of Fertilisers, and between 1,000 and 2,500 in three of the other four trades, the exception being Lead. Yet the fact remains that the combined labour-force of these thirteen trades with many units and large size-ratios only represents 4 per cent of total employment, so that their relative importance is again small.

Trades with few units and small size-ratios

Finally, there are the high-concentration trades which combine few units with small size-differences. Conditions in these trades seem favourable for collusion, but that does not rule out the possibility that active and fierce competition (of an oligopolistic kind) may in fact prevail. The seventeen trades in question are identified in Table 10, from which it may be seen that for nine of these trades the average size of units is large. Once again, the largest units are giants for these nine trades: they employ an average of 5–10,000 persons in three trades (Rayon, Nylon C.F. Yarn and Staple Fibre, Rubber Tyres and Tubes, and Ball and Roller Bearings), and in every case but one (Asbestos Cement Goods) have an average employment of more than 2,500. At the other extreme, there are the five trades with small average unit size and small size-ratios. Not only are the largest units comparatively small concerns (their average employment is less than 500 for four of the five trades), but the five trades are themselves small, since only one has a total employment of more than 2,500. Although the trades with large and medium unit size are, naturally enough, much larger, the aggregated employment of the seventeen trades with few units and small size-differences represents 3 per cent of the total for the 219 trades.

[1] The use of the term 'giant' is restricted in this chapter to those largest units whose average employment is more than 2,500.

Table 11. *Medium-concentration trades with many units and large unit size-ratios by average unit size, 1951**

Size-ratio of units	Average size of units: Large		Medium		Small	
16–20	—		Woven Cotton Fabrics—Printing	*17*	Tea Blending	*18*
			Plastics Materials	*18*	Electric Cookers and Heaters	*20*
21–30	Commercial Vehicles	*24*	Canal, Dock and Harbour Undertakings (Civil Engineering)	*22*	Agricultural Machinery	*21*
					Scrap Metal Processing	*27*
					Watch and Clock	*28*
31–40	Aircraft Manufacture and Repair	*32*	Aluminium and Magnesium	*35*	Wholesale Bottling of Beer	*32*
			Copper and Copper Alloys	*35*	Magazines and Periodicals	*33*
			Cocoa and Chocolate	*36*	Animal Feedingstuffs	*33*
			Metal Boxes and Containers	*36*	Toys and Games	*33*
					Milled Wheat	*38*
41–50	—	—	—	—	—	—
51 and over	—	—	Electrical Machinery	*65*	Dry Cleaning, Valeting, Dyeing	*53*
			Chemicals (General)	*90*	Motor Bodies, Sidecars, Trailers	*65*
					Glass (other than Containers)	*70*
					Textile Machinery and Accessories	*71*

* Figures in italics are the size-ratio of units for each trade.

Summary

To sum up, therefore, it may be said that there is a monopolistic element in the structure of all the high-concentration trades, but that need not mean that monopoly power is either present or exercised in every case. These trades account for a fairly small proportion—between 10 and 11 per cent—of the employment in all the 219 trades, although some of the fifty trades are individually important by any reckoning.

3. INDUSTRY STRUCTURE AMONG THE MEDIUM-CONCENTRATION TRADES

The sixty-nine medium-concentration trades also fall into three distinct groups: (*a*) the twenty-five trades with many units and large size-ratios; (*b*) the fifteen trades with few units and small size-ratios; and (*c*) the twenty-nine trades with many units and small size-ratios.

Trades with many units and large size-ratios

The twenty-five medium-concentration trades with many units and large size-differences are composed of a relatively few giant concerns and a considerable number of pygmies. As for the high-concentration trades with the same unit characteristics, tacit collusion or price leadership, and a significant degree of monopoly power, are likely to be found among these twenty-five trades.

The twenty-five trades are identified in Table 11, from which it may be seen that for eleven of them, the average unit size is medium or large. For two of these trades (Electrical Machinery, and Aircraft Manufacture and Repair), the three largest units have an average employment of more than 20,000, while in another two cases (Chemicals (General) and Commercial Vehicles), the average is more than 10,000. Three of the other seven trades (with medium-size units) have an average of 5–10,000 employed by the largest units, and in no case is it less than 3,000. Finally, among the fourteen trades where the average unit size is small, the existence of large size-ratios allows the largest units to have an average employment of 5–10,000 in three trades (Textile Machinery and Accessories; Motor Bodies, Sidecars, Trailers; and Glass (other than Containers)) and from 2,500–5,000 in another four trades (Dry Cleaning, Valeting, Dyeing etc.; Magazines and Periodicals; Milled Wheat; and Toys and Games).

On the whole, these trades tend to be larger than those with high concentration, so that together they account for 17·5 per cent of the total employment in the 219 trades, and two-thirds of the total employment in the medium-concentration trades.

Table 12. *Medium-concentration trades with few units and small unit size-ratios by average unit size, 1951**

Size-ratio of units	Average size of units					
	Large		Medium		Small	
5 and under	—	—	Fibreboard Packing Cases	*5*	Ice	*3*
			Electrical Ware	*5*	Sanitary Earthenware	*3*
					Roofing Felts	*5*
					Office Machinery Requisites	*5*
6–10	Steel Sheets	*9*	Preserved Meat	*6*	Mechanical Cloth and Wool Felts	*6*
			Gas Meters	*9*		
11–15	Coke Ovens and By-Products	*12*	Iron Ore and Ironstone	*11*	Slate Quarries and Mines	*11*
	Locomotive Manufacturing†	*13*			Other Optical Instruments and Appliances	*11*

* Figures in italics are the size-ratio of units for each trade.
† Excluding railway locomotive shops.

Trades with few units and small size-ratios

The fifteen medium-concentration trades with few units and small unit size-ratios may also have conditions similar to those in the high-concentration trades with the same unit characteristics. That is to say, the conditions are favourable to collusion, with the difference that the smaller share of the trade under the control of the largest units may not give them such influence as in the case of the high-concentration trades.

The fifteen trades in question are shown in Table 12. For eight trades, the average size of unit is medium or large, and the three largest units employ an average of 2,500–5,000 persons in each of the three trades where the average unit size is large (Locomotive Manufacturing; Coke Ovens and By-Products; and Steel Sheets). Similarly, for all but two of the five trades with medium unit sizes (Fibreboard Packing Cases and Preserved Meat) the average employment per largest unit is more than a thousand. Among the seven trades with small unit size, on the other hand, the three largest units have an average employment of more than a thousand only in the case of Slate Quarries and Mines, and Other Optical Instruments and Appliances. Once again, these trades tend to be the smaller trades, for together they account for only 2 per cent of the total employment among the 219 trades.

Trades with many units and small size-ratios

The combination of many units and small size-differences among the remaining twenty-nine medium-concentration trades might be interpreted as signifying the presence of competitive elements in their structure. On the other hand, the fact that the three largest units control at least one-third of the trade suggests, particularly if the trade or a sufficiently large part of it is collectively organised, that they may possess considerable influence in its affairs.

The twenty-nine trades are listed in Table 13, from which it may be seen that average unit size is large in two trades and medium in another ten. The three largest units have an average employment of more than 8,000 in the case of Electric Wires and Cables, and between 2,500 and 5,000 for Blast Furnaces; Glass Containers; and Biscuit. For the other eight trades, employment is between 1,000 and 2,500.

Among the seventeen trades with small average unit size, the three largest still employ more than one thousand apiece in five trades:

Steel Drop Forgings	Paper Bags
Toilet Preparations and Perfumery	Cordage, Cables, Rope, etc.
	Safes, Locks, Latches, etc.

For the rest, employment per largest unit is between 400 and 500 for four trades (Anchors and Chains; Textile Packing; Clay Roofing Tiles; and

Table 13. *Medium-concentration trades with many units and small unit size-ratios by average unit size, 1951**

Size-ratio of units	Average size of units: Large		Medium		Small	
6–10	Blast Furnaces	*9*	Glazed Tiles	*6*	Clay Roofing Tiles	*6*
			China and Porcelain	*6*	Ink	*8*
			Office Machinery	*7*	Photographic and Cinematograph Apparatus	*8*
			Jute	*10*	Pens, Pencils, Crayons	*8*
			Refrigerating Machinery	*10*	Cotton Yarn—Finishing	*9*
					Anchors and Chains	*9*
					Cordage, Cables, Rope, etc.	*10*
					Glue, Gum, Paste and Allied	*10*
11–15	Electric Wires and Cables	*15*	Cast Iron Stoves and Grates: Solid Fuel	*13*	Textile Packing	*11*
			Glass Containers	*13*	Cinematograph Film Production	*11*
			Electric Lamps	*15*	Blankets, Shawls, Travelling Rugs	*12*
			Cartons	*15*	Steel Drop Forgings	*12*
			Biscuits	*15*	Safes, Locks, Latches, etc.	*12*
					Polishes and Canvas Dressings	*13*
					Lubricating Oils and Greases	*13*
					Toilet Preparations and Perfumery	*13*
					Paper Bags	*15*

* Figures in italics are the size-ratio of units for each trade.

Photographic and Cinematograph Apparatus), and between 500 and 1,000 in the other eight trades.

Once again, the importance of these trades with many units and small size-differences is relatively slight, since they account for only 6 per cent of the total employment in the 219 trades.

Summary

Taking the medium-concentration trades together, therefore, it may be said that the most important group comprises the twenty-five trades whose structure embodies some significant monopolistic element by virtue of the size-differences that exist between the units composing those trades. For the rest, there is a possibility of collusion in one group, and of dominant influence, where collective organisation exists, in the other.

4. INDUSTRY STRUCTURE AMONG THE LOW-CONCENTRATION TRADES

Among the one hundred low-concentration trades are two groups: (*a*) the forty trades with many units and large unit size-ratios; and (*b*) the sixty trades with many units and small unit size-ratios.

Trades with many units and large size-ratios

Large differences in unit size may mean that conditions in many of the forty trades, despite their low concentration, are incompatible with the operation of perfect competition. Thus, where the largest units are absolutely as well as relatively large, it is possible that one or other of them may act as price-leader for the whole trade, or that singly or in combination they can threaten the existence of their smaller brethren by aggressive competition.

It will be seen from Table 14 that there are six trades for which the average size of units is medium, so that the large size-ratios indicate the presence of giant concerns. In fact, employment per largest unit is over 10,000 in the case of three trades: Iron and Steel (Melting and Rolling); Shipbuilding and Ship Repairing; and Cotton Spinners and Doublers. It is also between 5,000 and 10,000 for Radio Apparatus and Gramophone, and Paper and Board, and between 2,500 and 5,000 for Worsted Yarns.

Similarly, giant concerns are to be found among the thirty-four trades where average unit size is small. Employment per largest unit is between 5,000 and 10,000 for three trades (Wholesale Tailoring, Men's and Boys'; Newspapers; and Bread and Flour Confectionery) and between 2,500 and 5,000 in another thirteen trades:

Table 14. *Low-concentration trades with many units and large unit size-ratios by average unit size, 1951**

Size-ratio of units	Average size of units: Medium		Small	
16–20	Paper and Board	*17*	Medical, Surgical, Veterinary Instruments	*16*
	Worsted Yarns	*18*	Heating and Ventilating Apparatus	*16*
			Fish Curing	*17*
			Ophthalmic Instruments and Appliances	*17*
			Woven Worsted Fabrics	*17*
			Shop and Office Fittings	*17*
			Women's and Girls' Nightwear, etc.	*18*
			Saw Mill Products	*18*
			Preserved Fruit and Vegetables	*19*
			Boots, Shoes, Sandals, etc.	*19*
21–30	Radio Apparatus and Gramophone	*25*	Stone	*21*
	Cotton Spinners and Doublers	*26*	Wholesale Tailoring—Women's and Girls'	*21*
	Iron and Steel (Melting and Rolling)	*30*	Scientific, Engineering, Industrial Instruments	*22*
			Wire and Wire Manufactures	*22*
			Paint and Varnish	*23*
			Wooden Furniture	*24*
			Constructional Engineering	*24*
			Bacon Curing and Sausage	*25*
			Hosiery and Knitted Goods	*25*
			Making-up of Tailored Garments	*28*
			Drugs and Pharmaceuticals	*28*
			Machine Tools	*30*
31–40	—	—	Bolts, Nuts, Screws, Rivets	*31*
			Whole Milk (Bottled or Processed)	*32*
			Soft Drinks	*33*
			Laundry Work	*34*
			Clay, Sand, Gravel, Chalk	*36*
			Iron Engineering Castings	*36*
			Mechanical Engineering (Repairing)	*39*
41–50	—	—	Wholesale Tailoring—Men's and Boys'	*45*
			Newspapers	*50*
51 and over	Shipbuilding and Ship Repairing	*56*	Building Bricks	*55*
			Printing, Publishing, Bookbinding, Engraving	*66*
			Bread and Flour Confectionery	*91*

* The figures in italics are the size-ratio of units for each trade.

Printing, Publishing, Bookbinding, Engraving
Preserved Fruit and Vegetables
Scientific, Engineering, Industrial Instruments
Wire and Wire Manufactures
Iron Engineering Castings
Drugs and Pharmaceuticals
Bolts, Nuts, Screws, Rivets
Whole Milk (Bottled or Processed)
Boots, Shoes, Sandals, etc.
Hosiery and Knitted Goods
Machine Tools
Laundry Work
Constructional Engineering

Indeed, only in four of these thirty-four trades is employment per largest unit less than 1,000: Medical, Surgical, Veterinary Instruments; Fish Curing; Shop and Office Fittings; and Stone.

Out of the forty trades with many units and large size-ratios, therefore, the largest units have an average employment of more than 2,500 persons in twenty-two cases. Thus, the giant concerns may possess considerable power in trades accounting for nearly 35 per cent of the total employment for the 219 trades. Moreover, though the largest units are not absolutely so large in the other eighteen trades, their relatively greater size may still endow them with sufficient influence to make perfect competition improbable. Employment in these eighteen trades represents another 8 per cent of the combined total for the 219 trades.

Trades with many units and small size-ratios

Finally, there are the sixty low-concentration trades, identified in Table 15, which have many units and small differences in the sizes of

Table 15. *Low-concentration trades with many units and small unit size-ratios by average unit size, 1951**

Size-ratio of units	Average size of units: Medium		Small	
10 and under	Mining Machinery	*6*	Umbrella and Walking Stick	*2*
	Carpets, Rugs of Wool	*7*	Fellmongery	*5*
	Other Earthenware and Stoneware	*7*	Sanitary Ware	*5*
	Marine Engineering	*9*	Lime and Whiting	*6*
			Hosiery and Knitted Fabrics—Finishing	*6*
			Wooden Boxes, Packing Cases, etc.	*6*
			Men's and Boys' Shirts, etc.	*6*
			Heavy Overalls and Aprons	*6*
			Flock and Rag	*7*
			Gloves and Mittens	*7*
			Other Hollow-ware	*7*
			Woollen Yarns	*7*
			Linen and Soft Hemp	*7*
			Canvas Goods and Sack	*8*

* Figures in italics are the size-ratio of units for each trade.

Table 15* (*continued*)

Size-ratio of units	Average size of units: Medium		Small	
10 and under (*continued*)			Specialist Metal Finishers	*8*
			Lace	*8*
			Woven Woollen Fabrics	*8*
			Work Done—Dressmade Garments	*8*
			Springs, other than Laminated	*9*
			Woven Cotton Cloth	*9*
			Hair, Fibre and Kindred Trades	*9*
			Hats, Hoods, etc. of Fur Felt	*9*
			Knives	*9*
			Corsets and Brassières	*10*
			Brushes and Brooms	*10*
			Metal Furniture, etc.	*10*
			Narrow Fabrics	*10*
			Fur	*10*
			Retail Tailoring and Dressmaking	*10*
			Boot and Shoe Repairs for the Trade	*10*
11–15	Railway Carriages, Wagons, Trams†	*11*	Hats, Hoods, etc. of Wool Felt	*11*
	Brewing and Malting	*14*	Woven Woollen and Worsted Fabrics—Finishing	*11*
			Edge Tools	*11*
			Domestic Hollow-ware	*11*
			Motor Vehicles and Cycles (Repairing)	*11*
			Leather Goods	*11*
			Bedding	*12*
			Woven Cotton Fabrics (Dyeing)	*12*
			Upholstered Furniture	*12*
			Proofed Garments	*12*
			Needles, Pins, Fish Hooks	*12*
			Sugar Confectionery	*13*
			Jewellery and Plate	*13*
			Rigid Boxes	*13*
			Musical Instruments	*14*
			Sports Requisites	*14*
			Pre-cast Concrete Goods	*14*
			Brass Manufacture	*15*
			Wholesale Dressmade Garments	*15*
			Mechanical Handling Equipment	*15*
			Printing and Bookbinding Machinery	*15*
			Refractory Goods	*15*
			Plastic Goods	*15*
			Leather (Tanning and Dressing)	*15*

* The figures in italics are the size-ratio of units for each trade.

† Excluding railway establishments.

those units. These trades come closest to satisfying the theoretical definition of a perfectly competitive industry, and fall short of it mainly because there is considerable product heterogeneity in most cases. But provided there is not collective regulation, which in most cases would be very difficult to administer because of the large number of producers, there are only a few of these trades where any firm or group of firms would be capable of exercising any monopolistic influence.

Among the possible exceptions to the general rule are four trades where average unit size is medium and the size-ratios are sufficiently large to give the largest units an average employment of more than 2,500, namely:

Marine Engineering	Railway Carriages, Wagons and Trams
Brewing and Malting	Carpets, Rugs of Wool

But employment in these four trades only represents 3 per cent of the total for the 219 trades.

Employment in the other fifty-six trades accounts for nearly 18 per cent of the total, and employment per largest unit is less than 1,000 for thirty-seven of them and between 1,000 and 2,500 for the remainder.

Summary

For the low-concentration trades, therefore, it may be said that there are seventy-four trades, with just over one-quarter of the total employment in the 219 trades, where there is a likelihood that perfect competition, in the absence of collective regulation, will be operating. The presence of giant concerns in the other twenty-six trades suggests on the other hand, despite low concentration, that competition will not be fully operative, and employment in these trades accounts for nearly 38 per cent of the combined total.

5. SUMMARY

In the light of the preceding analysis, it is possible to make a number of general statements about the structure of the 219 trades in 1951, though it would be rash to pretend that they can be anything but tentative generalisations.

In the first place, the trades with strong elements of monopoly in their structure are comparatively few and relatively unimportant in terms of employment. At most, they account for little more than 10 per cent of the total employment.

At the other extreme, the trades which are essentially competitive in their structure are more numerous and important. They represent more than one-third of the total number of trades, though not much more than one-quarter of the total employment.

In between come the rest of the trades which, to one degree or another, embody monopolistic elements in their structure. Such trades account for over three-fifths of the total employment, but less than half the total number of trades.

Turning to the average size of units, there are only twenty-three trades where average unit size is large, and concentration is high for sixteen of them and medium for the others. On the other hand, the average size of units is small in 138 trades, and concentration is low in eighty-nine cases and high in twelve.

The existence of large unit size-ratios for ninety-eight of the 219 trades means, however, that the largest units in a trade are frequently not only relatively much larger than the others, but also absolutely large. Thus, there are nine trades (including three with low concentration) where the largest units have an average employment of 10,000 or over:

Tobacco
Wrought Iron and Steel Tubes
Commercial Vehicles
Aircraft Manufacture and Repair
Chemicals (General)
Cotton Spinners and Doublers
Iron and Steel (Melting and Rolling)
Shipbuilding and Ship Repairing
Electrical Machinery

For another twenty-one trades, of which five have low concentration, average employment per largest unit is between 5,000 and 10,000:

Boilers and Boiler-house Plant
Bicycles and Tricycles
Explosives and Fireworks
Sugar and Glucose
Prime Movers: internal combustion
Rayon, Nylon C.F. Yarn and Staple Fibre
Rubber Tyres and Tubes
Ball and Roller Bearings
Copper and Copper Alloys
Cocoa and Chocolate
Motor Bodies, Sidecars, Trailers
Glass (other than Containers)
Aluminium and Magnesium
Textile Machinery and Accessories
Electric Wires and Cables
Paper and Board
Radio Apparatus and Gramophone
Wholesale Tailoring—Men's and Boys'
Newspapers
Bread and Flour Confectionery
Marine Engineering

Last, there are forty-three trades where employment per largest unit is 2,500–5,000, so that giant concerns can be said to be operating in seventy-three trades, or one-third of the total number covered by this analysis.

CHAPTER VI

PLANT STRUCTURE IN 1951

I. INTRODUCTION

We have already seen in the previous chapter that the differences in size between the business units comprising a trade have an important bearing on its structure, and it is intended in this chapter to inquire to what extent these size-differences are due to technological, commercial and other factors which affect the relative number and size of plants[1] operated by different business units.

It was shown in Chapter II that the size-ratio of business units can be divided into two components: the number-ratio of plants (that is, the average number of plants of the three largest units divided by the average number for the other units), and the size-ratio of plants (that is, the average numbers employed per establishment of the largest units divided by the average numbers per establishment of the other units).[2] It is possible, therefore, to establish the relative importance of plant size differences and plant number differences in accounting for the disparity in the size of the units in each trade.

The size-ratio and number-ratio of plants are important for two reasons. Differences in the sizes of plants *within* a trade, when supplemented by average plant size, may suggest the importance of technological or locational factors in determining the size of the typical plant, as well as indicating whether entry into the trade is difficult or easy. Similarly, the number-ratio of plants is a measure of the importance of multi-plant operations in a trade, and when linked with plant size data, tentative conclusions can be drawn about the importance of managerial or commercial economies, transport costs, and monopolistic strivings, as reasons for these multi-plant operations.

The concepts to be used in this chapter have, for the most part, already been defined above, but it is necessary to emphasise that some of the classifications employed below are fairly arbitrary. Two categories of average plant size, for example, are distinguished: *small*, where the average number of persons per plant[3] is less than 250; and *large*, where it is

[1] The term 'plant' is used here to embrace all kinds of establishments covered by the Census of Production.

[2] See Chapter II, p. 39 and Appendix F.

[3] The reason for adopting the average number of workers per establishment, rather than some other measure such as Professor Sargant Florence's prevalent plant size, to denote the average or typical size of plant in each trade is given in Chapter II, p. 38.

250 or over.[1] Similarly, the number- and size-ratios of plants are divided into *small*, when they are 5 and under; and *large* when they are over 5.[2]

We shall proceed by treating the ninety-eight trades where large differences in unit size existed in 1951 separately from the other 121 where the differences were small.

2. PLANT STRUCTURE OF TRADES WITH LARGE DIFFERENCES IN SIZES OF BUSINESS UNITS

Trades with small plant size-differences

Thirty-six out of the ninety-eight trades with large unit size-ratios have only small plant size-ratios. Such relatively small differences in the sizes of plants within a trade may be taken as indicative of the operation of technological, locational or transport factors which set a pattern to which most of the plants conform. But in order to determine which of these factors are likely to be the more important, it is necessary to take into account the average size of plant.

For twenty-eight of the thirty-six trades, the average size of plant, as well as the plant size-ratio, is small.[3] These trades are identified in Table 16, which also gives their plant number-ratios and plants per unit.[4] There are, of course, several reasons why a trade may have small plants. The trade itself may be small, though only six of the twenty-seven with small plants and plant size-ratios have less than 10,000 employed. But it may also be that there are no technical advantages to be gained from increasing the size of plant. Where a trade must cater for a variety of consumer tastes, or produces a large number of different items, there is room for a number of small specialist plants. Alternatively, even where technical economies could be obtained by increasing the size of plant, it may be that these advantages would be more than offset by the increased transport costs involved in obtaining raw materials or distributing the finished product.

It is not surprising, therefore, to find among the twenty-eight trades with small plants and small plant size-differences, a considerable number to which such considerations obviously apply. There are, for example, extractive industries, such as Stone, and Clay, Sand, Gravel, Chalk,

[1] The fact that the average number of persons per plant among factory trades was 127 in 1951 (see Chapter XI, p. 171) might suggest that to call a plant with up to 250 persons 'small' is misleading. But it is also the case that the median worker in the factory trades is to be found among the establishments with 300–399 persons, which makes the 250 demarcation line for small plants appear more reasonable.

[2] The unweighted average number-ratio of plants for the 219 trades is 4·5, while the unweighted average size-ratio is 5·7.

[3] Thus, small plants represent between three-quarters and four-fifths of these trades, which corresponds to their proportion of all the 219 trades.

[4] The basic data for this and other tables are given in Appendix H.

Table 16. *Twenty-eight trades with large unit size-differences, small plant size-ratios and small average plants, by number-ratio of plants and concentration category, 1951*

	Number-ratio of plants	Plants per unit: Three largest units	Plants per unit: Other units
Low-concentration trades			
Bread and Flour Confectionery	22·6	27·3	1·2
Building Bricks	22·4	31·3	1·4
Soft Drinks	19·7	25·3	1·3
Whole Milk (Bottled or Processed)	18·5	27·0	1·5
Laundry Work	14·5	17·0	1·2
Clay, Sand, Gravel, Chalk	12·8	16·3	1·3
Saw Mill Products	10·5	13·7	1·3
Mechanical Engineering (Repairing)	9·9	11·3	1·1
Stone	9·1	11·7	1·3
Boots, Shoes, Sandals, etc.	7·2	9·3	1·3
Woven Worsted Fabrics	7·1	9·0	1·3
Ophthalmic Instruments and Appliances	6·9	9·0	1·3
Wire and Wire Manufactures	6·7	8·0	1·2
Paint and Varnish	5·7	6·7	1·2
Worsted Yarns	5·6	7·3	1·3
Fish Curing	5·4	6·3	1·2
Shop and Office Fittings	3·7	4·0	1·1
Medical, Surgical, Veterinary Instruments	3·2	3·7	1·2
Medium-concentration trades			
Canal, Dock and Harbour Undertakings (Civil Engineering)	13·5	19·0	1·4
Wholesale Bottling of Beer	13·7	17·3	1·3
Scrap Metal Processing	12·1	14·0	1·2
Milled Wheat	9·7	11·7	1·3
Woven Cotton Fabrics—Printing	4·8	6·0	1·2
High-concentration trades			
Spirit Distilling	14·9	18·7	1·3
Scales and Weighing Machinery	14·5	16·7	1·2
Fertilisers	14·3	16·0	1·1
Wallpaper	5·5	6·0	1·1
Precious Metals Refining	4·7	5·7	1·2

where the size of 'plant' is largely determined by the area of the mineral deposits, while other examples of this kind are as follows:

Dispersed materials	*Product differentiation*
Scrap Metal Processing	Boots, Shoes, Sandals, etc.
Saw Mill Products	Shop and Office Fittings
Whole Milk (Bottled or Processed)	Wallpaper
Building Bricks	Woven Worsted Fabrics
Milled Wheat	Medical, Surgical, Veterinary Instruments
Fish Curing	

Dispersed markets	*Service trades*
Soft Drinks	Wholesale Bottling of Beer
Bread and Flour Confectionery	Laundry Work
Fertilisers	Mechanical Engineering (Repairing)
	Woven Cotton Fabrics—Printing
	Canal, Dock and Harbour Undertakings (Civil Engineering)

In trades where both plant size and plant size-differences are small, it follows that multi-plant operation is likely to be a condition of growth for the individual firm. Where transport and locational factors restrict the sizes of plants, a firm must increase the number of its plants and disperse them if it is to serve a wider market. In fact, the number-ratio of plants is large for twenty-four of the twenty-eight trades[1] with small average plant size and plant size-ratios.[2] Since the other units also include a number of multi-plant concerns in some of these trades, the plants per unit of the three largest units is often considerably higher than the plant number-ratio. Thus, from Table 16, it may be seen that the largest units have an average of more than fifteen plants each in eleven out of the twenty-three trades, though the number-ratio is more than fifteen for only four of them.

In sixteen of the twenty-four trades, concentration is low despite the large unit size-differences. For them, the largest units have grown relatively large by multi-plant operation without securing control of the major part of the trade. Concentration, on the other hand, is medium or high in the other eight trades, and though transport and locational factors may again have been operating, it is also probably true that they do not wholly explain the number of plants operated by the largest units. The multi-plant growth may, in their case, have been prompted not merely by the desire of some units to grow but also by the desire to bring a large share of the trade under their control. Certainly amalgamations and acquisitions have been an important feature of the development of concentration in trades such as Milled Wheat; Spirit Distilling; Scales and Weighing Machinery; Wallpaper; and Fertilisers.

For eight of the thirty-six trades with small plant size-ratios, the average size of plants is not small but large; these trades are identified in Table 17. This combination of plant-size characteristics suggests that

[1] The four exceptions are Precious Metals Refining; Medical, Surgical, Veterinary Instruments; Shop and Office Fittings; and Woven Cotton Fabrics—Printing. For them, the number-ratio of plants (*R*) is small but, together with small size-differences in plants (*S*), still sufficient to result in 'large' differences in unit size. Indeed, the contributions of the two factors are more or less equal except in the case of Medical, Surgical, Veterinary Instruments, where the ratio of *S* to *R* is more than 1·5.

[2] The contribution of the plant number-ratio to the size-differences of units is markedly greater than the plant size-ratio for all but one of these twenty-three trades; the exception is Paint and Varnish, where the ratio of *R* to *S* is less than 1·5.

technical economies of scale may set a norm to which plants will tend to conform, and that entry may be more difficult than in the trades where average plant size is small. But it also suggests that if there are large unit size-differences, then the number-ratio of plants has to be large.

Table 17. *Eight trades with large unit size-differences, small plant size-ratios and large average plants, by number-ratio of plants and concentration category, 1951*

	Number-ratio of plants	Plants per unit: Three largest units	Plants per unit: Other units
Low-concentration trades			
Cotton Spinners and Doublers	21·0	32·3	1·5
Paper and Board	9·3	12·0	1·3
Radio Apparatus and Gramophone	5·2	7·0	1·3
Medium-concentration trades			
Aircraft Manufacture and Repair	9·8	14·7	1·5
Plastics Materials	3·8	4·3	1·1
High-concentration trades			
Sugar and Glucose	8·0	8·7	1·1
Prime Movers: internal combustion	5·9	6·7	1·1
Cast Iron Pipes and Fittings	4·5	5·0	1·1

As can be seen from Table 17, the number-ratio of plants is, in fact, large for six of these eight trades,[1] although its contribution to differences in the size of units is not markedly greater than that of the plant size-ratio in another two trades.[2] For the remaining four trades, where the large number-ratio is the more important factor in explaining size-differences between the units, locational considerations do not wholly explain the multi-plant operations of the largest units. They may have some relevance, it is true, in the case of Sugar and Glucose and Paper and Board, but in the former case, the history of mergers among the cane sugar-refiners as well as the statutory amalgamation of the beet-sugar concerns is probably the more important reason. Similarly, the pursuit of commercial economies may be the principal reason for multi-plant operations in the Cotton Spinners and Doublers and Paper and Board trades, while vertical integration may largely explain them for Aircraft Manufacture and Repair.

Trades with large plant size-differences

So far we have been concerned only with the trades which have large

[1] The two exceptions are Cast Iron Pipes and Fittings, and Plastics Materials.

[2] For Radio Apparatus and Gramophone, and Prime Movers: internal combustion, the ratio of R to S is less than 1·5.

size-differences between units and for which the differences in plant sizes are small. But for sixty-two of the ninety-eight trades with large unit size-differences, there are also large differences in the size of plants. It is convenient to divide these sixty-two trades into two groups, according to whether the plant number-ratio is also large or small.

The eighteen trades where the largest units are the largest because they operate both considerably more and larger plants than the other units are identified in Table 18. Large differences in the sizes of the plants within a trade may be due to the diversity of the product comprising the trade: some plants will be much larger than others because they are producing different things. A large concern may also find that in order to produce the largest possible range of products, it must operate a number of plants, or that there are important commercial economies to be gained from multi-plant operation.

Table 18. *Eighteen trades with large unit size-ratios and large plant number- and size-ratios, by number-ratio of plants and concentration category, 1951*

	Number-ratio of plants	Plants per unit: Three largest units	Plants per unit: Other units
Low-concentration trades			
Printing, Publishing, Bookbinding, Engraving	8·3	9·0	1·1
Newspapers	7·9	9·3	1·2
Shipbuilding and Ship Repairing	7·0	9·0	1·3
Wholesale Tailoring—Men's and Boys'	6·9	9·3	1·4
Machine Tools	5·6	6·3	1·1
Iron and Steel (Melting and Rolling)	6·0	8·0	1·3
Making-up of Tailored Garments	5·2	5·3	1·0
Medium-concentration trades			
Chemicals (General)	16·7	23·3	1·4
Electrical Machinery	8·4	10·7	1·3
Magazines and Periodicals	6·5	7·0	1·1
Textile Machinery and Accessories	6·2	7·3	1·2
Metal Boxes and Containers	6·1	7·0	1·2
High-concentration trades			
Explosives and Fireworks	10·3	10·7	1·1
Wrought Iron and Steel Tubes	8·4	12·7	1·5
Wholesale Bottling of Wines and Spirits	7·0	7·7	1·1
Tobacco	5·8	8·0	1·3
Primary Batteries	5·7	5·7	1·0
Seed Crushing and Oil Refining	5·6	6·7	1·2

Although the differences in plant size are large, the average size of plant is small for eleven of these eighteen trades, namely:

Seed Crushing and Oil Refining
Magazines and Periodicals
Metal Boxes and Containers
Making-up of Tailored Garments
Newspapers
Wholesale Tailoring—Men's and Boys'

Machine Tools
Wholesale Bottling of Wines and Spirits
Textile Machinery and Accessories
Printing, Publishing, Bookbinding, Engraving
Chemicals (General)

Some part of the multi-plant operations of the largest units in these trades may, therefore, be connected with the existence of locational, transport or demand factors (at present or in the past), though the various plants of the largest units may also be specialising in different lines among the trades' product-range. Nevertheless, there is little to choose between the contributions of the plant number- and size-ratios to the size-differences of the units in most of these trades. Indeed, there is only one trade, Chemicals (General), where the number-ratio is clearly the predominant factor, and in its case, multi-plant operations (perhaps due to commercial economies, vertical integration, product-heterogeneity as well as combination) are not confined to the largest units. Similarly, there is only one trade, Textile Machinery and Accessories, where the size-ratio of plants is the predominant factor, and here it is almost certainly the wider range of products produced in the larger plants that is the reason for the differences in plant size.

Locational and transport factors probably have little bearing on the multi-plant operations of the largest units in the other seven trades where plant number- and size-ratios are both large, and the average size of plants is also large. It would seem that substantial technical economies can be achieved by the largest plants in such trades, but that it is nevertheless worth while (in terms of commercial economies or a full product-range) to operate a number of plants. Yet in some cases there is still a place for the smaller plant, specialising in one or a few products, as in the following trades:

Primary Batteries
Iron and Steel (Melting and Rolling)
Tobacco
Wrought Iron and Steel Tubes
Electrical Machinery
Explosives and Fireworks
Shipbuilding and Ship Repairing

All the same, in only one of these trades is the number-ratio of plants sufficiently large to make it the predominant factor in the large unit size-differences. The exception is Explosives and Fireworks where, apart from the historical importance of combination, the explanation may be that safety considerations favour the dispersal of plants. For the rest, the size-difference between the units is not predominantly attributable to one factor rather than the other.

We turn next to the second group of trades among those with large unit and plant size-differences: that is, those for which the number-

Table 19. *Forty-four trades with large unit size-differences, large plant-size ratios* and small plant-number ratios, by average plant size and concentration category, 1951*

Average size of plant	Concentration category: High		Medium		Low	
Small	Lead	*6·5*	Tea Blending	*6·5*	Preserved Fruit and Vegetables	*5·7*
	Notepaper, Pads, Envelopes	*7·7*	Watch and Clock	*7·1*	Bacon Curing and Sausage	*5·7*
	Accumulators and Parts	*8·4*	Animal Feedingstuffs	*8·7*	Heating and Ventilating Apparatus	*5·8*
	Margarine	*11·2*	Agricultural Machinery	*9·5*	Hosiery and Knitted Goods	*5·9*
	Match	*11·6*	Copper and Copper Alloys	*9·5*	Wholesale Tailoring—Women's and Girls'	*6·1*
	Zinc	*11·8*	Electric Cookers and Heaters	*11·0*	Wooden Furniture	*6·1*
	Soap and Glycerine	*12·7*	Dry Cleaning, Valeting, Dyeing, etc.	*13·7*	Women's and Girls' Nightwear and Underwear	*7·6*
	Incandescent Mantles	*12·8*	Glass (other than Containers)	*14·4*	Constructional Engineering	*8·0*
	Bicycles and Tricycles	*15·6*	Toys and Games	*14·5*	Drugs and Pharmaceuticals	*8·5*
	Ice Cream	*19·8*	Motor Bodies, Sidecars, etc.	*25·3*	Scientific, Engineering, Industrial Instruments	*8·6*
					Iron Engineering Castings	*10·2*
					Bolts, Nuts, Screws, Rivets	*11·7*
Large	Asbestos Manufactures	*5·4*	Commercial Vehicles	*5·7*		
	Motor Cycles, etc.	*7·4*	Aluminium and Magnesium	*7·3*		
	Photographic Plates and Films	*8·7*	Cocoa and Chocolate	*9·9*		
	Transmission Chains	*12·6*				
	Abrasive Wheels, etc.	*12·7*				
	Small Arms	*13·3*				
	Razors (excl. Electric)	*14·5*				
	Boilers and Boiler-house Plant	*15·2*				
	Cotton Thread	*21·0*				

* The figures in italics give the size-ratio of plants for each trade.

ratio of plants is small. For these forty-four trades, identified in Table 19, it is clear that the large differences in unit size must be primarily (and with three exceptions predominantly) attributable to the larger plants of the biggest units.[1] For thirty-two of the forty-four trades, average plant size is small, so that while the largest units may be employing mass production techniques in their plants, there are also many small plants producing less standardised products. The possibility of this kind of situation seems obvious in such trades as Toys and Games; Motor Bodies, Sidecars, Trailers; Glass (other than Containers); Iron Engineering Castings; Scientific, Engineering, Industrial Instruments; and Drugs and Pharmaceuticals. In other trades, where the products are more homogeneous (for example, Ice Cream; Margarine; Bacon Curing and Sausage) the largest plants cater for a much wider territorial market than the smaller plants, with the result that scale economies are achieved in the former without prejudicing the survival of the latter.

For the other twelve trades where the average size of plants, as well as the plant size-ratio, is large, the technical economies of scale in the largest plants will be even more marked. The fact that the small plants can still survive, despite those economies, suggests that they may be on the periphery of the trade, or even undertaking subcontract work for the largest units. But certainly they can hardly be regarded as in the same class as the largest mass production plants.

3. PLANT STRUCTURE OF TRADES WITH SMALL DIFFERENCES IN SIZES OF BUSINESS UNITS

Trades with small plant size-differences

Eighty-two of the trades where there are only small differences in unit size also have small differences in plant size. But for fourteen of these eighty-two trades, the number-ratio of plants is large, so that whatever differences exist between units are predominantly due to the larger number of plants operated by the largest units.

The average size of plants is small for twelve of the above fourteen trades, which are listed in Table 20, so that for them multi-plant operation is probably a condition of growth for the largest units. The average number of plants operated by the largest units is particularly high for Railway Carriages, Wagons and Trams (38·7), Coke Oven and By-Products (20) and Brewing and Malting (11·3), but multi-plant concerns would also appear to be fairly common, as can be seen from Table 20, among the other units in the first and last of these trades. Even so, the number-ratio of plants for both Railway Carriages, Wagons and Trams

[1] The three trades where the ratio of S to R is less than 1·5 are Commercial Vehicles; Bacon Curing and Sausage; and Hosiery and Knitted Goods.

and Coke Ovens and By-Products is more than 15, so that the small size-differences between the units in these trades are due to the fact that the largest units have, on the average, considerably smaller plants than the others.

For the other two trades where average plant size is large, location and transport costs are probably less important than commercial economies and combination in explaining the large number-ratio of plants. For Cement, it is true that the other units have an average of 1·6 plants each compared with an average of 11 for the largest units, but for Tinplate the other units tend to be single-plant concerns while the largest have an average of 9 plants each. Moreover, both these trades are highly concentrated, whereas the other twelve have medium or low concentration.

Table 20. *Fourteen trades with small unit size-differences, large plant number-ratios and small plant size-ratios, by number-ratio of plants and concentration category, 1951*

	Number-ratio of plants	Plants per unit: Three largest units	Plants per unit: Other units
Low-concentration trades			
Railway Carriages, Wagons and Trams*	21·6	38·7	1·8
Boot and Shoe Repairs for the Trade	7·9	8·3	1·1
Gloves and Mittens	6·0	7·0	1·2
Leather (Tanning and Dressing)	6·0	6·7	1·1
Woven Cotton Fabrics—Dyeing	5·6	6·3	1·1
Brewing and Malting	5·4	11·3	2·1
Refractory Goods	5·4	7·3	1·4
Woven Cotton Cloth	5·1	6·7	1·3
Mechanical Handling Equipment	5·0	5·7	1·1
Medium-concentration trades			
Coke Ovens and By-products	16·8	20·0	1·2
Iron Ore and Ironstone	5·4	7·0	1·3
Gas Meters	5·0	9·3	1·9
High-concentration trades			
Tinplate	8·0	9·0	1·1
Cement	6·6	11·0	1·6

* Excluding railway establishments

We turn next to the sixty-eight trades for which the plant number-ratio as well as the plant size-ratio is small; these trades are listed in Table 21. For fifty-two of these sixty-eight trades, average plant size (as well as the size-ratio of plants) is small, so that for these trades it would appear that there are few technical economies of scale to be achieved or that the size of plant is limited by transport or demand factors. Once again, multi-plant operations will be a condition of growth, but, in fact,

Table 21. *Sixty-eight trades with small unit size-differences, small plant number- and size-ratios, by average plant size and concentration category, 1951*

Average size of plants	Concentration category: High	Medium	Low
Small	Spirit Rectifying Salt Mines, etc.	Mechanical Cloth and Wool Felt Clay Roofing Tiles Ink Jute Textile Packing Cotton Yarn—Finishing Ice Sanitary Earthenware Roofing Felts Office Machinery Requisites Fibreboard Packing Cases Preserved Meat Glazed Tiles Anchors and Chains Electric Lamps Pens, Pencils, Crayons Cordage, Cables, Ropes Glue, Gum, Paste, and Allied Cinematograph Film Production Blankets, Shawls, Travelling Rugs Lubricating Oils and Greases	Umbrella and Walking Stick Sanitary Ware Linen and Soft Hemp Canvas Goods and Sack Fellmongery Lime and Whiting Hosiery and Knitted Fabrics —Finishing Mining Machinery Woollen Yarns Wooden Boxes, Packing Cases, etc. Men's and Boys' Shirts and Underwear Flock and Rag Other Earthenware and Stoneware Woven Woollen Fabrics Edge Tools Upholstered Furniture Other Hollow-ware Hair, Fibre and Kindred Trades Corsets and Brassières Lace Narrow Fabrics Retail Tailoring and Dress-making Leather Goods Bedding Proofed Garments Needles, Pins, Fish Hooks, etc. Motor Vehicles and Cycles (Repairing) Wholesale Dressmade Garments Pre-cast Concrete Goods
Large	Rayon, Nylon C.F. Yarn and Staple Fibre Asbestos Cement Goods Cast Iron Stoves and Grates: Other Valves and Cathode Ray Tubes Mineral Oil Refining Ball and Roller Bearings	Electrical Ware China and Porcelain Office Machinery Carpets, Rugs of Wool Cast Iron Stoves and Grates: Solid Fuel Locomotive Manufacturing* Blast Furnaces Electric Wires and Cables Steel Sheets	Marine Engineering

* Excluding railway locomotive shops

there are only seven trades among the fifty-two where the plant number-ratio (while small) is even the predominant factor in explaining the size-differences between the units. They are

Mechanical Cloth and Wool Felts	Textile Packing
Clay Roofing Tiles	Cotton Yarn—Finishing
Jute	Narrow Fabrics
Needles, Pins, Fish Hooks, etc.	

For the rest, either the plant size-ratio is the predominant factor (as in nineteen trades) or its contribution is more or less equal to that of the number-ratio (as in twenty-six trades). Thus, there is little evidence of either technical or commercial economies of scale among these trades.

For the other sixteen of the sixty-eight trades, the combination of large average plant size and small plant size-ratios suggests that technical economies will be important and even a substantial obstacle to easy entry. Among these sixteen trades, there are only two where the size-ratio of plants (though small) is the predominant factor in the unit size-differences.[1] For the rest, neither the number-ratio nor the size-ratio of plants predominates. But there is still a substantial element of multi-plant operation by the largest units in these trades: they have an average of three or more plants each in twelve of the fourteen trades. Thus, it might be concluded that commercial economies as well as technical economies are exploited by the largest units, and by some of the other units, in these trades.

Trades with large plant size-differences

We are left with the thirty-nine trades, identified in Table 22, with small unit size-differences, small plant number-ratios, but large plant size-ratios. Multi-plant operations can be discounted for these trades, and attention concentrated on the size-differences between the plants which account for the predominant part of the admittedly small differences in the size of the units.

Although the plant size-differences are large, the average size of plants is small in all but five of these thirty-nine trades. The exceptions, as can be seen from Table 22, are:

Refrigerating Machinery	Biscuit
Glass Containers	Rubber Tyres and Tubes
Floor Coverings	

Moreover, the fact that the plant size-differences are large while the unit size-differences are small is due in eight trades to the number-ratio of plants being less than unity. That is to say, the other units have, on the average, more plants than the largest units in the following trades:

[1] They are Office Machinery and Cast Iron Stoves and Grates: Other.

Table 22. *Thirty-nine trades with small unit size-differences, small plant number-ratios and large plant size-ratios*, by average plant size and concentration category, 1951*

Average size of plants	Concentration category: High		Medium		Low	
Small	Starch	*5·5*	Other Optical Instruments and Appliances	*5·5*	Metal Furniture	*5·1*
	Vinegar and other Condiments	*5·9*	Steel Drop Forgings	*6·6*	Domestic Hollow-ware	*5·1*
	Tin	*6·0*	Paper bags	*7·1*	Hats, Hoods, etc. of Wool Felt	*5·5*
	Tramway, Trolleybus and Omnibus Undertakings (Civil Engineering)	*6·3*	Cartons	*7·6*	Rigid Boxes	*5·6*
	Cinematograph Film Printing	*8·5*	Polishes and Canvas Dressings	*7·8*	Plastic Goods	*5·6*
			Photographic and Cinematograph Apparatus	*8·8*	Springs other than Laminated	*5·8*
			Safes, Locks, Latches	*9·9*	Fur	*6·2*
			Toilet Preparations and Perfumery	*10·3*	Brushes and Brooms	*6·5*
			Slate Quarries and Mines	*10·7*	Jewellery and Plate	*6·8*
					Woven Woollen Fabrics—Finishing	*7·3*
					Heavy Overalls and Aprons	*7·9*
					Sports Requisites	*8·2*
					Brass Manufacture	*8·3*
					Specialist Finishers of Metal Goods	*8·5*
					Work Done—Dressmade Garments	*8·6*
					Hats, Hoods, etc. of Fur Felts	*9·3*
					Knives	*9·7*
					Musical Instruments	*9·8*
					Printing and Bookbinding Machinery	*12·7*
					Sugar Confectionery	*13·4*
Large	Rubber Tyres and Tubes	*6·4*	Glass Containers	*5·4*	—	—
	Floor Coverings	*8·4*	Refrigerating Machinery	*6·1*		
			Biscuit	*6·9*		

* The figures in italics are the size-ratio of plants for each trade

Cinematograph Film Printing
Photographic and Cinematograph Apparatus
Specialist Finishers of Metal Goods
Sugar Confectionery
Work done—Wholesale Dressmade Garments
Knives
Heavy Overalls and Aprons
Floor Coverings

Indeed, the largest units were, with the exception of Floor Coverings, single-plant concerns in these trades. The large plant size-differences suggest that entry into all these trades will be easy, except perhaps in the trades with large plants.

4. SUMMARY

The establishments data given in the two preceding sections can be summarised in a number of different ways. In the first place, it can be seen from Table 23 that among the 121 trades with small differences in unit size, the plant size-differences are also small in eighty-two trades (or 68 per cent of the cases), whereas among the ninety-eight trades with large unit size-differences they are small in only thirty-six trades (or 38 per cent of the cases). Thus, there is a significant positive association between unit and plant size-differences.[1] Similarly, the plant number-ratio is small for 107 (or 88 per cent) of the 121 trades with small unit size-differences, compared with fifty (or 51 per cent) of the ninety-eight trades with large unit size-differences. Here again there is a significant positive association.[2]

Table 23. *Distribution of 219 trades by size-ratio of units and the size- and number-ratio of plants, 1951*

Size-ratio of plants	Number-ratio of plants	Size-ratio of units: Small	Size-ratio of units: Large	Total number of trades
Small	Small	68	6	74
	Large	14	30	44
Large	Small	39	44	83
	Large	—	18	18
Total number of trades		121	98	219

Small plant size- and number-ratios occur together in seventy-four (or roughly one-third) of the 219 trades, and the size-differences of the units are also small in all but six cases. Large plant size- and number-ratios occur together in only eighteen trades, and in each case, the size-differences of the units are large. But for all the trades together there is a

[1] $\chi^2 = 19 \cdot 8$ (χ^2 for one degree of freedom and a 10 per cent level of significance equals $2 \cdot 71$).
[2] $\chi^2 = 35 \cdot 5$.

significant negative association between the plant size- and plant number-ratio.[1]

When average plant size is introduced into the analysis, it is found that for 169 of the 219 trades (or 77 per cent), average plant size is small. It can be seen from Table 24 that small plant size-differences are associated with large average plants in twenty-six trades. These plant size characteristics suggest that technical economies of scale may be a considerable factor governing the size of plant and conditioning entry to the trade, and, in fact, eleven of these trades have high concentration, and another ten medium concentration.

Table 24. *Distribution of 219 trades by average plant size and plant size-ratios, 1951*

Size-ratio of plants	Average size of plants		Total number of trades
	Small	Large	
Small	92	26	118
Large	77	24	101
Total number of trades	169	50	219

For the ninety-two trades which combine small plants and small plant size-differences, locational, transport and demand factors appear to be primarily important in determining plant size, and entry will be generally easy. For fifty-six of these trades, concentration is low, compared with twenty-nine with medium, and seven with high concentration.

Among the trades with large plant size-differences, the average size of plants is large in twenty-four cases. The largest plants in these trades probably enjoy considerable technical economies of scale, but that does not prevent the existence of small plants alongside them. Indeed, the continued survival of the latter may reflect the product-heterogeneity of these trades. Finally, for seventy-seven trades, the average size of plants is small, even though there are still considerable variations in size between them, so that in most cases entry will be easier than in those trades with large average plants.

The 219 trades are next arranged in Table 25 according to their average plant size and the number-ratio of plants, which is large for sixty-two (or 28 per cent) of the 219 trades; for them, multi-plant operation is an important element in the activities of the largest units. For forty-seven of these sixty-two trades, the average size of plants is small, so that there is a presumption that multi-plant operations will be a condition of growth for the concerns in many of these trades. But for the other fifteen trades where the average plant size is large, commercial economies and

[1] $\chi^2 = 9 \cdot 8$.

concentration for concentration's sake are probably a more important part of the explanation. Indeed, for ten of these fifteen trades, concentration is medium or high.

Table 25. *Distribution of 219 trades by average plant size and plant number-ratios, 1951*

Number-ratio of plants	Average size of plants: Small	Average size of plants: Large	Total number of trades
Small	122	35	157
Large	47	15	62
Total number of trades	169	50	219

While it is helpful to relate average plant size to the number- and size-ratio of plants when describing the plant structure of different trades, it must be emphasised that there is no significant statistical association between average plant size and either of the other two variables. Thus, from Table 24, it can be seen that the size-ratio of plants is small for only a slightly larger proportion of the trades with small average plants than for those with large average plants, while the same is true for the number-ratio of plants.

When the 219 trades are arranged (as in Table 26) according to the relative importance of the number- and size-ratio of plants in accounting for size-differences, it is seen that they are more or less equally important in sixty-six trades,[1] and that plant size-ratios are the greater for two-thirds of the other 153 trades. On the whole, therefore, it may be said that the relatively larger establishments of the largest units account for their predominance to a markedly greater extent than their relatively greater number of plants in twice as many trades as the reverse applies.

Table 26. *Distribution of 219 trades according to average plant size and the relative importance of the number- and size-ratio of plants, 1951*

Relative importance of number- and size-ratio of plants	Average size of plants: Small	Average size of plants: Large	Total number of trades
Number-ratio > Size-ratio	43	7	50
Size-ratio > Number-ratio	85	18	103
Size-ratio ≏ Number-ratio	41	25	66
Total number of trades	169	50	219

It might be imagined that the number-ratio of plants would be more important than the size-ratio in accounting for size-differences between units in trades where average plant size is small than where it is large.

[1] That is, the ratios $R : S$ or $S : R$ are less than 1·5 for these sixty-six trades.

But there is no significant association between average plant size and the relative importance of these two factors, for among the 153 trades where one or other factor predominates, the number-ratio is greater than the size-ratio for almost the same proportion of the trades with small average plants as for all 153 trades together.

Finally, the 219 trades are distributed in Table 27 according to the relative importance of the number- and size-ratio of plants and concentration category. Confining attention to the 153 trades where one or other factor is the more important, we find that where it is the plant number-ratio that predominates, concentration is low in 56 per cent of the cases, while out of the 103 trades where the plant size-ratio predominates, concentration is low in only 41 per cent of the cases. Thus, there would appear to be some association, though it is not quite significant at the 10 per cent level, between the relative importance of the number-ratio and size-ratio of plants and concentration.[1]

Table 27. *Distribution of 219 trades according to concentration category and the relative importance of the number- and size-ratio of plants, 1951*

Relative importance of number and size-ratio of plants	Concentration category			Total number of trades
	High	Medium	Low	
Number-ratio > Size-ratio	8	14	28	50
Size-ratio > Number-ratio	28	33	42	103
Size-ratio ≏ Number-ratio	14	22	30	66
Total number of trades	50	69	100	219

In conclusion, therefore, it may be stated that while unit size-differences are positively associated with both plant size- and plant number-differences, the latter two variables are themselves negatively associated. Thus, if one trade has a larger plant size-difference than another, it is likely to have larger unit size-differences, but its plant number-ratio is likely to be smaller. Moreover, neither plant size-ratios nor number-ratios are associated with the average size of plants; nor is their relative importance in accounting for unit size-differences associated with average plant size. But there would appear to be some slight association between their relative importance and concentration, concentration tending to be lower where the plant number-ratio predominates than where the size-ratio predominates.

[1] After merging high- and medium-concentration trades, $\chi^2 = 2\cdot56$.

CHAPTER VII

STATISTICAL ANALYSIS OF FACTORS RELATING TO CONCENTRATION

I. INTRODUCTION

In the three preceding chapters, the concentration data have been used, in conjunction with other factors such as the number, average size and size-ratio of units and plants, to analyse the industry and plant structure of the 219 trades in 1951. Indeed, it is evident from the preceding discussion that many of these factors are significantly associated with concentration, though no precise statistical analysis was made. The purpose of this chapter is to provide such an analysis and to try to discover whether any of the related variables can be regarded as factors determining concentration.

Some introductory remarks on the approach of this chapter may also help to set the investigations reported here into proper relation with those of Chapter XI below. Throughout the present chapter the data examined are the concentration statistics for 1951; that is, the method adopted is to compare trades with one another as they were at a single point in time. The kind of conclusion to be derived is, for example, that among trades in 1951 larger plant sizes occur in the more highly concentrated trades.

Cross-sectional analysis of this kind is often used in other branches of economics, especially in studies of consumer behaviour. But it is necessary to be very cautious before drawing any causal inferences from the relations discovered. The analysis of savings provides an example. One may find that richer people save a higher proportion of their income than poorer people. From this, it might be argued that greater wealth is a cause of a higher savings ratio, and that as a nation becomes richer it will save more. But an equally good causal explanation may be that savings are causally related to a person's position in the income scale but do not depend on the absolute level of income: in which case the inference that greater national wealth will lead to a higher national savings ratio may prove false.[1]

In Chapter XI we shall examine *changes* in concentration which have taken place over time (1935–51). To some extent Chapter XI may help us to discover whether any of the relationships established in this chapter permit causal inferences: for example, we find in this chapter that the size

[1] See J. S. Duesenberry, *Income, Saving and the Theory of Consumer Behavior* (Harvard University Press, 1949).

of a trade is significantly related to concentration, but in Chapter XI we fail to establish any significant relation between a change in size and a change in concentration. In itself, this does not disprove the proposition that greater size is a cause of lower concentration, for a real causal relation may have been masked by other factors operating in the period. But it certainly throws some doubt on the validity of any causal inference.

This example draws attention to another possible defect of the cross-sectional analysis of this chapter. The size of a trade in a given year is determined not only by purely objective factors such as the demand for its products, but also, as we have seen, by a decision defining which products are to comprise the trade. Thus an association between the size of a trade and concentration might merely reflect the enlargement of a trade by including more products: if this were the case (though we would not argue that it often is) then the cross-sectional correlation between size and concentration would give us no grounds to expect that a trade which had become larger through increased demand for its products would have lower concentration.

This problem of definition is not, unfortunately, confined to the size of trade. The choice of trade classifications by the Census authorities affects all the possible determining factors of concentration which we examine. If one merely wanted to predict the concentration of a trade in a given year (when, say, its concentration data were unknown) from other known variables, such as its size and plant size, the fact that all the variables are partly a matter of Census choice would not matter. One would be comparing like with like. But in order to predict what will happen to the concentration of a trade when the independent variables change as a result of, say, changes in demand, it is not entirely satisfactory to proceed on the basis of variables determined not only by demand but also by Census requirements. For this reason (among others) we have to be cautious about drawing any inferences from cross-sectional analysis as to what might happen over time. Without further warning we now pass to an analysis of the data.

Definitions

Although some of the variables to be studied in this chapter have already been defined and introduced in preceding chapters, the whole of the notation to be used is given here for convenience:

C = Employment concentration-ratio

E = Total trade employment

E_3 = Total employment of three largest units

M = Number of plants per unit

P = Number of plants

P_3 = Number of plants of three largest units

Q = Average size of plants

T = Size-ratio of plants (alternative definition: average size of plants of three largest units divided by average size of plants of *all* units)

U = Number of units

V = Average size of units

W = Size-ratio of units (average size of three largest units divided by average size of *other* units)

X = Size-ratio of units (alternative definition: average size of three largest units divided by average size of *all* units).

The two definitions of size-ratio of units

In Chapters v and vi, the size-ratio of units used is W; in the present chapter it is replaced by a very similar concept denoted by X which, though slightly less simple intuitively, has a simpler mathematical relation to other variables used in the analysis (the relation is linear in the logarithms instead of non-linear). The definitions are as follows:

$$W \equiv \frac{E_3}{3} \div \frac{(E - E_3)}{(U-3)}$$

On dividing both fractions by E and substituting C for $\frac{E_3}{E}$, it will be seen that this simplifies to

$$W \equiv \frac{CU/3 - C}{1 - C} \qquad \text{(1)}$$

On the other hand, we have

$$X \equiv \frac{E_3}{3} \div \frac{E}{U} \qquad \text{(2)}$$

$$\equiv CU/3$$

The relation between W and X is readily seen to be

$$W = (X - C)/(1 - C) \qquad \text{(3)}$$

Use of logarithms

The statistical analysis that follows is carried out on the logarithms of the variables. This has a number of technical advantages. First, the relations between many of the variables are additive instead of multiplicative, which facilitates the analysis throughout. Secondly, the coefficients obtained in a regression analysis of the data are at once in the familiar form of elasticities (showing that a 1 per cent change in X leads to a b per cent change in Y). Thirdly, the standard deviation of the logarithm of a variable provides a convenient measure of its variability, independent of its unit of measurement (it is thus like the more familiar coefficient of variation). Fourthly, the classical statistical tests which assume normality can be applied directly, since most of the variables approximately follow the log-normal distribution.[1]

In what follows, lower-case symbols are used to denote the logarithms of the quantities denoted by the corresponding capitals. Thus: $x = \log X$.

Definitional relations

From the definitions follow certain identities, and these have to be borne in mind throughout. The principal ones are as follows. First, between employment, and the sizes and number of units and plants:

$$e = u + v = p + q \qquad (4)$$

Secondly, the number of plants per unit is given by

$$m = p - u = v - q \qquad (5)$$

Thirdly, concentration can be identically analysed in a number of different ways.

$$c = \log 3 + x - u \qquad (6)$$

$$= \log 3 + x + m - p \qquad (7)$$

$$= \log 3 + x + m + q - e \qquad (8)$$

$$= p_3 + t + q - e \qquad (9)$$

Where such relationships exist, it is possible to partition the variability of any one of them into components that are entirely attributable to the others. For example, from (6) we have, on summing squares (and neglecting the constant term),

$$\Sigma c^2 = \Sigma x^2 - 2\Sigma xu + \Sigma u^2 \qquad (10)$$

which, in the usual variance notation, leads to

$$\sigma^2_c = \sigma^2_x - 2r_{ux}\sigma_u\sigma_x + \sigma^2_u \qquad (11)$$

But it is pointless to carry out a regression analysis between concentra-

[1] See J. Aitchison and J. A. C. Brown, *The Lognormal Distribution*, University of Cambridge Department of Applied Economics, Monograph 5 (Cambridge University Press, 1956).

tion and the entire set of factors that are specified on the right-hand size of an identity. The correlation would always be perfect, and the regressions would be ±1 according to the definitional construction of the dependent variable. This difficulty would not have arisen if concentration had been measured in some independent manner; as it is, if tautologies are to be avoided, care is necessary in selecting the hypotheses suitable for testing by regression methods.

2. THE NUMBER- AND SIZE-RATIO OF BUSINESS UNITS

It will probably assist the reader to have a diagram of the relationships to be discussed. In Fig. 2, on the lines connecting each pair of variables are written the values of the relevant simple correlation coefficients.[1]

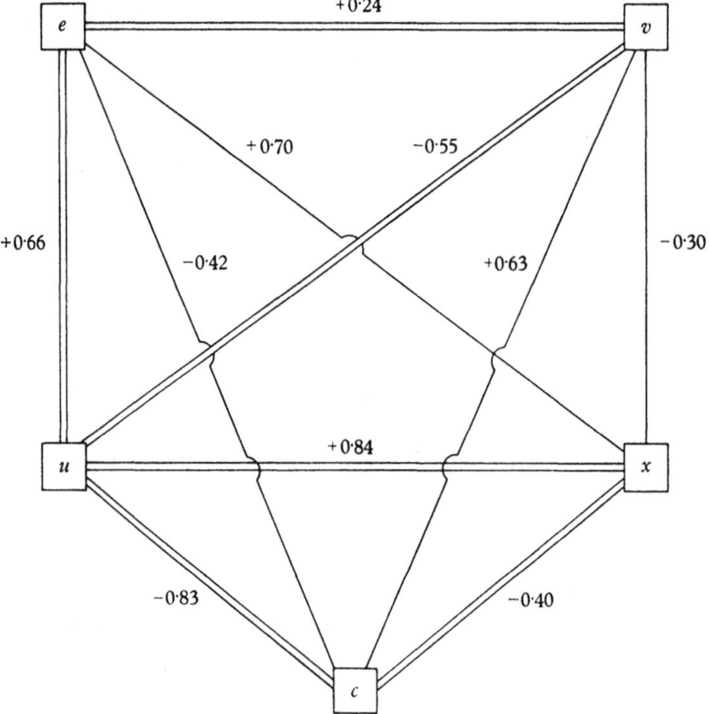

Fig. 2 Correlation coefficients between concentration and other variables

Where a space is enclosed by double lines it indicates that the variables on the boundaries of the space are mathematically connected (that is, the triangles *evu* and *uxc*).

[1] The coefficients yielded by the regression analysis are summarised in Appendix I.

There is a strong negative correlation ($r_{cu}=-0\cdot83$) between concentration and the number of business units in a trade, so that the smaller the number of units, the higher the concentration. To be precise, the regression coefficient $b_{cu}=-0\cdot50$ ($\pm0\cdot02$) shows that, on the average, a trade with 10 per cent fewer units than another will have a 5 per cent higher concentration.

Studies in other countries have also established a close association between concentration and the number of units. For example, the T.N.E.C. investigators in the United States found that 'the relationship between the number of companies manufacturing a product and its concentration-ratio is generally, though by no means perfectly, inverse in character'.[1] Similarly Dr Rosenbluth, working on a sample of ninety-six Canadian manufacturing industries, found a correlation coefficient of 0·96 between concentration and the number of firms.[2]

This relationship is hardly surprising. Low concentration cannot occur with few units. Concentration cannot be less than $3/U$, even if the size-ratio falls to unity (see identity (6)). Provided that there are some trades with few units, and some with low concentration, the correlation is inescapable.

Identity (6) shows us that concentration is higher in trades with fewer units, unless this is offset by a size-ratio that is sufficiently lower (which may not be possible). But equally it tells us that concentration must be higher in trades with a greater size-ratio unless the number of units is also higher.[3] Let us, therefore, now try to see which of these two factors accounts for the greater part of the observed concentration variance. To succeed in this demands that the co-variance term in (11) above, which depends upon the correlation between the number of units and the size-ratio, be relatively small. In fact we have:

Variance of size-ratio	0·104
Plus variance of number of units	0·286
Minus twice the co-variance	−0·287
Equals variance of concentration	0·103

Unfortunately the correlation between the number of units and the

[1] W. F. Crowder, 'The Concentration of Production in Manufacturing', in Temporary National Economic Committee Monograph no. 27 (Washington, 1941), p. 409.

[2] G. Rosenbluth, *Concentration in Canadian Manufacturing Industries*, N.B.E.R. (1957), p. 34. The correlation was positive because the index of concentration was defined as the number of firms accounting for 80 per cent of employment.

[3] It may be thought surprising that the correlation between concentration and the unit size-ratio is negative ($r_{cx}=-0\cdot40$), especially in the light of the discussion of Chapter v. But the change of definition of the latter variable must be borne in mind: indeed, the correlation on the basis of the former definition is positive ($r_{cw}=0\cdot16$). Moreover, on the present definition, the correlation between the unit size-ratio and the number of units is strongly positive, and this produces a negative correlation between concentration and the size-ratio.

size-ratio ($r_{xu}=0\cdot84$) is so large that one cannot assign greater importance to one factor rather than the other.[1]

However, as far as the simple correlations are concerned, it appears that the number of units is more closely associated with concentration than is the size-ratio ($r_{cu}=-0\cdot83$ while $r_{cx}=-0\cdot40$ only).

3. THE AVERAGE SIZE OF UNITS AND TRADE EMPLOYMENT

In relating concentration to the number of units and the size-ratio of units, as in the preceding section, no approach was made to any causal explanation. It would seem as reasonable, indeed perhaps more reasonable, to say that higher concentration resulted in fewer units, as the reverse.

From this point of view the average size of units may seem a more promising variable: it is nearly as well related to concentration ($r_{cv}=0\cdot63$) as is the number of units ($r_{cu}=-0\cdot83$).

Undoubtedly to a large extent, such factors as technology, geography, and selling and managerial economies, help to determine unit size. These factors may be regarded as a causative element in concentration, even in cases when the immediate cause of greater concentration is the desire for monopoly power, provided that such power could not be acquired in the absence of economies resulting from larger unit size. In other cases, however, it must be recognised that monopolistic yearnings may result in higher concentration, and hence in larger unit sizes, even in the absence of economic reasons for larger unit size.

Assuming that, to some extent at least, unit size may be regarded as a causal factor in determining concentration, we may ask in what manner it affects concentration. Fig. 2 and the analysis of the preceding section show that it might operate either through the number of units or the unit size-ratio. In fact, unit size is negatively correlated with both the size-

[1] This is at variance with the findings of Rosenbluth (*op. cit.* p. 34) who concludes: 'As a reasonable first approximation, one may regard difference in concentration among industries as reflecting purely differences in the number of firms, and need not inquire into the causes of inequality of firm size.' The reason for the difference appears to lie in the different measures of inequality used by him and by us. His measure is essentially like a Gini coefficient (it is the proportion of firms in the trade accounting for 80 per cent of the employment: that is, the reading from the Lorenz curve at the 80 per cent point). This varies within narrow limits between trades, and he finds it has only a negligible correlation with concentration and with the number of units.

Our measure, however, is related to the number of units in the trade as a simple example shows. Suppose the size of a trade is doubled by giving each unit a twin brother. The frequency distribution of sizes is unchanged, and so is the Lorenz curve and Rosenbluth's measure of inequality. However, our measure of inequality will increase, since it depends on the average size of the largest three firms and this is now necessarily larger (strictly, not smaller, if we allow for the possibility that the largest three were originally all of the same size). It is not therefore surprising that we find a marked positive correlation between the number of units and our measure of inequality.

ratio ($r_{vx}=-0\cdot30$) and with the number of units ($r_{vu}=-0\cdot55$). But we have already seen in Section 2 that these two latter variables are themselves highly correlated. Thus, for the same reason that we could not say whether variations in concentration mainly reflected variations in the number of units or in the size-ratio, so we cannot say whether any causal influence which unit size may have on concentration flows via the number of units or the size-ratio.

It is interesting to explore further the correlation between unit size and the number of units, because this leads us straight to a consideration of trade size and its influence—since $e=u+v$.

Trade size is correlated with concentration ($r_{ec}=-0\cdot42$) and the question arises as to how far it may be regarded as a causative factor in concentration.[1] Theoretically, if the concentration of a trade resulted in some kind of monopolistic control, output and employment might be reduced. In practice, it would seem highly doubtful whether this could be regarded as a significant part of the explanation of the correlation. If we rule out this possibility, and assume that any causation acts from employment to concentration, what can be the explanation of the correlation?

The prima facie explanation would seem to be that larger trades have, on the average, more units ($r_{eu}=0\cdot66$); and, as we have seen, more units are in fact (and it would be surprising if they were not) strongly associated with less concentration. On the other hand, larger trades also have on average larger units ($r_{ve}=0\cdot24$) as well as more units, and larger units are associated with higher concentration. But the first connection outweighs the second.

We can put the above arguments more precisely as follows. First, we estimate by regression analysis the relative change in the number of units and in the average size of unit, respectively associated with a given relative change in employment. Then, again by regression analysis, we estimate the relative change in concentration associated with the estimated relative changes in the number and size of units. This is illustrated in Fig. 3, which also shows the direct regression of concentration on employment.[2]

It thus seems that there is a negative correlation between employment and concentration mainly because, as employment rises, the number of units rises in greater proportion than the size of units. There is, of course, nothing necessary about this: indeed it is conceivable that the number of units should fall as employment rises.

[1] Rosenbluth (*op. cit.* p. 53) also finds a correlation equal to $0\cdot55$ between trade size and concentration.

[2] It will be seen that the direct regression of concentration on employment gives precisely the same result as that calculated via the two branches of the diagram. This is necessarily so; for if $u+v=e$, it can be shown that $b_{ue}+b_{ve}=1$, and that $b_{ue}b_{cu.v}+b_{ve}b_{cv.u}=b_{ce}$.

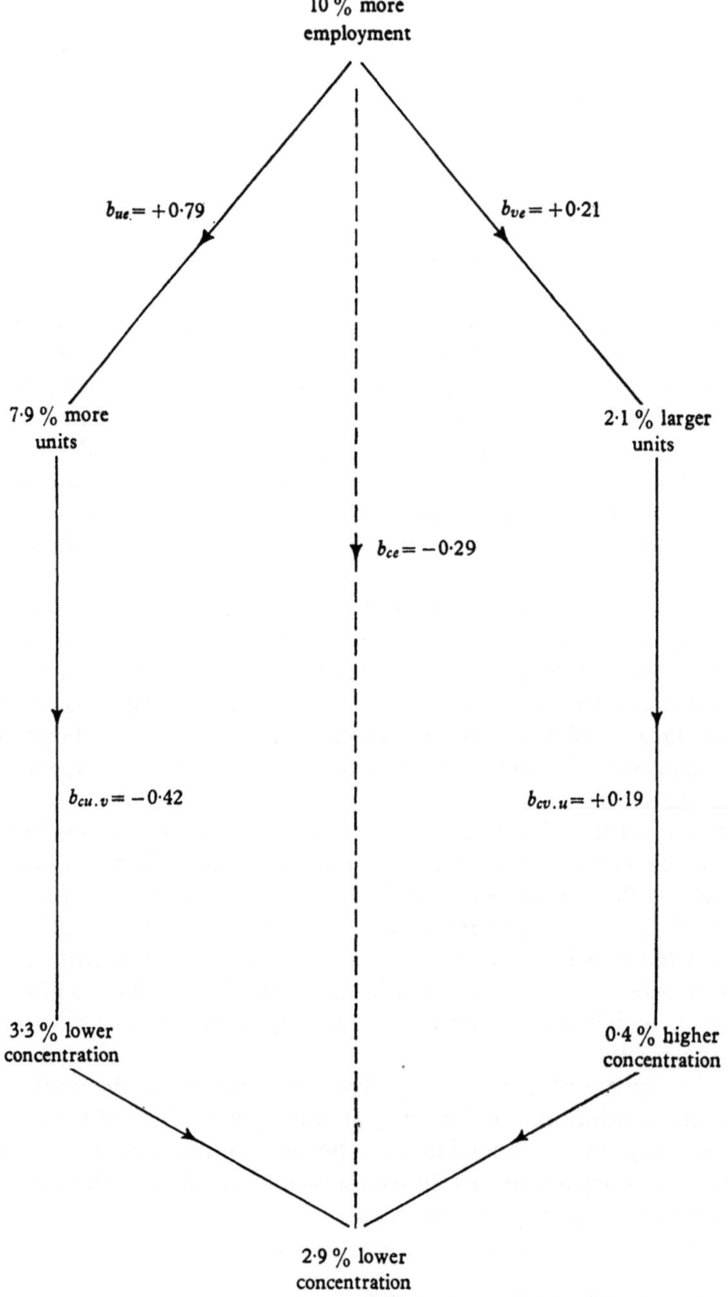

Fig. 3 The relation between concentration and employment

However the facts as found do not seem unreasonable. Suppose that trades are fairly homogeneous so far as production methods and techniques are concerned, and suppose that the average unit size in a given trade is largely determined by techniques, and by managerial and transport considerations.[1] Then we should expect a positive but imperfect correlation of trade and unit size, unit size being limited by the size of the market in the case of the smaller trades, and by geographical and managerial considerations in the case of the larger trades. From this it would follow that employment and the number of units would also be positively correlated. One might also have been prepared to guess that the size of the market is not a very strong influence in affecting unit size (that is, that average unit size would vary in much lower proportion than trade size[2]), so that the present result is what one might well have expected.

To sum up: a larger trade will be associated with lower concentration, provided that unit size does not increase too much with trade size. General considerations certainly suggest that larger trades will have both more units and larger units. Also, as one might have expected, the number of units varies in closer proportion to trade size than does unit size—and this in fact results in a negative correlation between concentration and trade size.

4. CONCENTRATION ESTIMATED FROM TRADE SIZE AND UNIT SIZE

Numerous qualifications have been made in the preceding sections as to the validity of regarding trade size and unit size as causal factors in concentration. Nevertheless it seemed worth while to calculate the multiple regression of concentration on these two variables, with the following results:

$$c = -0{\cdot}41(\pm 0{\cdot}03)e + 0{\cdot}61(\pm 0{\cdot}03)v + 1{\cdot}83 \quad \ldots\ldots\ldots (13)$$
$$R^2 = 0{\cdot}72$$

This equation shows that a 10 per cent increase in unit size (keeping trade size constant) is associated with a 6 per cent increase in concentration. Similarly, a 10 per cent increase in trade size (keeping unit size constant) is associated with a 4 per cent fall in concentration. The correlation coefficient shows that 72 per cent of the concentration variance is explained, in a statistical sense, by variations in trade size and unit size.

[1] We can admit, so far as the present argument is concerned, that monopolistic striving is also present and will affect unit size, so long as the former is uncorrelated with trade size.

[2] Rosenbluth (*op. cit.* p. 34) finds a remarkably similar correlation between trade size and unit size: $r=0{\cdot}27$ as compared with our $r=0{\cdot}24$.

5. CONCENTRATION, PLANT SIZE AND PLANTS PER UNIT

So far we have proceeded as if the average size of units were, at any rate to a large degree, a datum for each trade determined by technological and managerial or commercial factors. But the analysis of Chapter VI has shown that if it is desired to examine the two sets of factors separately we must look to plants rather than units. For the purposes of that chapter, the size-differences of units were analysed in terms of the number-ratio and size-ratio of plants, but since we are here concentrating attention on the relation between concentration and average unit size, we may begin by analysing the variability of average unit size among trades in terms of the average size of plants and the number of plants per unit.

Using the following identity, derived from (5) above,

$$q+m=v \quad \ldots\ldots\ldots\ldots\ldots\ldots\ldots (14)$$

we find that:

Variance of average plant size	0·137
Plus variance of plants per unit	0·011
Plus twice the co-variance	0·027
Equals variance of unit size	0·175

It will be seen, first, that unit sizes are more variable between trades than are plant sizes (note that this is quite separate from the question of variability *within* any trade); the standard deviation of the logarithms of the former is some 11 per cent greater.

Secondly, there is a moderate positive co-variance term, resulting from a positive correlation between the size of plant and the number of plants per unit ($r_{mq}=0 \cdot 34$). In fact, a 10 per cent greater plant size is associated with approximately a 1 per cent increase in the number of plants per unit, the regression estimate being $b_{mq}=0 \cdot 10$ ($\pm 0 \cdot 01$).

This positive association between plant size and the number of plants per unit suggests that the initiating cause of an increase in concentration is often a fall in the number of units (not necessarily for technological reasons) rather than an increase in average plant size. Certainly, if larger plants are always the initiating factor, it is hard to see why there should be an association between larger plants and more plants per unit. But if the initiating factor is a fall in the number of units, due to a combination or acquisition, there will be an immediate increase in the number of plants per unit. Further, as the new business units formed by combination concentrate production in their most efficient plants, or build new and larger plants, there is also likely to be an increase in average plant size.

The importance of combination as a prelude to reorganisation and 'rationalisation' is borne out by the experience of several industries, both among the high-concentration trades (see Chapter VIII), and among those whose concentration can be shown to have changed between 1935 and 1951 (see Chapter XI). In particular this is true for Tinplate, Wrought Iron and Steel Tubes, Metal Boxes and Containers, China and Porcelain, Transmission Chains, Fertilisers, Cement, Wallpaper, and Prime Movers: internal combustion. In some cases, however, the influence of technological considerations was considerable, and the need for larger plants may be regarded as a causal factor even if concentration in fact came first. In others it was surplus capacity which initially prompted amalgamation, but thereafter improved technology, which may itself have been encouraged by the amalgamation, led to larger plants.

Another way of assessing the importance of this factor (that is, the average number of plants per unit) is by asking to what extent an increase in average unit size is associated with an increase in plant size, and to what extent with an increase in the number of plants per unit. The regressions $b_{qv}=0\cdot 86(\pm 0\cdot 01)$ and $b_{mv}=0\cdot 14\ (\pm 0\cdot 01)$ show that a 10 per cent increase in average unit size is shared as to some 8·6 per cent by an increase in plant size, and as to 1·4 per cent by an increase in the number of plants per unit. Further, as shown by its variance (of 0·011) the number of plants per unit does not vary very much about its average value, which is 1·3 plants.

Although we may therefore dismiss variations in the number of plants per unit as a rather unimportant part of any explanation of concentration, the same does not of course necessarily follow if we look at variations in the number of plants per unit among the top three units in each trade—or what comes to the same thing, the variations in the number of plants owned by the top three.

At this stage it is worth recalling identity (9):

$$c=p_3+t+q-e$$

We may first concentrate on the two terms q and e and examine the multiple regression of c on q and e. This is obviously closely analogous to the regression of c on v and e, considered in the previous section (see equation 13). It might, however, be expected to reflect more accurately the influence of technological and geographical factors than equation (13). In fact, the numerical results are practically identical:

$$C=-0\cdot 41(\pm 0\cdot 03)e+0\cdot 66(\pm 0\cdot 04)q+1\cdot 81 \quad \ldots\ldots(15)$$
$$R^2=0\cdot 675$$

It may be noted that the simple correlation coefficient between c and q is 0·60, so that plant size alone 'explains' 36 per cent of concentration, while plant size and trade size together 'explain' 67 per cent. Unit size 'explained' 40 per cent of the variation in concentration, while unit size and employment together 'explained' 72 per cent. These differences are of little importance.

We have chosen (with reservation) the variables q and e as those which reflect best, though of course imperfectly, the objective factors technology and demand. What may we say of the other two variables in identity (9), namely p_3 and t?

If the number of plants belonging to the top three is large, this may, of course, be connected with managerial or with buying and selling economies, in which case the smaller single-plant concerns may maintain themselves by having other advantages; or because the trade is in fact sufficiently heterogeneous for them not to be very competitive with the larger firms; or because it does not suit the larger firms, for various possible reasons, to compete them out of existence. But it is also quite possible that the large units have many plants although no considerable economy is thereby realised. We must thus regard p_3 as reflecting not only managerial and marketing factors, but also concentration for concentration's sake.

The variable t is rather more difficult to interpret. It is a crude measure of the variability of plant size within a trade. To some extent it undoubtedly reflects the heterogeneity of the trade. If the top three have relatively very large plants, this suggests that many of the other units in the trade may be producing rather different things which do not require such large plants for efficiency. But there are several other explanations of a large plant size-ratio. One is that there is little competition so that the large firms with large plants do not drive out the less efficient small firms with small plants. Another is that the large plants are not in fact more efficient: a large unit may have a large plant just because it *is* a large unit; thus the large unit may, if transport costs are not important, have grown up on the same site, although it would have been at least as efficient to have several different establishments.[1] Finally it may be that the trade *is* homogeneous, that large plants *are* more efficient, and there *is* competition, so that the small firms with small plants are on their way out: but this is a process which takes time, and we have simply caught the trade at an historical moment when only some of the small fry have been eaten up.[2]

The influence of t on concentration, after allowing for trade and plant

[1] To the extent that this happens the association of large average plant size with high concentration is explicable on terms of high concentration causing large plants, and not vice versa.

[2] Bread baking is, perhaps, an example. The number of small craft-bakers has, for various reasons, been falling, and may be expected to continue to fall. Indeed, their continued survival is probably largely explained by the variety of their products (including flour confectionery) compared with those of the plant-bakery; or, in other words, with the element of heterogeneity in the trade's products.

sizes, appears to be small. This may be seen by comparing the following multiple regression with (15) above:

$$c=-0\cdot41(\pm0\cdot03)e+0\cdot65(\pm0\cdot04)q-0\cdot006(\pm0\cdot06)t+1\cdot82 \quad (16)$$
$$R^2=0\cdot675$$

The correlation has not risen noticeably; the coefficients attached to e and q have not changed; and the coefficient attached to t is not significant.

On the other hand, the influence of p_3 appears to be more substantial, as the following regression shows:

$$c=0\cdot54(\pm0\cdot03)e+0\cdot70(\pm0\cdot03)q+0\cdot33(\pm0\cdot04)p_3+1\cdot91 \quad (17)$$
$$R^2=0\cdot765$$

The coefficient attached to p_3 is clearly significant; and a comparison with (14) shows that the other coefficients have only changed slightly. From the correlation coefficients, it appears that p_3 accounts for a further 9 per cent of the concentration variance.

It might be thought that a good measure of the influence of p_3 could be obtained by a 'method of subtraction', by considering further the results of regression (15). For, if p_3 were also inserted into that regression, it follows from (9) that the correlation would rise to unity. Hence, $1-R^2_{c.eqt}$ $=0\cdot325$ could be taken to measure the importance of the remaining variable p_3, since it is the proportion of the variance that cannot be explained without introducing p_3. We would thus have a rough measure of the importance of 'concentration for concentration's sake'. This estimate is, however, almost certainly an over-estimate, since the residual variance in (15) will include, in addition to the effects of p_3, elements more properly ascribable to errors of measurement and the non-linear components of the other variables. The estimate of 9 per cent given in the preceding paragraph is therefore perhaps to be preferred.

6. CONCLUSION

It cannot be claimed that the analysis of this chapter is as rewarding as one might have hoped, although a large number of statistically significant associations have been unearthed. We have seen that both plant size and unit size 'explain' a little over one-third of the variance of concentration, and that either of these combined with the size of trade 'explains' a little over two-thirds. Plant size, the number of plants of the three largest units, and employment, together 'explain' about three-quarters.

What is unsatisfactory about these and similar results is that one cannot be sure that variations in concentration (not caused by variations in the so-called 'independent' variables) do not themselves affect the 'independent' variables. In this respect unit size is perhaps the most suspect variable (apart from the number of plants belonging to the three largest units, which is obviously not independent) and employment the least.

It may finally be noted that we have confined ourselves in this chapter to examining the relationship between concentration and other variables derived from Census data. But it is almost certainly the case that relatively few of the factors influencing concentration are susceptible to precise measurement, and to that extent, the limited causal explanation of concentration provided by Census variables is understandable. The diversity of those factors can, in fact, be seen from the two chapters that follow, where, mainly because of their intrinsic interest from the viewpoint of monopoly power, the high-concentration trades of 1951 are studied in greater detail.

CHAPTER VIII

THE GROWTH OF LEADING FIRMS IN THE HIGH-CONCENTRATION TRADES

I. INTRODUCTION

A special interest attaches to the high-concentration trades since it is among them that strong elements of monopoly power are most likely to be found. The fifty trades with high concentration in 1951 have already been identified in Chapter IV, and they have also been classified in Chapter V according to the number and the size-difference of the units that comprise the trade.

The purpose of this chapter is to examine the high-concentration trades in greater detail, and to carry the analysis a stage further by attempting to answer two questions that appear relevant and important. First, how did high concentration develop in these trades, and when did it emerge? Second, what are the factors which promoted high concentration in the first place?

To answer these questions, use can be made of descriptive material, but it must be emphasised that no attempt is made in the following sections of this chapter to provide a complete explanation of the circumstances in each and every high-concentration trade. The approach is illustrative and not comprehensive.

We have already observed that the high-concentration trades are characterised by a relatively small number of concerns, though there are notable exceptions to this general rule. In some cases, the number of firms has always been small, perhaps for technological reasons, so that concentration has always tended to be high. But more often the high-concentration trades were much more heavily populated in the past than they are today, and at some stage in their development may well have conformed closely to the competitive model.

The transition from the industry of the many to the industry of the few may have come about in various ways, depending largely on how the firms in the industry grew. Basically, there are two growth patterns. First, the individual firm may grow by internal expansion; that is, by the construction of new productive capacity, adding to the potential of the trade as well as the firm. Second, it may grow by external expansion, combining with other firms through acquisition or merger, without necessarily increasing the capacity of the trade.

The two methods of growth are clearly not mutually exclusive even for the same firm. It may grow by internal expansion at one stage of its development, and then proceed to grow still larger by acquisition. Alternatively, it may begin life as the result of a merger, but then grow almost exclusively by internal expansion. It is, however, often possible to judge fairly confidently whether internal or external expansion has played the greater part in the rise of individual firms, and thus to decide whether the trades to which they belong have become highly concentrated primarily because of internal or external expansion by the leading firms. But there are trades where the growth pattern of the leading firms is more confusing, since one leading firm may have grown large by expanding internally while others have developed by external expansion.

It is possible, even so, to take these latter trades into account, so that the high-concentration trades can be examined from two points of view: first, according to the growth pattern of the leading firms (that is, internal or external expansion, or combination of both), and second, according to whether the number of firms in the trade was once large or has always been relatively small.

2. HIGH-CONCENTRATION TRADES WITH EXTERNALLY EXPANDED LEADING FIRMS

It is perhaps significant that the trades where external expansion has been the principal method by which the largest firms have grown have all been much more heavily populated at some stage in the past. But the reduction in the number of concerns populating the trade, as well as the growth of the leading concerns, may have occurred in several different ways, ranging from the simultaneous amalgamation of many firms to gradual and piecemeal acquisition over a period of years.

The multi-firm amalgamation

In the closing years of the nineteenth century there occurred a series of amalgamations without precedent in British industry, whereby a number of producers in the same trade combined in a single undertaking. This trust movement, which paralleled developments in the United States and Germany, occurred after manufacturers had tried, but largely failed, to solve through looser forms of association the problems that beset their trades. One of the most common of those problems was surplus capacity, due partly to the over-expansion of the domestic industry and partly to the growth of international competition. The surplus capacity frequently made itself felt in cut-throat competition, and large amalgamation seemed to be a method of eliminating excess capacity and raising prices to more profitable levels.

The monster combines which were created were often responsible for a very large proportion of their trades. Their object was frankly monopolistic: to secure a share of the trade sufficient to give them control over prices and output. Thus, Wall Paper Manufacturers, formed in 1899 by a merger of thirty-one firms, claimed to be responsible for over 90 per cent of the trade, while the Salt Union, amalgamating sixty-four firms in 1888, claimed a similar proportion of the salt trade at its inception. But neither the salt nor the wallpaper combine was able to maintain such a large share of the trade for long.

The Salt Union attempted to increase salt prices, and for a while it was successful. Yet within twelve years of its formation, it had lost nearly half its trade and most of its capital, 'due to the development of new domestic sources of supply and improved methods of utilisation, and the rapid growth of the industry abroad'.[1] Even attempts at cartel arrangements proved futile until the formation of the Salt Manufacturers' Association in 1915, which controlled about 90 per cent of the salt marketed. There were, however, several important concerns that emerged in the inter-war period mainly as the result of mergers, including Cerebos and Imperial Chemical Industries (I.C.I.), the latter through the interests of Brunner Mond and the United Alkali Company. Yet the trade did not rank as highly concentrated in 1935, though it certainly gained that distinction two years later when I.C.I. acquired the Salt Union.

The monopoly position of Wall Paper Manufacturers (W.P.M.) also proved shortlived. In the decade following its formation many new concerns embarked on wallpaper manufacture, while imports also tended to increase. In 1915, however, W.P.M. regained a very large proportion of the trade by acquiring a number of the newcomers. But its position was undermined again in the post-war period as new firms started production, and intensive price competition developed. Once again, acquisition provided the solution for W.P.M.'s difficulties; several firms were acquired in 1934, to give it 85–90 per cent of the trade in 1935. Although the wallpaper trade remained highly concentrated throughout this period and up to 1951, there was some tendency for concentration to decrease after 1935, and for W.P.M.'s share of the total trade to decline as well.

Surplus capacity and its attendant price-cutting were also the main reasons for mergers in the cement trade, where high concentration was attained by two distinct stages. In 1900, the Associated Portland Cement Manufacturers was formed to purchase the undertakings of twenty-seven firms, and at its foundation it controlled 45 per cent of the total trade. Even so, competition remained severe, and in 1912 it amalgamated another thirty-three cement firms in a subsidiary company, British Portland Cement Manufacturers, to give it three-quarters of the total production. Once again, this high share was not maintained, for new firms entered the

[1] P. Fitzgerald, *Industrial Combination in England*, 2nd ed. (London, Pitman, 1927), p. 72.

trade, particularly during the building boom of the 1920's. In the ensuing slump surplus capacity again emerged, and in order to offset its consequences and restore its share of the trade Associated Portland acquired the Allied Cement Manufacturers group (Red Triangle) in 1931. Its position was still further strengthened by its acquisition of a majority shareholding in Alpha Cement in 1938, which itself had grown by absorbing other cement concerns. By 1947, therefore, Associated Portland group owned about two-thirds of the industry's productive capacity, which was only a slightly smaller share than in 1912 despite the overall expansion of the trade, to which it had itself contributed by new building.

There are two other trades where high concentration dates back to large mergers in the closing years of the nineteenth century, and in each case the resulting combines have been able to maintain their position without the difficulties encountered in the cement, salt, and wallpaper trades.

In the tobacco trade, the Imperial Tobacco Company (of Great Britain and Ireland) originated as a defensive combination of the thirteen leading British manufacturers (headed by W. D. and H. O. Wills) against the invasion of their domestic market by the American Tobacco combine in 1901. After a keen battle for that market, the two protagonists came to an agreement, by which Imperial took over the British interests of the American concern, while the export business and foreign interests of the two concerns were acquired by the British American Tobacco Company. By 1920, Imperial comprised eighteen manufacturing companies and controlled 55–60 per cent of the tobacco consumed in the United Kingdom market. It increased its share of the expanding trade still more in the inter-war years, largely without further acquisitions.

Two important mergers in the cotton thread trade resulted in the establishment of an effective duopoly which has been maintained more or less intact ever since. The firm of J. and P. Coats was already by far the largest in the trade when it amalgamated with its three principal rivals in 1896, and in the following year the majority of the other thread concerns combined to form the English Sewing Cotton Company. By 1920, it was reported that Coats alone controlled 80 per cent of the trade in household thread, as well as a very considerable proportion of factory thread, and in 1935 sewing cotton was listed by Leak and Maizels as one of the commodities whose output was concentrated in one or two firms. Similarly, although there were twenty-seven business units in the cotton thread trade in 1951, the three largest of them accounted for over 90 per cent of its activity.

Amalgamations involving considerable numbers of firms at one time are not confined to the pre-1914 period (although there were few during the inter-war years so spectacular as those of the 1890's). In 1919, for example, a number of lead concerns merged into Associated Lead Manufacturers, which acquired Walkers, Parker and Company in 1929, before itself amalgamating with Goodlass Wall and Company in 1930. Even so, high concentration in the lead trade did not emerge until much later and then mainly as the result of the contraction of the trade.

There were also mergers during the inter-war period in the cast iron pipes and fittings trade. Thus, Allied Ironfounders was formed in 1929 by the merger of a number of light foundry concerns, including ten producers of cast iron pipes and fittings, while in 1935, another batch of companies, six of them making cast iron pipes, came together in Federated Foundries. Here again, it was the intense competition springing from surplus capacity that encouraged amalgamation, though the same problems were also tackled through restrictive cartel arrangements.

Finally, mention may be made of the voluntary amalgamation of fifteen beet-sugar concerns in the British Sugar Corporation in 1936 as part of the statutory reorganisation of the sugar industry in this country. Though it did not cause the industry to become highly concentrated, for it was that already, the merger was responsible (as will be described in Chapter XIV) for some part of the increase in trade concentration.

Large-firm amalgamations

The stage may be reached in an industry's development where it consists to all intents and purposes of a few large concerns. But the process of concentration may be carried still further by the merger of the leading firms, either because they prefer combination to competition, or sometimes because the actual or potential contraction of the trade almost forces it upon them.

Such was the experience of the match trade, where the number of manufacturing concerns was reduced by merger and acquisition, under pressure of foreign competition in the domestic market, from forty in 1895 to seventeen in 1920. Fifteen of these seventeen manufacturers were associated, however, in three groups: Bryant and May (with seven concerns), Maguire, Paterson and Palmer (with five concerns) and J. John Masters (representing the British interests of the Swedish Match Company, with three concerns). In 1922, Bryant and May acquired the Maguire interests, and five years later it merged with Masters to form the British Match Corporation as part of a revised wider agreement with the Swedish Match Company.

There was also only a handful of producers in the transmission chains trade by the end of World War I, of which the most important were Hans Renold, Coventry Chain Company, Brampton Bros., Alfred Appleby Chain Company and Perry and Company. In 1925, Coventry Chain and Brampton Bros. were amalgamated, and after intensive price competition, the resulting combine was merged with Hans Renold in 1930. Three years later, Renold and Coventry Chain acquired three other chain manufacturers, including Alfred Appleby, thereby obtaining a very high proportion of the total trade.

There were also several combines in the explosives trade before the final act which created a near-monopoly in the production of commercial and military explosives in 1918. The Nobel Dynamite Trust Company was formed in 1886 to unite four explosives concerns, while Curtis's and Harvey amalgamated eight leading manufacturers of explosives in 1898. But competition remained keen until the outbreak of World War I, when the various domestic producers began to work as a single unit under government control. With the approval of the Government, the various firms were amalgamated in 1918 in Explosives Trades (which as Nobel Industries was itself later to form part of the I.C.I. merger in 1926), the main object being to cushion the effect of redundant capacity after the War.

In the incandescent mantle trade, Curtis's and Harvey was the leading manufacturer of incandescent mantles by 1920, when it formed Lighting Trades, to which it transferred its own and two acquired mantles businesses, the Volker Lighting Corporation and the Ramie Company. Lighting Trades subsequently became part of the I.C.I. combine, which also included the Welsbach Incandescent Gas Light Company, though I.C.I. ceased to manufacture gas mantles in 1930.

In two of the non-ferrous metals trades, high concentration has been associated with the merger of relatively large concerns at a time when refining activity in this country was declining. The leading concern in the zinc trade, Imperial Smelting Corporation, was formed in 1916, and in 1924 it acquired a partly completed government smelter at Avonmouth (which commenced production in 1928) and the Swansea Vale Smelter Company. These two smelters were the only ones able to survive the end in 1930 of the government-negotiated contract, under which the industry had obtained its concentrates on advantageous terms. Subsequently, Imperial Smelting extended its interests still further by take-overs. Similarly Consolidated Tin Smelters was formed in 1929 to acquire three smelting companies, and proceeded to concentrate production at the Williams, Harvey plant at Bootle. As a result of this merger, Consolidated accounted for 90 per cent of the total British production of refined tin.

Another example of large-firm amalgamation comes from the margarine trade. For many years before World War I, the British market was very largely supplied by imports from two Dutch margarine concerns, Anton Jurgens and Van den Berghs, the only important British producer being the Maypole Dairy Company, which had acquired Otto Monsted's factory at Southall. During the War, the difficulties of export persuaded the two Dutch concerns to establish factories in this country, while the need for greater supplies provided the opportunity for Lever Bros., with the support of the Government, to enter the trade through Planter's Margarine Company in 1914. The expanding market also induced Jurgens to make a number of acquisitions, culminating in 1924 with its absorption of Maypole which had tended to lose ground after claiming about one-quarter of the market in 1920. The two Dutch concerns had been linked by a profits pool agreement for some years, but there had always been difficulties about its operation, and in 1927 they merged in Margarine Union. Although Lever Bros.' margarine interests were comparatively small, the merger concluded in 1929 between it and the Margarine Union established Unilever as the largest margarine producer in this country.

In the sugar-refining trade there was a large element of internal expansion in the early growth of the firms which later merged to become the dominant concern. Up to 1921, both the Henry Tate and Sons and the Abram Lyle and Sons businesses grew by new building, and each reached an impressive size by exploiting new techniques and improving the quality of sugar products. As they grew, other concerns went out of the trade of their own accord, until by 1900 Tate and Lyle were the only two refiners left in London. The merger of the two businesses in 1921 was prompted by the desire for greater economies of operation, and subsequently led to further acquisitions including Fairrie and Company in 1929 and Macfie and Sons in 1938.

Growth by piecemeal acquisition

In some trades the process of combination has been more protracted than in the case of the overnight consolidation of large numbers of small concerns, or the merger of a small number of larger concerns. One firm may grow large by a consistent policy of acquisition over a period of years, until it reaches the point where it alone accounts for the greater part of a trade's activity.

Such has been the case in the spirit distilling trade. The Distillers Company was formed by a merger of six Scotch whisky concerns as long ago as 1877, but it was still unable to deal with the effects of over-production from which the trade tended to suffer. It embarked, therefore, on a programme of acquisition, closing down some of the distilleries and concentrating production in the others, which was to continue for half a century. In 1907, it entered the industrial spirit trade by acquiring a Liverpool distillery, and during World War I made a number of other purchases. The policy of acquiring competitors was accelerated in the immediate post-war years, culminating in 1925 in the absorption of Buchanan-Dewar and John Walker and Sons. By that time, Distillers could claim more than 80 per cent of the country's grain and malt whisky production, as well as a predominant share of the blending and distributing sections of the trade.

The same pattern of growth marked Distillers' emergence as the most important concern in the spirit rectifying trade, whose principal product is gin. After acquiring Tanqueray Gordon and Company, it took over Sir Robert Burnett and Company and Boord and Sons in 1924, to which it later added Booth's Distilleries.

It was also a consistent policy of acquisition, coupled with a substantial measure of internal expansion, that enabled W. and T. Avery to become, by the beginning of this century, the largest producer of scales and weighing machinery in the world. Then, in 1913, it acquired its most important rival, Henry Pooley and Son, which itself had absorbed a number of other producers a few years earlier. Moreover, when Avery's principal rival, George Salter and Company, which specialises in spring-operated weighing machines, became a public company in 1953, it was revealed that the two companies were linked by an exchange of shares.

Combination in the soap trade was preceded by the internal growth of Lever Bros., which up to 1906 expanded without making a single acquisition at home. In that year, however, after a period of intense competition, the idea of a soap trust was mooted in which eleven leading firms (accounting for two-thirds of total output) intended to participate. But the public reaction was so adverse that the idea was abandoned. Instead Lever Bros. proceeded to acquire by 1911 all but two of the ten other concerns in the proposed trust, and acquired them, as well as others in later years, to give it more than 70 per cent of the trade by 1921. Even though Lever's share of the trade (despite subsequent additional acquisitions) was afterwards reduced by the growth of rivals, such as the Co-operative Wholesale Society and Thomas Hedley, the trade itself has remained highly concentrated ever since.

Two or more firms may also grow by acquisition until between them they are responsible for a large part of the trade. In the fertilisers trade, the emergence of high concentration has been associated with the growth of the interests of two concerns—I.C.I. and Fisons. I.C.I.'s interests in fertiliser production originated in the Brunner Mond synthetic sulphate of ammonia plant which commenced production in 1923, but they were substantially extended when it acquired eight Scottish superphosphates concerns and merged them into its subsidiary, Scottish Agricultural Industries, in 1928. Similarly, three old-established businesses combined to form Fison, Packard and Prentice (later Fisons) in 1929, which thereafter made many acquisitions in different parts of the country, as well as building new plants and expanding others. By 1939, Fisons was responsible for more than one-third of the fertiliser trade, and by the end of the War its share had risen to between 40 and 50 per cent.

The same pattern of development can be observed in the wrought iron and steel tubes trade. One of the leading concerns in the industry, Stewarts and Lloyds, was created by a merger in the early years of this century, and in the late 1920's and early 1930's it made a number of important acquisitions, including the two largest English as well as the largest Scottish tube producers. The other leading concern, Tube Investments, was also formed as the result of a merger in 1919, and its growth was also marked by the acquisitions that it made in the next ten to fifteen years. There were close ties between these two concerns after 1930, and, as described in Chapter XIV, they made a number of joint acquisitions in subsequent years. The progressive concentration of the trade in these two concerns, as in the case of fertilisers, enabled rationalisation and modernisation to proceed.

Surplus capacity and later the rationalisation and modernisation of the industry have also been potent factors prompting mergers in the tinplate trade. By 1925, the leading concern in the industry, Richard Thomas, already controlled about one-third of total capacity, and ten years later its share was nearer two-fifths. Much of its growth was due to the acquisition of other businesses, and the same was also true for the other two largest concerns, Baldwins and the Briton Ferry Steel Company. The process of concentration through acquisition continued in the late 1930's and in 1939 there was another merger of four concerns creating Llanelly Associated Tinplate Companies. Towards the end of the War, Richard Thomas and Baldwins (R.T.B.) joined forces, after each had made further acquisitions, while in 1947 the Steel Company of Wales was formed to which both R.T.B. and Llanelly Associated transferred old-type tinplate mills. As a consequence of these mergers, the tinplate industry became highly concentrated during the 1935–51 period.

In the motor-cycle trade, the Birmingham Small Arms Company (B.S.A.) became the largest manufacturer in the 1920's, and was responsible for about one-quarter of the total production. During the 1930's, however, another concern developed rapidly, for by 1937 Associated Motor Cycles (A.M.C.) comprised the businesses of Matchless Motor Cycles (Colliers), A. J. Stevens and Company (acquired in 1931), and the Sunbeam interests of John Marston (acquired in 1937). Although the Sunbeam goodwill, designs and trade-mark were later sold to B.S.A., A.M.C. continued its policy of acquisition after the War by absorbing Francis and Barnett in 1947, the James Cycle Company in 1950 (later selling the bicycle section to Tube Investments), and Norton Motors in 1953. Similarly, B.S.A. took over the New Hudson and Ariel Motors businesses during the War, and later the Triumph Engineering Company. The purpose of these acquisitions was twofold: to obtain the valuable goodwill and trade-marks of the absorbed concerns, and to widen the range of machines supplied to the market. But their effect was to increase the degree of concentration in the industry, and to enable B.S.A. and A.M.C. between them to claim as much as two-thirds of the trade.

Turning to the floor-coverings trade, each of the two largest producers of floor coverings was stated in 1953 to be responsible for not much less than one-third of the trade. In each case, merger has played a significant part in their growth. Thus, the Barry and Staines Linoleum group was formed by the merger, in 1930, of the pioneer Linoleum Manufacturing Company and Barry, Ostlere and Shepherd (which was itself an amalgamation of three Kirkcaldy linoleum firms in 1899). Moreover, in 1937, Barry and Staines acquired the Corticine Floor Covering Company. Similarly, the other leading concern, Michael Nairn and Greenwich, was formed by merging two important firms in 1922, and acquired the Fife Linoleum Company in 1933.

3. HIGH-CONCENTRATION TRADES WITH INTERNALLY EXPANDED LEADING FIRMS

Among the trades where high concentration has been associated with the emergence of firms that have grown primarily by internal expansion, it is possible to distinguish those where the number of firms was once (or is still) large, from those where it has always tended to be small; that is, the many- and the few-firm trades.

The many-firm trades

It has already been demonstrated in the preceding section that the number of firms in a trade can be reduced, and large firms can grow, through amalgamation and acquisition. But firms can grow large without recourse to merger, expanding from within until they control the major part of a trade's activity. The number of firms in the trade may or may not be affected by such a development.

The growth of the leading firms is frequently attributable to their exploitation of new techniques or development of new products, which gives them a lead over the others. Although it may be within their ability to acquire their smaller competitors, they may not be concerned to do so since the latter's capacity is unwanted or unsuitable to the new technique. Thus, their own growth is centred on internal expansion, and their share of the trade increases as the smaller concerns dwindle in numbers or relative importance.

Take the razors trade, for example, where Gillette Industries has emerged as the leading concern through a process of internal expansion.

As will be more fully described in Chapter xv, Gillette's success has been based on the technological advantage that it gained as the result of the merger of its parent company with another American concern. Other razor blade concerns could not match the quality of Gillette's product, so that they abandoned the trade in considerable numbers even before the outbreak of World War II forced the closure of many additional works. As a consequence, Gillette was able to secure a large share of the trade for itself without recourse to merger or acquisition.

In the ice cream trade, the emergence of a few large concerns has not meant that the total number of producers is very small, though it is certainly much lower than pre-war. The opportunities for large-scale operation in this trade date from the introduction to this country of the 'American' ice which, thanks to mechanical refrigeration, could be produced in factories, stored, and widely distributed. One of the leading firms, T. Wall and Sons, was acquired by Lever Bros. soon after it commenced ice cream manufacture in the early 1920's, and developed its own distinctive form of distribution by tricycle. The other, J. Lyons and Company, sold a large part of its output through its chain of tea-shops. Both have expanded their trade through extensive advertising, designed particularly to increase off-season sales, but acquisition has played no part in their growth.

The few-firm trades

More often the high-concentration trades, where internal expansion has been the principal method of growth of the leading firms, have never had large numbers of producers. The relatively small number of firms can be explained in various ways: the trades themselves may be relatively new industries; or their early development may have been governed by patents which restricted entry, subsequent entry becoming difficult because of the scale of operations of the established concerns; and so on. In any case, the leading producers have either grown with the trade or entered it on a large scale, so that a high degree of concentration has been maintained throughout.

In the rubber tyres trade, for example, the Dunlop Rubber Company has been the largest concern in the trade ever since it began manufacture in 1900. Indeed, by the end of World War I, it was the only large-scale manufacturer in this country, though some firms which were older than Dunlop were still active. In the early 1920's, other firms entered the trade, but Dunlop's main competitors were European and American concerns exporting to this country. The imposition of an import tariff in 1927 was designed to check this competition, but several foreign firms thereupon established factories in this country. Two of the newcomers, the Goodyear Tyre and Rubber Company (Great Britain) and the Firestone Tyre and Rubber Company (both subsidiaries of American concerns), became the second and third largest concerns in the industry; another, the India Tyre Rubber Company, was acquired by Dunlop in 1933. Though Dunlop's share of the trade was less than 50 per cent in 1951, the scale of operations of the other leading concerns has kept concentration high, despite the growth in the trade itself and in the number of firms.

Similarly, the rayon trade throughout its development has been dominated by Courtaulds which, after acquiring the British rights to the patents for viscose rayon manufacture, began production in 1904. For several years, there was only one other rayon yarn producer in this country, an associate of a German firm, which was acquired by Courtaulds in 1917. During the 1920's, there was a considerable influx of newcomers into the trade, but most of them did not last for long. Of the twenty-five firms in the trade in 1929, thirteen had closed down by 1931 after a period of fierce price competition. But among those which survived were British Celanese (which entered the trade in 1920 and specialised in acetate yarn) and British Enka (a subsidiary of a Dutch concern which commenced production in 1926). These two firms between them accounted for about one-quarter of rayon yarn output by World War II, compared with Courtaulds' share of more than one-half. In addition, Courtaulds was responsible for nearly the whole output of staple fibre.[1] Thus, Courtaulds has retained its position in the trade without engaging much in acquisition, although in the spring of 1957, it was announced that Courtaulds and British Celanese were to merge. Like rayon, nylon manufacture is also highly concentrated, since I.C.I. is the sole producer of nylon polymer, while the polymer is turned into yarn solely by British Nylon Spinners, a joint subsidiary of I.C.I. and Courtaulds.

In mineral oil refining, the number of concerns has never been large. The principal concerns in the industry today were also active before the War; two of them built refineries in the early 1920's, and the other somewhat later. But since 1945 these same concerns, with their international connections and extensive interests in oil distribution, have grown with the trade by building new and large-scale refineries. Consequently, Shell, British Petroleum and Esso have tended to increase their share of the trade compared with pre-war, purely by internal expansion.

Another trade which has always consisted of a small number of firms is asbestos cement goods. Developing as an industry in the inter-war years, its most important producers are Turners Asbestos Cement Company (formed by Turner and Newall in 1929), Tunnel Asbestos Cement Company (a subsidiary of Tunnel Portland Cement Company, formed in 1936), Universal Asbestos Manufacturing Company, and

[1] H. A. Silverman, 'The Artificial Textile Industry' in *Studies in Industrial Organisation*, ed. by H. A. Silverman (London, Methuen, 1946), pp. 321–2.

Atlas Stone Company. Indeed, in 1948, the Simon Committee on the Distribution of Building Materials reported[1] that there were only five manufacturers of asbestos cement goods, and that four of them accounted for 95 per cent of the trade. Although the number of business units had increased to nine by 1951, the share of the four largest was only a little lower, at 92 per cent, than in 1948.

4. HIGH-CONCENTRATION TRADES WHERE LEADING FIRMS HAVE EXPANDED IN DIFFERING WAYS

There are, as already stated in Section 1, a number of trades where the leading firms have grown in differing ways, so that it would be misleading to classify them to either of the preceding sections. Examples of such trades are given below, distinguishing again between the many- and the few-firm trades.

The many-firm trades

In the starch trade, external expansion has been the primary method of growth for two of the largest producers which themselves merged in 1938. Reckitt and Sons entered starch production in 1840, and early in this century made a number of acquisitions from among its rival starch and blue producers. Similarly, J. and J. Colman, which started starch production even earlier than Reckitts, acquired another important producer, Keen, Robinson, in 1903. After the merger of the trading interests of Reckitts and Colman in 1938, other acquisitions were made by Reckitts in order to offset the loss of capacity caused by damage to its own factories during the War. But whereas Reckitts and Colman have expanded externally, the largest starch producer, Brown and Polson, has grown by internal expansion. Recognising that the demand for starch in traditional uses was limited, Brown and Polson sought to increase its trade by finding new applications, and today some four hundred different starch products are used in eighty different industries.

Another example comes from the photographic plates and films trade, where one of the industry's leaders is Kodak, a subsidiary of the American Eastman Kodak concern, which began production in Britain in 1890 and has expanded by new building. The other major concern, Ilford, entered the trade in 1880, but in the 1920's acquired a considerable number of other concerns. Moreover, Ilford, in collaboration with BX Plastics, formed Bexford in 1946 to produce film base in this country.

In the bicycle trade, too, there is a difference between the growth patterns of the leading firms. Raleigh Industries has grown almost entirely by internal expansion; the labour-force at its Coventry factory rose from

[1] Ministry of Works, *The Distribution of Building Materials and Components* (London, H.M.S.O. 1948).

5,000 in 1946 to 7,000 in 1951, while its output of bicycles rose from 60,000 in 1914 to 100,000 in 1926 and to one million in 1951. Another major producer, B.S.A., made more use of acquisition in its growth, for after its re-entry into cycle manufacture (after a lapse of twenty years) in 1908, it acquired the Eadie Manufacturing Company, famous for its coaster hub, as well as making a number of subsequent acquisitions. Similarly, the interests of Tube Investments in the bicycle trade have been developed through acquisition over a long period of years.

The seed-crushing trade witnessed an amalgamation of seventeen firms to form the British Oil and Cake Mills (B.O.C.M.) as long ago as 1899, and at that time the combine claimed about half of the nation's seed-crushing capacity. But with the expansion of the industry, B.O.C.M. continued to acquire other mills, until in 1921 it entered soap manufacture. This venture brought it into conflict with Lever Bros., and in 1925 B.O.C.M. amalgamated with Lever's on a share-exchange basis. Meanwhile, Anton Jurgens had acquired another major seed-crushing concern, the Olympia Oil and Cake Company. Thus, at the time of the Unilever merger of 1929, a considerable part of the seed-crushing industry came under the control of the new combine. Another of the leading concerns in the trade is the family business of J. Bibby and Sons which, unlike the Unilever interests, has grown through internal expansion.

The few-firm trades

Cinematograph film printing, despite its expansion, has never been a highly populated trade. As can be seen from Chapter XIV, its high degree of concentration can be associated with the entry into the trade on a large scale of Technicolor in 1936, the consolidation of a group of laboratories through the amalgamation of film producing concerns in the Rank Organisation, and the internal growth of George Humphries and Company.

There has been a similar mixture of experience among the leading concerns in the radio valves and cathode ray tubes trade. The largest producer is Mullard, which has been a subsidiary of the Dutch N. V. Phillips since 1927. Mullard, largely (though not entirely) by internal expansion, has increased its share of the trade in valves and cathode ray tubes from 40 per cent pre-war to nearly 60 per cent in 1954. The interests of another large producer, Associated Electrical Industries, stem, on the other hand, from the merger in 1928 of Edison Swan Electric Company (Ediswan), British Thomson-Houston Company (B.T.H.), and Metropolitan-Vickers Electrical Company. After the merger, the radio valve departments of the three concerns were rationalised, Ediswan concentrating on valves, with B.T.H. later specialising on special types of electronic valves.

5. SUMMARY AND CONCLUSION

From the preceding discussion emerges the major importance of external expansion in the growth of the leading concerns in the highly concentrated trades. There are few firms indeed among the leaders in the trades surveyed which were not created by amalgamation or have not resorted to acquisition and merger at some stage during their development.

There are a variety of reasons why firms have expanded in this way. Surplus capacity has been one of the most potent reasons, particularly in inducing a number of firms to amalgamate in a combine. In a number of instances the immediate aim was to provide a floor to prices, to end 'ruinous price competition', but where this was attempted without tackling the excess capacity, the amalgamation frequently proved to be vulnerable. Rationalisation has been, however, a more positive reason for amalgamation in some trades, though the lead in this case has been generally taken by one or two firms anxious to introduce new or improved techniques of production. In other cases, amalgamation has occurred either in order to meet foreign competition, to cushion the effects of a change in demand, or simply because it was more comfortable to combine than to compete. Finally, external expansion may have been adopted by a firm in order to widen its range of products, to extend the geographical spread of its operations, or to secure the goodwill attaching to a rival's products.

Internal expansion, on the other hand, has been associated with the exploitation of the opportunities afforded by early entry into a developing trade, or the advantages of introducing a new technique or product into a technically stagnant trade. Where there are also technological factors determining that the productive unit should be large, the growth of the leading firms by internal expansion suggests that there are good reasons why the firms should be few and concentration high, while it has also been suggested that growth by internal expansion, unlike growth by external expansion, means that the firm grows in the face of competition. Finally, it is relevant to note that in a striking number of instances the firms which have grown internally have been subsidiaries of American or European companies, or have had access to the technical know-how of foreign concerns which are among the industry-leaders in their own countries.

It may be seen that the tendency for firms to grow by external expansion has not been confined to any one period of time, though the frequency of amalgamations appears to have been most marked fifty or sixty years ago and again in the 1920's, when surplus capacity plagued many industries. In addition, as will be seen in Chapter XII, growth by external expansion does not appear to have been so important during the

1935–51 period, at least among those trades where concentration changed to a measurable degree.

Finally, there has been a marked tendency for high concentration, once attained, to persist. A considerable number of the trades which were highly concentrated in 1951 attained that distinction before World War I or in the early years of the inter-war period, notwithstanding some temporary or permanent loss of ground by the leading concerns. The persistence of high concentration, particularly in trades which have tended to expand as most of them have, clearly calls for some explanation, and to this we turn in the next chapter.

CHAPTER IX

FACTORS CONTRIBUTING TO THE MAINTENANCE OF HIGH CONCENTRATION

I. INTRODUCTION

At the end of the last chapter we observed that when a trade has once become highly concentrated, and the firms comprising it have been reduced to a small number, there is a marked tendency for these conditions to persist. The purpose of this chapter is to explain, as far as possible, this phenomenon with the help of empirical data relating to the highly concentrated trades of 1951.

Although the maintenance of high concentration is consistent with a change in the identity or ranking of the three largest concerns, in general it appears that once a firm has become one of the leaders in a highly concentrated trade it is not easily displaced. If it is assumed, for the sake of argument, that there is no change in the identity of the three largest units, then the maintenance of high concentration depends on their ability to keep their combined share of the trade. Where a trade's level of activity has contracted, or remained unchanged, they will be able to do so merely by maintaining their own production at the same absolute level, or reducing it proportionately with the trade as a whole. But when the trade has expanded, to keep their share they must expand at least at the same rate as the trade.

In theory, when the trade expands rapidly, it would seem difficult to attain the required rate of growth, for it might be anticipated that new enterprises would be attracted into the trade, with other established firms also doing their best to exploit the opportunity to grow. If this were in fact the case, concentration would tend to fall in expanding trades and if the decrease was sufficiently great, the trade might cease to be highly concentrated. But in practice this tendency is not apparent,[1] so that there would seem to be factors operating which frustrate the development of new competition.

The explanation of the persistence of high concentration may be sought, therefore, in two directions: first, stagnation or decline in trade activity, and second, the factors which make it difficult for newcomers to enter the trade or, even if entry is relatively easy, hamper the rate of growth of the new or established concerns. These factors can, moreover, be divided into two categories: those which operate on the side of production, and those which operate on the side of the market.

[1] See Chapter XI, p. 156.

2. THE STATE OF TRADE ACTIVITY

Where the long-term trend of demand for an industry's products is falling, or at best remains fairly stationary, there is an incentive for the firms in the trade to rationalise production through amalgamation and acquisition. There is also little to attract newcomers to the trade, unless they possess some new technique or product which will revitalise the trade and revive demand. Despite the absence of any general association between changes in concentration and in trade employment,[1] there is little doubt that for a few trades the contracting or stationary level of activity has been either the dominant or a contributory factor in the continuation of high concentration. Among these trades are the following:

Incandescent Mantles	Cotton Thread
Tin	Wallpaper
Cast Iron Stoves and Grates: Other	Vinegar and Other Condiments

A decline in demand may be temporary rather than sustained, with the result that the trade may suffer periodically from surplus capacity. It might be expected that entry into trades liable to periodic surplus capacity would also be unattractive to newcomers. But that is not always so. Even if the trade became highly concentrated as the result of measures to prevent 'cut-throat competition', it may still have to reckon with the entry of new firms as trade revives. When surplus capacity again emerges with the slackening of demand, the newcomers may not quickly disappear, unless the largest firms acquire them (as in wallpaper, soap and cement), or temporarily undersell them in their main markets through the introduction of special brands (as in matches), a special 'fighting company' (as in cast iron rainwater goods), or by a more general price-war (as in rayon during the inter-war years).

The fact remains, however, that for the great majority of the highly concentrated trades, the long-term trend of demand has been rising rather than falling so that the explanation of the maintenance of high concentration must be sought in the operation of the production and market factors restricting entry and limiting the growth of the smaller firms in these trades.

[1] See Chapter XI, p. 156.

3. PRODUCTION FACTORS RESTRICTING ENTRY AND HAMPERING GROWTH IN THE HIGH-CONCENTRATION TRADES

There are a variety of factors operating from the side of production which, by restricting new entry or limiting the growth of smaller established concerns, serve to maintain high concentration. The most important of these factors, examined below in turn, are: (*a*) the economies of large-scale operation; (*b*) capital requirements; (*c*) patents, technical know-how and essential equipment; (*d*) access to raw materials; (*e*) restrictive arrangements; and (*f*) State regulations.

(*a*) *Economies of large-scale operation*

In some industries, there is a tendency for the plants to be very large, indicating that economies of large-scale production are important. Where such conditions are found, entry may be difficult for the newcomer. To compete successfully with the established leaders of the industry, he must operate on a large scale from the very beginning. To do so, he must not only meet the initial capital outlay on buildings and plant, but also face the problem of recruiting and paying the substantial labour-force required. Moreover, he must always reckon with the possibility that to build a large plant will mean such an addition to the existing capacity that total supply will become more than the market can absorb.

We have already suggested in Chapter VI that economies of large-scale production can be detected by the combination of a large average plant size (250 persons or over) and a small plant size-ratio (5 and under). There are twenty-six trades where such a combination exists, and concentration is high for the following eleven of them:

- Rayon, Nylon C.F. Yarn and Staple Fibre
- Asbestos Cement Goods
- Cast Iron Stoves and Grates: Other
- Valves and Cathode Ray Tubes
- Mineral Oil Refining
- Ball and Roller Bearings
- Tinplate
- Cement
- Sugar and Glucose
- Prime Movers: internal combustion
- Cast Iron Pipes and Fittings

The average size of plants is not, however, fully satisfactory as an indicator of the typical plant in a trade and, as an alternative, the high-concentration trades have been classified in Table 28 according to whether their 'prevalent' plant size is large, largish or biased towards larger plants.[1] A distinction has been made between Census Trades and

[1] For the rules by which trades are assigned to prevalent plant size grades, see P. Sargant Florence, *Investment, Location and Size of Plant*, p. 17.

Sub-Trades in this table, since the estimation of prevalent plant size requires a size-distribution of establishments which is available only for Census Trades. Thus, the high-concentration trades that are Sub-Trades have been classified according to the prevalent plant size of the Trades of which they form part, except where reference to the average plant size data indicates that it would be misleading to do so.

Table 28. *High-concentration trades with high prevalent plant sizes, 1951*

Prevalent plant size grade	Trades	Sub-trades
Large (50 per cent or more of employment in establishments with 1,000 or more persons)	Mineral Oil Refining Tobacco Asbestos Manufactures	Motor Cycles Valves and Cathode Ray Tubes Prime Movers: internal combustion Rubber Tyres and Tubes Bicycles and Tricycles
Largish (50 per cent or more of employment in establishments with 500 or more persons)	Ice Cream Tramway, Trolleybus, Omnibus Undertakings (Civil Engineering)	Primary Batteries Accumulators and Parts Floor Coverings Rayon, Nylon C.F. Yarn and Staple Fibre Soap and Glycerine Boilers and Boiler-house Plant Transmission Chains
Bias toward larger (75 per cent of employment with over 200 persons)	Explosives and Fireworks Wallpaper Match Margarine Wrought Iron and Steel Tubes Tinplate Sugar and Glucose Salt Mines, etc. Precious Metals Refining Starch Small Arms Seed Crushing and Oil Refining	Abrasive Wheels, etc. Ball and Roller Bearings

In all the Trades listed in Table 28, which includes thirty-two of the fifty trades with high concentration, the economies of scale may be sufficiently large to constitute some difficulty in the way of newcomers entering the trade, at least at a level where they would constitute a threat to the established large concerns.

(*b*) *Capital requirements*

Where prevalent plant size is high, it is usually the case that the capital needed to enter the trade is also high. But capital requirements may also constitute an obstacle to easy entry in trades which are very capital-intensive even though their prevalent plant size is low, since the latter is measured in terms of numbers employed.

According to the estimates of Dr T. Barna, the value of fixed capital assets per employee in manufacturing industry as a whole amounted to £1,830 in 1955.[1] But there are several trades among the highly concentrated where the capital assets per employee are above average, and in some cases markedly so:[2]

Mineral Oil Refining	Soap and Glycerine
Sugar and Glucose	Ice Cream
Fertilisers	Starch
Rayon, Nylon C.F. Yarn and Staple Fibre	Seed Crushing and Oil Refining
	Cotton Thread
Wallpaper	Match
Cement	Margarine
Floor Coverings	

It will also be the case that entry may be more difficult because more costly at one rather than another stage of the same trade. Thus, in the non-ferrous metals trades, entry at the primary stages of production would require more capital per head than at the fabricating stages.

The capital required to enter the trade will not, in all instances, be indicated by the value of fixed assets (that is, buildings and plant) per worker. In some trades, it may be largely determined by the high cost of the principal raw materials (for example, in precious metals refining) or the necessity to finance the holding of stocks (for example, in spirit distilling, where the stocks of maturing whisky must be held for a legal minimum period of three years).

There seems to be little doubt that capital requirements do constitute an obstacle to entry for many of the highly concentrated trades.

(c) *Patents, technical know-how and essential equipment*

When a firm is granted a patent to produce a new article or use a new process, it receives an absolute legal monopoly for that product or technique for sixteen years. This legal monopoly may be dispersed if it decides to grant licences, against payment of royalties, to other firms. But either way, the firm which has a valuable and unbreakable patent is in a strong position: it is able, if it chooses, to refuse to license new entrants or rival firms, or to afford them the right only on the payment of royalties which place them at a disadvantage. The importance of patents as an

[1] T. Barna, 'The Replacement Cost of Fixed Assets in British Manufacturing Industry in 1955', *Journal of the Royal Statistical Society*, Series A (General), vol. 120, part 1, 1957, p. 17, table 3.

[2] We are indebted to Dr Barna for his assistance in determining the trades listed.

obstacle to new entry or growth will, however, depend on their intrinsic value and the extent to which they can be evaded, and that is often very difficult to assess.

In several cases, leading firms in the highly concentrated trades enjoy the exclusive right to use certain patents as the result of their ties with foreign undertakings. An outstanding example are the patents under which I.C.I. and British Nylon Spinners enjoy the exclusive rights of nylon manufacture in the British Commonwealth, excluding Canada; these came under their control as the result of the I.C.I.-du Pont patents and processes agreement. Other trades where British concerns are beneficiaries of patents belonging to their foreign parent or affiliated companies are ball and roller bearings, valves and cathode ray tubes, and matches.

Quite apart from patents, new firms coming into an industry may find it difficult to acquire the necessary technical know-how. Indeed, the production processes themselves may be so involved and intricate that newcomers hesitate to embark upon them; or existing firms may be operating secret processes. They may also find it difficult to obtain the machinery or equipment they need, because their supply is controlled by the established concerns. Thus, the Monopolies Commission found that 'the development of competition by independent British match manufacturers has been hampered by their being unable to buy machinery from manufacturers controlled by Swedish Match—the main source of supply in Europe—as a consequence of agreements between Swedish Match and the British Match Corporation'.[1] Even where supplies of machinery are available to newcomers, the machines themselves may not be so efficient as those used by established concerns which, as in the case of the razor trade, either make their own or adapt the standard designs to increase production.

All in all, it would appear that patents, secret processes, technical know-how and allied factors have operated to one degree or another as obstacles to entry and growth in the following high-concentration trades:

Transmission Chains	Match
Explosives and Fireworks	Primary Batteries
Photographic Plates and Films	Accumulators
	Incandescent Mantles
Precious Metals Refining	Razors (excl. Electric)
Sugar and Glucose	Starch
Scales and Weighing Machinery	Tinplate
	Valves and Cathode Ray Tubes

[1] Monopolies Commission, *Supply and Export of Matches* (1953), par. 215.

Mineral Oil Refining	Cinematograph Film Printing
Rayon, Nylon C.F. Yarn and Staple Fibre	Ball and Roller Bearings
	Rubber Tyres and Tubes

It must, however, be recognised that the importance of patents, if not of technological know-how, as an obstacle to entry and growth may easily be overrated, since in several of the trades listed above it has been the practice to issue non-exclusive licences to other concerns in the trade.

(*d*) *Access to raw materials*

Vertical integration, whereby a manufacturing concern controls its own supplies of raw materials, is a feature of many highly concentrated trades. Indeed, in some cases it provides a link between one high-concentration trade and another. Thus, Unilever, as the principal concern in both the Soap and the Margarine trades, is also the largest concern in the Seed Crushing and Oil Refining trade, which produces the raw materials common to both soap and margarine manufacture. Similarly, the Distillers Company is not only the largest concern in both the Spirit Distilling and Spirit Rectifying trades, but also possibly the largest in the Wholesale Bottling of Wines and Spirits trade.

Vertical integration may have developed in different ways and for a variety of reasons. It may have been due to manufacturing concerns which have integrated backwards into the production of their own raw materials. The need to safeguard their supplies of those raw materials has frequently been the principal motive; thus, the Dunlop Rubber Company began to acquire rubber plantations in Malaya before World War I, while Turner and Newall have owned asbestos mines in South Africa and Canada for many years. Acquisition of raw materials has also been prompted by the desire to stabilise costs, for some raw materials tend to fluctuate widely in price. The soap and margarine makers acquired their own plantations overseas at an early stage in their development for that reason. Or again, firms may have been forced to produce their own raw materials, either because existing supplies were insufficient in quantity or unsatisfactory in quality, as in the case of Nobels in the explosives trade.

Another way in which vertical integration has developed is where a raw materials producer has embarked on the manufacture of the finished products. Thus, Curtis's and Harvey started to manufacture incandescent mantles largely because the nitro-cellulose it produced was used in the coating of mantles, while the seed-crushing activities of J. Bibby led it into the manufacture of soap and edible fats. Finally, vertical integration may arise as the result of an international consolidation of interests extending from raw materials to finished product, such as occurred in the tin and zinc trades between the wars.

Where vertical integration results in a leading concern controlling a substantial proportion of the raw materials essential for the manufacture of its product, it can frustrate a newcomer's progress by denying it access to these raw materials or by charging it a discriminatory price. The restrictive control exerted by the British Match Corporation over supplies of certain chemicals used in match manufacture has already been mentioned.[1] But whether or not the vertically integrated concern chooses to use its control of raw materials restrictively, it almost certainly possesses an advantage over the non-integrated concern. The nature of this advantage is clearly demonstrated in the mineral oil refining trade. Most of the main refineries are owned by international companies which also produce crude oil in the Middle East, and though refining in Western Europe is itself of doubtful profitability, any losses made are offset by the high profits earned on crude oil. The non-integrated refiner enjoys no such advantage, and so his ability to operate is restricted. Indeed, it has been stated that some of them are occupied mainly with work on behalf of the major integrated companies.[2]

Vertical integration is common among the leading concerns in the following high-concentration trades:

Explosives and Fireworks	Soap and Glycerine
Fertilisers	Margarine
Tinplate	Seed Crushing and Oil Refining
Wrought Iron and Steel Tubes	Photographic Plates and Films
	Rubber Tyres and Tubes
Mineral Oil Refining	Match
Asbestos Manufactures	Cement

Asbestos Cement Goods

It is reasonable to suppose, therefore, that in these trades the leading concerns, through their control of raw material supplies, enjoy at least a cost-advantage compared with non-integrated concerns, which may hinder the latter's growth.

(*e*) *Restrictive arrangements*

Restrictive arrangements in particular trades, though not designed to advance the cause of leading concerns, may nevertheless have had the effect of helping them to maintain their share of the trade. Such arrangements may involve, by agreement between a number of firms representing the predominant part of an industry's activity, the division of its output through production or sales quotas. In the cast iron rainwater goods trade, for example, the British Ironfounders' Association between 1933

[1] See Chapter III, p. 43.

[2] See Economic Commission for Europe, *The Price of Oil in Western Europe* (Geneva, United Nations, 1955), pp. 30–2.

and 1942 aggregated the total home sales of its members and every year 'each concern was allocated a percentage share based on previous trade'; up to 1940, the firm which delivered in excess of its quota was fined and the firm which undersold its quota was compensated.[1] Similar quota arrangements have operated also in the tinplate and cement trades, as well as in grain milling, though the latter has not become a highly concentrated trade.

The Monopolies Commission has stated, in the case of rainwater goods, that there were appreciable changes in the share of the total trade held by individual concerns during the operation of the quota scheme, and comparable statements have been made regarding the cement quota system.[2] But it can be argued, on the other hand, that a quota system not only hinders the entry of newcomers but introduces a high degree of rigidity into the trade. Moreover, it tends to preserve the proportion of the industry in the hands of the largest concerns, as well as encouraging growth by merger.

(*f*) *State regulations*

The State may act in a way that either restricts entry into particular trades or serves to protect established concerns. The creation of the British Sugar Corporation in 1936 with a statutory monopoly of beet-sugar manufacture, as well as the Refining Agreement establishing quotas among the cane sugar-refiners, has restricted entry into the sugar and glucose trade. Similarly, import restrictions which resulted in leaf quotas for tobacco manufacturers tended to maintain the established pattern of the trade and restrict the expansion of individual firms except by acquisition.

The necessity to obtain licences and satisfy certain onerous conditions before operating as a spirit distiller or rectifier is also likely to restrict entry to those two trades. The restrictions over the operation of public service vehicles have also contributed to the high concentration in the Tramway, Trolleybus and Omnibus Undertakings (Civil Engineering) trade. Similarly, the elaboration of safety regulations, as in the case of explosives and abrasive wheels, or hygiene regulations, as in the case of ice cream, may also act as a deterrent to entry.

Finally, protective tariffs may also tend to shield established concerns although, as already seen in the preceding chapter, they may also have the effect of inducing foreign firms to embark upon production in this country. But these newcomers often start on such a scale that high concentration is maintained, even though the share of the largest established concerns may be reduced.

[1] Monopolies Commission, *Report on the Supply of Cast Iron Rainwater Goods* (London, H.M.S.O. 1951), pars. 90–1.

[2] Ministry of Works, *Cement Costs* (London, H.M.S.O. 1947), par. 112.

4. MARKET FACTORS RESTRICTING ENTRY AND HAMPERING GROWTH IN THE HIGH-CONCENTRATION TRADES

The principal factors operating from the side of the market which tend to restrict new entry or limit growth are: (*a*) advertising and sales promotion; (*b*) distribution methods and service facilities; and (*c*) restrictive arrangements in distribution.

(*a*) *Advertising and sales promotion*

It is generally accepted that advertising yields increasing returns to scale, which means that the large firm has an advantage over the small. Moreover, once a manufacturer has established a reputation for his product, the goodwill attaching to his brand-name can be transferred by skilful advertising from one product to another. Advertising acts, therefore, as a barrier to entry since a new firm, if it is to compete on equal terms, may need to create goodwill quickly by advertising on a large scale from the start. In other words, as Professor Scitovsky has stated, 'the need for advertising in the uninformed market creates the same protection for established firms and the same obstacles to the entry of new firms as the existence of technological economies of scale'.[1]

Among the high-concentration trades, there are several where established brand-preferences and the need for advertisement and sales promotion would appear to constitute an advantage to existing large firms:[2]

Razors (excl. Electric)	Tobacco
Margarine	Bicycles and Tricycles
Soap and Glycerine	Rubber Tyres and Tubes
Spirit Distilling	Primary Batteries
Spirit Rectifying	Accumulators and Parts
Mineral Oil Refining	Photographic Plates and Films

The importance of advertising and sales promotion is by no means uniform among these trades, and in general it appears possible for firms to enter and survive in the trades without substantial advertising. But their growth will be limited unless they are able to make the large advertising appropriations which are characteristic of the big concerns.

(*b*) *Distribution methods and service facilities*

Where distribution is integrated with production, there is an additional obstacle to the entry of new, and the growth of smaller, concerns. The

[1] T. Scitovsky, 'Ignorance as a Source of Oligopoly Power', *American Economic Review*, vol. 40, no. 2, May 1950, p. 50.

[2] Based on data in N. Kaldor and R. Silverman, *A Statistical Analysis of Advertising Expenditure and of the Revenue of the Press*, National Institute of Economic and Social Research, Economic and Social Studies, 8 (Cambridge University Press, 1948), table 75, pp. 144–7.

integration may extend to the ownership of chains of retail shops, but if the established pattern of distribution is direct from the point of production to the point of sale or use, that alone may act as a deterrent to new entry. Once again, mineral oil refining provides a good example, since the major concerns have intervened in distribution without taking over the retail outlets. Instead, the outlets are 'backed financially (mainly in respect of their investment in storage and retailing equipment)' and enjoy 'sales assistance by the supplier', and 'in return they use (and by using strengthen) the suppliers' brand'.[1] The result is that 'no refiner who lacks an already established motor spirit network can hope to create one quickly, and even then the expense of doing so is prohibitive except for very large companies'.[2]

Direct sales from producer to retailer or user are, in fact, important in a number of the high-concentration trades, including the following:[3]

Mineral Oil Refining	Soap and Glycerine
Photographic Plates and Films	Wallpaper
	Margarine
Floor Coverings	Asbestos Cement Goods
Motor Cycles, etc.	Salt Mines, etc.
Notepaper, Pads, Envelopes	

In such trades, therefore, the new entrant must take into account not merely the capital costs of embarking upon production, but also (unless it is prepared to ignore the accepted pattern of distribution) the capital costs of organising and creating its own distributive machinery.

A somewhat similar obstacle to new entry is the importance attached in some trades to the provision of servicing or repair depots for the convenience of their customers, or a large number of geographically scattered wholesale or distributing depots for speedy supply. Among the trades where such factors appear to be significant are:

Primary Batteries	Scales and Weighing Machinery
Accumulators and Parts	Fertilisers
Ice Cream	Bicycles and Tricycles

Once again, the leading firms often enjoy a distinct advantage over the smaller firms in these respects.

[1] P. H. Frankel, 'Integration in the Oil Industry', *Journal of Industrial Economics*, vol. 1, no. 3, July 1953, p. 210.

[2] Economic Commission for Europe, *op. cit.* pp. 33–4.

[3] The trades cited are those for which 60 per cent or more of the characteristic products are distributed direct to retailer or user, based on data taken from J. B. Jefferys, *The Distribution of Consumer Goods*, National Institute of Economic and Social Research, Economic and Social Studies, 9 (Cambridge University Press, 1950), p. 18; and from Ministry of Works, *The Distribution of Building Materials and Components* (H.M.S.O. 1948), pp. 53–5.

(c) *Restrictive arrangements in distribution*

There are a considerable variety of restrictive arrangements which may impede a newcomer's access to the market, and these arrangements are frequently present among high-concentration trades. According to the Monopolies Commission, exclusive dealing arrangements, particularly where they are collectively organised, create

> 'an excessive rigidity and go far to eliminate possible competition from traders outside the group.... Once a large group of buyers are committed to buy only from the suppliers who are members of the group it becomes extremely difficult for any independent producer to find a market. He will be particularly handicapped if the supplier members of the group supply a wide range of qualities or sizes of the goods while he produces only a few qualities or sizes.'[1]

Similarly, aggregated rebates (again particularly where collectively organised) offer strong economic incentives to buyers to confine their purchases to established concerns and to ignore the attention of new enterprises. A potential newcomer to the cement industry, for example, would find that its prospective customers were faced 'with the difficulty that by accepting supplies from the new manufacturer they would lose whatever rebates they were entitled to' under the Cement Makers' Federation rebate scheme. In particular, 'a new cement works would be unlikely to attract custom from large customers who required deliveries at all points in the country', since they could not afford to forgo their right to rebate unless the new works were able (and it would almost certainly be unable) to supply them with all their needs.[2]

In the tobacco trade, the Imperial Tobacco Company (I.T.C.) has operated a Customer Bonus Scheme, whereby retailers receive a bonus in return for undertaking to display I.T.C. products prominently and generally to promote the sale of its goods. This system has undoubtedly given I.T.C. an advantage over smaller tobacco manufacturers.

Various types of restrictive arrangements affecting distribution, which are likely to have influenced the ease of entry or conditions of growth, can be stated to have existed in the following high-concentration trades:

Wallpaper	Bicycles and Tricycles
Floor Coverings	Motor Cycles, etc.
Mineral Oil Refining	Valves and Cathode Ray Tubes
Cement	Primary Batteries
Asbestos Cement Goods	Accumulators and Parts

Tobacco

[1] Monopolies Commission, *Collective Discrimination*, Cmd. 9504 (London, H.M.S.O. 1955), par. 115.

[2] Ministry of Works, *Cement Costs* (1947), pars. 115 and 116.

At the same time, it must be stressed that their influence may not have been very strong, and that the passage of the Restrictive Trade Practices Act, 1956, is likely to have removed it altogether in most instances.

5. SUMMARY AND CONCLUSION

It is clear that there are a variety of obstacles to new entry and to growth which appear to be significant in the case of the high-concentration trades, though it is much more difficult to assess their relative importance in the same trade or between one trade and another. There are, however, a number of trades where their incidence appears to be most marked, and where their cumulative effect may be very considerable. These trades are as follows:

Mineral Oil Refining	Bicycles and Tricycles
Cement	Ice Cream
Primary Batteries	Tobacco
Accumulators and Parts	Tinplate
Wallpaper	Rubber Tyres and Tubes
Soap and Glycerine	Floor Coverings
Photographic Plates and Films	Sugar and Glucose
	Match
Explosives and Fireworks	

At the same time, it must be stressed that the obstacles are not insuperable. Firms do enter many of the high-concentration trades, and firms do grow despite the obstacles and difficulties. But it may be easier to enter the trade by purchasing a going concern than by starting from scratch, though it may still need considerable financial resources to grow after that. It is significant, for example, that the firm that has grown in the soap trade to the extent of reducing the share controlled by Unilever was Thomas Hedley, after it had been acquired by one of the leading American soap concerns, Procter and Gamble. Thus, although the obstacles are not insuperable in every trade, they are formidable in many of the high-concentration trades, and for that reason, they can be held to contribute substantially to the maintenance of high concentration.

PART III

CHANGES IN CONCENTRATION, 1935–51

CHAPTER X

CHANGES IN CONCENTRATION: SOME PROBLEMS OF METHODOLOGY

In the two preceding chapters, we have been concerned with developments over a fairly long period of years in the trades with high concentration in 1951. But, given the concentration data for 1935, it is clearly desirable that a more systematic attempt should be made to establish what changes in concentration took place among Census trades between 1935 and 1951, as well as to relate those changes to changes in other measurable factors during the same period.

The concentration-ratios at each of the two dates are of course subject to the limitations described in Chapter I. But there are additional factors which complicate the assessment of changes in concentration and industrial structure over a period of time, let alone changes in the degree of monopoly power. In the main, these factors may be examined under two heads: first, the adequacy of the concentration-ratio in revealing changes in concentration and industry structure; and second, the effect of changes in the definitions and comprehensiveness of Census trades.

I. THE CONCENTRATION-RATIO AND CHANGES IN CONCENTRATION

The concentration-ratio, measuring the share of the three largest units in a trade's activity, is neither a sensitive indicator of changes in the size-relationship of the concerns in an industry nor an adequate indicator of the changes in the structure of the industry.

Take, for example, a trade with a concentration-ratio of 70 per cent, divided between the three largest units, A, B, and C, on a 4 : 2 : 1 basis. If a merger occurs between A and B, the two largest units in the trade, it is an event of obvious significance for the industry as a whole. Yet the concentration-ratio may be very little altered. It will be raised by the share of what was previously the fourth largest unit, but this share may have been quite small. Indeed, in the absence of mergers, important changes in the relative importance of the three largest units can occur without changing the concentration-ratio.

A comparison of concentration-ratios at two dates, therefore, neither reveals changes in the relative sizes of the three largest units nor changes in their identity. Yet these changes in identity or rank may be very important, for they can qualify any conclusions reached on the evidence of a change, or absence of change, in the concentration-ratio itself. Thus, in a trade where concentration has remained high over a number of years, changes in the identity of the leading concerns suggest that conditions in the trade have been far more dynamic than would be supposed from its unchanged concentration-ratio.

Knowledge of changes in the number of units in a trade is of some help in interpreting changes in concentration-ratios. Thus, a decrease in the number of units in a trade, but with little or no change in concentration, may significantly alter its structure. Such a change will also be reflected in the size-ratio of the business units at the two dates. For example, if a trade's concentration-ratio remains unchanged at 70 per cent, but its number of units falls from thirty to ten, then its unit size-ratio will be reduced from twenty-seven at the beginning to six at the end of the period, suggesting that its structure has become less monopolistic and more oligopolistic in character.[1]

Although the number of business units in each trade is given for 1951, the same information is not generally available for 1935. For a number of trades, however, the Board of Trade has provided data on which an estimate of the number of business units in 1935 can be based, so that it is possible in these cases to establish the direction and magnitude of the change in the number of business units and their size-ratios between 1935 and 1951.[2]

Even with this additional information, our knowledge of important aspects of changes in industrial structure remains deficient. In particular, changes in the identity of the leading firms in an industry are most relevant in discussing the experience of a trade, but Census data do not, of course, help us in this connection. Thus, once again, changes in concentration-ratios and numbers of business units must be supplemented by other and more descriptive material if there is to be any reliable appreciation of the significance of the changes.

2. THE EFFECTS OF CHANGES IN THE DEFINITION AND COMPREHENSIVENESS OF CENSUS TRADES

One of the principal factors which complicate the determination of changes in concentration from Census data is the periodical redefinition

[1] In fact, however, its structure may have become even more monopolistic if one of the three largest units has increased its share of the 70 per cent to a sufficient degree.

[2] See Chapter XI, p. 153.

of Census trades. The definition of a Census trade may be changed for a number of reasons, such as an increased diversification of its output, the introduction of new techniques, or the growth of one part of its production to such an extent that it attains the status of a separate trade.

Suppose, for example, that trade A is redefined by virtue of the fact that one of its principal products is now classified to another trade, B. Some of the establishments initially classified to trade A will be transferred to trade B, since their output consists wholly or mainly of the principal product that has been switched from trade A to trade B. If the establishments transferred belong entirely to the three largest units, their share of the redefined trade A will be less than their share of the original trade A. Indeed, it is possible, as a result of the redefinition of the trade, that the three largest units lose their pre-eminence and are replaced by different concerns. Yet there might have been no real change whatever.

It is important, therefore, in considering changes in concentration, to establish the extent to which the trade of 1951 is the same as the trade of 1935; otherwise quite misleading conclusions may be reached. An initial check on the existence of changes in definition between 1935 and 1951 can be made by using the 1948 Census of Production. This Census gives for each trade not merely the 1948 data, but also comparable data for 1935. Thus, the existence of any change in definition is revealed by comparing the 1935 data according to the 1948 Census with the 1935 data according to the 1935 Census.

The degree of comparability, which may be defined as the ratio between the 1935 sales of principal products by establishments in the Census trade according to the 1948 Census, and the same data for 1935 according to the 1935 Census,[1] has been calculated to reveal and measure changes in the definition of Census trades. It is, however, an accurate measure of changes in definition only where the reclassification of products has been in one direction: that is, where principal products have only been added to, or taken from, the trade. Where some products have been added but others taken away, the differences in the 1935 sales of principal products by the trade's establishments will be a net figure. The change in definition, as denoted by the degree of comparability, will consequently appear to be less than it is in reality. Thus, in assessing the extent of redefinition, account must be taken of the gross change in its product-structure, as well as the net change indicated by the degree of comparability.

Changes in specialisation and exclusiveness

A further complication in comparing concentration-ratios over time stems from the fact that, independent of changes in its definition, the

[1] In the case of Sub-Trades, for 'principal products' read 'characteristic products'.

specialisation and exclusiveness can also change over time. The effect of specialisation and exclusiveness on the validity of a trade's concentration-ratio for a single year has already been examined in Chapter 1, where it was also pointed out that it was possible within limits to estimate, using the degrees of exclusiveness and specialisation, a principal product concentration-ratio for each trade.

The way in which the principal product concentration-ratio underlines the importance of changes in specialisation and exclusiveness can best be illustrated by a specific example: the Cars and Taxis Sub-Trade of the Motor Vehicles and Cycles (Manufacturing) Trade. For this Sub-Trade, there was apparently a large increase in concentration between 1935 and 1951: from 47 to 82 per cent in terms of gross output and from 48 to 69 per cent in terms of employment. When the principal product concentration-ratios were calculated, using the formulae of Appendix D, it was estimated that the three largest units' combined share of the principal products produced lay somewhere between 30 and 64 per cent in 1935 and between 47 and 55 per cent in 1951.

For the Cars and Taxis Sub-Trade, therefore, the principal product concentration-ratio does not confirm the large increase in concentration denoted by the gross output ratio. Concentration in terms of principal products may have increased; but it may equally well have decreased. The explanation of this result lies in the difference between the Sub-Trade's specialisation and exclusiveness in the two years. In 1935 the Sub-Trade was virtually 100 per cent exclusive: that is, only a very small fraction of the total output of cars and taxis was produced by establishments outside the Sub-Trade. On the other hand, its specialisation was much lower at 77 per cent. In 1951 the Sub-Trade was much less exclusive: only 63 per cent of the total output of cars and taxis came from the Sub-Trade's establishments, while the establishments themselves were even less specialised (at 69 per cent) than in 1935. Thus the Sub-Trade's gross output concentration-ratio in 1951 referred only to a relatively small part of all the cars and taxis produced in this country.

Finally, to confirm this explanation of the divergence between the gross output and principal product concentration-ratios, a more detailed study of the car industry was undertaken. Its conclusion was that the share of the total output (by value) of cars and taxis held by the three largest producers fell between 1935 and 1951.[1] It is therefore fair to conclude that the rise in the concentration-ratio was the direct opposite of what in fact took place in the car industry.

[1] It may be noted that the merger of the Nuffield and Austin interests in the British Motor Corporation took effect in 1952. If it had taken place in 1951, there would then have been an increase in concentration in the motor car industry (that is, in terms of the share of the three largest producers) compared with 1935.

Changes in the definition of a Census trade may also affect its specialisation and exclusiveness, so that the formulae presented in Sections III and IV of Appendix D are designed to estimate a revised principal product concentration-ratio for 1935 where the trade has changed from its original composition. There is, however, one qualification to which the formulae in Sections III and IV of Appendix D are subject: namely, that the change in the definition of the trade has not been sufficiently great to change the identity of the three largest units as a result. Attention has been paid to this point and some trades, otherwise eligible for selection, have been rejected from the analysis of 1935–51 concentration-changes on these grounds.

To sum up: in comparing concentration-ratios for Census trades over time, it is necessary and desirable to establish what has happened to the concentration of principal products. Only by that means can it be determined whether a change in trade concentration implies a change in the concentration of the principal products of the trade. To this end, it is necessary to take account of three factors:

(*a*) changes in the definition of the trade, in terms of its principal products, which affect the establishments classified to it;

(*b*) changes in its degree of specialisation; that is, the extent to which the output of the establishments of the trade consist of principal products; and

(*c*) changes in its degree of exclusiveness; that is, the extent to which its establishments are responsible for the total output of the principal products appropriate to the trade.

These three factors have been covered by the formulae of Appendix D which have been applied to gross output concentration-ratios in 1935 and 1951 in order that the principal product concentration-ratios in the two years can be established. The results of the application of these formulae are surveyed in the following section.

3. THE SELECTION OF TRADES FOR THE ANALYSIS OF CHANGES IN CONCENTRATION, 1935–51

Concentration-ratios provided by the Board of Trade relate to 147 Trades and 200 Sub-Trades of the 1951 Census of Production, outnumbering the 302 Trades and Sub-Trades covered by the Leak and Maizels study of concentration in 1935. For several reasons, many of the 1951 trades have no direct counterpart in terms of 1935 data. In some instances a Sub-Trade of 1935 has become a fully fledged Trade by 1951 and while such trades can be compared one with the other where data for both years exist, it sometimes becomes impossible to compare the remainder of the 1935 Trade with any particular Trade or Sub-Trade in

1951. Conversely, some of the 1935 Trades have lost their identity, mainly through incorporation with another Trade in a reshuffle of establishments between several Census Trades. Finally, data for 1951 have not been provided by the Board of Trade for certain Census Trades, which existed in both 1935 and 1951, because the concentration data would not be particularly meaningful in the latter year; the outstanding example is Coal Mines.

After account has been taken of these various factors, there remain 185 Census Trades and Sub-Trades for which data relating to 1935 and 1951 exist on a prima facie basis of comparability. These 185 trades are listed in Appendix J, which shows their degree of comparability, their gross output concentration-ratios and their estimated principal products concentration-ratios for 1935 and 1951. For the reasons described in the preceding section, attention must be paid to these principal product concentration-ratios to determine whether a positive or negative change in gross output concentration for the trade coincides with a corresponding concentration-change in terms of the trade's principal products.

There are sixty-one trades among the 185 for which a change in principal product concentration can be claimed. The claim is easily substantiated in forty-seven cases where there was a clear gap between the minimum and maximum of the estimates for the two years. For the other fourteen trades, where the maximum of 1935 was the same as the minimum for 1951, or vice versa, it is assumed (in view of the corresponding change in gross output concentration) that principal product concentration has changed over the period.

There is yet another stage in the selection of trades for the analysis of concentration-changes, comparable to the procedures adopted in the case of the 1951 analysis. Where concentration-changes are established both for a Trade and one or more of its Sub-Trades, the Sub-Trades are preferred and the Trade itself rejected from the analysis.[1] Similarly, where a trade has degrees of specialisation or exclusiveness of less than 67 per cent in one or both years, it is deemed to be unsatisfactory and is also rejected.[2] For some trades, too, the degree of comparability suggests that the definition of the trade has changed sufficiently to make it likely that the identity of the three largest units in 1935 would have changed as a consequence, and these trades are rejected as well.[3] Finally, there is one trade, Tin, which has been removed for a particular reason: namely, that

[1] The Trades rejected are: Brick and Fireclay; Soap, Candle and Glycerine; and Cutlery.

[2] Low specialisation and exclusiveness caused the omission of the Fertiliser, Disinfectant, Insecticide, etc., Trade, and the Fertilisers; Motor Cycles, etc.; Metal Door and Window Frames; Sausages; and Rayon, Nylon, etc. Woven Cloth, Sub-Trades.

[3] Poor comparability was the reason for the rejection of the Salt Mines, etc.; Small Arms; Printing Machinery; Shipbuilding; Musical Instruments; and Springs, other than laminated, Trades.

the largest concern in the trade did not rank as one of the three largest units in 1935 because of its relatively small labour-force, and the concentration-ratio for 1935 is misleading as a result.

The result of these selection procedures is that there are only forty-five trades that are comparable between 1935 and 1951 and for which concentration-changes have been established in terms of principal products. But for four of these trades, the concentration-change in terms of principal products is not consistent in direction with the change in terms of employment.[1] Moreover, there are considerable differences in the magnitude of these concentration-changes, so that these four trades have also been omitted. Accordingly, the analysis of the following chapter relates, in the main, to the forty-one trades where principal product concentration changed, and employment concentration changed in the same direction, between 1935 and 1951.

[1] The magnitude (in percentage points) and direction of the concentration-changes by principal products, employment and net output for these four trades are:

	Principal products	*Employment*	*Net output*
Tobacco	−3	+4	−9
Precious Metals Refining	−4	+12	+18
Fellmongery	+10	−1	−4
Umbrella and Walking Stick	+1	−4	−1

CHAPTER XI

CHANGES IN CONCENTRATION AND FACTORS RELATING TO CONCENTRATION, 1935–51

I. INTRODUCTION

The purpose of this chapter is to explore some of the relationships which exist between changes in concentration and in other variables among the forty-one trades identified in the manner explained in the preceding chapter. It is therefore analogous to Chapter VII, with the important difference that we deal here with *changes* in the logarithms of the variables. In other words, we are concerned with the percentage changes in concentration and other variables which have occurred in the various trades between 1935 and 1951. The relations established are not, as in Chapter VII, based on comparisons between trades, but on comparisons of the same trades at different dates. The results of these two different kinds of analyses will be compared as we go along.

There are other differences between the chapters which should be noted. First, this chapter is concerned with changes in principal product concentration, not employment concentration. Principal product concentration cannot be precisely estimated: it can only be stated to lie within a certain range. Strictly speaking, therefore, one can only say (in some cases) whether it has changed or not: one cannot say precisely by how much it has changed. Secondly, in Chapter VII differences in the size of trades were measured by the relative number of persons employed. To use the same measure of the relative size of a given trade at two dates may be rather misleading, for a trade may have become smaller in terms of its employment although its output of principal products has increased considerably.

For both these reasons, regression analysis of the 1935–51 data, on the lines of Chapter VII, has certain disadvantages. In particular any magnitude assigned to the change in concentration is rather arbitrary. Consequently, we present in this chapter two kinds of analysis: first, an 'association' analysis which takes account only of the direction of the changes in concentration, trade size, etc. (Section 2 below); and, secondly, a regression analysis (permitting a closer comparison with Chapter VII) in which the magnitude of the concentration change is determined arbitrarily, and in which changes in the size of a trade are measured by employment (Section 3). In Section 4 there is a more detailed discussion than emerges from the bare statistics of changes in concentration and in unit and plant size, while in Section 5 we sum up the results.

The variables

The methods of measuring changes in concentration, the number of business units, trade size, unit size, and plant size, require some further discussion.

Table 29. *Changes in principal product concentration for forty-one comparable trades, 1935–51*

Trades with increased concentration	1935	1951	Trades with decreased concentration	1935	1951
Coke Ovens and By-Products	14–30	51–74	Polishes and Canvas Dressings	65–81	42–54
Razors (excl. Electric)	45–59	87–97	Wallpaper	95–96	77–88
Incandescent Mantles	68	91–100	Clay Sanitary Ware	15–29	8–15
Mineral Oil Refining	65–75	93–96	Bacon Curing and Sausage	19–29	10–18
Watch and Clock	27–32	50–61	Carpets, Rugs of Wool	21–32	14–21
Ice	27–29	53	Biscuit	27–35	19–27
Glass Containers	19–22	40–48	Linoleum, Leathercloth and Allied Trades	55–56	40–55
Spirit Rectifying	61–70	83–91	Rubber	43–50	36–42
Metalliferous Mines and Quarries	24–25	32–58	Grain Milling	40–43	33–35
Lead	21–44	49–67	Match	95	88–89
Building Bricks	9–18	29–34	Glove	12–14	6–10
Metal Boxes and Containers	39–51	52–74	Fur	9–15	5–9
Tinplate	52–61	71–77	Boots, Shoes, Sandals, etc.	9–11	4–7
China and Porcelain	7–14	18–36	Textile Finishing	24–26	22–24
Cattle, Dog and Poultry Food	34–35	47–53			
Cinematograph Film Printing	51	65–67			
Toilet Preparations and Perfumery	8–16	21–31			
Sugar and Glucose	74–77	87–90			
Fish Curing	8–9	17–26			
Wrought Iron and Steel Tubes	66–72	75–88			
Bread and Flour Confectionery	3–9	15–18			
Cement	68–79	79–89			
Soap and Glycerine	64–74	74–84			
Drugs and Pharmaceuticals	10–14	15–29			
Textile Packing	28–29	36			
Sports Requisites	12–19	19–26			
Slate Quarries and Mines	57–59	59–67			

Note: Upper and lower limits are given for most trades; these are determined as described on p. 147.

In the last chapter, it was shown that there are only forty-one trades on which to base our analysis of concentration-changes between 1935 and 1951, and these trades are listed according to the direction, and in the order of magnitude,[1] of their principal product concentration-changes in Table 29. There is, however, a further restriction on the number of trades for any analysis involving the number or size of business units, due to the fact that data on the number of business units in 1935 are not available in every case. The number of business units given by Leak and Maizels for individual trades in 1935 referred only to the units which (either in that trade, or that and other trades) employed more than 500 persons. But with additional information supplied by the Board of Trade for the present inquiry, it has been possible to make a rough estimate of the total number of business units in 1935[2] for thirty-five of the forty-one trades listed in Table 29.[3]

It may be stressed here that these thirty-five (or forty-one) trades constitute a sample from the total population of 186 trades which are prima facie comparable between 1935 and 1951. The sample has obviously not been chosen in a manner intended to be random. But we do not know any reason why a sample of trades chosen because of their comparability should bias the estimate of any specific variable in any particular way.

Turning to the measurement of trade size in the association analysis, a trade is said to have expanded when its employment has risen by more than 10 per cent. But where employment has fallen, a check has been made on the volume of production of the principal products to confirm that trade activity (and hence size) has not risen despite the fall in the labour-force. Where the change in trade employment has been less than 10 per cent either way, the volume of production has also been the factor determining the classification of such trades, but if the percentage change is still less than 10 per cent the trade's size is described as 'unchanged'.

The measurement of plant size and unit size by the numbers employed per plant and unit respectively is reasonably unexceptionable in a cross-

[1] The magnitude of the change in principal product concentration, which is generally expressed as a range in both years, is determined here and in the later regression analysis by the difference between the mid-points of the ranges in the two years.

[2] These estimates probably overstate the true number of business units in 1935, from which it follows that the average size of those units is understated, and the size-ratio of those units overstated in 1935. Thus, the additional information supplied by the Board of Trade is the number of returns (y) after ignoring those made by units included in the Leak and Maizels analysis (that is, by units employing more than 500 persons) or by the three largest units if there are not more than three units employing over 500 persons. If (x) is the number of business units covered by the Leak and Maizels analysis, then the estimated total of business units in 1935 is assumed to be $x+y$. The 1935 estimate, however, overstates the true 1935 total of business units for two reasons: (*a*) because in some instances, one firm will have made more than one return, and (*b*) a business unit, by definition, may include more than one firm.

[3] The exceptions are Mineral Oil Refining, and Watch and Clock, among the trades with increased concentration; and Bacon Curing and Sausage; Carpets, Rugs of Wool; Rubber; and Glove, among the trades with decreased concentration.

sectional analysis. But when we come, as in this chapter, to consider changes in plant size and unit size for given trades, the measure is clearly open to the objection that greater productivity per man in a given unit or plant may well be represented as a fall in unit or plant size. Since there have been considerable increases in productivity in the 1935–51 period, our size measures clearly tend to underestimate increases in unit and plant size, and overestimate the decreases. So far as the analysis is concerned, this is not important if changes in productivity are uncorrelated with other variables. But if they *are* correlated, our results could be misleading. For instance, we find that changes in concentration and plant size are positively correlated. In theory this might be the result of a negative correlation between changes in concentration and in productivity. We do not, of course, suggest that this is the case: but it is nevertheless necessary to bear in mind that our size measures might produce some bias.

2. ASSOCIATION ANALYSIS

Changes in concentration, number- and size-ratio of units[1]

In Chapter VII we saw that there was a strong negative correlation between concentration and the number of business units among the 1951 trades. The thirty-five trades for which data are available are arranged in Table 30[2] according to changes in concentration and in the number of units between 1935 and 1951. We find that concentration rose in thirteen out of the twenty cases in which the number of units rose. But it also rose in twelve out of the fifteen cases in which the number of units fell. These figures are inadequate either to confirm or deny the thesis that changes in concentration are negatively associated with changes in the number of units.[3]

On the other hand, when the trades are arranged according to changes in concentration and unit size-ratios, as in Table 31, we find that a positive and significant association exists.[4] Concentration rose in twenty-two out of twenty-seven of the cases in which the unit size-ratio rose; whereas it rose in only three out of the eight cases in which the unit size-ratio fell.[5]

[1] The size-ratio of units is, for the purposes of this section of the chapter only, defined as the ratio of the size of the top three to the size of the other units. There is thus no linear analytical relation between the three variables, as there was in Chapter VII. Indeed, since we are here dealing with principal product concentration, not employment concentration, no exact analytical relation exists at all between the three variables under consideration.

[2] The basic data for this and other tables are given in Appendix K.

[3] $\chi^2=0\cdot35$ (χ^2 for one degree of freedom and a 10 per cent level of significance equals $2\cdot71$).

[4] $\chi^2=3\cdot89$.

[5] It may be noted that, given the same definition of the unit size-ratio, there was also a positive, though slight, correlation between concentration and the size-ratio ($r_{cw}=0\cdot16$) among the 1951 trades.

Changes in concentration, unit size, and trade size

Among the 1951 trades, there was a good positive correlation between average unit size and concentration, and this relationship is confirmed by the changes in concentration and in unit size between 1935 and 1951.[1] Thus, from Table 32, it may be seen that concentration rose in sixteen out of the eighteen trades in which average unit size rose, while it rose in only nine out of the seventeen trades in which average unit size fell.[2]

Table 30. *Distribution of thirty-five trades according to changes in concentration and number of units, 1935–51*

Changes in number of units	Changes in principal product concentration, 1935–51: Increased	Decreased
Increased	Spirit Rectifying*	Polishes and Canvas Dressings*
	Metal Boxes and Containers	Clay Sanitary Ware
	China and Porcelain	Biscuit
	Cattle, Dog and Poultry Food	Match
	Cinematograph Film Printing	Fur
	Toilet Preparations and Perfumery	Boots, Shoes, Sandals, etc.
	Sugar and Glucose	Textile Finishing
	Fish Curing	
	Wrought Iron and Steel Tubes	
	Bread and Flour Confectionery	
	Drugs and Pharmaceuticals	
	Sports Requisites	
Decreased	Coke Ovens and By-Products	Wallpaper
	Razors (excl. Electric)	Linoleum, Leathercloth and Allied Trades
	Incandescent Mantles	Grain Milling
	Ice	
	Glass Containers	
	Metalliferous Mines and Quarries	
	Lead	
	Building Bricks	
	Tinplate	
	Cement	
	Textile Packing	
	Slate Quarries and Mines	

* The number of units estimated for 1935 was the same as in 1951, but since the 1935 figure is likely to be an over-estimate (see footnote on p. 153), it is assumed that there was an increase in numbers over the period.

It might be expected that if a trade is declining, with plants being closed down and employment falling, concentration would be more likely to rise than fall as a result, especially if, as is generally believed, the larger concerns have greater powers of resistance. Similarly, in an expanding trade, it might be expected that opportunities for the entry of new firms

[1] $\chi^2=2\cdot45$. [2] $\chi^2=3\cdot93$.

and the expansion of small firms would be greater, and that, if other things were equal, concentration would be more likely to fall than rise.[1]

In Table 33 the forty-one trades are arranged according to the direction of the change in concentration and trade size. Concentration increased in seventeen out of the twenty-four expanded trades, in three out of the eight unchanged trades, and in seven out of the nine contracted trades. Thus, the negative relationship in 1951 between concentration and trade size is not confirmed (or denied) by the changes as between 1935 and 1951.[2] Similarly, although they offer no support for the *a priori*

Table 31. *Distribution of thirty-five trades according to changes in concentration and size-ratio of units, 1935–51*

Changes in size-ratio of units	Changes in principal product concentration, 1935–51: Increased	Changes in principal product concentration, 1935–51: Decreased
Increased	Coke Ovens and By-Products Razors (excl. Electric) Incandescent Mantles Glass Containers Spirit Rectifying Metalliferous Mines and Quarries Lead Building Bricks Metal Boxes and Containers China and Porcelain Cattle, Dog and Poultry Food Cinematograph Film Printing Toilet Preparations and Perfumery Sugar and Glucose Fish Curing Wrought Iron and Steel Tubes Bread and Flour Confectionery Cement Soap and Glycerine Drugs and Pharmaceuticals Textile Packing Sports Requisites	Clay Sanitary Ware* Biscuit Fur* Boots, Shoes, Sandals, etc. Textile Finishing
Decreased	Ice Tinplate Slate Quarries and Mines	Polishes and Canvas Dressings Wallpaper Linoleum, Leathercloth and Allied Trades Grain Milling Match

* The unit size-ratio estimated for 1935 was the same as in 1951, but since the 1935 figure is likely to be an over-estimate (see footnote on p. 153), it is assumed that there was an increase in numbers over the period.

[1] See Chapter IX, p 132.

[2] If we merge the stationary and declining trades, $\chi^2=0\cdot22$.

arguments of the previous paragraph, they do not, on the other hand, disprove them.

We suggested in Chapter VII that if unit size were, in general, fairly closely determined by technical and managerial considerations, then trade size and concentration might be negatively associated, since larger trades would be more closely associated with a greater number of units

Table 32. *Distribution of thirty-five trades according to changes in concentration and average size of units, 1935–51*

Changes in average size of units	Changes in principal product concentration, 1935–51	
	Increased	Decreased
Increased	Coke Ovens and By-Products Razors (excl. Electric) Glass Containers Spirit Rectifying Building Bricks Metal Boxes and Containers Tinplate China and Porcelain Cattle, Dog and Poultry Food Cinematograph Film Printing Toilet Preparations and Perfumery Sugar and Glucose Wrought Iron and Steel Tubes Bread and Flour Confectionery Cement Drugs and Pharmaceuticals	Linoleum, Leathercloth and Allied Trades Grain Milling
Decreased	Incandescent Mantles Ice Metalliferous Mines and Quarries Lead Fish Curing Soap and Glycerine Textile Packing Sports Requisites Slate Quarries and Mines	Polishes and Canvas Dressings Wallpaper Clay Sanitary Ware Biscuit Match Fur Boots, Shoes, Sandals, etc. Textile Finishing

than with larger units, and *a priori* considerations suggested that a greater number of units would be associated with less concentration. This question will be examined at greater length in the next section, but here we may note that the argument is *not* supported by the data for the direction of changes between 1935 and 1951, which fail to show any association between either changes in trade size or in the number of units and changes in concentration. The only significant associations demonstrated have been between changes in average unit size, in relative unit size and in concentration. It would therefore appear likely that any tendency for a rise in trade size to imply more units, and hence lower concentration, has been offset by a tendency for the average size of units and the size-differences between them to rise between 1935 and 1951.

Table 33. *Distribution of forty-one trades according to their changes in concentration and trade size, 1935–51*

Changes in trade size	Changes in principal product concentration, 1935–51: Increased	Decreased
Expanded	Coke Ovens and By-Products Razors (excl. Electric) Watch and Clock Cement Cinematograph Film Printing Spirit Rectifying Metal Boxes and Containers Toilet Preparations and Perfumery China and Porcelain Bread and Flour Confectionery Drugs and Pharmaceuticals Glass Containers Wrought Iron and Steel Tubes Cattle, Dog and Poultry Food Soap and Glycerine Mineral Oil Refining Sugar and Glucose	Polishes and Canvas Dressings Linoleum, Leathercloth and Allied Trades Rubber Bacon Curing and Sausage Match Biscuit Carpets, Rugs of Wool
Unchanged	Incandescent Mantles Tinplate Sports Requisites	Glove Wallpaper Fur Textile Finishing Boots, Shoes, Sandals, etc.
Contracted	Textile Packing Fish Curing Ice Metalliferous Mines and Quarries Building Bricks Lead Slate Quarries and Mines	Clay Sanitary Ware Grain Milling

Changes in concentration and in plant size

In Chapter VII we found that there was a good positive correlation between average plant size and concentration ($r_{cq}=0\cdot60$). This relationship is confirmed as between changes in plant size and in concentration.[1] As can be seen from Table 34, out of the forty-one trades, concentration rose in twenty-one of the twenty-seven cases in which average plant size rose, and rose in only five out of the fourteen cases in which average plant size fell.

[1] $\chi^2=4\cdot59$.

Summary of the association analysis

We find that the 1935–51 comparison shows that percentage changes in concentration are significantly and positively associated with percentage changes in (*a*) the unit size-ratio, (*b*) average unit size, and (*c*) average plant size.

Table 34. *Distribution of forty-one trades according to changes in concentration and average size of plants, 1935–51*

Changes in average size of plants	Changes in principal product concentration, 1935–51: Increased	Decreased
Increased	Coke Ovens and By-Products	Wallpaper
	Razors (excl. Electric)	Clay Sanitary Ware
	Incandescent Mantles	Bacon Curing and Sausage
	Mineral Oil Refining	Linoleum, Leathercloth and Allied Trades
	Watch and Clock	Grain Milling
	Ice	Fur
	Glass Containers	
	Spirit Rectifying	
	Lead	
	Building Bricks	
	Metal Boxes and Containers	
	Tinplate	
	China and Porcelain	
	Cattle, Dog and Poultry Food	
	Cinematograph Film Printing	
	Toilet Preparations and Perfumery	
	Fish Curing	
	Bread and Flour Confectionery	
	Cement	
	Drugs and Pharmaceuticals	
	Textile Packing	
Decreased	Metalliferous Mines and Quarries	Polishes and Canvas Dressings
	Sugar and Glucose	Carpets, Rugs of Wool
	Wrought Iron and Steel Tubes	Biscuit
	Soap and Glycerine	Rubber
	Sports Requisites	Match
	Slate Quarries and Mines	Glove
		Boots, Shoes, Sandals, etc.
		Textile Finishing

On the other hand, the figures do not show a significant negative association between percentage changes in concentration and percentage changes in either (*a*) the number of units or (*b*) trade size, both of which relationships might have been expected to hold on the basis of the cross-sectional analysis of the 1951 trades.

3. REGRESSION ANALYSIS

The same symbols are used throughout this section as were used in Chapter VII (see pp. 101–2), except that they are dashed to indicate that they refer to differences in the variables (or their logarithms) between 1935 and 1951 and not to absolute values. The same definitional relations hold between differences in the variables as hold between the variables themselves (see Chapter VII, p. 103), except that C' is not analytically related to the other variables since it stands for principal product concentration and not employment concentration. As in Chapter VII, the analysis is conducted in terms of the logarithms of the variables.[1]

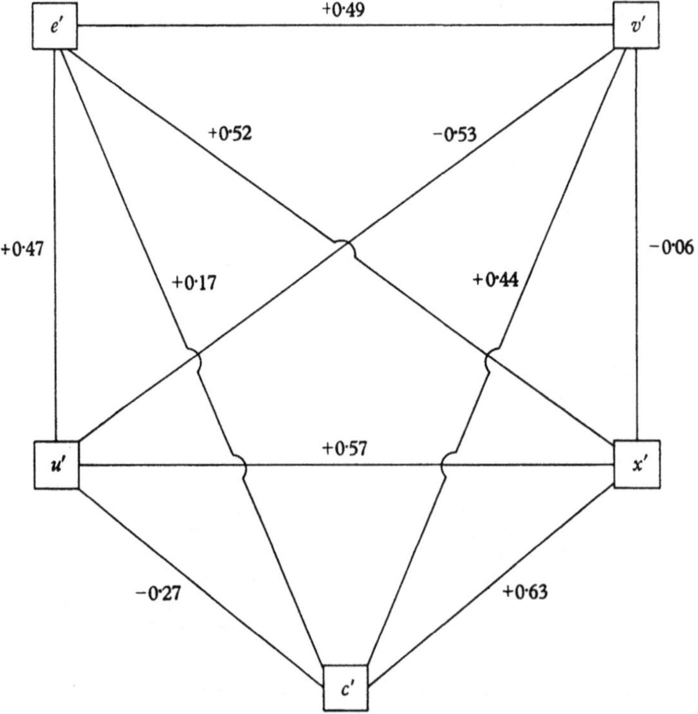

Fig. 4 Correlation coefficients for changes in concentration and in other variables

The correlation coefficients between changes in employment, number of units, average unit size, the unit size-ratio and concentration are shown in Fig. 4, which should be compared with Fig. 2 in Chapter VII.[2]

[1] The coefficients yielded by the regression analysis are summarised in Appendix L.

[2] The triangular relationship between u', x', and c' is not indicated by double lines. This is because no analytic relationship holds between these variables now that we are not dealing with employment concentration.

The number- and size-ratio of business units

Our sample shows only a weak and scarcely significant correlation between changes in concentration and the number of units ($r_{c'u'} = -0 \cdot 27$: $b_{c'u'} = -0 \cdot 29 \pm 0 \cdot 17$). This confirms the results of the association analysis of the previous section, but is considerably different from the relation between concentration and unit numbers among the 1951 trades ($r_{cu} = -0 \cdot 83$: $b_{cu} = -0 \cdot 50 \pm 0 \cdot 02$). At the same time, one should not make too much of the difference. It is not impossible that the lower figures for the 1935–51 comparison result from sampling errors, while they might also partly result from measuring the change in concentration in terms of principal products rather than employment.

However, let us suppose that all trades had remained comparable from 1935 to 1951 and that we then found a much weaker correlation between changes in employment concentration and in unit numbers than between concentration and unit numbers among the 1951 trades. If this supposition is correct, there would seem to be two possible explanations. The first is that the negative correlation of concentration and unit numbers results mainly from the structure of trades at their birth (or their invention by the Census authorities), and depends to a relatively small extent on any subsequent change in that structure. Thus if a trade, by reason of its product composition, consists originally of a relatively few units, it is always likely to have relatively few units and high concentration, because of the operation, as we saw in Chapter IX, of factors which constitute advantages for the established firms or obstacles to newcomers.

The second possible explanation is that the forces which have tended to associate low numbers with high concentration were stronger in the period before 1935 than subsequently. Thus the correlation, even if it does not result mainly from the birth of trades, may already have been high in 1935, and possibly higher than in 1951. We do not know whether this is true or not, though it seems very possible in view of the extent of merger activity before 1935.

Let us turn now to the unit size-ratio. We find there is a good positive correlation between changes in concentration and in the unit size-ratio ($r_{c'x'} = 0 \cdot 63$: $b_{c'x'} = 0 \cdot 54 \pm 0 \cdot 11$). This confirms the association analysis of the preceding section (although the unit size-ratio was not the same as here). The sign of this relation is actually reversed as compared with the analogous relation among the 1951 trades ($r_{cx} = -0 \cdot 40$: $b_{cx} = -0 \cdot 40 \pm 0 \cdot 06$). There is, however, little point in trying to give an economic explanation of this, for it is not more than a by-product of the facts (*a*) that the positive correlation between changes in the unit size-ratio and in unit numbers is considerably weaker than the analogous relation among the 1951 trades ($r_{x'u'} = +0 \cdot 57$ compared with $r_{xu} = +0 \cdot 84$), and (*b*) the already examined fact that the correlation between changes in unit numbers and concentration is far weaker than the analogous relation among the 1951 trades ($r_{c'u'} = -0\cdot27$ against $r_{cu} = -0\cdot83$).

Finally we may note that because of the good correlation between x' and u', the variance of c' cannot be satisfactorily apportioned between u' and x'. The same was true of the variables c, u, and x in Chapter VII.

Changes in the average size of units and trade employment

As we remarked in Chapter VII, the number of units and the unit size-ratio cannot be regarded as exogenous determining factors in concentration. Unit size and trade size are at least a little more promising from this point of view.

Changes in concentration and in unit size are fairly well correlated ($r_{c'v'} = +0\cdot44 : b_{c'v'} = 0\cdot46 \pm 0\cdot16$), a result which was foreshadowed in the previous section, and was also true of concentration and unit size among the 1951 trades ($r_{cv} = +0\cdot63$). Assuming, as in Chapter VII, that unit size may to some extent be regarded as a causal factor in concentration, we may ask in what manner it affects concentration. There is, in fact, no significant direct correlation between changes in unit size and in the size-ratio ($r_{v'x'} = -0\cdot06 : b_{v'x'} = -0\cdot05 \pm 0\cdot14$). Thus, to the extent that a rise in unit size is a causative factor, it may probably be said to increase concentration through reducing the number of units (the correlation between u' and v' is in fact quite good, $r_{u'v'} = -0\cdot53 : b_{u'v'} = -0\cdot53 \pm 0\cdot14$), although it must be remembered that the direct link between changes in the number of units and concentration is itself weak.

Following the analysis of Chapter VII, let us now consider further the relation of changes in unit size and changes in unit numbers, and the manner in which they are related to changes in trade size. As we might expect, changes in trade size result in changes in the same direction for both unit numbers and unit size:[1] but to some extent unit size varies independently of trade size, and this results in the negative correlation of changes in unit size and in unit numbers referred to above.

The association analysis of Section 2 of this chapter established no connection between changes in trade size and concentration. Correlation analysis yields a small *positive* correlation ($r_{e'c'} = +0\cdot17$) which is the reverse of what might have been expected on the basis of the 1951 results ($r_{ec} = -0\cdot42$). Before analysing this apparent difference it is as well to be sure that there *is* a difference. In fact, $b_{c'e'} = +0\cdot19$ with a standard error of $0\cdot19$. Thus, no more can be said than that the correlation of changes in trade size and in concentration is probably positive, and is almost certainly less negative than the correlation of trade size and concentration in 1951.

[1] Thus, $r_{u'e'} = +0\cdot47$ and $r_{v'e'} = +0\cdot49$, and $b_{u'e'} = +0\cdot49 (\pm 0\cdot16)$ and $b_{v'e'} = +0\cdot52$ ($\pm 0\cdot16$).

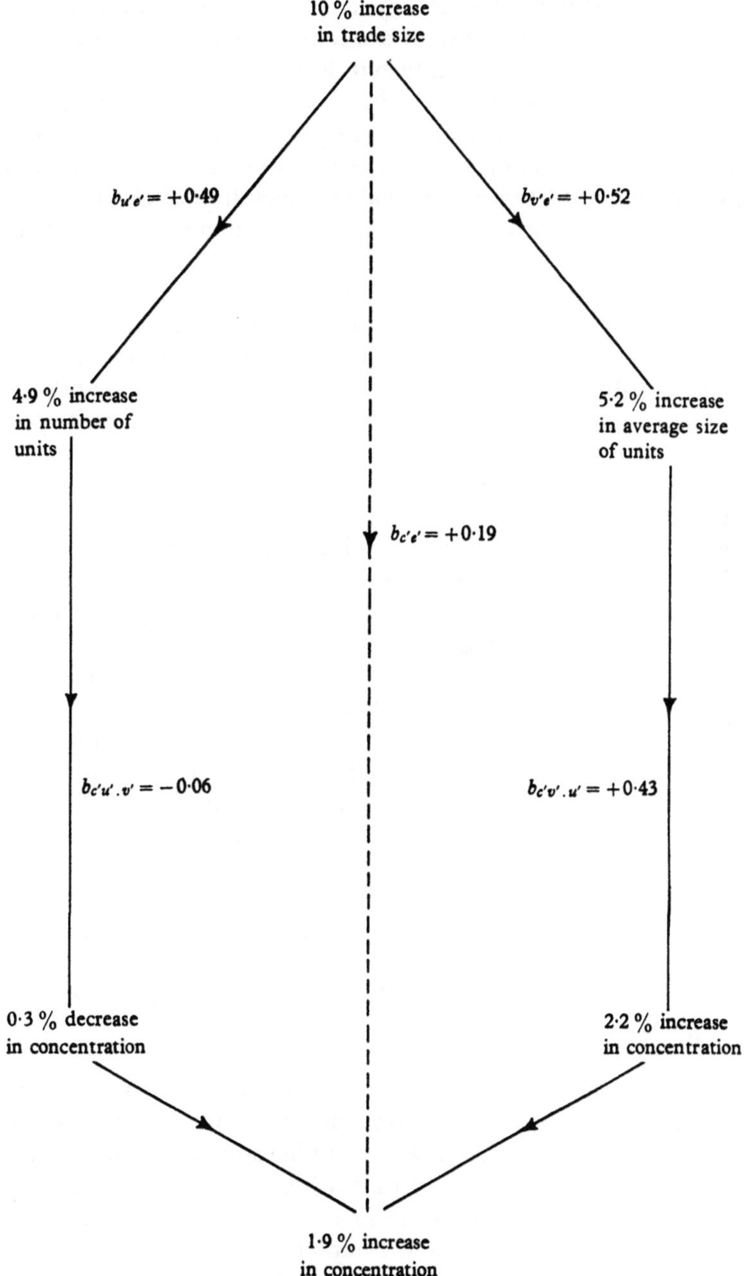

Fig. 5 The relation between changes in concentration and changes in employment

In Chapter VII we showed how any effect of trade size on concentration could be shown as the sum of its effects via changes in unit size and unit numbers. Fig. 5 presents the same analysis for changes in trade size, and should be compared with Chapter VII, Fig. 3.

We can see that, as compared with the results for the 1951 trades, an increase in trade size in the 1935–51 sample tends to come about more by an increase in average unit size and less by an increase in unit numbers. This, combined with the much weaker association of changes in unit numbers and in concentration, is a sufficient explanation of the fact that, for the thirty-five trades in the sample, changes in trade size are positively correlated with changes in concentration.

There is, however, no certainty that all the coefficients used above would be, for the whole population, significantly different from the analogous coefficients for the 1951 trades. Thus both $b_{v'e'}$ and $b_{u'e'}$ are within two standard errors of b_{ve} and b_{ue} respectively. It is quite possible that what needs explanation (the significant difference between b_{ce} and $b_{c'e'}$) is merely a result of the already discussed weaker correlation of concentration and unit numbers $(r_{c'u'} < r_{cu})$.

However, it remains much more probable than not that in the 1935–51 period a growth in trade size was more closely linked with larger units than any naïve application of the cross-sectional analysis of the 1951 trades would have suggested. But there seems to be little reason why a cross-sectional relationship should be expected in this instance to apply over time. Indeed, it may reasonably be presumed that new techniques are both favourable to larger units and likely to be more important in prosperous and expanding trades. This would be a sufficient reason to expect a closer correlation between changes in trade and in unit size than between trade size and unit size themselves.

Changes in concentration estimated from changes in trade size and in unit size

The following equation is analogous with equation 13 of Chapter VII:

$$c' = -0\cdot07(\pm 0\cdot20)e' + 0\cdot49(\pm 0\cdot19)v' + 1\cdot25(\pm 0\cdot40) \quad \ldots\ldots (1)$$

$$R^2 = 0\cdot20$$

The simple correlation coefficient $r^2_{c'v'} = 0\cdot19$, so it can be seen that in the 1935–51 sample a change in unit size alone is almost as good an indicator of a change in concentration as any combination of both trade size and unit size. It should also be noted that, whereas equation (1) above 'explains' only 20 per cent of the variations in concentration changes in the 1935–51 sample, equation (13) of Chapter VII explained 72 per cent of the concentration variations in 1951. Similarly changes in unit size alone 'explain' 19 per cent of the variation in changes of concentration, while unit size alone explained 40 per cent of the variation of concentration among the 1951 trades.

Changes in concentration and plant size

As stated in Chapter VII plant size might be expected to be more closely determined than unit size by 'objective' factors such as technology, transport cost, managerial cost, and the size of the market. If, therefore, it is intended to see how much of the variation in concentration is explicable in these terms, it is probably better to relate concentration to plant size than to unit size.

As in Chapter VII, we may begin by seeing how much of the variation in unit size is due to variations in plant size, using for this purpose the identity

$$q' + m' = v'$$

The results are as follows:

Variance of changes in average plant size	0·020
Plus variance of changes in plants per unit	0·017
Plus twice covariance	0·000
Equals variance of changes in average unit size	0·037

The first thing to note is the zero covariance, and hence zero correlation, of changes in plant size and plants per unit. In contrast, there was a positive correlation of average plant size and plants per unit among the 1951 trades ($r_{mq} = 0 \cdot 34$). We suggested that this correlation might reflect a process of 'rationalisation', mergers and acquisitions causing a fall in the number of units and hence a rise in plants per unit, and subsequently a rise in the size of plants as production was concentrated in the larger and more efficient plants.[1] In formal terms we suggested in fact that the positive correlation of m and q arose from both these variables being negatively correlated with the number of units.

The 1935–51 comparison is not in conflict with the above theory. For, although there is no correlation between m' and q', there is still a negative correlation between both q' and u' ($r_{u'q'} = -0 \cdot 26$) and m' and u' ($r_{u'm'} = -0 \cdot 50$). Thus, during this period, the greater the percentage fall in the number of units, the greater tended to be the percentage rise in plants per unit and to a lesser extent in plant size. In fact, in the majority of trades the number of units rose: but the smaller the rise the more likely was it that plants per unit and plant size would rise. The fact that in most trades the number of units rose is not inconsistent with a process of 'rationalisation'—the concentration of production in larger units and

[1] It may be noted that, since the number of plants always exceeds the number of units, the death of a single-plant firm by merger or bankruptcy reduces the number of units proportionately more than the number of plants, even if the plant ceases to exist. Consequently the purchase of small single-plant units for closure raises both plants per unit and average plant size.

plants—if such 'rationalisation' on the part of the older units in a trade is combined with entry on the part of new smaller units.

As a result of there being no correlation between q' and m', we can say that 42 per cent of the variation of v' results from variations in m' and 58 per cent from variations in q'. Also the variance of v' was 85 per cent greater than the variance of q'. In contrast, in the cross-sectional data of 1951, the variance of v was only 11 per cent greater than the variance of q. Thus changes in the number of plants per unit between 1935 and 1951 were of far greater importance than difference in plants per unit as between trades in 1951.

In Chapter VII we were able to dismiss the relatively small variation in m as an unimportant factor in explaining differences in concentration between trades. But its greater variability over time suggests that it may play some part in explaining changes in concentration.

The simple regression of changes in concentration on changes in plant size ($b_{c'q'}=0\cdot74\pm0\cdot10$) 'explains' 27 per cent of the variance of changes in concentration ($r^2_{c'q'}=0\cdot27$). In the light of the above paragraph we have worked out a multiple correlation of concentration on plant size and plants per unit. The result is:

$$c'=0\cdot74(\pm0\cdot21)q'+0\cdot13(\pm0\cdot23)m'+0\cdot32(\pm0\cdot64) \quad \ldots.(2)$$
$$R^2=0\cdot28$$

It appears, therefore, that despite its greater variability m' is not significant in explaining changes in concentration. Nor is the explanatory value of trade size raised by being associated with plant size rather than unit size, as equation (3) shows:

$$c'=0\cdot82(\pm0\cdot24)q'-0\cdot14(\pm0\cdot19)e'+0\cdot67(\pm0\cdot45) \quad \ldots.(3)$$
$$R^2=0\cdot28$$

In other words, the introduction of trade size does not improve on the 'explanation' afforded by plant size alone, any more than it improved on the explanation offered by unit size alone.

In Chapter VII we went on to examine the influence of p_3 and t in the identity $c=p_3+t+q-e$. But this line of inquiry cannot be here pursued, because the values of the variables p_3' and t' are not available.

4. CHANGES IN PLANT AND UNIT SIZES AND CONCENTRATION FOR THIRTY-FIVE TRADES WITH CONCENTRATION-CHANGES, AND FOR ALL FACTORY TRADES, 1935–51

Of all the variables whose connection with concentration we have examined, there are two which to a limited extent may be regarded as independent or exogenous, and which are fairly well correlated with concentration. They are average unit size and average plant size. Among the 1951 trades, the regression of concentration on both these variables was not significantly different from +0·5, and the correlation coefficient for both not significantly different from 0·6. Average plant size and average unit size were themselves very highly correlated (r_{qv}=0·97).

For the 1935–51 comparison, the sample shows a regression of concentration on plant size of 0·74 and on unit size of 0·46; the correlation coefficients are 0·52 and 0·44 respectively. These results are not significantly different from those for the 1951 trades. Changes in plant size and in unit size were also highly correlated ($r_{q'v'}$=0·74), but significantly less highly correlated than plant and unit size themselves.

The remainder of this section will be mainly concerned to put some flesh on the bones of these statistical relations by identifying the trades which conform and conflict with the ruling association of concentration with plant size and unit size, and of these two latter variables with each other. It will also be tentatively suggested how it was that concentration changed as it did for the different categories of trades, though in doing so we do not dig below the surface of Census data or attempt to give any complete causal explanation. Then lastly we compare the aggregated changes in the number and average size of plants and units for the sample of thirty-five trades, with the corresponding changes for all factory trades between 1935 and 1951.

Trades with increases in average plant size

From Table 35, it will be seen that there are fourteen trades where the average size of plants and units both increased, and concentration rose as well. Among these fourteen trades there are seven where the relative rise in average unit size was greater than the relative rise in average plant size, so that the number of plants per unit rose. These seven trades, where the rise in unit concentration cannot therefore be wholly explained by technological factors increasing the size of plants, are:

Coke Ovens and By-Products | Tinplate
Razors (excl. Electric) | Cement
Glass Containers | Building Bricks
Drugs and Pharmaceuticals

In particular, the rise in the number of plants per unit was marked for Cement, Tinplate, and Coke Ovens and By-Products, and it will be seen in Chapter XII that mergers and acquisitions were, in fact, important in these three trades during the 1935–51 period. For the other seven trades, average plant size rose relatively more than unit size; in other words, plants per unit fell for:

Spirit Rectifying
Metal Boxes and Containers
China and Porcelain
Cinematograph Film Printing
Toilet Preparations
Bread and Flour Confectionery
Cattle, Dog and Poultry Food

Table 35. *Changes in concentration, plant size and unit size for thirty-five trades, 1935–51*

Changes in: Plant size	Changes in: Unit size	Changes in concentration, 1935–51: Increased	Changes in concentration, 1935–51: Decreased
Increased	Increased	Coke Ovens and By-Products Razors (excl. Electric) Glass Containers Building Bricks Tinplate Cement Drugs and Pharmaceuticals Spirit Rectifying Metal Boxes and Containers China and Porcelain Cattle, Dog and Poultry Food Cinematograph Film Printing Toilet Preparations Bread and Flour Confectionery	Linoleum, Leathercloth and Allied Trades Grain Milling
	Decreased	Incandescent Mantles Ice Lead Fish Curing Textile Packing	Clay Sanitary Ware Fur Wallpaper
Decreased	Increased	Sugar and Glucose Wrought Iron and Steel Tubes	
	Decreased	Metalliferous Mines and Quarries Slate Quarries and Mines Soap and Glycerine Sports Requisites	Biscuit Boots, Shoes, Sandals, etc. Polishes and Canvas Dressings Match Textile Finishing

All these trades expanded between 1935 and 1951 and in each case the number of units rose. So it appears that, despite the rise in average plant size, it was still possible for newcomers to enter the trade on a small scale. The rise in concentration was due, therefore, to some firms growing faster than others; indeed, as can be seen from Table 31, the size-ratio of the units increased for these seven trades between 1935 and 1951.

In another five trades, where average plant size and concentration both increased, the fall in the number of plants per unit was so great that average unit size actually fell.[1] The five trades in question are:

[1] No doubt these five trades are a good part of the explanation of why changes in plant size in the sample are better correlated with changes in concentration than are changes in unit size.

Incandescent Mantles Fish Curing
Ice Lead
Textile Packing

Four of these five trades contracted between 1935 and 1951 and the other (Incandescent Mantles) remained unchanged. As trade fell away, it is reasonable to suppose that the number of units tended to fall and that output was concentrated in fewer and larger plants by some of the units that remained. Thus the average size of plants rose, while the number of plants closed was great enough for plants per unit to fall. Although this explanation probably holds good for four of the five trades, it does not fit the circumstances of the Fish Curing trade. In its case there were more units in 1951 than in 1935, but fewer plants. Fish curers tended to be multi-plant concerns in 1935, so that the fall in plants per unit was due not only to there being more units but also to the closure of plants that were active in 1935. Moreover, the rise in the average size of plants was probably due not merely to the fall in the number of plants but also to the fact that the plants of the new entrants to the trade tended to be larger than average.

Still confining attention to trades where the average size of plants rose between 1935 and 1951, there are five non-conformists with reduced concentration. In two cases—Linoleum, Leathercloth, etc., and Grain Milling—there was an increase in average unit size as well as plant size. Since concentration fell these increases were not due to extended operations of the largest units; indeed, their employment fell while that of the rest rose between 1935 and 1951. So it seems that the fall in concentration occurred because the other units lessened the difference in size between their plants and those of the largest units, possibly by taking advantage of the technological economies of scale already attained by the largest concerns.

In the other three trades, the rise in average plant size was relatively small, but a fall in the number of plants per unit resulted in a reduction in the average size of units. In two of these trades—Clay Sanitary Ware and Fur—there were fewer plants, but more units, despite a fall in total employment. Thus, it seems that newcomers entered on a relatively small scale while other units concentrated their output in fewer and larger plants. In the third trade, Wallpaper, the number of units as well as plants fell between 1935 and 1951, but the number of plants fell relatively more. However, the employment of the three largest units fell absolutely while that of the rest rose absolutely, with the result that concentration fell despite the increase in average plant size.

Trades with decreases in average plant size

From Table 35, it will be seen that concentration fell in five of the eleven trades where the average size of plants fell between 1935 and 1951:

Biscuit
Boots, Shoes, Sandals, etc.
Polishes and Canvas Dressings
Match
Textile Finishing

A fall in average plant size may occur either because the number of plants rises faster than trade employment (as for Biscuit; Boots, Shoes, Sandals, etc.; and Match) or because the number of plants falls more slowly (as for Polishes and Canvas Dressings, and Textile Finishing). An increase in the number of plants may be due, moreover, to a rise either in the number of units or in the number of plants per unit. For Biscuit, and Boots, Shoes, Sandals, etc., both factors operated; indeed, the rise in plants per unit made the fall in unit size smaller than the fall in plant size. Nevertheless, the influx of new concerns, even though their plants were small, served to reduce concentration in both these trades. In the Match trade, the number of units rose, but plants per unit fell, so that unit size fell more than plant size. Thus in this case also, newcomers to the trade caused a fall in concentration.

For the other two trades, Polishes and Canvas Dressings, and Textile Finishing, the number of plants fell but, since the number of units either rose or was unchanged, plants per unit fell. The fall in average unit size was, therefore, greater than the fall in average plant size. Thus the largest firms, despite some concentration of production in fewer plants, have lost ground to the small-scale entrants to the trade with the result that concentration has fallen.

Turning to the trades where a fall in average plant size has been accompanied by a rise in concentration, there are two where the average unit size rose. For Sugar and Glucose, and Wrought Iron and Steel Tubes, a rise in plants per unit has, in other words, more than offset the fall in average plant size. Thus, despite an influx of new concerns operating on a small scale, the largest concerns have been able to increase their share of the trade by increasing the number of plants they operate.

Finally, there are four trades where a fall in average plant size has been accompanied by a fall in unit size, yet concentration has still increased. In two cases, Metalliferous Mines and Slate Mines, there has been a rise in plants per unit. Thus it seems probable that concentration has increased because the largest firms have acquired more plants.

For Soap and Glycerine, the fall in average plant size has been accompanied by a rise in the number of plants and a fall in plants per unit. But, despite the number of units having almost doubled, the largest concerns have increased their share of the trade. For Sports Requisites the number of plants fell as the number of units increased, so that there was also a decrease in plants per unit. In this case, the largest concerns have operated

Table 36. *Changes in average size of establishments and business units for thirty-five trades and all factory trades, 1935–51*

	Thirty-five trades with concentration changes, 1935–51			All factory trades		
	1935	1951	1951 as percentage of 1935	1935	1951	1951 as percentage of 1935
Total employment (thousands)	718·1	804·3	112	5,157·6	7,331·3	142
Number of establishments	8,356	6,932	83	48,944	57,691	118
Number of business units	5,103*	5,097*	100	33,275–36,840§	44,734*	121–134§
Average size of establishments (numbers employed)	86	116	135	105	127	121
Average size of business units (numbers employed)	141†	158†	112	140–155‡	164†	106–117
Number of plants per unit	1·64†	1·36†	83	1·34–1·47	1·29†	88–96

* Over-estimate.
† Under-estimate.
‡ See Appendix M for basis of this estimate.
§ This estimate is a consequence of the estimated size. See footnote ‡ above.

fewer plants and yet increased their share of the trade, in spite of a rise in the number of firms.

Aggregated changes in the average sizes of plants and units

The number of plants and units on the one hand and employment on the other have been aggregated for the thirty-five trades, and the estimated average sizes of plants and units are given in Table 36. It must be noted that the average size of units is probably understated for both years since it is assumed (in the absence of better information) that no business unit is active in more than one trade, while the 1935 estimate is further subject to error for reasons already given.[1] Subject to these qualifications, however, it may be seen from Table 36 that the number of plants in the thirty-five trades fell by 17 per cent between 1935 and 1951, whereas the fall in the number of units was negligible. Since the aggregated employment of the thirty-five trades rose by 12 per cent, the average size of units also rose by 12 per cent and that of plants by 35 per cent: the number of plants per unit fell in consequence by 17 per cent.

For all factory trades[2] covered by the Census of Production in both 1935 and 1951 the number of plants rose by 18 per cent and the number of units by between 21 per cent and 34 per cent. Plant size rose by 21 per cent, and unit size by between 6 per cent and 17 per cent. The number of plants per unit fell by between 4 per cent and 12 per cent.

Employment in the sample rose considerably less than in all factory trades. Unit size rose to about the same extent, but plant size rose more than in all factory trades so that plants per unit fell more.

The fact that the average size of units rose less than that of plants is perhaps contrary to general expectation. The explanation would appear to be that the tendency for output to be concentrated in larger plants at one end of the scale has frequently been offset by the entry of new enterprises with smaller plants at the other. The change in concentration will then depend on whether the new enterprises are sufficiently large in numbers and size to offset or more than offset what would otherwise be the increased share of the three largest units.

It should be noted that the newcomers may often be former small firms (employing ten or fewer persons) which have grown into larger establishments (employing eleven or more persons), thereby increasing both the number of establishments and the number of units. Some such development may well have taken place since the number of small firms

[1] See footnote on p. 153.

[2] It is necessary to restrict attention to factory trades, since data are not available for 1935 on the number of business units in non-factory trades. The number of business units in 1935, moreover, has been estimated on the basis of Leak and Maizels' data which referred to the number of business units employing more than 500 persons in all trades. The methods employed in these estimates are described in Appendix M.

in factory trades fell from more than 132,000 in 1935 to around 80,000 by 1951.

Indeed when the small as well as the larger establishments are taken into account, it is found that for all factory trades there was a fall in the number of plants and units between 1935 and 1951. But unit size now increased more than plant size, while there was also a small increase in the number of plants per unit. Thus much of the change between 1935 and 1951 for the larger establishments is almost certainly due to the transformation of small firms into larger establishments.

5. SUMMARY AND CONCLUSIONS

We have related changes in concentration to changes in other variables identifiable from Census data. Some of these other variables are clearly by no means independent. The size-ratio of units, in particular, is tautologically related to concentration via the number of units in a trade. While we have put most emphasis on concentration, it would have been equally valid to concentrate on the unit size-ratio as the main dependent variable: indeed the unit size-ratio may be as important a concept (for example, as an indicator of forms of market behaviour) as concentration.

In the 1935–51 period, changes in these two variables were fairly highly correlated ($r_{x'c'}=0\cdot63$). At the same time, and rather surprisingly, there was only a weak and scarcely significant negative correlation of changes in concentration and in unit numbers ($r_{c'u'}=-0\cdot27$). We refer to this again below.

Only variables which are at least partly independent of concentration (and the size-ratio) can be regarded as being of explanatory value. These are trade size, plant size and unit size—the first being perhaps most independent, and the latter least. Changes in employment could not, on the basis of the trades studied, be shown to be significantly related to changes in concentration. But changes in both plant size and unit size were significant, the former 'explaining' some 27 per cent of the changes in concentration. But, to repeat, unit size and plant size, especially the former, are undoubtedly influenced by as well as influencing concentration.

If we stick strictly to explaining changes in concentration, there is nothing more of a positive nature to be said. But the analysis brings out various other interesting features of the 1935–51 period. The more employment rose in a trade, the more likely that both unit numbers and unit size would rise, and the more unit size rose the more likely that both plant size and the number of plants per unit would rise. On the average for the sample (and this is also true for all factory trades), employment, unit size and plant size all increased, but the number of plants operated per unit fell.

From the above it seems that there was a tendency for a concentration of production in larger plants by the older and larger units in a trade, some of which would themselves amalgamate, together with an entry of comparatively small newcomers. The latter were often sufficient to result in an increase in unit numbers, but generally insufficient to prevent average plant size rising. Whether or not concentration increases in such circumstances depends on both the size and number of the new entrants and on the degree of 'rationalisation' among the older units.

We also saw that the more the number of units tended to fall or the less they rose, the more likely it was that both plant size and plants per unit would rise. This is consistent with the operation of a process of amalgamation and the concentration of some production at least in larger and more efficient plants.

We turn now to consider the more important similarities and differences between the inter-temporal analysis of this chapter and the inter-trade analysis of Chapter VII. The most important similarity is that plant and unit size both 'explain' roughly two-fifths of the variance of concentration among trades in 1951—which, in view of the standard errors involved, is not significantly different from the one-fifth to one-quarter of the variance of changes in concentration 'explained' by changes in the same variables between 1935 and 1951. On the other hand, as between trades, a larger trade tends to have lower concentration, while an increase in the size of a given trade does not, so far as the analysis of this chapter shows, tend to result in a fall in concentration. As a result of this, trade size and plant size together 'explain' much more (about 70 per cent of the variance of concentration between trades) than changes in these two variables together explain changes in concentration (about 30 per cent).

The other most important difference, which has already been noted, is that the association between changes in the number of units and changes in concentration over the 1935–51 period is very much weaker than that between unit numbers and concentration among the trades in 1951. Indeed, our association analysis showed that a change in unit numbers is a very poor indicator of a concentration change. In contrast, changes in the size-ratio of units were correlated more closely (though with a change of sign) with changes in concentration than were concentration and the size-ratio in 1951. This shows up not only in the statistics, but also in the more detailed discussion in Section 4.

While the above differences are, perhaps, the most important, one must add that disappointingly few of the cross-sectional relationships extant in 1951 seem to have been, as it were, in process of formation since 1935, though often the standard errors are large enough to prevent one saying with much certainty that they were not. Only the significance of unit size and plant size is confirmed by both types of analysis: and they do not explain a very large part of the variations in concentration. The 1935–51 period was, of course, exceptional for various obvious reasons. Even so, our results suggest that it is risky to argue from differences between trades as to what may happen over even a considerable period of time, especially in view of the fact that our cross-sectional study related to the last year of the period.

The results of this chapter (and Chapter VII) are rather insubstantial. There are probably two different reasons for this. First, there is the fact that we have restricted ourselves, in this statistical analysis, to Census data, so that many factors which might be useful in explaining concentration have not been considered. Secondly, it may very well be that a considerable part of the variation in concentration is, and always will be, inexplicable in terms of easily measurable economic facts. For these reasons, a more detailed examination of a selection of trades with concentration changes has been undertaken. This series of industry case-studies is presented in Part IV. But in the following chapter, we examine the main factors contributing to changes in concentration during this period which have been identified from the case-studies.

CHAPTER XII

FACTORS CONTRIBUTING TO CHANGES IN CONCENTRATION, 1935–51

1. INTRODUCTION

The purpose of this chapter is to discuss the factors, particularly as revealed by the industry studies of Part IV, which seem to have contributed to the changes in concentration that have occurred between 1935 and 1951 among the forty-one trades discussed in the preceding chapter.

There are, however, two points which must be noted at the outset. First, the factors which are identified below are illustrative rather than comprehensive: to produce a definitive list of such factors, let alone to assess their relative importance, would require a much larger body of trades, a longer time-period and more thorough investigation than has been possible in this study. Second, the time-period over which changes in concentration have been measured is dictated by the fact that 1935 and 1951 were both years in which a Census of Production was taken and for which the necessary concentration data were available. But it is frequently the case that the most significant events affecting concentration in individual trades have occurred outside the 1935–51 period. Where such events occurred before 1935 their effects may have been working themselves out during the 1935–51 period so that they should properly be noted as contributory factors. But, where they have occurred after 1951, they have generally been ignored, except where they are the ultimate result of forces active in the 1935–51 period.

2. THE GENERAL CHARACTERISTICS OF THE 1935–51 PERIOD

The 1935–51 period falls naturally into three divisions—pre-war, war, and post-war—each with its own characteristics relevant to discussions of changes in concentration.

The pre-war years were characterised by a change in the attitude of governments towards two questions of major importance as far as concentration is concerned: protection and industrial reorganisation. It has been stated that 'the Twenties were the last period in which *laissez-faire* was official policy'.[1] Its abandonment was made manifest by the Import Duties Act, 1932, which imposed a 10 per cent *ad valorem* duty on all non-Empire goods, and by a readiness on the part of the Government 'to

[1] P. J. D. Wiles, 'Pre-War and War-Time Controls' in *The British Economy, 1945–1950*, ed. by G. D. N. Worswick and P. H. Ady (Oxford University Press, 1952), p. 134.

encourage schemes of self-government in particular industries and to assist *ad hoc* schemes for the reduction of plant'.[1] Both developments tended to increase the chances of greater concentration in industry, though it is probably the case that their effects were reflected mainly in concerted action through trade associations rather than by combination among individual firms.

The War forced drastic changes upon industry. The output of all kinds of civilian goods was severely curtailed, and many were rationed. There were concentration schemes for particular industries, price controls and Utility goods. Government ownership and management were considerably extended. In general, however, such changes were intended 'only for the duration'. The principle which governed official policy towards industry was 'to alter the basic structure as little as possible... non-interference with ownership and the channels of trade was the rule'.[2]

The end of the War did not mean an end to all the problems of industry. True, there was a sellers' market at home and abroad. But shortages of raw materials frequently persisted, controls were maintained and various forms of rationing were also continued for particular commodities. Capacity destroyed by enemy action during the War was sometimes slow to be replaced, while the nation's balance-of-payments difficulties placed a premium on exports.

There were other and more direct points of contact between government and industry. The nationalisation of coal, gas, electricity and transport removed a large sector of industry from private ownership and introduced an element of public ownership into other trades where the nationalised concerns had ancillary interests. There was a change, too, in the official attitude towards self-government in industry. On the one hand, there were the moves to establish statutory Development Councils in the industries reviewed by the Working Parties immediately after the War, but 'this attempt to provide industry with powers of self-government under statute, and at the same time to inject a broader control over policy making, lost the support of industry almost before it had been properly started'.[3] On the other hand, there was the much more hostile attitude towards restrictive practices in industry that found legislative expression in the Monopolies and Restrictive Practices (Inquiry and Control) Act, 1948, which established a permanent body to investigate restrictive practices in particular trades, as well as the procedure whereby they might be brought to an end.

Taking the 1935–51 period as a whole, there was a general expansionist

[1] Federation of British Industries, Trade Organisation Committee, Appendix to *The Background of the British Trade Organisation Movement*, 1944, quoted in PEP (Political and Economic Planning), *Industrial Trade Associations* (London, Allen and Unwin, 1957), p. 29.

[2] Wiles, *op. cit.* p. 151. [3] PEP, *op. cit.* pp. 41–2.

tendency in British industry. By 1951, manufacturing output was around 60 per cent higher than in 1935, while for all industries the rise was about 50 per cent. But the period was also full of changes, normal and abnormal, which might be expected to have some effect on industrial concentration.

So far only the effects of such changes as a rise or fall in the number or size of plants and units in individual trades have been noted. But in the following sections an attempt is made, on the basis of the evidence supplied by the industry-studies, to identify the factors which have caused these effects and thereby contributed to the changes in concentration that have occurred.

3. THE EFFECTS OF WORLD WAR II

For six of the sixteen years between 1935 and 1951, Britain was at war. It might be anticipated, therefore, that the dislocation and disturbance caused by total warfare would have left a permanent mark on the structure of many industries. Certainly every trade was affected in some degree by the War, but in most cases the effects were immediate rather than lasting, though equally they were not confined to the period of hostilities.

It is convenient to review the consequences of war under three main heads: (*a*) the destruction of capacity; (*b*) the concentration schemes; and (*c*) shortages and restrictions.

(*a*) *Destruction of capacity*

During the War a considerable amount of manufacturing capacity was destroyed and few trades escaped without a scar. Often, however, the plants that were damaged or destroyed were either too small to affect concentration significantly or were quickly repaired or replaced.

An exception to this general rule was grain milling, where nearly three-quarters of productive capacity was concentrated at the ports in the first line of air attack. A considerable proportion of this port mill capacity was consequently destroyed or severely damaged, and rebuilding and repairs were delayed by building restrictions after the War so that the share of the trade controlled by the largest units was not restored to the 1935 level by 1951.

In the match industry, too, enemy action destroyed the largest factory of Bryant and May, but here, as possibly in other trades, it subsequently proved possible for the largest units to maintain or increase production by a fuller use of their other capacity.

(*b*) *Concentration schemes*

As a result of restrictions on civilian goods, surplus capacity emerged in many trades, and in order to release labour and factory space for war work, it was decided to concentrate the essential production in a limited number of firms. 'Firms were asked to arrange among themselves, or failing that were compelled to transfer their current civilian outputs to one of their number, the "nucleus" firm, which, of course, had to compensate them.'[1]

Among the forty-one trades with concentration-changes to which concentration schemes were applied were boots and shoes, carpets, razors, linoleum, china and porcelain, toilet preparations, lead, sports requisites, tinplate, textile finishing, and building bricks. The extent of the concentration varied, however, very greatly between trades. It was possibly most severe in the case of building bricks, tinplate, and textile finishing. The number of brickworks active in 1942, for example, was one-third less than in 1938, while a comparable reduction was effected in the number of tinplate works, together with a 50 per cent fall in the labour-force. Similarly, in the finishing section of the cotton industry, 25 per cent of the normal dyeing capacity, 35 per cent of the bleaching capacity, 50 per cent of the printing capacity and 33⅓ per cent of the yarn-processing capacity was closed down.[2] In some trades, on the other hand, concentration existed only on paper,[3] while in others the envisaged concentration had to be virtually abandoned because of the ensuing shortage of essential civilian goods.

The subsequent effects of the war-time concentration schemes have varied between trade and trade. In general, most of the concentrated firms resumed operations, as was envisaged at the inception of the schemes. Thus, in the linoleum trade, three of the four concentrated firms resumed operations after the War while the fourth was acquired by another manufacturer in 1949. Yet there can be no doubt that for tinplate, building bricks and textile finishing, and possibly to a lesser extent for carpets, the concentration schemes reduced the number of plants operating in the post-war period. This may have partly resulted from the concentrated firms being acquired by the nucleus firms, but, in addition, some of the concentrated firms began to produce other products during the War and have not reverted since.

(c) *Shortages and restrictions*

Coupled with the attempts to concentrate production of civilian goods were extensive regulations limiting or prohibiting the use of scarce raw materials for non-essential production. Many of these restrictions per-

[1] Wiles, *op. cit.* p. 149.

[2] Board of Trade, *Cotton*, Working Party Reports (London, H.M.S.O. 1946), p. 43.

[3] See E. L. Hargreaves and M. M. Gowing, *Civil Industry and Trade*, History of the Second World War, United Kingdom Civil Series (London, H.M.S.O. and Longmans Green, 1952), ch. x, pp. 202–33.

sisted into the post-war period and were still present, though considerably modified, for some trades in 1951. While they lasted, these restrictions affected individual firms in various ways and to differing degrees.

Shortages of raw materials cramped the activities of some of the largest firms to the detriment of their business. The demand for biscuits, for example, increased during the War and new firms entered the trade to meet it. They were allocated a share of the common pool of raw materials and, with imported unrationed ingredients, were able to produce lines which sold under conditions of shortage. The smaller concerns were able, therefore, to increase their business even at the expense of the largest producers, since the latter were unable to expand their production without jeopardising the good name of their products.

Shortages also encouraged the entry of small concerns in other trades, such as polishes and toilet preparations, particularly since no licence was required for operations below a certain level of production. Many such concerns could flourish only while shortages persisted, so that they have tended to disappear.

Restrictions have reduced the number of firms in other trades, and here bread and flour confectionery is perhaps the prime example. Although there is a long-term trend for bread consumption to fall, and a marked tendency for plant bakeries to replace the craft baker, the reduction in the number of craft bakers was accelerated by the controls on the types of flours used and bread baked which continued for ten years after the War. Bakers were given a subsidy to reduce the price of flour used in price-controlled bread, but such was the method of determining the subsidy that the smallest bakers found it difficult to produce bread except at a loss. As a consequence, many small bakers have ceased to bake bread; the number of applications for the subsidy fell from nearly 21,000 in 1942 to 14,500 ten years later.

In other trades restrictions on raw material supplies, which took the form of quotas and allocations, may have encouraged mergers and acquisitions in order to increase output. Finally, there have been instances where war-time shortages of imported materials necessitated the increased use of domestic resources or the establishment of facilities to produce them for ourselves. Thus, the demands of the steel industry during the War accelerated the rate at which the domestic reserves of hematite and other iron ores were exploited, thereby tending to reduce the number of concerns as reserves were exhausted. On the other hand, it became essential during the War for the Ministry of Supply to establish a factory to manufacture jewels for watches and instruments, thereby laying the foundations for a flourishing new line of production in the post-war period.

4. TECHNOLOGICAL FACTORS

Technological factors as they affect concentration may be divided into two broad types: first, the major advances in technology which revolutionise the methods of manufacture and either threaten the survival or reduce the importance of the concerns which cling to the old processes; and second, the improvements in techniques which can increase the efficiency and advantage of the firms that adopt them without necessitating or causing the elimination of others in the trade.

Major technological advances

Major advances in technology will, by their very nature, be comparatively rare, but where they occur and particularly where they involve a change in the size of the production unit, they are likely to be a prime influence in changing the trade's degree of concentration.

A case in point is the tinplate industry, where the continuous strip mill and, possibly to a lesser extent, electrolytic tinning have contributed greatly to the concentration-change in the trade. It was clearly apparent in the pre-war decade that the future of the industry lay in the introduction of continuous strip mills, but the surplus capacity among the old-type and relatively inefficient hand mills of South Wales was a formidable obstacle to the adoption of the new technique. In the event, the necessary prelude to the building of the strip mill at Ebbw Vale was a series of amalgamations and acquisitions which made room for the new plant by closing down some of the old mills.

The same pattern has applied in the post-war years. The new capacity has been introduced into the industry by the Steel Company of Wales, which was formed in 1947 when four steel companies transferred to it certain of their assets, including a number of old tinplate works. As the new capacity has come into operation, so some of the old mills have been closed down. The new and larger plants necessitated by the new technology have been integrated into the industry without too much pain, though both directly, and indirectly through the accompanying moves towards combination, they have contributed to the increased concentration in the trade.

Somewhat similar considerations apply in the watch and clock industry, except that here new techniques have made possible a new industry as well as resurrecting an old. Clockmaking was a dying trade in the 1920's, and the domestic market was almost entirely dependent on imports. The advent of the synchronous electric clock provided an opportunity for British firms to regain part of the domestic market, but the lead came from firms from outside the ranks of mechanical clock producers. The older enterprises in the trade, tied more firmly to craft methods and catering largely for specialised markets, were unable to adopt the new mass-production methods on which the expansion and growth of both the firm and the industry depended.

The process of mechanisation and mass production has been intensified since the War and applied to watches as well as clocks. Successful watch manufacture now depends on quantity production and it is significant that the largest watchmakers are all post-war entrants to the trade, operating from the outset on a large scale. Thus, the new technology in both watch and clock manufacture, by largely determining the scale of plant required, has made a major contribution to the rise in the trade's degree of concentration.

Mineral oil refining is also virtually a new industry compared with pre-war, since the large programme of post-war refinery building has changed it out of all recognition. Though the new refineries have, in the main, been built by firms active in the industry before the War, it has been the scale of those plants, determined by technology, which can be held to account for the rise in concentration in the trade between 1935 and 1951.

Another example of the effect of a major technological advance on concentration is provided by the cinematograph film printing trade. One of the largest units in this trade has been Technicolor which, since its formation, has enjoyed under licence the exclusive use of the Technicolor process of colour printing for the whole of Europe. Technicolor has thus operated on a large scale from the outset, significantly changing the structure of the industry after its entry into production in the late 1930's.

For wrought iron and steel tubes, it has been stated that before the latest methods of tube-making could be introduced in the 1930's, concentration in large units was essential since the economies of mass production could not be achieved with small scattered works. It was also argued that demand for merchant pipe had to be consolidated as well, so that the principal units at both ends of the trade made a series of acquisitions as a preliminary to the introduction of mass-production techniques. The result was a highly concentrated trade as early as 1935, though by increasing their capacity by new building as well as acquisitions, the level of concentration was slightly increased by 1951.

Improvements in techniques

Improvements in techniques may be less spectacular than the major technological advances, but they are no less important a factor contributing to concentration since they are a large part of the explanation of firms' differing fortunes.

Take the razor industry, for example. While Gillette Industries started with a technological advantage in razor blade manufacture, its subsequent progress has been linked with the efforts it has made not merely to maintain that lead, but to increase it. Although razor blade manufacture is not a costly or difficult trade to enter, the gap between the technology of the leading concerns and the newcomer is therefore likely to be so large that the latter's growth will be limited.

Similarly, the growth of the Metal Box Company in the metal boxes and containers trade is attributable to the fact that it enjoyed access to the developing know-how of one of the leading American manufacturers of open-top cans, as well as to its continual and vigorous promotion of new uses for containers which, through large-scale production and specialisation, it is able to produce economically.

There is, in fact, an *a priori* reason to suspect the influence of technological factors in trades where plant concentration has increased between 1935 and 1951, since the concentration of output in larger plants suggests the presence of technological economies of scale. But though technological improvements have been present in such trades as bread and flour confectionery, cement, china and porcelain, where both plant and unit concentration have increased, they have not been absent from other trades, such as sugar and glucose, where plant concentration decreased but unit concentration increased, nor from biscuits where both plant and unit concentration decreased between 1935 and 1951.

5. STATE ACTION

Many of the factors already discussed as the effects of World War II have close connections with State action to the extent that they derive from official war-time policy. But there are other aspects of State action which have a bearing on concentration, of which the most important are: (*a*) tariffs and import quotas; (*b*) subsidies and statutory reorganisation schemes; and (*c*) nationalisation.

(*a*) *Tariffs and import quotas*

The main objects of tariffs and import quotas have been to protect domestic industry against foreign imports and, in the post-war period, to conserve scarce currencies. In a protected home market, it is of course possible that the domestic firms will attempt and more easily achieve amalgamations or cartel arrangements, but it is also possible that a larger number of firms will continue to populate the trade than would have survived if foreign competition had continued unchecked.

It is very difficult to determine, therefore, the effect of the Import Duties Act, 1932, on the development of concentration in British industry, even among the trades where changes in concentration took place between 1935 and 1951. But there is one consequence of protection and import restrictions that demands comment: namely, the encouragement they provide for foreign firms to establish manufacturing plants here instead of supplying the British (or even the European) market at a distance.

This consequence can be seen particularly clearly in the razor industry. Although a number of important American safety-razor manufacturers had British manufacturing subsidiaries before World War I, it was the imposition of a 33⅓ per cent duty on imported cutlery in 1926 that encouraged the American firms to embark on mass production of blades in this country. Similarly, the tariff on toilet preparations and perfumery made foreign firms establish manufacturing plants in this country, while the same considerations probably also apply to drugs and pharmaceuticals. Furthermore, the soap firm of Thomas Hedley was acquired by Procter and Gamble in 1930 with considerable subsequent effects on concentration in the soap trade.[1]

Since the War, American participation has made the most marked contribution to increased concentration in the watch and clock trade. In order to encourage the establishment of the industry on modern lines, the Government increased the duty from 20 to 25 per cent on alarm clocks and from 20 to 33⅓ per cent on other clocks, as well as imposing quotas on imports of all but electric clocks. Similarly, the existing 33⅓ per cent duty on watches was reinforced by import quotas. Partly in order to jump the tariff wall and partly to supply the European market (where shortages of dollars restricted imports of United States products), two American concerns established manufacturing subsidiaries in Britain to produce alarm clocks and low-priced watches. Both subsidiaries started and have continued operations on a large scale and must be counted as among the largest units in the trade in 1951.

(b) *Subsidies and statutory reorganisation schemes*

Tariffs and import quotas are not the only means by which the State protects domestic industry. Particularly in the field of agriculture, subsidies have been employed to support home producers and have frequently been accompanied by producers' boards. Agriculture is very largely outside the industries in which we are interested, but in one case State action in the interests of the farmers has greatly affected the structure of the trade which processes their produce.

That trade was the beet-sugar industry which forms part of the Census trade of Sugar and Glucose. After a ten-year subsidy had been granted in 1924 to the beet-sugar factories, mainly in order to support the sugar-

[1] For a comprehensive survey of the effect of the United Kingdom tariff policy on the establishment of American productive facilities in this country, see J. H. Dunning, *American Investment in British Manufacturing Industry* (London, Allen and Unwin, 1958).

beet producers against the competition of imported cane-sugar, the number of growers increased fivefold and thirteen new factories were built in three years. But the subsidy was expensive—it cost £30 million in the ten years—and in 1936, the Government decided to reduce the subsidy by effecting a reorganisation of the industry. The Sugar Industry Reorganisation Act, 1936, provided for the voluntary amalgamation of the fifteen companies operating the beet-sugar factories into the British Sugar Corporation, with the Corporation receiving Exchequer assistance in respect of the raw sugar it produced each year. The result was an immediate increase in the degree of concentration, which was accentuated by the division of the refining trade between the Corporation on the one hand and the refiners of cane-sugar on the other.

The development of the watch and clock industry has also been assisted by State subsidy in the post-war years. The Government announced in October 1945 that a fund of £1 million was being established to buy factories and special plant to be rented to watchmakers and to found a horological college to train technicians. Two years later, an agreement was concluded with Switzerland whereby Swiss machines were hired for the British industry in return for a limited market (guaranteed by quota) for Swiss watches in Britain and an undertaking to limit exports of British watches to non-Commonwealth countries.

(c) *Nationalisation*

Nationalisation must clearly have a direct and major effect on the degree of concentration by virtue of the fact that a whole industry is transferred to the control of a single body, such as the National Coal Board. The direct effect has, however, been eliminated from the present analysis by the removal of the trades concerned from those for which concentration data have been supplied by the Board of Trade. But nationalisation can also have an indirect effect on concentration for trades in which the nationalised undertakings have ancillary interests.

Thus, a considerable part of the change in concentration in the coke ovens and by-products, and building brick trades can be attributed to the nationalisation of the coal industry. After 1947, the National Coal Board became possessed of a large number of coke ovens and brickworks which had formerly been owned and operated by the colliery companies, and were responsible for more than two-fifths of the national output of hard coke as well as some 8 per cent of the national output of building bricks.

It must be noted, however, that the nationalisation of the steel industry was not reflected in the concentration data for the various iron and steel trades. This was not because the different method of public ownership adopted precluded treatment of the holding company, the Iron and

Steel Corporation, as a single unit, but because the transient nature of nationalisation, as well as the fact that the firms retained their identity, suggested that it would be more useful to continue to treat the steel concerns as individual business units.

6. MERGERS, ACQUISITIONS AND JOINT ENTERPRISES

As we saw in Chapter VIII, firms may either grow by internal expansion or by merger and acquisition. Acquisition may simply be a matter of the strong absorbing the weak, and since it goes on all the time it is slow and unspectacular. But when a large number of firms combine forces, or two or more large concerns merge their interests in a single undertaking, the resulting industrial giant may effect an immediate change in the concentration of the trade in which it is engaged.

There is no shortage of examples of amalgamations which have led to the overnight creation of industrial giants during the last fifty or sixty years in British industry, and some of them have already been noted in Chapter VIII. Although there have been few monster mergers during the 1935–51 period comparable to the creation of Imperial Tobacco Company in 1901 or of I.C.I. in 1926, mergers and acquisitions have been a feature of many of the trades under consideration.

Without resorting to a merger of all their interests, firms sometimes come together and form a jointly-owned enterprise for specific purposes. Such joint enterprises provide an opportunity for the firms to pool their specialised knowledge, whether it concerns the productive techniques or the market for which the product is destined, and also to share the heavy capital costs involved in developing a new process or launching a new product.

The motives for mergers, acquisitions and joint enterprises are manifold and the predominating causes may vary with general economic conditions and the circumstances of individual trades. For the 1935–51 period, it is possible to distinguish a number of factors common to several trades which help to explain why mergers and acquisitions have taken place, and these are discussed in the following sections.

Reduction of excess capacity

The existence of surplus capacity in an industry offers a powerful inducement for firms to combine as a means of rationalising production and eliminating redundant plants. But excess capacity may itself arise for a variety of reasons, including a long-term tendency for demand to fall, increased foreign competition, over-expansion of the trade in the past or the introduction of new or improved technological methods.

There was surplus capacity in a number of trades before the War, and among those where the problem was most severe were tinplate and grain milling. The loss of traditional export markets was the initial cause of the surplus capacity in the tinplate trade, but the difficulties were intensified by the technological developments which threatened to make the old hand mills redundant. The result, as we have already seen, was a number of mergers and acquisitions between tinplate producers both to reduce the surplus capacity by shutting some of the acquired mills and to pave the way for the building of the larger and more efficient continuous strip mills.

The surplus capacity in grain milling was due to different reasons. Even before World War I, flour-milling capacity was increasing at a faster rate than flour consumption in this country, while during the War itself the inland mills increased in number and size as a result of the restricted operations of the larger mills at the ports. The capacity of the industry exceeded requirements by about one-quarter in the post-war decade and, with a considerable quantity of imported flour reducing the demand for home-produced flour still further, price competition was extremely severe.

The main attack on this surplus capacity came after the establishment of the Millers' Mutual Association (M.M.A.) in 1929, whereby a quota scheme was introduced and redundant mills purchased and closed down. The two largest units in the trade—Ranks and Spillers—anticipated the policy of the M.M.A. when they jointly acquired a group of mills in 1928, and made a number of additional acquisitions separately both before and after 1935. Although the degree of concentration in the trade increased as a consequence of these acquisitions and new building by the largest units, by 1951 it was lower than in 1935 because, as already noted, of the damage sustained by the industry during the War.

The brick industry was another victim of surplus capacity, due partly to the increasing competition from alternative building materials and partly to the growth of Fletton brick production at the expense of the traditional brick producers. The largest unit in the trade—the London Brick Company—was formed by merger in 1923 and extended its interests by further acquisitions. Other concerns followed its example, although acquisitions and amalgamations have been less important in the 1935–51 period than earlier and have been more common among the medium-sized than the largest concerns.

Accompaniment of technological change

Technological change, by intensifying the problem of surplus capacity as in the case of tinplate, may accelerate the process of combination. But mergers and acquisitions, or the formation of joint enterprises, may be regarded as an accompaniment of technological change to the extent that they are a convenient way of introducing the new techniques with the least disturbance to the trade as a whole.

The introduction of mass-production techniques in the wrought iron and steel tubes trade was preceded by concentration among both the tube producers and tube fabricators. The two major concerns—Stewarts and Lloyds, and Tube Investments—that emerged as a result were complementary to each other, but instead of merging their interests, they concluded a working agreement which provided for the exchange of liaison shares and for interlocking directorships and jointly-owned subsidiaries. In the ensuing years, they continued to expand by acquisitions, both singly and jointly, as well as by the formation of new joint ventures, and in this process technological considerations have ranked high.

The joint enterprise is also to be found in the watch industry, where Smith's and Ingersoll, and for a time Vickers-Armstrongs, jointly formed and owned the Anglo-Celtic Watch Company, which produces about one-third of all Britain's watches. Here again the technical know-how of the partners was one of the main reasons for their collaboration in the establishment of a new concern on large-scale lines, although financial considerations also probably played a part.

In cinematograph film printing, the concentration of laboratory facilities by one of the largest units was prompted by the necessity to utilise new techniques to the full in order to secure efficient operation. But the laboratory interests of the Rank group were built up by its growth through amalgamation and acquisition on the production and exhibition side of the film industry.

Finally, in the china and porcelain trade, the adoption of improved methods of production which involve substantial investment expenditure has prompted the development of mergers and acquisitions among the concerns in the industry.

Acquisition of quotas or additional raw materials

Where the operations of an industry are governed by quota arrangements which provide for a division of the trade available or for the allocation of scarce raw materials, mergers and acquisitions may be the easiest way for a firm to expand its share of the trade. Among the trades with concentration-changes are two—cement and grain milling—which had privately-organised market-sharing arrangements, as well as another, the sugar industry, where the arrangements were officially sponsored, and in each case acquisitions to obtain quotas were made.

The Cement Makers' Federation, for example, fixed production quotas as well as prices after 1934, and in this industry Associated Portland Cement Manufacturers and the Rugby Portland Cement Company both acquired other concerns in the 1935–51 period. Similarly, the operations of the Millers' Mutual Association envisaged that no new milling capacity should be built without the elimination of a comparable amount of old, and here again acquisitions were frequent. Again, the Sugar Refining Agreement of 1937, by fixing quotas for all the refining concerns, encouraged acquisition as a method of expansion. In 1938 Tate and Lyle purchased and closed the Macfie refinery in order to secure its quota, and with Westburn Sugar Refineries assumed joint control of the Glebe Sugar Refining Company. Similarly, control of the Sankey Sugar Company was acquired by Manbré and Garton.

Selected method of expansion

Although there is an element of growth in all forms of combination, mergers and acquisitions may be selected as the most convenient method of expansion by some firms, particularly in trades which are already well populated. There may, in fact, be considerable advantages in acquiring existing firms as going concerns rather than building up a business from scratch or launching out on a large scale from the start.

An example is the development of the Weston interests in the bread trade and in the biscuit industry. Allied Bakeries was formed in 1935 to acquire a number of bakery businesses in seven cities as far apart as London and Edinburgh, and has continued to acquire other bread and cake concerns as its main method of expansion, since it enables them to use established retail outlets and benefit from existing goodwill. The method of development adopted by Westons was more varied in the biscuit industry. By 1938 it possessed four new biscuit factories, the first of which was built in 1933, but since the War it has acquired an established business, Burton's Gold Medal Biscuits. The biscuit industry also witnessed in 1948 a merger between two old-established concerns, Macfarlane, Lang and Company and McVitie and Price, but despite these combinations concentration fell between 1935 and 1951.

Another trade in which acquisitions have occurred without effecting an increase in concentration is polishes, where Blyth and Platt acquired the William Wren concern, thereby compensating themselves for the loss of a part of their oversea business as a result of political changes in some of their most important markets.

Concentration has, however, increased in both drugs and pharmaceuticals and in toilet preparations and perfumery, where a particular feature has been the development of the Beecham Group. From the time of the merger of Beecham's Pills and Veno Drug Company (1925) in 1928, the business has grown by mergers and acquisitions, and in the above closely connected trades, it acquired between 1935 and 1951 such important concerns as Macleans, Eno Proprietaries, County Perfumery

Company (makers of the Brylcreem products), Harwoods Laboratories, Endocrines-Spicer and Silvikrin Laboratories.

Strengthening control of the trade

Every merger or acquisition may embody an element of the desire to restrict competition. But this motive may be most evident when a concern has a near monopoly of a particular product. In the circumstances, any move to eliminate potential or actual competitors by acquisition is open to the interpretation that the motive is to procure the monopoly.

The British Match Corporation (B.M.C.) was certainly responsible in 1935 for at least 90 per cent of the match production in Britain, but the remaining output was shared between a number of independent manufacturers. Some of these independent concerns were acquired by B.M.C., but in two instances B.M.C. concluded agreements with the independent concerns whereby, *inter alia*, it acquired a minority interest in them. While the agreement between B.M.C. and United Match Industries (U.M.I.) was ended before its expiry in 1947, the minority interest has continued, although B.M.C. has stated that U.M.I. 'now competes quite freely'. A minority interest is not, of course, sufficient for these two concerns to be aggregated with B.M.C. as a single business unit, while the real explanation of the decreased concentration recorded lies in the relative growth of the firelighters section of the Census Match Trade.

7. OTHER FACTORS

It will already be apparent that some of the most easily recognisable factors contributing to concentration-changes may be found in association, but serving opposing ends in the same trade. Such considerations make classification difficult and the task is still further complicated by additional factors which, since they appear to be significant among the present body of trades, must briefly be noted.

Changes in the pattern of trade demand

The fortunes of particular firms may be severely affected by changes in the pattern of demand for their products. In the simplest case, when a trade is contracting as the result of a long-term decline in the demand for its products, there is likely to be a drift of firms away from that trade. The number of firms will fall and the strongest of the surviving firms may then account for an increasingly large share of the industry, as in the case of the slate trade. But in order to compensate for a fall in the demand for their traditional products, some concerns may produce new lines or variants of the old which nevertheless belong generically to the same trade. Thus, in the fish curing trade, the output of quick-frozen fish has been expanding while sales of salt and cured fish have been declining. Since the new products may involve large-scale methods of production, it is possible that they will be developed by newcomers to the trade and concentration may increase despite a rise in the number of concerns.

Within an industry it may be found that some firms will be catering almost exclusively for the home market, while others are geared more closely to exports. A change in world markets may therefore variously affect the fortunes of different concerns. Mainly as a result of political and economic nationalism, some markets have been lost to British firms without being replaced by others or by an expansion in home sales. The firms may, of course, jump the tariff walls and establish factories in the markets to which they previously exported, but either way the production in their home factories has to be reduced. Such factors have operated in the polishes trade and have contributed to the decline in its degree of concentration. But in addition there have been changes in the relative importance of different types of polishes, which again have variously affected the development and importance of the concerns in the trade.

Advertising and sales promotion

The importance of advertising and sales promotion as a condition of growth, if not a condition of entry, has already been discussed in Chapter IX. In many consumer goods trades among those with concentration-changes, advertising and sales promotion have an obvious importance in maintaining or improving the position of the leading concerns. In the razor trade, Gillette has advertised extensively and increased the number and variety of retail outlets for its products, with the result that it is harder for the smaller firms to sell razor blades than to make them.

Extensive advertising and sales promotion are important, too, in such trades as soap, toilet preparations, drugs and pharmaceuticals, spirit rectifying, and watches and clocks, in all of which concentration has increased.

Trade association activity

The quota arrangements which have already been noted as contributing to changes in concentration in the grain-milling, cement, and tinplate trades were organised by trade associations. In other ways, the activities of trade associations may act as an obstacle to the easy entry of new concerns into a trade. As we have already seen in Chapter IX, exclusive dealing and aggregated rebates may have this effect, though in the wallpaper trade such practices have not prevented the rise of a major competitor and a decline in concentration.

8. CONCLUDING COMMENTS

It was not the purpose or intention of this chapter to draw conclusions about the relative importance of the various factors contributing to concentration-changes in the 1935–51 period. Indeed, any attempt to do more than illustrate their diversity would be hazardous for two reasons: because the same factor may have different effects in different trades, and because the various factors may produce opposing tendencies within a specific trade. Moreover, for such as the Match Trade or Linoleum, Leathercloth and Allied Trades, the main explanation of the observed concentration-change lies not so much in the operation of the factors themselves as in some peculiarity in the composition of the Census Trade.

General conclusions are, therefore, better avoided. But two comments must be made. In the first place, for the majority of the trades covered by the case-studies, it was not merely the proportion of the trade covered by the three largest units that changed between 1935 and 1951. There were also changes in the identity or ranking of the three largest units, suggesting that there is considerable mobility among firms in many trades with changes in concentration.

In the second place, events subsequent to 1951 may have intensified the established trend for concentration to increase or decrease but, on the other hand, they may have worked against the observed movement between 1935 and 1951. In the latter case, if concentration data were available for later years, it might be found that the change compared with 1935 had disappeared or even altered in direction. Some of the forty-one trades would as a result no longer qualify as trades with concentration-changes, though their places might well be taken by others where post-1951 events have produced a change in concentration which had not been fully established by 1951.

PART IV

CASE-STUDIES OF TRADES WITH CHANGES IN CONCENTRATION, 1935–51

CHAPTER XIII

INTRODUCTION TO INDUSTRY CASE-STUDIES

In the following Chapters XIV and XV are presented twenty case-studies of industries selected from among the Census trades with changes in concentration between 1935 and 1951. It is not intended that these case-studies should provide a comprehensive analysis of all the various aspects of an industry's development over a long period of years. They are concerned much more with one aspect of that development: the change in concentration during the 1935–51 period. Their purpose, therefore, is to identify the leading concerns in the trades at the two dates, to explore the factors which have contributed to the concentration-change and to assess their relative importance in the individual trades. Similarly, attention has been confined in the main to the 1935–51 period, except where it is necessary to an understanding of that period to take into account events before 1935 or after 1951. It must too be emphasised that the trades investigated are as defined by the concentration data. That is to say, they are Census trades, which may or not conform to the general conception of the industry.

We should have liked to cover all the forty-one trades where concentration could be shown to have changed between 1935 and 1951, but time prevented any such attempt at complete coverage. It has been necessary, therefore, to select the twenty trades for study. In the first place, it was decided that a trade should be reasonably homogeneous in its product-composition; if its principal products were too varied (as, for example, in the case of sports requisites or rubber), it would become exceedingly difficult to assess the effects of various developments or the relative importance of firms engaged in different sections of the trade. Secondly, some trades were so unimportant in their size or economic significance that it appeared there would be relatively little interest in an investigation of their concentration-changes. Thirdly, the availability of published material was an important consideration in determining the choice of trades for detailed investigation.

More positively, an attempt has been made to ensure that the trades selected are representative as far as the direction of the concentration-change, the nature of the products produced and the level of their activity are concerned. Thus, fourteen of the twenty-seven trades with increased concentration and six of the fourteen trades with decreased concentration have been covered by case-studies. Similarly, ten of the trades can be roughly classified as consumer goods trades and ten as producer goods trades. The division is less balanced, however, as far as trade activity is concerned. Among the forty-one trades, twenty-four expanded, eight were stationary and nine contracted, but of the twenty trades covered by the case-studies, fourteen expanded, two were stationary and four contracted.

Finally, the material used in these case-studies has come almost entirely from published sources: books, trade journals, press-cuttings, and company reports. There has been no systematic approach by questionnaire to the principal firms in the trades, though individual companies have assisted with points of detail in particular instances, either by letter or by interview.

CHAPTER XIV

TRADES WITH INCREASED CONCENTRATION, 1935–51

I. COKE OVENS AND BY-PRODUCTS

The carbonisation of coal is principally carried on at gasworks, where the main product is town gas, and at collieries and steelworks, where the main product is metallurgical coke. Gas undertakings are in fact specifically excluded from the Coke Ovens and By-Products Trade which consists, therefore, of establishments wholly or mainly engaged in the manufacture of metallurgical coke, crude coal tar, ammoniacal liquor and low-temperature carbonisation products. Metallurgical coke represented about 70 per cent of the Trade's gross output in 1951 and the other principal products contributed a further 10 per cent. The remaining 20 per cent consisted of the secondary production of the Trade's establishments: that is, their output of crude and refined benzole, coal-tar distillates, coke-oven gas and other products, which the Census authorities treat as principal to other Trades.

The Coke Ovens and By-Products Trade expanded between 1935 and 1951. Employment rose from 14,100 in 1935 to 18,700 in 1951, and the output of metallurgical coke from 12·4 million to 16·5 million tons. Most of the crude by-products and refined substances also increased in quantity between 1935 and 1951. The number of establishments, on the other hand, fell from 113 to eighty-five during this period, while the decline in the number of business units from eighty-one to twenty-four was even greater.

Concentration increased sharply between 1935 and 1951: the three largest units were responsible for 17 per cent of the Trade employment in 1935 but 63 per cent in 1951, while their share of net output similarly rose from 18 to 63 per cent. Thus, in this Trade increased concentration has been associated with a fall in the number of plants and business units, despite an expansion in the output of the Trade.

The production of metallurgical coke has long been technically and financially integrated with coal mining on the one hand and the iron and steel industry on the other. Thus it was reported in 1925 that 'four-fifths of all the metallurgical coke produced at home came from ovens owned, directly or indirectly, by colliery companies', and of this output nearly half was made by those colliery concerns also engaged in iron and steel making. 'Only 14 per cent of the output was wholly independent.'[1] About

[1] Committee on Industry and Trade (the Balfour Committee), *Survey of Metal Industries*, Part IV of a Survey of Industries (London, H.M.S.O. 1928), p. 433.

Table 37. *Number of units and concentration-ratios for fourteen case-study trades with increased principal product concentration, 1935–51*

	Number of units*		Gross output concentration-ratios		Net output concentration-ratios		Employment concentration-ratios	
	1935	1951	1935 (%)	1951 (%)	1935 (%)	1951 (%)	1935 (%)	1951 (%)
Coke Ovens and By-products	81	24	21	60	18	63	17	63
Razors (excl. Electric)	25	11	59	98†	60	99†	55	94†
Mineral Oil Refining	..	8	78	93	84	35‡	82	84
Watch and Clock	..	61	36	60	42	62	38	60
Metalliferous Mines and Quarries	44	33	26	46	27	41	32	50
Lead	46	40	35	69	30	69	38	53
Building Bricks	672	397	18	33	19	32	14	30
Metal Boxes and Containers	73	83	46	68†	51	61†	45	60†
Tinplate	34	18	59	74	61	72	57	71
Cinematograph Film Printing	10	18	50	66	47	70	42	61
Sugar and Glucose	22	25	73	88	62	82	71	84
Wrought Iron and Steel Tubes	62	81	71	84†	70	79†	71	77†
Bread and Flour Confectionery	1,430	1,512	8	18	10	17	6	15
Soap and Glycerine	39	74	76	85	81	80	70	72

* Estimated in 1935; see footnote, p. 153.
† For four largest business units.
‡ Not comparable.

this time, too, some two-thirds of the metallurgical coke produced came from coke ovens sited at collieries, with the remaining one-third from ovens attached to iron and steel works.

The number of plants had already fallen substantially by 1935, largely because the old beehive coke ovens (which did not permit by-products to be recovered, or heat to be recuperated) had been replaced by the larger and more economical regenerative ovens which made possible the full utilisation of by-products. The utilisation of surplus gas also prompted a change in the location of coke ovens, for when they were sited alongside the blast furnaces and steelworks, the surplus gas could be used for heating purposes throughout the steelmaking and rolling processes. So not only did the number of coke ovens fall, but more of them were sited at steelworks: by 1939, some 60 per cent of total coke-oven capacity was sited alongside blast-furnaces.

The degree of integration between colliery companies, steel concerns, and coke-oven operators in 1935 was indicated in the Leak and Maizels paper. There were, for example, sixty-seven units employing more than 500 persons active in both the Coal Mines and Coke Ovens and By-Products Trades, and these sixty-seven units accounted for 84 per cent of the employment in the latter Trade. Similarly, there were fifteen units active in both the Iron and Steel (Smelting and Rolling) and the Coke Ovens and By-Products Trades, accounting for 33 per cent of the total employment in the latter Trade. Some of these units were, of course, interested in all three Trades, as well as in the Blast Furnace Trade, so that there is an element of duplication in the figures. It was also stated that the ten concerns (each with more than 1,000 employees) engaged in each of the four Trades were responsible for 30 per cent of the total employment in the Coke Ovens and By-Products Trade in 1935.

The identity of two of the three largest units in the trade in 1935 has also been given by Leak and Maizels: they were Dorman Long and Company and the United Steel Companies. Both were primarily iron and steel concerns, though each owned collieries as well. The other largest unit in 1935 was almost certainly the Consett Iron Company, which again combined colliery and steel interests and, according to the *Coke-Oven Managers' Year Book*, possessed nearly 1·9 million tons of coking capacity.

Although the number of coke ovens continued to decline after 1935, the principal cause of the decline in the number of business units between 1935 and 1951 was the nationalisation of the coalmining industry in 1947. In its second Annual Report, the National Coal Board (N.C.B.) stated that on Vesting Day it became the owner of fifty-five coking plants which had belonged to the colliery companies and thereby became responsible for 'more than two-fifths of the national output of hard coke'. Naturally enough, the N.C.B. became the producer of the by-products, too: 'about a sixth of the tar, a third of the benzole, and a fifth of the sulphate of ammonia produced in the country'. So, by the single stroke of coal nationalisation, the degree of concentration in the Coke Ovens and By-Products Trade was substantially increased.

By 1951, the number of the N.C.B.'s active coke ovens had been reduced to fifty-one, despite the fact that one plant was acquired in 1949 and another had been built and operated for the first time. Three-fifths of the eighty-five establishments in the Trade were thus owned and operated by the N.C.B. in 1951, making it by far the largest unit in the industry. In its 1951 Report, furthermore, the N.C.B. claimed that its share of the total output of metallurgical coke still remained at about 40 per cent, compared with nearly 50 per cent produced at coke ovens 'owned by, and often integrated with steel works', the remainder coming from a few independently-owned plants.

The nationalisation of the coalmining industry did more than make the N.C.B. the largest unit in the Coke Ovens and By-Products Trade, since it also reduced the coking capacity of iron and steel firms with colliery interests. The ranking of these concerns in the Trade now rested solely on the coking capacity which they operated directly rather than through colliery companies. It would appear, judging from the *Coke-Oven Managers' Year Book*, that the largest coke-oven capacities in 1951 were owned, apart from the N.C.B., by Dorman Long, Stewarts and Lloyds, Richard Thomas and Baldwins, United Steel Companies, and the Steel Company of Wales, probably in that order.

The ranking of the steel concerns, on the basis of their coke-oven capacity, has certainly been affected by the loss of their colliery coke ovens. But it has also been affected by the expansion of their own integrated coke-oven capacity and by mergers and acquisitions between themselves. For example, Stewarts and Lloyds' probable claim to third place in 1951 has been due both to expansion of their coke-oven plant at Corby and to their acquisition of the Stanton Ironworks Company shortly before the outbreak of World War II. But since 1951 the same factors may have again changed the ranking of the largest units, apart from the N.C.B.

Although it would have been preferable to rank the units in the trade according to their production of metallurgical coke and by-products, the coking capacity figures are sufficient to indicate the relative importance of the leading concerns at the two dates. In any case, the primary cause of the change in concentration is evident enough. Although technological factors favouring larger plants as well as mergers and acquisitions have been present in this trade, it was the nationalisation of coalmining (which centralised the ownership of the colliery coke ovens in the N.C.B.) that has contributed the major part of the increase in concentration between 1935 and 1951.

2. RAZORS AND RAZOR BLADES

The safety razor established its ascendancy in the 1920's, and by 1935 the competition of the 'cut-throat' had practically vanished. The establishment of the safety razor industry owed much to American firms which established manufacturing subsidiaries in this country before or during World War I. The Sheffield cutlers who made the traditional razor knew their trade was disappearing, but in the main they did not attempt to manufacture safety razors. Instead they began to make the blades, for which there was a tremendous and growing demand as the safety razor increased in popularity. By 1927, there were fifteen plants making safety razor blades in Sheffield alone. But Sheffield was not destined to become the only, or even the main, centre of the safety razor trade; by 1934, razor blades were being manufactured in London, Birmingham, Southampton, Norwich, Morecambe and Glasgow, and the combined production in these centres was greater than in Sheffield itself.

The establishment of the new industry was not hampered by foreign competition. The more important American companies had British manufacturing subsidiaries. The other important foreign rival was Germany, but its internal economic and financial difficulties hindered its export trade. Moreover, the home industry was helped by the 33⅓ per cent tariff imposed on imported cutlery in 1926, though the prime purpose of the tariff was to assist the depressed Sheffield cutlers.

The number of manufacturers of razors and razor blades continued to increase in the early 1930's, but it was the blade section of the trade that showed the greatest increase and was the most heavily populated in 1935. Razor blade manufacture was particularly attractive, not merely because of the favourable demand conditions, but also because entry was easy. Little capital equipment was needed, and each firm could make its products readily distinguishable by the use of a brand-name and a distinctive wrapping. It was possible to buy blanks (that is, pieces of steel the size and shape of a blade), to finish them and market them under a proprietary name. Small wonder, indeed, that there were more than a hundred brands of safety razor blades on the market in 1934.

The manufacturers of razor blades at the time were of three main types: (*a*) firms making cutlery and similar products which, faced with a general depression in cutlery, welcomed this opportunity for profitable activity; (*b*) steel firms, such as Darwins, which claimed in 1929 to have the largest safety razor blade plant in Britain; and (*c*) the specialist producers of razors and razor blades.

Although the present mass-production techniques of razor blade manufacture bear little resemblance to the cutlers' craft, the historical connection between the two trades is maintained by the Census of Production since the 'specialist producers of razors (excluding electric) and parts' form a sub-division of the Cutlery Trade. Employment in this Sub-Trade was just under 3,000 in 1935, or nearly 30 per cent higher than five years earlier. The number of establishments classified to the Sub-Trade also increased from seventeen in 1930 to twenty-nine in 1935.

Not all razors and blades came from the establishments classified to the Sub-Trade. In 1935, some 12 per cent of the total sales of razors and blades were produced in establishments outside the Sub-Trade, but more than half of these sales still came from other establishments in the Cutlery Trade. By 1951, less than 3 per cent of the total sales came from outside the Sub-Trade, and less than 2 per cent from outside the Cutlery Trade. Thus, the establishments in the Sub-Trade were responsible for a greater proportion of the total sales of razors and blades in 1951 than in 1935, indicating that their manufacture had become less widespread and diversified during the period.

Between 1935 and 1951, output more than trebled in quantity, with blades increasing their share of total sales from 75 per cent in 1935 to 83 per cent in 1951. Home demand rose during this period for both safety razors and safety razor blades, but whereas the quantity of razors sold on the home market in 1951 was more than double the 1935 sales, the increase was only in the region of 70 per cent for blades. But exports of blades increased more than exports of razors. Although exports of razors increased from 55 per cent of home production in 1935 to 65 per cent in 1951, the proportion for blades rose from under one-quarter to over half in the same period.

The employment of the Sub-Trade has increased with rising production, though the rise in numbers employed from 2,920 in 1935 to 3,860 in 1951 is very much less than the increase in output would suggest. The number of establishments in the Sub-Trade has, on the other hand, fallen from twenty-nine in 1935 to thirteen in 1951; so, too, has the number of business units, from twenty-five to eleven.

It is not surprising, therefore, to find that there has been a substantial increase of concentration in the Sub-Trade between 1935 and 1951. The three largest units accounted for 55 per cent of employment and 60 per cent of net output in 1935. In 1951 the four largest units were responsible for 94 per cent of employment and 99 per cent of net output. Thus, in 1935 the share of the Sub-Trade left to the twenty-two other units was approximately 40 per cent, but by 1951 the seven other units only shared 1–2 per cent of the total trade between them.

The fall in the number of establishments and business units in the Sub-Trade is explained by several factors. In the first place, the supply of both safety razors and blades seems to have caught up with demand soon after 1935. For safety razors, this simply meant a halt to any further increase in the number of establishments. But among the blade manufacturers, where the greatest expansion in terms of both new entrants and extensions to existing plants had taken place, fierce competition developed. 'High quality blades continue to sell very well,' it was reported in 1936, 'but the trade in blades is menaced by ultra-cheap goods and price cutting. It is difficult to believe that the prices at which some blades are put on the market allow makers anything like a reasonable profit.'[1] It was also suggested that the public appreciated the reliability of goods that bore a well-known trade-brand and were backed by the names of reputable manufacturers.

At all events, it appears that many small manufacturers of blades abandoned the trade before the outbreak of war. In some cases, the failure of such concerns was due to the poor quality of their products. In others, it is attributable to neglect of the need for adequate advertisement. Although many small concerns lacked the resources to finance an extensive sales campaign, there is also evidence that they did not fully appreciate the importance of advertising. As a consequence, the largest

[1] *Sheffield Chamber of Commerce Journal*, May 1936.

concerns, which did engage in extensive advertising, tended to gain at their expense.

During World War II, the number of manufacturing concerns was further reduced by the concentration scheme which was applied to the industry in order to release labour and raw materials for other work. Many of the smaller firms which stopped making razor blades did not re-enter the trade after the War because of the continued shortage of steel, their lack of trained staff, their selling difficulties or the greater profitability of their new lines of production. One well-known firm, James Neill and Company, makers of the 'Eclipse' blade, lost all their machinery in an air raid, and though for a time they continued to market a blade produced by another manufacturer, they eventually decided to concentrate on other products and finally left the trade.

The largest units in the trade benefited from the disappearance, for one reason or another, of some of the smaller concerns. There is no doubt that the largest concern in 1935 was Gillette Industries, and that its principal rival was Ever-Ready Razor Products. Both were subsidiaries of American concerns which had been created or involved in merger activity. Thus, Gillette Industries was formed in 1931 to take over the British enterprises of the Gillette Safety Razor Company[1] and the Auto-Strop Safety Razor Company, following the amalgamation of the parent companies in the United States. Gillette had started a London branch and begun to make blades in Leicester as early as 1905, while Auto-Strop commenced blade manufacture in London in 1917. Similarly, Ever-Ready Razor Products, registered in 1920 as the British-American Safety Razor Corporation, was a subsidiary of the American Safety Razor Corporation, formed by the merger in 1919 of three United States concerns which marketed the Ever-Ready, Gem and Star blades.

Apart from Gillette and Ever-Ready, the largest units in the trade in 1935 included the Wilkinson Sword Company, Thomas Ward and Sons ('Wardonia'), James Neill ('Eclipse'), Darwins, George H. Lawrence ('Laurel', 'Velvet') and Rolls Razor, but their individual importance was much less than that of the two leaders.

By 1951, Gillette had done more than maintain its position as the leading producer: it had increased its share very considerably. In 1948, Gillette employed more than 2,000 persons, constituting approximately three-fifths of the total employment in the Sub-Trade in that year and more than the total of the three largest units combined in 1935. It has also been stated that as long ago as 1946 Gillette was responsible for more than 70 per cent of the total razor blades exported from Great Britain,[2] and it is understood that its share later increased to well over

[1] Now the Gillette Company.

[2] Ian Coster, *The Sharpest Edge in the World* (London, Gillette Industries Ltd, 1948), p. 75.

90 per cent. As far as the home market is concerned, its four brands, Blue Gillette, Red Gillette, Seven O'Clock, and Valet, were credited with some three-quarters of razor blade sales in 1953.[1]

Second place was still held by Ever-Ready in 1951, though it had certainly not increased its share of the trade to the same extent as Gillette. Indeed, in 1953, the sales of its Ever-Ready and Star blades have been placed at around 11 per cent of the total sales in the British market.[2] The holder of third place in 1951 was another subsidiary of an American concern, Pal Personna Products, which was credited with 9 per cent of the home market in 1953 though it did not start manufacture in this country until 1945. Moreover, in 1953, Pal Personna was acquired by Ever-Ready.

It is abundantly clear, therefore, that the increase in concentration in the razor industry has been associated with the growth in the importance of Gillette. It is consequently relevant to determine the various factors which have contributed to Gillette's position of strength. In the first place, Gillette has succeeded in making a reliable high-quality product available at all price levels, except the very cheapest. In this country, it markets four different blades, thus catering for all types of customer. Secondly, it began production with a technical advantage, which it has improved rather than neglected. In 1931, when the present company uniting Gillette and Auto-Strop was founded, Auto-Strop had developed machinery for making double-edged blades in long strips, separating them only for packing. This not only speeded up the manufacturing process but facilitated further mechanisation and the automatic testing of the blade during manufacture. Previously the first process had been to cut a piece of steel to the size of a blade (the blank) and each blade was then finished individually. Such technical improvements were exploited to the full in the factory built by the new Gillette company with an initial capacity of 1½ million blades a day. Gillette has continued this policy of research, improving both its product and its methods of production, thereby ensuring that its technical position is maintained. It now makes most of its own machinery or rebuilds standard machines to its own requirements.

Finally, by vigorous sales promotion and the exploration of new retail outlets, Gillette has kept its products continuously in the public eye. This last factor may possibly have been the most important. It would be difficult, but not impossible, for a new firm to compete with the efficiency and expert knowledge of Gillette in terms of production, though Gillette's exact production methods cannot be repeated since the machinery re-

[1] Based on *The Buying Habits and Purchasing Power of Daily Herald Readers*, New Series, Report no. 8: *Razor Blades* (London, Daily Herald, 1954), p. 8.

[2] Based on *ibid.* p. 8.

quired cannot be bought. But the problem facing other firms is not so much how to make razor blades, but how to sell them. In the past they tended to lose ground steadily to Gillette, and the high level of advertising and sales promotion needed to combat the sustained Gillette campaign acts as a bar to new entrants. Some idea of the magnitude of Gillette's advertising can be gained from the fact that it was responsible for over 35 per cent of the total spent on press advertising by makers of razors and blades in the last quarter of 1935, and as much as 70 per cent of the total in the comparable period of 1951.[1]

It is possible to conclude, therefore, that the large increase in concentration in this industry has been directly associated with the emergence of one dominant firm, at a time when the number of manufacturers has been declining. Amalgamations and acquisitions have played no part in the growth of that firm during the 1935–51 period, though its technological advantages stem from the merger which created it in 1931. In a trade which had already changed from a craft producing instruments intended to last to a mass-production industry concentrating on a cheap expendable blade, the largest firms have benefited from the cost advantage that they enjoy compared with their smaller rivals. The result has been a decline in the number of producers, accentuated by the circumstances of war, leaving the surviving manufacturers free to increase their trade as the market expands, protected against new entrants by the high costs of selling.

The safety razor has, it is true, had to reckon in recent years with the growing popularity of the electric razor. In general, the safety razor manufacturers have not entered into this new field, but there is no indication that the market for razor blades, which forms the largest part of their business, has been adversely affected by the new products. Indeed, it may well be that the relatively high initial cost of an electric razor is, at least at the present time, sufficient protection to the safety razor manufacturers, although the intensive advertising that they practise is a further safeguard of their position.

3. MINERAL OIL REFINING

In the post-war decade the oil refining industry in Britain has changed out of recognition. It is not merely that its output has expanded greatly; its character has changed as well. Whereas most of the small refineries of pre-war days produced only a few specialised products, the large-scale modern refineries built since 1945 produce a full range of petroleum products, including materials for the manufacture of petroleum-based chemicals.

[1] Based on information given in the *Statistical Review of Press Advertising* (London, Legion Publishing Company).

The reasons for this remarkable and sudden change in the stature of the United Kingdom mineral oil refining industry are well known. The compelling motive for developing large-scale refining in this country was the necessity to save dollars by importing comparatively cheap crude oil instead of expensive refined products from the United States and the Caribbean. The opportunity was provided by the rapidly rising availability of Middle East crude oil, and by higher costs in the United States which reduced the pressure of American competition. Moreover, there had been a big increase in the size and diversity of the market for refinery products; the danger of producing large and unmarketable surpluses of residual fuel and other oils diminished with the increased use of heavy fuel oils and the development of the petroleum-chemicals industry.

Some idea of the magnitude of this change in the scope and size of the oil refining industry is given by the Census data, though the principal product composition of the Mineral Oil Refining Trade was not the same in 1935 as in 1951. For instance, crude shale oil was treated as a principal product in 1935, and this introduced an element of duplication into the principal product data since the refined products made from that shale oil were also taken into account. On the other hand, bitumen and bituminous products were not regarded as principal products in 1935 as they were in 1951.

The changes in the definition of the Trade have meant that the Trade as originally defined in 1935 had more establishments and a larger labour-force than it has when defined in the same way as in 1951. Even so, its employment in 1951 was nearly treble the employment of the original 1935 trade, while in terms of the comparable data employment rose from less than 3,400 to more than 12,000 between 1935 and 1951. The number of establishments in the Trade, on the other hand, fell from twenty-five on the original basis in 1935 (and from twenty on the revised basis) to fifteen in 1951.

The increase in the labour-force of this capital-intensive trade is a poor indication of its growth. More significant is the extent to which the output of the home refineries has satisfied the increased demand for petroleum products. In 1938, the inland consumption of refined products amounted to just under 9 million tons; in 1951, it was nearly 16·9 million tons. The proportion of this total consumption represented by home refinery output was only 27 per cent in 1938, but by 1951 it had risen to 97 per cent.

There has also been a radical change in the pattern of output of the oil refining industry between 1935 and 1951. Refinery operations can, within certain limits, be technically adjusted to yield varying proportions of the different refined products from a ton of crude oil. But the main determinant of that change in the output pattern has been the increased demand for fuel, gas and diesel oils which accounted for 54 per cent of the value of refined petroleum products in 1951 compared with 21 per cent in 1935. The importance of motor and aviation spirit has correspondingly fallen during the same period: from 50 per cent to 29 per cent of the total value of refined products.

A final indication of the expansion in the oil refining industry is given by the rated capacity of the refineries, though it must be borne in mind that in pre-war years output was at levels far below capacity. The rated annual capacity of the twelve major refineries active in 1938 has been put at 3,785,000 tons, and at 4,360,000 tons in 1946. By 1953, as a result of the post-war expansion programme, the rated capacity of the fifteen major refineries had risen to 26,535,000 tons—a sevenfold increase compared with 1938.[1]

It is against this background of a rapidly expanding industry—both in terms of capacity and actual output—that the increase in concentration between 1935 and 1951 must be viewed. The trade was already highly concentrated in 1935; the three largest units were responsible for 78 per cent of the gross output, 84 per cent of the net output and 82 per cent of the employment. Between 1935 and 1951 the degree of concentration increased still further, the rise being slight in terms of employment (2 percentage points) but large (15 percentage points) in terms of gross output.[2]

The distribution of refinery capacity according to ownership is shown for both pre-war and post-war years in Table 38. The identity of the three largest units before the War is immediately apparent; the Shell Petroleum Company, the British Petroleum Company and the Esso Petroleum Company were far and away the most important concerns, and together were responsible for some 85 per cent of the total rated capacity in 1938.

The interests of the British Petroleum Company (formerly the Anglo-Iranian Oil Company) in the refining industry in Britain date back to the early 1920's, when its subsidiary, National Oil Refineries, began operating the first large-scale refinery in Britain for the treatment of imported crude oil (at Llandarcy in South Wales). The other pre-war refineries of British Petroleum (B.P.) were operated through Scottish Oils and were situated at Grangemouth (opened in 1924) and Pumpherston, the latter processing Scottish shale oil and other indigenous crudes.

By 1938, the three refineries of B.P. had a rated refining capacity of 870,000 tons—or some 23 per cent of the national total. Since then it has built a new refinery at the Isle of Grain, Kent, with a capacity in 1953 of 4 million tons, and has vastly expanded its plants at Llandarcy and Grangemouth. As a result, it has raised its capacity to 10,680,000 tons, or

[1] 'Oil Refining in Britain', *The Times Review of Industry*, November 1952, p. 10.

[2] The net output concentration-ratio for 1951 is not comparable with that for 1935.

some 40 per cent of the national total, as shown in Table 38. In 1951, however, these extensions and new building were not complete; indeed, construction on the Isle of Grain refinery did not begin until the middle of 1950 and production until early in 1953.

Table 38. *Capacity of major oil refineries, 1938–53**

Company	Plant	Refining capacity (thousand tons) 1938	1946	1953
Shell Petroleum	Stanlow	750	925	3,800
	Shellhaven	800	800	3,000
	Heysham	—	—	1,500
	Ardrossan	200	200	200
		1,750	1,925	8,500
British Petroleum	Llandarcy	360	360	4,000
	Isle of Grain	—	—	4,000
	Grangemouth	360	360	2,500
	Pumpherston	150	150	180
		870	870	10,680
Esso Petroleum	Fawley	600	900	6,000
Mobil Oil†	Coryton	250	250	850
Lobitos Oilfields	Ellesmere Port	130	130	160
Manchester Oil Refinery	Trafford Park	—	100	150
Berry Wiggins and Company	Kingsnorth	90	90	95
	Weaste	60	60	65
Wm Briggs and Sons	Dundee	35	35	35
	Total	3,785	4,360	26,535

* Based on information given in 'Oil Refining in Britain', *T.R.I.* Nov. 1952, p. 10.
† Formerly Cory Bros. plant.

The refining interests of the Shell Petroleum Company[1] in Britain originated in the Stanlow plant built in 1922 for the manufacture of bitumen, and later extended to include petroleum spirits with special distillation ranges. With the general expansion in the 1930's, the Shellhaven plant was built to produce bitumen, paraffin wax, lubricating oils and special boiling point spirits. The smaller Ardrossan plant, on the other hand, was a topped crude refinery mainly devoted to bitumen production.

During the War the Government built a refinery at Heysham, but this was closed down in 1946 and then bought by Shell for its own use in 1948. The extensions at the Stanlow refinery, which were to raise its capacity to 3·8 million tons by 1953, began in the same year, followed shortly afterwards by the Shellhaven expansion to 3 million tons in 1953. Therefore Shell's total refining capacity stood at 8·5 million tons, or 32 per cent of the national total, in 1953, compared with 1·75 million tons and 46 per

[1] Part of Royal Dutch-Shell Group.

cent in 1938. Prior to the War, Shell had the largest refining interest in Britain, but it could claim only second place in 1953.

The third largest refiner both in 1948 and since the War is Esso Petroleum (formerly Anglo-American Oil)[1] whose crude oil refinery at Fawley had a capacity of 600,000 tons in 1938. Post-war construction at Fawley has made the refinery there the largest in Europe, with a capacity of 6 million tons in 1951 and 8 million in 1956. The new refining capacity came into large-scale production in 1951, and by 1953 Esso was responsible for some 22·5 per cent of the total United Kingdom capacity, compared with 16 per cent in 1938.

Of the other refining concerns identified in Table 38, Berry Wiggins and Company embarked on the production of bitumen in 1920, and opened a refinery at Kingsnorth on the Medway in 1929, followed later by another at Weaste on the Manchester Ship Canal. Lobitos Oilfield similarly erected and operated an oil refinery at Ellesmere Port in 1934, while Manchester Oil Refinery began production of lubricating oils and white oils shortly before the outbreak of war in 1939. None of these concerns has joined the big three in large post-war expansion; their combined share of the trade has consequently fallen from more than 8 per cent in 1946 to less than 2 per cent in 1953. Far larger than the refineries of these concerns is that of the Mobil Oil Company (formerly Vacuum Oil) at Coryton. This refinery, whose products consist mainly of lubricating oils, did not begin production until 1953, when it replaced an earlier plant of Cory Bros. which had a capacity in 1938 of 250,000 tons.

Although the refining capacity data and the concentration data refer to two different time-periods, it is possible to relate the one to the other fairly satisfactorily. Even so, two points must be noted. First, rated capacity cannot be equated with actual production, particularly for the pre-war years when the level of operation was low; and second, the 1953 capacity figures cannot be held to apply to 1951 when some considerable part of that capacity was under construction but not yet in production. Bearing these qualifications in mind, the rated capacity data give the three largest units some 83 per cent of the total capacity in 1938 and 94 per cent in 1953; this corresponds fairly closely with the change in concentration between 1935 and 1951.

Conclusion

The increase of concentration in this trade has been associated with the expansion of the refining industry after the War. Mergers played no part in this expansion, nor were small concerns acquired by large, save in the case of Mobil Oil's purchase of the Cory Bros. plant. To some extent, expansion has taken the form of adding to existing capacity in such a way

[1] Controlled by the Standard Oil Company of New Jersey.

as to amount to the building of a new refinery, but even the completely new refineries have been built by concerns which were already among the leaders before the War. It is significant that by far the larger part of the additional refinery capacity has been installed by Shell, B.P. and Esso, which, through their marketing subsidiaries,[1] accounted for 80–90 per cent of the pre-war sales of petroleum in this country. The other large international oil concerns, with the exception of Mobil Oil, did not between 1935 and 1951 attempt to enter the United Kingdom refining industry, while the smaller independent refiners have also not shared in the expansion because refining, divorced from production and distribution, is scarcely profitable.[2] Accordingly, the change in concentration in this industry is associated both with the scale of the additional refinery capacity installed since the War, which was determined by technological factors, and the fact that it has been undertaken by the concerns which already possessed some refinery capacity in Britain before the War, even though they were mainly important as distributors of products imported from their refineries overseas.

4. WATCHES AND CLOCKS

Thirty years ago the British watch and clock industry had almost ceased to exist. Clockmaking, which had been a thriving craft industry for centuries, seemed destined for complete extinction, while there was scarcely any output of home-produced watches.

By 1951, the position was vastly different. In that year, more than 5 million clocks and more than 1·7 million watches were produced in this country, and within four years watch output was to reach 3 million a year. Similarly, imports which before the War accounted for more than 80 per cent of the domestic supply of clocks, and more than 95 per cent of the domestic supply of watches, had fallen by 1951 to less than 15 per cent for clocks and around 40 per cent for watches.

There are many reasons for the decline of the watch and clock industry in this country, and its revival in the last quarter of a century. While other countries introduced various mechanical devices in the second half of the nineteenth century, British craftsmen in a Luddite mood resisted such changes. The result was that the British industry declined as foreign competition developed, and at the time of the first Census of Production in 1907, employment in the trade had fallen to 5,300 compared with about 20,000 at the beginning of the nineteenth century.[3]

[1] The Royal Dutch-Shell and B.P. groups have marketed their products since 1931 in the United Kingdom through a jointly-owned subsidiary, Shell Mex and B.P.

[2] See Economic Commission for Europe, *The Price of Oil in Western Europe* (1955), pp. 30–2.

[3] 'Race against Time', *Future*, vol. 4, no. 5, October 1949.

Although clocks, watches and components became subject to the McKenna duties of $33\frac{1}{3}$ per cent in 1915, the purpose was to restrict luxury imports rather than to protect the domestic producers. Although the duties lapsed in 1924 they were reimposed for protective purposes in the following year, subject to a preferential rebate in favour of Empire products (amounting to one-third of the full duty). The Anglo-German Trade Agreement of 1933, however, reduced the duty to 20 per cent on clocks imported from Germany, and other countries were able to take advantage of the reduced rate under most-favoured-nation arrangements.

Despite the tariff, the penetration of the British market by foreign producers was almost complete up to 1930, while even the small amount of British production was dependent on imports of vital components. But the large volume of imports prompted firms from outside the trade to speculate on the possibilities of developing the production of synchronous electric clocks in Britain. Here was a new field of manufacture which British makers could enter on more or less equal terms with foreign producers and, it was hoped, recapture part of the domestic market. By 1935, some 100,000 electric clocks were being produced in this country, and by 1937 output was up to nearly 165,000. Even so, home-produced electric clocks had to compete not merely with the very cheap and sometimes subsidised foreign mechanical clocks, but also with imported electric clocks, which increased their share of home supply from 17 per cent in 1935 to 40 per cent in 1937.

The limited recovery of clock production did not mean that watch output also increased. It has been rightly stressed that watchmaking 'is not a simple extension of clock-making; it is qualitatively different'.[1] Indeed when war came in 1939, as Sir Stafford Cripps later commented, 'the inadequacy of the clock and watch making industry left a very serious gap in what may be termed our industrial armoury'. Stocks of Swiss timepieces were accumulated in the pre-war period, and, even more important, Swiss machinery was imported up to 1940 to provide the essential equipment for maintaining production of aviation clocks and watches. Such foresight enabled the industry to keep going, and before the War ended, the principal concern was making around 1,000 watches a week.

The lesson of an inadequate watch and clock industry was learnt, and the Coalition Government considered what assistance might be given to the industry after the War. In the event, the assistance took several forms. First, a £1 million fund was established by the Government to buy factories and special plant to be rented to watchmakers, and to found a horological college to train technicians. Second, the import duty on clocks was raised and import quotas imposed on watches and mechanical clocks.

[1] 'Race against Time', *Future*, October 1949.

Third, an agreement was concluded with Switzerland in 1947 whereby Swiss machines were hired to the British industry in return for a guaranteed quota for Swiss watches in Britain, and an undertaking that British watch exports to non-Commonwealth countries would not exceed 5 per cent of total production.

This government assistance greatly helped the expansion of the industry in the post-war years. Two-and-a-half times as many complete clocks were made in 1951 as in 1946, and nearly three times as many in 1955; while twenty times as many clocks were exported in 1951 as in pre-war years. Similarly, the output of complete watches had risen from 300,000 in 1947 to 1,720,000 in 1951, although only 2 per cent of the home production was exported in the latter year.

The increased importance of the industry is reflected in the data for the Census Trade. Employment in the larger establishments (that is, those employing eleven persons and over) rose from 4,000 in 1935 to 11,100 in 1951, while the number of larger establishments increased from sixty-six to eighty-two. In this trade, however, the smaller establishments have been relatively important. In 1935, there were 941 small establishments with ten or fewer persons, accounting for more than two-fifths of the total employment in all establishments large and small. By 1951, the number of small establishments was very much lower at 232, and their share of the total employment was less than one-tenth. Probably most of these smaller establishments only do repair work.

Concentration in this expanding trade increased substantially between 1935 and 1951. In 1935, the three largest units accounted for 38 per cent of the employment and 42 per cent of the net output of the larger establishments of the trade; by 1951, the comparable share was 60 per cent for employment and 62 per cent for net output. In order to identify the factors that have contributed to this increase in concentration, it is convenient to treat the two major sections of the trade separately, beginning with clocks.

Clocks

Before the advent of the synchronous electric clock the trade comprised a few makers of ordinary domestic clocks, the specialist manufacturers of turret clocks, time-recorders and clock-systems, and one or two makers of car clocks. One of the first firms to become interested in electric clock manufacture was S. Smith and Sons (Motor Accessories),[1] which formed a subsidiary to develop this business. In 1931, Smith's acquired a controlling interest in English Clock and Watch Manufacturers, an old-established Coventry business, and in the following year it opened a factory to mass-produce lever escapements.

[1] Since 1944, S. Smith and Sons (England).

Even at this time, there were other manufacturers of electric clocks, among them electrical engineering concerns like Ferranti and the General Electric Company, as well as the Telephone Manufacturing Company, and at the end of 1932 eight British makers formed the Synchronous Clock Conference to popularise electric clocks. But other concerns were entering clockmaking for the first time in the early 'thirties, such as Enfield Clock (soon to become associated with Smith's), Perivale Clock, and Garrard Clocks (whose parent company made gramophone motors and other engineering products). Thus, with such old-established concerns as Rotherham and Sons of Coventry, F. W. Elliott of Croydon, and Ingersoll which assembled clocks from imported movements and components, the clock trade was a much more thriving and populated trade in 1935 than it had been for generations past.

The main feature of the post-war period has been the development of alarm clock manufacture on a large scale by a few concerns: a development prompted by the disappearance of Germany as a major exporter of this type of clock. Although Smith's were making alarm clocks before the War, their post-war output has been vastly greater. At their Carfin factory the weekly output of alarm clocks rose from 20,000 soon after the end of the War to 55,000 in 1951. 'Operations that had formerly required skilled workers', it has been reported, were made 'capable of being performed by unskilled men and women', while machinery was evolved by Smith's to reduce the labour content of clocks.[1] But then Smith's transferred alarm clock production from Carfin to a new factory at Wishaw, which was laid out on true flow lines using mechanical handling both by conveyors and palletisation. It was hoped that output in the new factory would rise to 90,000 a week, but in 1955 Smith's output was said to be only about 40,000 a week, or 15,000 fewer than in 1951.

The other major producer of alarm clocks had been Westclox (a subsidiary of the General Time Instrument Corporation of New York) which began production at Strathleven in 1947. Other firms also entered this trade after the War, but some were forced to abandon alarm clock manufacture after making considerable losses, owing to their inability to meet the prices which the quantity production of the largest producers made possible. One concern which proved its staying power was John D. Francis of Liverpool; in 1955, its output of all types of clocks was stated to be more than 500,000 a year.

Alarm clocks apart, there is a considerable number of producers of other types of electric and mechanical clocks. Even so, it has been repeatedly stated that Smith's can claim some 90 per cent of the production of electric clocks, and though its importance in the mechanical clock

[1] 'Clockmaking: an Industry Revives', *Manchester Guardian Survey of Industry, Trade and Finance, 1956*, p. 107.

field is nowhere near as great, there is no doubt that it was the largest clock producer in 1935 and 1951 alike.

Watches

Turning now to watchmaking, it is important to emphasise that there was no mass production of watches in this country before the War. Apart from Rotherhams of Coventry who marketed an English watch, and Ingersoll who assembled substantial quantities of watches from imported movements and British cases, there were only a few specialist concerns at that time. During the War, Smith's began to produce watches (reaching a thousand a week by 1945) and the Ministry of Supply established a factory to manufacture jewels, but the main developments in watchmaking did not occur until after the War.

The promise of government assistance stimulated activity and in 1945, Smiths English Clocks[1] and Ingersoll jointly formed the Anglo-Celtic Watch Company. In the following year, they were joined by Vickers-Armstrongs in controlling the new company, but Vickers-Armstrongs sold their interest to the other two partners in 1954. The Anglo-Celtic factory began production in 1947, and although initially only pocket-watches were produced, wrist-watches were added in 1950. From this one factory, which claims to be the world's largest production unit for complete watches, can come about one-third of all Britain's watches.

A slightly smaller proportion of the total output is contributed by Timex (formerly U.K. Time), a subsidiary of the United States Time Corporation. With a factory near Dundee, this concern was producing around 400,000 wrist-watches a year in 1949, when Anglo-Celtic's output of pocket-watches was about 600,000. Another newcomer to the watch industry is Louis Newmark, with a factory at Croydon producing around 500,000 watches a year. In addition, Smith's decided to manufacture fully-jewelled lever watches at its Cheltenham factory in 1949, and output has recently been about 250,000 a year.

Three firms, 'whose projects and resources showed promise of success in building up a new watch making industry', had received government assistance by 1948,[2] and a feature of the new large-scale plants has been the banks of specialised Swiss machinery, much of it on hire from the Swiss makers or leased by the United Kingdom Government. On the other hand, there have been instances where specialised components produced in this country for the first time since the War have been sold to Switzerland.

Conclusions

Taking the watch and clock trade as a whole, there can be no doubt

[1] A subsidiary of S. Smith and Sons (England).

[2] *House of Commons Debates*, 25 March 1948, col. 367.

that Smith's were the largest unit in 1935, and were still the largest unit in 1951. Starting modestly in the early 1930's, they now possess fifteen factories producing jewels, springs, components, parts and complete watches and clocks. Although they have made some acquisitions in the past, by far the larger part of their growth is attributable to internal expansion. Undoubtedly that expansion has been very large in absolute terms, but it is by no means established that Smith's increased their share of the trade between 1935 and 1951. Their relative importance was probably greater in 1947 than in either 1935 or 1951 since, as we have seen, some new large-scale undertakings have entered the trade since 1947.

Among these new entrants, furthermore, are to be found the second and third largest units in 1951. Second to Smith's in that year was Westclox, with Anglo-Celtic (which since it was not a subsidiary of either Smith's or Ingersoll must be treated as a separate business unit) claiming third place, though neither started production until 1947. After Anglo-Celtic came Timex, John D. Francis and Louis Newmark, probably in that order as far as their share of the whole trade was concerned.

The need for large-scale production to achieve low costs has compelled the new entrants to start in a big way. The older enterprises in the trade, tied more firmly to craft methods and catering largely for specialised markets, have not been able to adopt the newer mass-production methods on which the growth of both firm and industry depended. Coming into the developing field of electric clock production in the 1930's, Smith's succeeded by a process of internal expansion over a period of years; other newcomers in the immediate pre-war years did less well, though several have survived. The most important post-war entrants to the trade, however, have either been backed by foreign capital or assisted by the Government, and it is doubtful to what extent they would have embarked on their ventures without such support. The increase in concentration in this trade owes little, therefore, to merger and acquisition; it is more closely associated with its transformation from a craft to a highly mechanised mass-production industry where both considerable capital and substantial sales promotion are conditions of success.

5. METALLIFEROUS MINES AND QUARRIES

The metalliferous mining industry today is almost entirely concerned with the extraction of iron ore and ironstone. The once prosperous lead and tin mining trades have declined almost to the point of extinction: together they accounted for less than a quarter of the total value of metalliferous mineral output in 1955, and still less in 1951. The production of iron ore, by deep mining or by opencast working, was responsible, on the other hand, for four-fifths of the total output value of the Metalliferous Mines and Quarries Trade of the Census of Production in 1951. Indeed, the specialist producers of iron ore and ironstone—a subdivision of the Trade recognised in 1951 but not in 1935—accounted for 85 per cent of its employment in 1951, though for little more than 75 per cent of its net output.

Although the total tonnage of iron ore and ironstone production increased by 30 per cent between 1935 and 1951, the value of that output (after adjustment for price changes) fell by some 5 per cent. The explanation lies in the changing pattern of British ore production, even in the last twenty years. Since 1935, hematite production in South Wales and Cumberland (with an iron content of 48–50 per cent) has accounted for a much smaller proportion of total output: 3 per cent in 1951 compared with nearer 10 per cent in 1935. Similarly, the output of Cleveland ores (with an iron content of 27·7 per cent) has fallen from 15 per cent of total output in 1935 to 7 per cent in 1951. Production from the fields of Scotland and Staffordshire ceased altogether during this period. On the other hand, there has been a very considerable increase in the production of the lower-grade ore-fields of Lincolnshire, Northamptonshire, Oxfordshire and Rutland: these areas contributed virtually 90 per cent of total output in 1951 compared with 75 per cent in 1935.

When the decline in the output of other metalliferous minerals is also taken into account, there can be no doubt that in terms of the value of its output, the Metalliferous Mines and Quarries Trade tended to contract during the 1935–51 period. Thus, it is estimated that, in terms of 1951 prices, the output of the principal products of the trade in 1951 was only half what it was in 1935. Since the establishments classified to the trade accounted for a very high proportion of the total output of its principal products in both years, the trade itself contracted by much the same extent.

The number of mines and quarries comprising the trade fell from 128 in 1930 to eighty-five in 1935 and to sixty-four in 1951, while the numbers employed also dropped from 10,850 in 1935 to around 8,000 in 1951. But while the trade has contracted between 1935 and 1951, the degree of concentration has increased. Employment concentration has risen from 32 to 50 per cent, and net output concentration from 27 to 41 per cent. Moreover, concentration at 58 per cent for employment and 55 per cent for net output was higher in 1951 among the specialist producers of iron ore and ironstone than for the trade as a whole. Indeed, it is clear from the data that the three largest units in the Iron Ore Sub-Trade were also the three largest units in the whole trade in 1951.

Although the changes in concentration in this trade may be explained almost entirely in terms of developments in the iron ore industry, it is interesting to note briefly the experience in tin and lead mining. In 1935 there were some 1,850 persons employed in tin mining, and well over 70 per cent of the total tin output came from three Cornish mines. By 1938 there were only four tin mines operating in Cornwall and Devon, and ten years later only two were active, with an output of 800 tons (metal content).[1]

Similarly, there were only four lead mines of any importance at work during 1935, and some 96 per cent of the output in that year came from two of them, one owned by Mill Close Mines (in Derbyshire) and the other by Halkyn District United Mines (in Flintshire).[2] In 1935 the output of the Mill Close mine was slightly greater than that of the Halkyn mine. During the War several mines closed down, including Mill Close, Halkyn and another, the Parc mine (also in Flintshire).[3] The more important mines operating in 1951 were accordingly the Greenside mine (owned by Goodlass Wall and Lead Industries), the Trecastill mine (in Flintshire) and the Coldberry mine in the North Pennines, from which came virtually the whole of the national output.

Iron ore mining and quarrying was, however, in the hands of a comparatively large number of concerns in 1935; there were over sixty undertakings listed as iron ore producers in *Ryland's Directory of the Coal, Iron, Steel, and Allied Trades* for that year. There was, however, a considerable degree of integration between iron ore mining and the production of iron and steel. There were, for example, fourteen business units which were engaged in both the Blast Furnaces and the Metalliferous Mines and Quarries Trades in 1935, accounting for no less than 54 per cent of the employment in the latter trade. Indeed, it has been estimated that 73 per cent of iron ore and ironstone was produced by these fourteen integrated businesses in 1935.[4]

In a number of cases, integration extended forward into steel smelting and rolling as well as backwards into iron ore mining. Seven concerns of the fourteen fall into this category: their share of the employment in the Metalliferous Mines and Quarries Trade amounted to 35 per cent in 1935. Finally, there were five concerns—Dorman Long and Company, Guest, Keen and Nettlefolds, Richard Thomas and Company, Stewarts and Lloyds, and the United Steel Companies—which operated as well in the Brick and Fireclay, Iron and Steel Foundries, Coal Mines, and Coke and By-Products trades, and together accounted for 33 per cent of the total employment in Metalliferous Mines and Quarries.[5]

[1] Ministry of Fuel and Power, *Report of the Mineral Development Committee*, Cmd. 7732 (London, H.M.S.O. 1949).

[2] *Fifteenth Annual Report of the Secretary for Mines for year ended 31 December 1935* (London, H.M.S.O. 1936), p. 45.

[3] Ministry of Fuel and Power, *op. cit.* pars. 180 and 187–9.

[4] Leak and Maizels, 'The Structure of British Industry', *J.R.S.S.* 1945, pp. 169–71. [5] *Ibid.*

The identity of two of the three largest units in the Metalliferous Mines and Quarries trade in 1935 has also been revealed as Dorman Long and the United Steel Companies.[1] There is little doubt that the third largest concern was Stewarts and Lloyds, which owned the Lloyds Ironstone Company in 1935, as well as a substantial (though not a controlling interest) in the Oxfordshire Ironstone Company. Dorman Long's main ore interests were in the Cleveland area of Yorkshire, where ore was gained by underground mining. United Steel, on the other hand, was principally interested in hematite production on the North-West coast (where its operations were conducted through the Beckermet Mining Company and the Bigrigg Mining Company) and in open-cast workings on the lower-grade deposits of the Midlands (through its subsidiary, Appleby-Frodingham Steel Company).

Among the important non-integrated iron ore producers in 1935 were three hematite producers—Millom and Askam Hematite Iron Company, the Hodbarrow Mining Company and the Glamorgan Hematite Iron Ore Company—as well as the Frodingham Ironstone Company, the Kettering Iron and Coal Company and the Midland Ironstone Company.

The change in the main centres of British iron ore production, occasioned by the gradual exhaustion of the higher-grade deposits, has greatly affected the control of the industry itself. The problem that it posed for United Steel, for example, has been stated in the following terms. During the latter part of the 1930's the Company began to take serious stock of its raw material supplies. For its Workington branch, 'the availability and quality of the local iron ore reserves had become a matter of serious concern. The older mines were becoming worked out, the quality of their ores was becoming more difficult and the blast furnaces had come to depend increasingly upon foreign supplies. After the 1930 depression the branch began to make systematic exploration of other possible local supplies, with a view to finding replacements for its reserves. Heavy costs were incurred on exploration. The hematite ore deposits are patchy and more difficult to assess than those of other deposits where the mineral lies in more continuous beds. Between 1933 and 1950, the Beckermet Company spent over £400,000 on drifting, exploration and surface boring. Further in 1937, the Company purchased from an exploring company the mining rights to work iron ore which had been proved in a large area adjoining the Beckermet mines.'[2]

It was the United Steel Companies' own prospecting that proved the existence of the ore, and led to the exploitation of the new Haile Moor mine. 'It was realised that the new mine would not then be an economic

[1] Leak and Maizels, pp. 158–9.

[2] P. W. S. Andrews and E. Brunner, *Capital Development in Steel: a Study of the United Steel Companies Ltd* (Oxford, Blackwell, 1951), p. 225.

proposition by itself, but the possibility of not being able to import supplies and the importance of steel supplies in war-time were taken as justifying working known reserves of any size almost regardless of cost.'[1] The Haile Moor mine came into operation in 1942, but the great bulk of the war-time output still came from Beckermet.

The War proved the importance of hematite ore production and accelerated the rate at which domestic reserves were exploited. Production at the North-West coast deposits increased from nearly 680,000 tons in 1938 to a war-time peak of over 700,000 tons (though this was 140,000 tons less than the 1935 output). In 1947, by comparison, only 365,000 tons were produced and only three companies with six mines were in operation there. Output at the Llanharry mine of the Glamorgan Hematite Iron Ore Company similarly increased from 188,000 tons in 1938 to a war-time peak in 1940 of nearly 234,000 tons; by 1947, however, output had fallen to 95,000 tons.[2]

The main activity in locating and exploiting new reserves was, however, already concentrated in the pre-war years on the belt of leaner ironstones in the Midlands. United Steel was active here in the 1930's, developing through the Appleby-Frodingham branch the Colsterworth and Cottesmore open-cast workings in Northamptonshire. 'The developments at Colsterworth, because of its heavy overburden, required relatively heavy outlays on new machines to strip the surface . . . [while] a good deal of smaller expenditure was required continuously at the ore mines as development and extraction of ores proceeded in step with the requirements of the branch.'[3] During the war period, new ore-quarries in South Lincolnshire and Rutland were developed and output reached new heights. But the more extended quarrying of the ore-fields during the War necessitated the earlier introduction of underground mining, as distinct from the previous open-cast operations, since the more easily available ore was beginning to be worked out.

To complete the account of developments in the United Steel Companies' ore interests, mention must be made of its purchase of the Frodingham Ironstone Mines, 'one of the last "non-captive" (i.e. not already tied to iron-works) ore reserves in the North Lincolnshire field. Already an important supplier of the Appleby-Frodingham branch, its acquisition brought a considerable increase in the reserves owned by the Company.'[4]

The result of these various developments was to raise United Steel's output of iron ore from over 1·25 million tons in 1937–8 to 1·95 million tons at the end of the War and to 3·25 million tons by 1951. Its share of the total national output rose at the same time from less than one-tenth

[1] Andrews and Brunner, *op. cit.* p. 225.
[2] Ministry of Fuel and Power, *op. cit.* par. 174.
[3] Andrews and Brunner, *op. cit.* pp. 227–8.
[4] *Ibid.* p. 316.

before the War to one-eighth at the end of the War and afterwards to over one-fifth.

The activities of Stewarts and Lloyds since 1935 show a similar concern to safeguard their ore supplies by acquiring additional reserves. The development of the Corby ore-fields was already well under way in 1935; output there had increased from 632,000 tons in 1932 to nearly 1 million tons in 1935. By 1938, however, the Corby fields were producing 1·7 million tons, or nearly 15 per cent of the national output in terms of tonnage. Shortly before the outbreak of war, Stewarts and Lloyds acquired the Stanton Ironworks Company which, apart from its important interests in cast-iron and spun-iron pipe production, owned large ore resources in Northants. Like United Steel, Stewarts and Lloyds increased the rate of ore production dramatically during the War; up to the end of 1944 its output averaged more than 500,000 tons a month, or more than 50 per cent greater than in 1938. Finally, in 1945, Stewarts and Lloyds acquired full control of Bowne and Shaw (with which it had been associated since the Stanton take-over in 1939) with extensive ironstone quarries in Derbyshire.

Although the war-time level of output was not maintained in the post-war period, Stewarts and Lloyds' 1949 production amounted to 4·5 million tons, or approximately one-third of the national production. It is almost certain that its share remained at this level in 1951.

In contrast to United Steel and Stewarts and Lloyds, Dorman Long does not appear to have increased its iron ore interests during the 1935–51 period.[1] Although it appears likely that it remained as one of the three largest units in the trade in 1951, its share was probably considerably less than in 1935.

The result has been a change in the order of importance of the three largest units between 1935 and 1951. Undoubtedly Stewarts and Lloyds had gained first place with their one-third share of total iron ore production in 1951, with United Steel Companies remaining in second place and Dorman Long moving from first to third place.

In the denationalisation of the iron and steel industry United Steel Companies acquired a further stake in iron ore production when it obtained from the Realisation Agency, at a cost of £331,000, the whole of the issued share capital of the Santon Mining Company, which owned large reserves of iron ore contiguous with United Steel's existing reserves. As a consequence, United Steel was able to record an iron ore output in 1955 (from the Frodingham and Northants fields) of nearly 4 million tons, or just under one-quarter of the total national output, compared with Stewarts and Lloyds' 5·1 million tons, or 31 per cent.

[1] In 1952, Dorman Long acquired Lingdale Ironstone Mines, which formerly belonged to Pease and Partners, from the Iron and Steel Realisation Agency.

Conclusion

The change in concentration in the Metalliferous Mines and Quarries trade between 1935 and 1951 can be wholly explained in terms of the concentration-change in the iron ore industry. The three firms which controlled 27 per cent of the trade's net output in 1935 were steel concerns which controlled their own supplies of iron ore. The fact that those three concerns had increased their combined share to 41 per cent by 1951 testifies to their success in safeguarding and augmenting those supplies, partly through acquisition of formerly independent concerns, and partly by increased exploitation of reserves which they already possessed or subsequently acquired.

Moreover, the Metalliferous Mines and Quarries trade tended to contract between 1935 and 1951, although subsequently iron ore production had risen in tonnage terms by more than one-eighth by 1957. In an extractive industry where reserves are limited, mines or other workings have to be abandoned as reserves are exhausted; consequently the number of concerns in the trade will probably continue to fall. Besides, it is not an easy trade to enter even if mineral rights are possessed. Even open-cast working of iron ore is becoming increasingly costly, for the largest types of draglines which admittedly can 'extract ore that would at one time have been written off as inaccessible except by deep mining . . . cost nearly £750,000'.[1] In any case, though 90 per cent of iron ore production is by open-cast working at the present moment, recourse to underground mining remains but a matter of time.

In such circumstances, the future may see a continuing tendency for concentration to increase, partly as the result of concerns going out of production as reserves are exhausted or operations become uneconomic, and partly through the extended production of the established concerns with reserves in hand and the financial resources necessary to exploit them.

6. LEAD

A century ago more lead was mined in Britain than in the rest of Europe put together, and the lead-smelting trade was thriving and important. The decline of the home lead-mining industry was accompanied, however, by a fall in domestic smelter production. To meet the growing demand for lead—and the range of its uses is very large—more and more lead had to be imported from abroad, mainly in the form of pig lead. Consequently, in the decade before World War II, domestic smelter production was responsible for little more than 4 per cent of the total lead smelter consumption; since the War it has been less than 1 per cent.

[1] PEP, 'Britain's Iron Ore Supplies', *Planning*, vol. 22, no. 395, 9 April 1956, p. 56.

Lead is used in the production of certain chemical compounds—such as white lead, red lead and litharge—as well as in the metallic state, but the Lead sub-division of the Non-Ferrous Metals (Smelting, Rolling, etc.) Trade covers only the metallic lead products. Apart from unwrought lead (pig lead, ingots, bars, slabs and cakes) which accounted for nearly one-third of the total sales of the principal products of the Lead Sub-Trade in 1951, the most important among the other of those products were antimonial and tinny lead, lead sheet and lead pipes.

Despite the variety of metallic lead products, the Lead Sub-Trade is comparatively small. In 1951, it accounted for less than 6 per cent of the net output, and 3 per cent of the total employment, of the Non-Ferrous Metals Trade. Moreover, the importance of the sub-trade has undoubtedly declined between 1935 and 1951. After adjusting for price-changes, it would appear that the total sales of the principal products of the sub-trade in 1951 were only two-thirds of what they were in 1935.

While the production of the principal products of the Lead Sub-Trade by establishments outside the Non-Ferrous Metals Trade was unimportant in both 1935 and 1951, there has been a decrease in the proportion of the total production in establishments classified to the Lead Sub-Trade from 94 per cent in 1935 to 86 per cent in 1951.

The decline in the importance of the trade, as well as its lower degree of exclusiveness, is reflected in other of the Census data. The number of establishments in the sub-trade fell from seventy-three in 1935 to forty-eight in 1951, while employment decreased from nearly 3,900 in 1935 to 3,200 in 1951, a fall of 17·5 per cent.

Concentration in the lead trade increased between 1935 and 1951 from 30 to 69 per cent in terms of net output, and from 38 to 53 per cent in terms of employment, while the number of business units fell from forty-six to forty in the same period.

In order to identify the principal concerns and the extent of their interests, it is necessary to examine the various sections of the industry in turn. The first stage in the production of lead is the smelting of lead concentrates, a continuous operation generally conducted in blast furnaces after the concentrates have been roasted to remove most of the sulphur they contain. The semi-finished product of smelting is known as base bullion, which contains silver and other impurities which are removed by refining to produce a commercial lead. After refining, the lead may be cast into pigs and sold as such, or in the form of bars, slabs, cakes, etc. Since lead is easily recoverable from scrap, there is also a considerable amount of secondary production, while the alloying of lead with antimony or tin is also an important part of the trade. The fabrication of lead products in the form of sheets, pipes, lead shot, etc. is carried on by a larger number of producers than are the earlier stages of production, but in the main and with one important exception, fabrication is conducted by concerns which are not engaged in smelting or refining.

In 1935, domestic smelter production was higher than for many years previously: the output was nearly 26,000 tons compared with less than 11,000 tons in 1929 and 6,500 tons in 1933. The lead smelter capacity, however, was very much greater than the output, the level of operation being less than 30 per cent of capacity in 1935. There were three main smelters in that year: Goodlass Wall and Lead Industries, H. J. Enthoven and Sons, and the Mill Close Mines.

The largest of the three principal smelters was Goodlass Wall; its smelting capacity was estimated at 60,000 tons a year (or two-thirds of the total United Kingdom capacity) in 1933.[1] Goodlass Wall's interest in the lead industry was acquired in 1930 when it merged with Associated Lead Manufacturers to form Goodlass Wall and Lead Industries. In 1935, Goodlass Wall numbered amongst its subsidiaries such concerns as Cookson Lead and Antimony Company; Locke, Blackett and Company; Alexander Fergusson and Company; and Foster, Blackett and James. In fact, Goodlass Wall already possessed in 1935 interests in the lead industry which extended far beyond the smelting stage.

The second largest smelting capacity in 1935 was possessed by Mill Close Mines (in which a substantial interest was held by the Consolidated Gold Fields of South Africa). Mill Close was one of the largest producers of lead ore in Britain, but the greater part of its output was exported before it installed a smelting plant with a maximum capacity of 30,000 tons a year. It has been stated that the whole of the large increase in smelter production during 1935 was due to the operation of this new plant of Mill Close.[2]

The third most important lead smelter in 1935 was almost certainly H. J. Enthoven and Sons (a subsidiary of the French Penarroya concern) whose Rotherhithe smelter had a maximum annual capacity in 1933 of 11,000 tons. There were, however, a number of other concerns which smelted varying quantities of lead (including secondary), among them Capper, Pass and Son; St Helens' Smelting Company; and Quirk, Barton and Burns (St Helens).

There was similarly a high degree of concentration in lead refining in 1935. The concern with the largest refining capacity, though not necessarily the greatest output, was the Britannia Lead Company, a subsidiary of the Mining Trust which was also largely interested in Mount Isa Mines of North Queensland from which Britannia drew its bullion lead.[3]

[1] Imperial Institute, *Lead* (London, H.M.S.O. 1933), p. 44.

[2] A. Butts, 'Lead' in *The Mineral Industry during 1935* (New York, McGraw-Hill, 1936), p. 382.

[3] In 1951, Mount Isa Mines gained control of the Mining Trust and has since itself become a subsidiary of the American Smelting and Refining Company.

Britannia Lead commenced operations at its Northfleet refinery in November 1931, but although its plant had a capacity of 75,000 tons a year, production was not reckoned to be much more than 25,000 tons.

The refining capacity of Goodlass Wall at 65,000 tons a year ran Britannia a close second, and its actual output may have exceeded Britannia's. Once again, H. J. Enthoven claimed third place with a refining capacity of some 30,000 tons a year, and among the other smaller refiners were to be found Capper Pass and St Helens' Smelting, the latter's main interest being in the production of antimonial and tinny lead.

At the fabricating end of the industry, Goodlass Wall was interested in the production of lead foil, sheets, shot and pipes. Among the other more important lead fabricators were Betts' British Foil Factories, George Farmiloe and Son (lead sheets), T. and W. Farmiloe (lead sheets and pipes), Quirk, Barton and Company (lead sheets, foil, strip and pipes), W. G. Frith (lead foil), British Lead Mills (sheets), and I.C.I. (lead sheet and pipes, mainly for its own use).

In view of the range and size of its interests, it is certain that Goodlass Wall ranked as the largest unit in the lead sub-trade in 1935. The identity of the other two largest units is less certain, but it would appear probable that H. J. Enthoven and Britannia Lead would have occupied the next two places.

Although lead consumption increased sharply between 1935 and the outbreak of World War II, domestic smelter production fell away equally sharply. Against the 26,000 tons production of 1935, output was under 11,000 tons in 1938, and during the War it fell still further until in the post-war period it has been as low as 2,000–2,500 tons. Lead consumption also fell during the War—in 1944, it was 17 per cent below the 1938 level—and had not returned to the pre-war level by 1951.

The restrictions on imports necessitated by the War tended to increase the importance of secondary production, and refinery capacity was increased.[1] It is unlikely, however, that the refinery capacity of the principal refiners—Goodlass Wall, Britannia Lead and H. J. Enthoven—changed greatly between 1935 and 1951, but their combined share of the total output may well have increased.[2] On the other hand, the smelter capacity has certainly declined: the Mill Close Mines smelter, for example, has gone out of production.

For unwrought lead in pigs, ingots, blocks, bars, slabs and cakes, production and available supplies for consumption were lower in 1951 than 1935, but domestic production was responsible for 40 per cent of con-

[1] 'Lead and its Manifold Uses', *Glasgow Herald Trade Review, January 1955*, p. 107.

[2] Britannia's output of refined lead is reported to have been 35,300 tons in 1949 (40 per cent more than in 1935) and possibly as much as 30 per cent of total United Kingdom output.

sumption in 1951 compared with 30 per cent in 1935. While Goodlass Wall undoubtedly maintained (if it did not increase) its predominant interest in these products over the period, there were two concerns which were becoming increasingly important by 1951.[1] One was British Lead Mills (now a subsidiary of Firth Cleveland) which at its Welwyn Garden City plant was both smelting and refining lead and producing tin/lead alloys as well as sheets. The other was Platt Metals, with a plant at Enfield for secondary production having a capacity in the region of 30,000 tons.

The number of establishments producing sheet lead almost certainly fell between 1935 and 1951, and both production and supplies available were halved during the same period. The decrease in the production and available supplies of lead pipes has been even greater. Although British Lead Mills has also become a more important producer of these two products it is doubtful whether Goodlass Wall's share of the trade has suffered as a result.

Although the lead industry as a whole was declining between 1935 and 1951, the general impression is that the period was marked by a considerable mobility among the concerns comprising the industry. While some of the more important producers of 1935 (such as Mill Close Mines) have disappeared, newcomers have entered the industry (such as Platt Metals) while others (such as British Lead Mills) have increased in importance.

The general absence of production data for individual concerns precludes any attempt to estimate the division of the trade between them. On the other hand, it can be fairly confidently stated that Goodlass Wall and Lead Industries was the largest concern in both years. In fact it is probable that the identity of the three largest units was the same in 1951 as in 1935, and that alongside Goodlass Wall stood Britannia Lead and H. J. Enthoven at both dates.

Conclusion

It would appear fairly clear that mergers and acquisitions have played a negligible role in the increased concentration in the lead trade between 1935 and 1951. There is no evidence either of any technological change that might have prompted the plant and unit concentration that sometimes accompanies it. Entry into the trade on a small scale, particularly at the refining end, is not particularly costly, and the trade is generally regarded as highly competitive.

The fact is that lead was a contracting industry during the 1935–51

[1] In 1949, the subsidiaries of Goodlass Wall concerned in the production of metals and their compounds were merged in a single subsidiary, which was given the previously used name of Associated Lead Manufacturers.

period, and in such circumstances, the larger firms may sometimes possess certain advantages which assist them in acquiring a larger share of the trade. Quite apart from their greater staying power, some of the trading practices of the larger units in the lead trade have probably worked to their advantage. Not only does Goodlass Wall, for example, sell a reasonably complete range of lead products and possess a sufficient number of plants to cover the country, but it is a practice of the trade for suppliers to conclude arrangements with their customers for the return of scrap. Since secondary production comprises the bulk of production, adequate supplies of scrap are a necessary condition of operation, and the arrangements between them and their customers stand the largest units in good stead.

In conclusion, therefore, it appears that the rise in concentration in the lead trade between 1935 and 1951 is principally attributable to the natural growth of some of the largest units, or possibly even mainly to the growth of the largest of them, Goodlass Wall and Lead Industries.

7. BUILDING BRICKS

Building bricks form part of the Brick and Fireclay Trade of the Census of Production,[1] and, with a labour-force of more than 39,000, the sub-trade accounted for slightly more than half of the Trade's total employment in 1951. The employment of the sub-trade in 1951 was 28 per cent lower than in 1935, while the volume of production of the principal products of the sub-trade was nearly one-fifth lower. Since 1951, however, the production of bricks has increased to much nearer the 1935 level, though it remains substantially below the 1938 total.

It is customary to distinguish several types of bricks and two main groups of producers. The most common type of brick is made from clay and shale; in 1951, this type accounted for 96 per cent by quantity and value of the total output of building bricks. Bricks made from siliceous sand and slaked lime are much less important. Among the clay and shale bricks, three distinct types are recognised: common, engineering and facing bricks. But more relevant is the division of the clay and shale brick-makers into two groups of undertakings: the Fletton and the non-Fletton sections of the industry.

The non-Fletton section of the industry is the most diversified and widely scattered, and in 1951 it accounted for 54 per cent of the total quantity of building bricks produced and 60 per cent of their total value. Included in the non-Fletton section are 'a considerable number of relatively small undertakings which, for one reason or another, have not been

[1] The full description of the Census sub-trade is: 'Specialist producers of building bricks (including flooring and wall partition blocks)'.

greatly affected by the trend towards mechanisation', as well as others as 'efficient as any group in the industry in skilful management and, so far as the nature of their raw material permits, in the employment of modern machinery and production methods'.[1] But large and small, efficient and not so efficient, in the non-Fletton section of the industry all hold the view that the brick market is 'essentially a regional affair', so that manufacture is differentiated to meet local building needs and traditions.

By contrast, the Fletton producer aims at a national rather than a regional market, although originally this group of producers with their works in the vicinities of Peterborough and Bedford developed as a typical regional section of the industry serving the London market. The Fletton producers had several advantages which led them to seek a national market. First, their costs of production were comparatively low since the raw material of the areas concerned had a carbonaceous content which permitted full burning of bricks with less fuel, as well as a high degree of mechanisation. Secondly, 'the Fletton brick weighs less than the average common brick' and that fact 'combined with the quantities involved has permitted advantageous transport terms and consequently widespread distribution'.[2] The result has been that the Fletton makers have become increasingly important, save for the period of the War when restrictions on transport worked to their disadvantage. In 1938, the Fletton producers were already responsible for nearly one-third of the total sales of building bricks; by 1951, they had increased their share to nearly one-half.

The decline in the size of the sub-trade between 1935 and 1951 has been reflected in the number of its establishments, which fell from over 1,000 in 1935 to less than 650 in 1951. The prime cause of this fall was the concentration of the industry that took place during World War II. Between 1938 and the end of 1941, the number of undertakings fell from 907 to 604, and the number of brickworks operated from 1,147 to 781.[3] The works which were closed during this period represented approximately one-eighth of the national output in 1938, but since the level of production in 1941 was only two-thirds of 1938, it is clear that the works which remained in operation ran at far below capacity. Since the end of the War there has been a severe labour shortage, with the result that many of the plants have remained closed or have been diverted to other purposes.

The physical concentration of production through the closure of brickworks has obviously contributed to the increase in unit concentration

[1] Ministry of Works and Buildings, *Second Report of the Committee on the Brick Industry* (London, H.M.S.O. 1944), par. 90.

[2] *Ibid.* par. 91.

[3] Ministry of Works and Buildings, *First Report of the Committee on the Brick Industry* (London, H.M.S.O. 1942), par. 10.

which rose between 1935 and 1951 from 14 to 30 per cent by employment, and from 19 to 32 per cent by net output, while the total number of business units fell from 672 to 397.

During the inter-war years, combination was common in the brick trade, of which the most striking example is provided by the London Brick Company. In 1923 two brickmaking concerns—B. J. Forder and Son and the London Brick Company—together with five other companies, were merged, and in the next six years the new combine acquired the assets, works or businesses of another ten brickmaking undertakings. By 1931, the London Brick Company and Forders had a productive capacity of 1,200 million bricks a year, equivalent to more than one-fifth of the current national production. It employed some 5,400 workpeople in its twenty works, and was far and away the largest brickmaking concern in this country.

Despite the general expansion in the industry, the London Brick Company (as it became known in 1936) maintained its one-fifth share of the total trade. In that year, it announced that its production amounted to just over 1,500 million bricks, while its acquisition of the Bedford Brick Company, whose Stewartby plant had an output of 80 million in 1936 (soon to be extended to a capacity of 125 million), enabled it to keep pace with the increased output of the industry as a whole. The importance of London Brick was, however, even greater in the Fletton section of the industry, where its share of total production before the War was reputed to be as high as 70 per cent.

Among the other more important producers in the Fletton group were Eastwoods (and its subsidiary, Eastwoods Flettons), Flettons, Bletchley Flettons, and the Marston Valley Brick Company. The Eastwoods brickmaking interests enabled it to claim to be the largest stock-brickmaker in the country in 1935, as well as owning the monopoly-rights for the Fletton section of the industry of a patented process for the manufacture of multi-coloured facing bricks.

In the non-Fletton section of the industry there were several relatively large concerns, though none of them approached the size of London Brick. One such was the Yorkshire Brick Company which, after acquiring eight companies between 1920 and 1933, operated eleven brick- and tileworks, and claimed to be the largest manufacturer in this country of high-grade architectural and engineering bricks. Similarly, the merger of the National Brick Company and the Star Brick and Tile Company in 1934 gave the resulting combine four works in the Newport area and two in Leicestershire, with a total capacity of 33 million bricks a year. Mention must also be made of the Allied Brick and Tile Works (formed in 1934) and of the Sussex Brick Company (1927) which quadrupled its labour-force between 1903 and 1928 and in 1929 acquired Thomas

Mitchell and Sons (Guildford) followed by the Dorking Brick Company in 1935.

The process of amalgamation and acquisition has continued during and since the War. In the early war years, London Brick acquired two brickmaking concerns and the Aylesford Pottery Company, and in 1950 it acquired a brickworks from Bletchley Flettons. In that year, London Brick claimed a total brickmaking capacity of 1,750 million a year (compared with 17 million in 1900), equivalent to one-quarter of the national output of bricks.

The Yorkshire Brick Company also made a number of acquisitions after 1935, while Sussex Brick increased its total labour-force to nearly 1,000 by 1953 compared with 400 a quarter of a century before. Similarly Eastwoods, with three Fletton works and five stock-brickworks, have claimed that their outputs are substantially in excess of pre-war.

Although the increased output of London Brick and Eastwoods in a trade where total output has fallen would alone account for a large part of the rise in concentration, there is a further factor which must be taken into account. Since bricks can be made from the shale and clay produced at many collieries along with the coal, it had long been the custom of colliery companies to operate their own brickworks, selling what they did not need in the open market. The extent of this activity is indicated by the fact that 117 coalmining concerns were engaged in the Brick and Fireclay Trade in 1935, and that together they accounted for 15 per cent of the Trade's employment. It is doubtful, however, whether any of the colliery concerns were sufficiently important as brickmakers to warrant comparison with the largest specialist makers in 1935.

The situation was transformed by the provisions of the Coal Industry Nationalisation Act, 1946, whereby the National Coal Board was given the option of acquiring the brickworks owned by colliery companies. By 1951 the N.C.B. was operating seventy-five brickworks with a total output of 473 million bricks, or 8 per cent of the national output in that year. On the average, the N.C.B. sells about three-quarters of all the bricks it produces, so it is clear that it can be regarded as second only to London Brick in the brickmaking industry. Thus, by centralising the ownership of the colliery brickworks in the N.C.B., the Nationalisation Act has contributed substantially to the observed increase in the degree of concentration in the Census sub-trade.

Conclusion

Several different factors have contributed to the increased concentration in the building bricks trade between 1935 and 1951. First, while the trade itself has not expanded, there has been a tendency for the largest concerns in the industry to grow. Acquisition and amalgamation have played some part in that growth, though less in the 1935–51 period than in the inter-war years and possibly less in the case of the largest units than the medium-sized concerns. Secondly, the war-time concentration of production, involving the closure of hundreds of works, has greatly reduced the number of units as well as the number of establishments. Thirdly, the nationalisation of the coal mines has also reduced the number of separate business units in the trade (though not necessarily the number of establishments), and may indeed have made the largest contribution to the increased concentration.

For all the changes that have taken place, concentration is still low in this trade, although it is certainly higher in the expanding Fletton section than in the older and more traditional non-Fletton section. In addition, the brick industry has long been characterised by price-fixing associations, most of them regional, but including the nationally organised Pressed Brick Makers' Association (whose five members were stated in 1948 to control 100 per cent of Fletton brick production) and the Sand Lime Brick Manufacturers' Association (with twenty-six members and 100 per cent of production).[1] On the other hand, the national market gained by the Fletton makers has introduced a disturbing element of competition into the markets of the non-Fletton producers, though the effectiveness of that competition is qualified by the transport costs which the Fletton producers must bear.

It is difficult, therefore, to assess the overall effect of the changes in the structure of the industry on the market for its products, but it is doubtful, particularly when the development of substitute building materials is taken into account, whether the trade is less competitive than it was before the War.

8. METAL BOXES AND CONTAINERS

The oldest part of the metal boxes and containers trade[2] is the making of tin boxes, which was carried on by generations of tinsmiths before the introduction of highly mechanised and automatic methods of production during this century. A more recent development has been the manufacture of open-top cans, particularly as containers for processed food, the output of which has risen from about 150 millions in 1924 to 600 millions in 1935 and to more than 3,000 millions in the middle 'fifties. In addition, aluminium has joined tinplate, blackplate, and terneplate as a

[1] Ministry of Works, *The Distribution of Building Materials and Components* (1948), app. II, p. 56.

[2] The full description of the trade which in the Census forms part of the Hardware, Hollow-ware and Sheet Metal Trade was 'the specialist producers of metal boxes and containers (excluding composite containers partly of metal)'; in 1935, it was more simply 'Tin boxes and containers'.

material from which boxes and containers may be made, although its importance as an alternative to tin is limited, the sales of aluminium containers representing less than one-eighth of the total sales of all types in 1951.

It is convenient, therefore, to distinguish two sections of the metal boxes and containers trade: (*a*) the manufacture of 'open-top' cans for processed food, and (*b*) the manufacture of 'general-line' containers for products other than processed food, products which may range from polishes and tobacco to biscuits and toffees.[1]

The production data on metal boxes and containers in the Census are not comprehensive, since they do not generally 'include the output of general-line or open-top containers by manufacturers of canned foods, syrup, polish, biscuits, etc., who also manufacture the containers in which they pack their products'.[2] For 1948, it has been estimated that this omitted production figure was probably in the region of 80,000 tons, or about 20–25 per cent of the total output of tin boxes and containers in that year. Similarly, the Census of Production states that in 1951 some 37,600 tons of tin boxes and containers were made for their own use by firms in five food trades,[3] equivalent to 16 per cent of the output made for sale by establishments classified to the Hardware, Hollow-ware and Sheet Metal Trade. When the additional output for their own use by firms in other food and non-food trades is also taken into account, it is possible that the output for sale included in the Hardware, Hollow-ware and Sheet Metal Trade represented 75–80 per cent of the total output of tin boxes and containers in 1951.

The Census data refer, therefore, only to what may be termed the commercial side of the trade—that is, production for sale—and in assessing the changes in the trade's structure, the proportion of output outside the trade must be borne in mind. Comparison of the output of metal boxes and containers between 1935 and 1951 is, however, complicated for two reasons: first, that the 1935 Census gave only one figure for tin boxes and containers, and second, that there is an element of duplication in the output data.[4] For these reasons, it is best to indicate the expansion of the trade in terms of its employment, which has risen by more than one-quarter from 20,560 in 1935 to 26,120 in 1951. The number of establishments in the trade was the same at the end as at the beginning of this period, and though the average size of those 113 establishments increased, they still employed on average less than 250 persons each in 1951.

[1] John Ryan, 'Statistics of Tins and Cans', *Journal of the Royal Statistical Society* (Series A, General), vol. 115, part 4, 1952, p. 475.

[2] Ryan, p. 475.

[3] The Trades were Milk Products; Cocoa, Chocolate and Sugar Confectionery; Sugar and Glucose; Biscuit; and Preserved Fruit and Vegetables.

[4] See Ryan, p. 475.

The number of business units in the metal boxes and containers trade has, however, increased from seventy-three in 1935 to eighty-three in 1951. Concentration has also increased between 1935 and 1951, though the extent of the rise is masked by the fact that the 1951 data refer to the share of the four largest units. Thus, employment concentration rose from 45 per cent for the three largest units in 1935 to 60 per cent for the four largest in 1951, and net output concentration from 51 to 61 per cent. A feature of the trade is the multi-plant operation among the largest concerns; thus, the four largest units operated twenty-three of the 113 establishments in 1951, while the remaining ninety establishments were shared between seventy-nine other business units.

By far the biggest producer of metal boxes and containers since the beginning of the 'thirties has been the Metal Box Company. Formed in 1921 by the amalgamation of four concerns, Metal Box acquired seven important firms—I. A. Hodgson and Company (Newcastle), E. T. Gee and Sons (Liverpool), Edward C. Barlow and Sons (London), T. F. Boutle and Company (London), British Sure Seal Company (London), Excel Canister Company (London) and G. H. Williamson and Sons (Worcester)—before becoming a public company in 1930.

This combination of interests was partly in response to the invasion of the British market by an American firm; for in 1929 the American Can Company (acting in conjunction with an associate company, the Thermokept Corporation) formed the British Can Company to acquire an old-established Liverpool business. Armed with the exclusive right to the patents and special machinery of its American parents, British Can was intended to capture a substantial part of the British market for the old-type containers as well as open-top cans.

To meet this threat, Metal Box concluded an agreement in 1930 with the Continental Can Company of America (American Can's principal rival), whereby it received the exclusive right to use its methods, patents, and processes in the British Isles as well as in certain overseas countries. This agreement ran originally until 1945, but it was then extended for a further twenty-one years. The importance of this agreement to Metal Box lay in the fact that the patents and processes referred to the manufacture of open-top cans for processed food, and in this developing field Metal Box assumed the lead from the start. In 1930, it was already producing some 23 million cans for fruit and vegetable canning,[1] and in 1931 it opened its first specialised food can factory at Worcester to raise production to 65 million cans.[2]

It soon became apparent, however, that British Can was finding it

[1] Prospectus of Metal Box Company Ltd, May 1932.

[2] Chairman's Speech, Ordinary General Meeting, Metal Box Company Ltd, for the year 1952–3.

difficult to obtain a sufficiently large share of the market to absorb its output. As a consequence, Metal Box was able to obtain control of British Can and its three factories in Liverpool, Manchester and Acton, as well as obtaining an undertaking from American Can 'not to become interested in or to assist can-making plants in the British Isles for 21 years'.[1]

By 1935, Metal Box had made a few minor acquisitions to raise the number of its subsidiaries to sixteen, operating eighteen factories in all. While it claimed to be 'by far the largest group of companies engaged in metal box manufacturing and printing',[2] it is impossible to be precise about its share of the trade in 1935, but certainly it would not have been less than 35–40 per cent.

It is equally difficult to determine the identity of the other two largest units in 1935, but among the claimants for this distinction must have been Reads of Liverpool, F. Robinson and Company of Hull, Barringer, Wallis and Manners, and the two principal Scottish manufacturers, John Drummond and Sons of Greenock, and Wilkie and Paul of Edinburgh.

Early in 1936, Metal Box acquired F. Robinson and Company and three years later added Barringer, Wallis and Manners to its group of companies. By the end of the inter-war period, Metal Box was probably responsible for one-third of the total output of general-line containers and 50–60 per cent of 'open-top' cans. Since then Metal Box has increased its output of metal boxes and containers by opening new factories rather than by acquiring other concerns, and indeed acquisitions have been insignificant compared with new building during its history.

The development of the industry was hampered by the shortage of tinplate throughout the post-war period: indeed, it was stated in 1952 that 'the tin-box industry has sufficient excess capacity both in the U.K. and abroad to fabricate the increased supply of tinplate' which would come from the new tinplate plants, since 'the true demand in most countries for tinplate and for tin boxes has been frustrated by quotas and packaging restrictions'.[3] Even so, some indication of Metal Box's expansion may be gained from the fact that its output of open-top cans rose from 100 millions in 1932[4] to more than 1,300 millions in 1949–50.

In 1951, Metal Box was operating six open-top can factories, while general-line containers were produced in thirteen other factories as well as in four of the open-top can factories. It would appear, therefore, that Metal Box accounted for nineteen of the twenty-three establishments belonging to the four largest units in the trade. On this basis, it may be esti-

[1] Prospectus of Metal Box Company Ltd, May 1932.

[2] *Ibid.* [3] Ryan, p. 494.

[4] Prospectus of Metal Box Company Ltd, May 1932.

mated that Metal Box alone was responsible for at least half of the employment of the trade in 1951.

In 1955, Metal Box reported that more than 2,000 million food cans had been produced in 1954–5, an increase of 20 per cent compared with the previous year. In that year, the new Wisbech factory had come into production, to be followed in 1955–6 by another at Westhoughton, while yet another was being erected at Rochester. So, in 1955–6 Metal Box was operating eight open-top can factories, while general-line containers were being produced in fifteen plants, including a newly-opened factory at Leicester for confectionery and biscuit containers.

The identity of the other two largest units in this trade, which is 'ill-provided with statistical information',[1] is obscure. The leading contenders are Reads of Liverpool, Huntley, Boorne and Stevens, A. Lloyd and Sons, E. Illingworth, Barnsley Canister Company, John Feaver, and F. Francis and Sons. At all events, Metal Box is clearly the dominant concern in the trade, particularly in the commercial manufacture of open-top cans.

Conclusion

The principal concern in the trade, the Metal Box Company, was formed by a merger of four old-established tin-box concerns, and acquisition played a major part in its early growth. The greatest contribution to Metal Box's development lay, however, not in the number of concerns it acquired but in the agreement that it concluded with Continental Can, whereby it obtained the benefit of the experience and technical advice of one of the leading American manufacturers of open-top cans, which enabled it to expand with the development of food canning.

Without this access to the developing expertise of the American industry, it is doubtful whether Metal Box would have grown so fast, although it has always been possible for other firms to obtain American machinery from other makers. At the same time, Metal Box has worked hard for its success, and has played a major role in developing the food canning industry in this country by its research and advisory facilities. Indeed, it has lost no opportunity for promoting new uses for containers which, through large-scale production and specialisation, it is able to produce economically. Similarly, Metal Box has enjoyed a substantial advantage over other domestic manufacturers in the geographical spread of its productive units, partly due to the early mergers but maintained by subsequent new building.

The dominant position of Metal Box is qualified by the production of containers for their own use by a number of leading processed-food, bis-

[1] Ryan, p. 477.

cuit, and polish manufacturers. Its position, on the other hand, has been strengthened both by the large financial resources required to embark on the manufacture of open-top cans, and the fact that for the greater part of the 1935–51 period there has been a shortage of tinplate, which has restricted entry into the tin-boxes-and-containers section of the trade. It is clear that the rise in concentration in this trade is directly associated with the growth of Metal Box and that this growth has been influenced greatly by technological factors and an ability to create and satisfy new uses for metal containers.

9. TINPLATE

For a generation or so at the end of the nineteenth century, Britain was the undisputed leader of the world's tinplate industry. From the mills of South Wales, where the industry had been very largely based from the beginning, came 85 per cent of the world's tinplate. Three-quarters of Britain's output, in fact, was exported, and among the principal customers was the United States. By 1913, however, Britain had been replaced by the United States as the leading tinplate producer, and after doubling its capacity during World War I, the United States began to challenge Britain successfully in its traditional export markets.

The consequences for the Welsh industry were serious, particularly as other countries followed the American example in developing their own tinplate industries. Even the expansion in home consumption could not prevent the emergence of surplus capacity, though this did not present quite such severe problems as in other more capital-intensive trades. In this industry the basic unit of production is the mill rather than the works (which may consist of a number of mills), and since the capital cost of a mill is small, 'expansion and contraction of the industry has normally taken the form of opening, closing or adding to the number of mills'.[1]

Nevertheless, the Welsh Sheet and Tinplate Association (to which all the firms in the industry belonged) organised the Tinplate Conference in an attempt to offset the problems created by surplus capacity. From 1927 onwards, the Conference fixed production quotas (expressed in terms of the percentage of total capacity at which the mills might work) with the usual provisions for payments of fines and compensation where the quotas were exceeded or not met; in addition, it fixed minimum prices for tinplate.

By 1935, the position of the industry had deteriorated and it was operating at little more than 50 per cent of capacity. It was against this background that the leading concern (which had absorbed a number of works in South Wales) announced in the middle of 1935 its intention to

[1] Welsh Reconstruction Advisory Council, *First Interim Report* (London H.M.S.O. 1944), par. 149.

erect a strip mill and tinplate works not in Wales but in Lincolnshire. To excess capacity was added the threat of redundancy, and although the new strip mill was eventually built at Ebbw Vale, the new methods of tinplate manufacture were in 1935 already threatening the old mills of South Wales.

The Tinplate trade in the Census of Production covers 'establishments engaged wholly or mainly in the rolling from the bar or slab of tin, terne and blackplate and the production of tinned sheets and terne sheets'.[1] The output of the principal products of the trade was only 1 per cent greater in 1951 than in 1935 both in quantity and in value, after adjusting for price-changes. But this small change in the output of the trade conceals substantial changes in both its structure and its methods of production.

The number of establishments in the Tinplate trade fell from sixty-six in 1935 to forty-one in 1948, rising again to forty-four in 1951. Similarly, the numbers employed in the Tinplate trade decreased from just under 22,000 in 1935 to less than 17,000 in 1951. In view of the slight increase in output, this indicates a considerable increase in productivity stemming from technological change.

The two technological changes in question were distinct but associated. First, the introduction of the continuous strip mill, and second, the development of electrolytic tinning. The traditional method of tinplate manufacture before the advent of the continuous strip mill was by the hand pack-mill, through which steel bars cut to size are, after heating and re-heating, progressively extended, doubled together and flattened, to form a thick pack of blackplates which are torn apart and subsequently pickled, annealed, cold-rolled and dipped in molten tin. This method depended substantially on manual skill and strength, and there was almost inevitably a large proportion of 'wasters' as the result of the harsh treatment to which the blackplates were subjected as the pack was split.[2]

By contrast, the continuous strip mill method is essentially a mechanised mode of manufacture. At one end of the mill goes in the steel ingot; at the other, reduced in thickness to 0·050 in. and increased in length up to 1,500 ft, emerges the steel strip to be coiled or cut into lengths. The manual handling of the steel bar is eliminated from the strip mill method, and the resulting product, ready for tinning, has a high and uniform standard of quality. There is no doubt that the tinplate produced from

[1] For a concise description of these products see L. Rostas, *Productivity, Prices and Distribution in Selected British Industries*, N.I.E.S.R. Occasional Papers, 11 (Cambridge University Press, 1948), p. 91.

[2] For a more detailed description of the two methods of tinplate manufacture, see Welsh Reconstruction Advisory Council, *First Interim Report*, pars. 156–7; and for the full advantages of the continuous strip method, see Rostas, *op. cit.* p. 100.

continuous strip is better and cheaper to make than the product of the old pack-mills.

Of course, the continuous strip mill is a far more expensive piece of capital equipment than the pack-mill. The tinplate mills of South-West Wales (representing 80 per cent of the whole industry before the War) were built on a capital of about £5 million, but the continuous strip mill and the integrated steel works at Ebbw Vale needed a capital investment of £12 million.[1] It is not surprising, therefore, that the introduction of continuous strip rolling was looked upon with disfavour by concerns with old-type mills. It was pointed out that the continuous strip mill had certain disadvantages compared with the pack-mills: not only was it costly to install but high-grade steel, continuous operation, and a reasonably assured market for the large quantities of tinplate produced were essential to its successful operation.[2]

The strip produced by continuous rolling was initially tinned by the same hot-dipped method as used with the blackplates of the old pack-mills. But from the United States, where the continuous strip mill was first developed, came the other great technological advance—electrolytic tinning. The strip mill produced a cold-reduced steel base to which tin could be applied by electrolysis. Not only could this process be applied to coiled strip thereby eliminating the separate handling of the small sheets as in hot tinning, but 'perhaps most important of all, it used the minimum amount of tin consistent with the degree of protection required'.[3]

The impact of these two technological changes on the industry has been great, though their full effect was not felt until after 1951. The continuous strip mill at Ebbw Vale began production in 1938; the first electrolytic tinning line was installed there ten years later. At the same time, the old pack-mills have not been eliminated even though another strip mill and electrolytic tinning line have come into production since 1948. Certainly, in 1951 the pack-mills were still responsible for more than half of the total output, though by 1955 their share had been reduced to a third. Even after a third strip-mill and electrolytic tinning plant came into production in 1956, the pack-mills were still responsible for one-sixth of the total output in 1957, mainly in the form of special requirements which it was uneconomic for the modern plants to produce.

These technological changes have greatly contributed to the increased concentration that has occurred in the industry between 1935 and 1951.

[1] M. P. Fogarty, *Prospects of the Industrial Areas of Great Britain* (London, Methuen, 1945), p. 122.

[2] W. R. Brown, 'The Tinplate Trade in 1935', *Iron and Coal Trades Review*, 17 January 1936, p. 136.

[3] C. J. Kavanagh and R. A. Hacking, 'Steel and the Consuming Industries', *Iron and Coal Trades Review*, 30 September 1949, p. 183.

Employment concentration rose from 57 to 71 per cent, and net output concentration from 61 to 72 per cent. The number of units on the other hand fell from thirty-four in 1935 to eighteen in 1951. Yet other factors have also been operating, as becomes apparent when the events of the 1935–51 period are considered in detail.

In 1935, the tinplate industry was already fairly highly concentrated. The dominant concern was Richard Thomas and Company, which had by a process of acquisition built up its tinplate interests to the extent that it controlled one-third of the 480 mills in South Wales by 1925[1], and nearer two-fifths of the 554 mills in the whole industry by 1935. To its control of the Grovesend Steel and Tinplate Company (secured in 1933) it added W. Gilbertson and Company, the Cardonnel Tinplate Works and the Melingriffith Company in 1934. Indeed, it reported in 1936 that in the previous four years it had purchased fifteen businesses previously under independent control, including the derelict steelworks of the Ebbw Vale Steel, Iron and Coal Company.[2]

Next in importance in 1935 was Baldwins, which had acquired in the previous year all the shares of Robert B. Byass and Company and a direct controlling interest in the Fairwood Tin Plate Company, thereby adding thirteen tinplate mills to its control. On the other hand, it sold the Eaglesbush Tinplate Works (with nine mills) to the Metal Box Company in the course of 1935, on the understanding that Metal Box would take its steel requirements from Baldwins. Altogether, Baldwins controlled seven works with fifty-five mills—or some one-tenth of the total capacity—in 1935. In addition it jointly controlled, with the Anglo-Saxon Petroleum Company, the Elba Tinplate Company whose sixteen mills were largely engaged in producing plates for oil-drums for use at the Llandarcy oil refinery.[3]

The third largest unit in 1935 was the Briton Ferry Steel Company, which had recently acquired six tinplate works with thirty-nine mills (or 7 per cent of the industry's capacity), as well as possessing a substantial interest in two other concerns comprising five sheet and seven tinplate mills. There were, in addition, three more concerns (apart from Elba) with more than ten mills apiece, of which the most important was Partridge, Jones and John Paton with four works containing twenty-two mills.

Thus it may be estimated that the three largest units in the tinplate industry—Richard Thomas, Baldwins, and Briton Ferry—controlled in

[1] Committee on Industry and Trade, *Survey of Metal Industries*, p. 37.

[2] Report of the Annual General Meeting, Richard Thomas and Company Ltd, July 1936.

[3] The Elba interests would not appear, however, to be included under Baldwins in the computation of the Board of Trade concentration-ratio since its interest did not exceed 50 per cent.

the region of 55 per cent of the industry's total capacity in 1935; and that the seven largest units controlled roughly 66 per cent.[1]

Amalgamation and acquisition continued after 1935. Richard Thomas bought the Morfa works of John S. Tregoning and Company in 1936, later adding three other concerns as well. The new integrated steel plant built on the old site of the Ebbw Vale company came into production in 1939, its tinplate capacity alone equivalent to the output of fifty of the old-type mills. Briton Ferry similarly acquired the Villiers and Gwynne concerns in 1936–7.

The Old Castle Iron and Tinplate Company absorbed the Western Tinplate Company in 1937 to bring its total number of mills to twenty-six, replacing for a time Partridge, Jones as the fourth largest concern in the industry. In 1939, however, Old Castle was one of the four concerns (the Ashburnham, Kidwelly and Teilo businesses were the others) to merge their interests under the style of the Llanelly Associated Tinplate Companies.

Although the number of tinplate works in existence did not change greatly between 1935 and 1939, the number of old-type tinplate mills decreased by nearly one-tenth—from 554 to 505. However, the reduction in the old-type capacity merely made room for the entry of the Ebbw Vale plant into the industry.[2] On the basis of the old-type mills, the three largest units—Richard Thomas, Briton Ferry and Llanelly Associated—represented 58 per cent of total capacity in 1939 compared with 54 per cent in 1935, with Baldwins reduced to fourth place. When Ebbw Vale is taken into account, the three largest units' share was 62 per cent (of which Richard Thomas, 46 per cent), an increase of 8 percentage points compared with 1935.

The outbreak of World War II accelerated the process of concentration. The loss of South-East Asian tinfields forced the country to economise in the use of tin, and it was the tinplate industry that had to bear the brunt. From the imposition of government control in December 1941, 'production was drastically curtailed and, from 1943, its output was stabilised at 10 million boxes. This was brought about by the closure of works and the dispersal of the workers. . . Some of the factories which were closed were used by various ministries for storage purposes. As a result the productive capacity of the industry was reduced. The number employed

[1] These estimates are based on the number of works and tinplate mills for firms listed in *Ryland's Directory*, assuming that each mill has the same weekly capacity of 1,000 base boxes of tinplate.

[2] Richard Thomas declared its intention to work the Ebbw Vale plant fully, though it expressed its willingness 'to restrict production at our old type plant on a *pro rata* basis with old type plant owned by competitors, so as to maintain, in co-operation with them, orderly competition'. (Prospectus, *The Times*, 27 January 1937.) Quoted in D. L. Burn, *The Economic History of Steelmaking, 1867–1939* (Cambridge University Press, 1940), p. 462.

dropped from about 21,000 in 1939 to about 10,000 in 1943. Further, from 1943, the industry was not able to recruit and train workers.'[1]

In 1944, there occurred the merger of the Richard Thomas and the Baldwins interests. By that time, Richard Thomas had acquired the Clayton Tin Plate Company, while Baldwins had taken over the Beaufort Works. As a result of this merger and the closure of many works during the War, the structure of the industry in 1946 had changed considerably. The number of tinplate works, according to *Ryland's Directory*, was forty-nine in 1946 compared with seventy-four in 1939, and among the old-type mills, the three largest units—Richard Thomas and Baldwins (R.T.B.), Llanelly Associated, and Briton Ferry—owned 64 per cent of the total capacity, compared with 58 per cent in 1939. Again, taking Ebbw Vale into account, the capacity concentration-ratio was higher still at 69 per cent in 1946.

After the War certain problems remained. There was a severe shortage of labour in the old-type mills. The labour dispersed during the War did not readily return to the industry. Female labour was also more attracted by the lighter work in the modern factories of South Wales. Nor did the foreign labour brought into the industry do more than ease the situation. As a consequence, the number of workers employed in tinplate manufacture rose only slowly from 10,500 in 1946 to 13,100 in 1950, and whereas the pre-war industry had excess labour and capacity because demand was low, in the post-war period the excess capacity remained because there was insufficient labour to man the mills.

More serious than the labour shortage was the need for the industry to rid itself of the old-type mills and to replace them by continuous strip mills and electrolytic tinning lines in order to provide a higher-quality product able to compete in world markets. It was recognised by the Welsh Reconstruction Advisory Council that such a programme of modernisation would require a grouping of the various interests in the industry on a geographical basis. Mergers and amalgamations were to be the order of the day.

In 1947, the Steel Company of Wales was formed, to which four steel companies—R.T.B., Guest Keen Baldwins Iron and Steel Company, John Lysaght, and Llanelly Associated—transferred certain of their assets. As a result, the Steel Company of Wales became possessed of eighteen tinplate works: fourteen (with 114 mills) from R.T.B. and four from Llanelly Associated. Meanwhile, R.T.B. itself installed the first electrolytic tinning line at Ebbw Vale in 1947, which by 1949 was producing 60,000 tons of tinplate a year.

Although tinplate production was slow to revive during the post-war

[1] W. E. Minchinton, 'The Tinplate Industry: its Present and Future Prospects', *National Provincial Bank Review*, May 1951, pp. 11–12. See also *The British Tinplate Industry* (Oxford University Press, 1957), by the same author.

period—indeed, it did not exceed the 1935 level until 1950—the industry's structure was very different from before the War.[1] The number of works listed in *Ryland's Directory* amounted to thirty-nine (as against forty-four establishments in the 1951 Census) controlled by fifteen concerns (as against eighteen business units in the Census trade).[2] By 1951, the Steel Company of Wales (S.C.W.) was producing nearly 260,000 tons of tinplate (or more than one-third of the total national output), mostly from the 130 old-type hand mills that it was still operating at that time. Another 203,000 tons came from the Ebbw Vale works of R.T.B., to which must be added the output from its two other old-type works. Indeed, the share of S.C.W. and R.T.B. together was probably about two-thirds of the total trade in 1951, which was as much as the seven largest units could claim in 1935. The third largest unit in 1951 was Briton Ferry, but its importance was very much less than that of its two larger brethren since it possessed only twenty-eight hand mills in that year, or less than one-tenth of the total capacity.

It is necessary to go beyond 1951 in order to assess the full significance of the developments in the tinplate industry during the post-war period. The first stage of the S.C.W.'s modernisation programme was the building of a new 80 in. continuous strip mill at Margam. The second and more relevant stage was the building of a cold-reduction mill and tinplate works at Trostre, near Llanelly. The Llanelly site was chosen because of the need to provide work for those made redundant by the closure of the old-type mills. The Trostre tinplate works, with their electrolytic tinning lines, did not come into full production until 1953, and output has continued to expand there since. But as the Trostre works came into production, S.C.W. closed six of the old-type works with thirty-eight mills.

A later stage in the modernisation of the industry was the construction by S.C.W. of another tinplate plant, again equipped with electrolytic tinning lines, at Velindre, which necessitated the closure of S.C.W.'s remaining pack mills earlier than anticipated. In 1956–7 the Trostre and Velindre works produced over 700,000 tons of tinplate, or more than two-thirds of the national output. Meanwhile at Ebbw Vale R.T.B. installed a new tinplate mill in 1953–4 to raise capacity there from 200,000 tons to 400,000 tons a year. Even so, there was still room for many old-type mills (of which 108 were operating in 1955) and it was not until the recession

[1] When the Iron and Steel Nationalisation Bill was put forward in 1948, the British Iron and Steel Federation stated that nine of the seventeen producers of tinplate, terneplate and blackplate were scheduled for nationalisation, and that these nine concerns accounted for 87 per cent of the £23 million gross value of tinplate output.

[2] The discrepancy between the *Ryland's Directory* number of tinplate works and the Census total of establishments is probably explained by the exclusion from the *Directory* of works which produce other of the principal products of the Tinplate trade. Thus, it seems possible that the two works of R.T.B. making heavy-coated steel sheets by old-type hand-mill methods were included in the Census trade though not in the *Directory*.

of 1958 that they were more or less totally eliminated. By 1958, therefore, S.C.W. and R.T.B. were responsible for virtually the whole of tinplate production in this country.

Conclusion

Many factors have contributed to the sweeping changes that have marked the history of the tinplate industry in the past quarter of a century. Surplus capacity, technological changes, closure of works during the War, labour shortages, and mergers and amalgamations have all helped to reduce the number of units and produce the situation where two concerns dominate the trade. There is, however, no doubt that technological change, requiring such large plants that the continued existence of older-type mills would have been very uneconomic, has been the most dynamic force promoting concentration. Although amalgamations and acquisitions occurred during the inter-war period, the existence of the quota system hampered the process, as well as keeping in existence some of the less efficient mills. It was, to repeat, the emergence of the continuous strip mill which accelerated the process of amalgamation as the most painless way of accommodating the new and larger plants in an old and relatively inefficient industry.

10. CINEMATOGRAPH FILM PRINTING

Some indication of the growth of the Cinematograph Film Printing Trade can be gained from the fact that the number of plants increased between 1935 and 1951, and the whole industry in 1935 was only a little larger than the biggest plant in 1951. The industry is still not a large employer of labour: its total labour-force was less than 2,400 in 1951, compared with 850 in 1935 and 600 in 1924. Yet the expansion suggested by the employment figures probably understates the real position, since the growth in employment has been accompanied by the introduction of labour-saving automatic machinery which has increased productivity.

There are many factors which have contributed to the trade's expansion. The fluctuating fortunes of the British film industry are well known, but the laboratory side of the trade is not entirely dependent on the level of production in this country. Foreign films are imported as negatives and printed here, so that the laboratories can offset any decline in the production of British films with the likely accompanying increase in the import of foreign films. Similarly, the laboratories are not entirely dependent on the number of prints of films required by exhibitors for commercial showing. The great increase in the production of sub-standard films by the Armed Services and industrial concerns for propaganda and educational purposes has probably contributed substantially to the rise in the trade's activity between 1935 and 1951.

The trade has benefited also from the exploitation of colour photography and the development of television as an alternative medium for the use of film. Yet both these developments are likely to be more relevant to the further expansion of the trade after 1951 (by 1955, employment had reached 2,800) rather than to its earlier growth. It is the availability of Eastmancolor since 1951 that has led to the greater interest in colour work, while commercial television, which did not start until 1955, has been the principal exponent of filmed rather than 'live' broadcasts. On the other hand, during the 1935–51 period the processing of films in Technicolor for the whole of Europe was concentrated in this country.

In 1935, the three largest units were responsible for more than two-fifths of the total employment in the trade, but for nearer one-half of its net output. By 1951, concentration was 61 per cent for employment, and 70 per cent for net output, despite an increase in the number of business units from ten to eighteen.

In 1935, the British film production industry operated at a high level of activity. In that year alone, 108 new production companies were registered, while the exhibitors' and renters' quotas of British films over 3,000 feet in length reached their maximum level.[1] On the laboratory side of the trade, the three largest units were almost certainly the Gaumont-British Picture Corporation, Olympic Kinematograph Laboratories, and George Humphries and Company. The Gaumont-British laboratories were at Shepherd's Bush, while Olympic was associated with the Paramount concerns. The other leading concern, George Humphries, was independent of producing interests, but since its formation in 1923 it had kept in close touch with the development of film printing and processing in the United States.

Among the other film laboratory concerns in 1935 were the Kay Film Printing Company and Pathé Laboratories (associated with the Movietone and Pathé newsreel producing interests respectively), the British Lion Film Laboratories, and the Associated British Laboratories at Elstree, as well as a number of smaller specialist concerns.

In the next few years there were a number of events which directly or indirectly affected the film printing trade. In the first place, the Technicolor Motion Picture Corporation of the United States registered Technicolor as a private company in 1935 and granted it rights under licence to the Technicolor process of film printing for the whole of Europe. Consequently, from its inception, the Technicolor laboratory business was one of the largest units, if not the largest, in the film printing trade, although its activities were confined to colour work. In the second place, the emergence of Mr J. Arthur Rank as a power in the production and exhibition sections of the film industry also had an effect on the film printing trade.

[1] PEP, *The British Film Industry* (London, 1952), p. 60.

It is unnecessary to describe here the complicated process by which the Rank interests were developed, but it must be noted that the Rank group acquired control of General Film Distributors (G.F.D.) in 1936 and, more important, the Gaumont-British Picture Corporation in 1941. In addition, the studios and laboratories at Denham, opened by London Film Productions in 1936, also came into the Rank group of companies shortly afterwards.

In 1948, the Rank group carried out a reorganisation of its laboratory interests. At that time, the processing and printing of films for Rank's was carried on partly by the Denham laboratories (by then owned by Denham Laboratories, a subsidiary of the British and Dominions Film Corporation) and partly at the Shepherd's Bush laboratories (owned by Gaumont-British and operated by G.F.D.). It was decided to close the Shepherd's Bush laboratories and, since 'efficiency and economy of operation require printing and processing to be concentrated' to enlarge the Denham laboratories 'so that all feature films can be dealt with there'.[1]

By 1951, the reorganisation at Denham had been effected so that Rank Laboratories (Denham) can be regarded as one of the three largest units in that year. It would appear, however, that its share of the trade was smaller than that of Technicolor, for statistics of Technicolor's production in 1951 suggest that it processed between one-quarter and one-third of the total footage of 35 mm. (apart from newsreels) and 16 mm. film.[2] Moreover, the labour force at Denham Laboratories—about 600 in 1956—was considerably smaller than that of Technicolor in 1951. Thus, it may be concluded that Technicolor was the largest and Denham Laboratories the second largest unit in the trade in 1951.

There is no doubt that the third largest unit in 1951, as in 1935, was George Humphries and Company, which in 1948 employed some 250 persons, or nearly 11 per cent of the total labour-force in the trade at the time. The other concerns in the trade in 1951 were relatively less important, but among the more prominent were Kodak (which handles all the master prints in Kodachrome), Kay (West End) Laboratories (with two establishments), Associated British Pathé, and Olympic Kinematograph Laboratories. In addition, the Armed Services and the B.B.C. are known to operate their own laboratories, though in the case of the B.B.C. the laboratory is used only for the processing of 'rush' films.

Conclusion

Technological factors have clearly played a major role in determining the pattern of concentration in the Cinematograph Film Printing Trade

[1] *Report of Odeon Theatres Ltd for the year ending 26 June 1948*, p. 4.

[2] Technicolor Ltd, Prospectus (*The Times*, 30 July 1952).

between 1935 and 1951. In one way or another, they have affected the fortunes of the leading units in the trade and contributed to the situation where only one of the leaders in 1935 was still at the top in 1951.

The claim of Technicolor to first place in 1951 stems directly from the right it has enjoyed under licence to the exclusive use of the Technicolor process of colour printing for the whole of Europe. This technological monopoly enabled it to operate on a large scale from the outset, so that its entry into production after 1935 immediately changed the structure of the industry to a significant degree.

Although the second largest unit in 1951 owes much to the process of concentration on the production and exhibition side of the film industry, technological advances have determined that it should centralise its laboratory facilities in order to secure efficient operations. Similarly, the third largest unit in both years has maintained that position only by keeping abreast of technological changes.

Intensive competition has generally been a feature of cinematograph film printing, and despite the general expansion of the trade, a number of concerns which were active before the War have gone out of business. Since 1951, the introduction of Eastmancolor on a non-exclusive basis has increased competition still further, for many of the black-and-white processors are now printing in colour as well. On the other hand, the advent of commercial television has increased the demands on the trade, though there is little reason to suppose that either factor has lessened its degree of concentration.

II. SUGAR AND GLUCOSE

In 1935, the sugar industry in this country was on the brink of reorganisation. The report of an official Committee of Inquiry appeared in the spring of that year, the Government announced its own policy in the summer and the Sugar Industry (Reorganisation) Act was passed by Parliament in 1936. Apart from amendments introduced during World War II, it was this Act which governed the operations of the industry throughout the 1935–51 period.

The sugar industry has two sections: the first is concerned with the manufacture of raw sugar from beet; the second refines raw sugar derived from either beet or cane. This division of the trade is not hard and fast: the beet-sugar factories refine part of their own raw sugar production (the rest being sold to the refiners) as well as refining imported cane-sugar from time to time.

Raw and refined sugar accounted for four-fifths of the total value of sales of the principal products of the Sugar and Glucose Trade in 1951; the proportion was even higher at 85 per cent in 1935. The greater part of the remaining one-fifth consisted of by-products of raw sugar production (such as beet-pulp and molasses) on the one hand, and of sugar-refining (such as syrup, treacle, invert sugar and sugar extracts) on the other. Glucose is the other important principal product, but its contribution to the total value was less than 5 per cent in 1951.

The sugar industry has been expanding, both in the production of raw sugar from home-produced beet and in its refining activities, over the last quarter of a century, although raw sugar production tends to fluctuate year by year, according to the state of the sugar-beet crop. In the year ending 31 March 1952, the production of raw sugar was equivalent to more than 600,000 tons of white sugar, or about the same as in 1934–5 which was a pre-war record. But in 1950–1 the output of raw sugar was 10 per cent higher than the pre-war peak and in 1954–5 a record of nearly 720,000 tons was achieved. Despite the restrictions on imports of cane-sugar during the war and post-war years, the output of refined sugar was 17 per cent higher in 1951 than in 1935, nearly 29 per cent of the output being exported in 1951 compared with 15 per cent in 1935.

A small change in the definition of the Census trade[1] has been responsible for some of the apparent increase in employment between 1935 and 1951 but, even on the basis of comparable data for the two years, there has been a rise of 6 per cent in the labour-force. Similarly the number of establishments rose from forty-three to fifty in the 1935–51 period, while the volume of production rose by about one-fifth.

There was a considerable increase in concentration between 1935 and 1951, the rise being greater in terms of net output (from 62 to 82 per cent) than in terms of employment (from 71 to 84 per cent), indicating an increase in the relative productivity of the three largest units. For 1935 separate concentration-ratios are available for beet-sugar firms and for other firms (principally the refiners). In both sections, concentration had already reached a high level in 1935: on the employment basis, 72 per cent for the beet-sugar producers and 83 per cent for other firms.

There were eighteen beet-sugar factories in 1935, owned by fifteen concerns; these concerns were in turn controlled by five financial groups. Largest of the five was the Anglo-Dutch group with five factories and a rated beet capacity in 1933–4 of 950,000 tons, or 32 per cent of the total capacity, followed by the Anglo-Scottish Beet Sugar Corporation with six factories and 29 per cent of the total capacity. The group with the third largest rated capacity, but whose production in 1933–4 entitled it to second place, was the Bury group, whose four concerns were controlled

[1] The changed definition of the trade entails the inclusion in 1951 of establishments engaged wholly or mainly in grinding sugar (used for icing, fondants, etc.); these establishments were, in 1935, classified to the Preserved Foods Trade.

by Tate and Lyle.[1] These three groups would, of course, constitute the three largest units in the beet-sugar section of the trade in 1935.

Turning to the refining section of the sugar industry, one concern—Tate and Lyle—stood out as the principal refiner even in 1935. Formed in 1921 by the merger of the family businesses of Henry Tate and Sons and Abram Lyle and Sons, it acquired Fairrie and Company in 1929, as well as controlling the Greenock firm of John Walker and Company. The other refining concerns in 1935, though very small compared with Tate and Lyle, were Westburn Sugar Refineries, Macfie and Sons, Sankey Sugar Company, the Glebe Sugar Refining Company, Martineaus, Merton Grove Company, and Manbré and Garton.

As already stated, some of the beet-sugar factories were also refiners of raw sugar, and the competition between them and the orthodox refiners had become so intense by 1932 that the Minister of Agriculture persuaded the two sides to negotiate and conclude an Industrial Agreement in 1933. Under that Agreement, the factories were allotted a quota whereby they were entitled to refine 500,000 tons of the 1,900,000 tons of refined sugar annually consumed in Britain. Some factories did not use all their quotas and sold them to refiners, and from the Census data for 1935 it may be seen that the factories were responsible for only 18 per cent of the tonnage of refined sugar produced (compared with their permitted 26 per cent).

The division of the refining trade between the factories and the refiners in the proportions of the 1933 Agreement was subsequently confirmed by the Sugar Refining Agreement of 1937. The share of fourteen-nineteenths allotted to the refiners was, moreover, divided into quotas for each of the main refining concerns, so that it becomes possible to gauge their relative importance. The quotas laid down in 1937 were as follows:[2]

	%
Tate and Lyle	74·965
Walker	4·654
	79·619
Westburn	5·735
Macfie	5·501
Sankey	5·482
Glebe	2·434
Martineaus	1·229
	100·000

[1] *Report of the United Kingdom Sugar Industry Inquiry Committee*, Cmd. 4871 (London, H.M.S.O. 1935), par. 89.

[2] In addition, Merton Grove Company was allowed 1,050 tons a year, while Manbré and Garton was given a maximum liquid sugar production of 14,970 tons (refined equivalent) and maximum candy sugar quotas of 2,661 tons to brewers and 30 tons to other customers.

If it is assumed that the orthodox refiners' trade was divided between them in these proportions in 1935, the predominance of Tate and Lyle is immediately apparent. If its 79·6 per cent share is applied merely to the output of refined sugar in 1935 (and not to any of the by-products of refining) and its stake in the raw sugar production by the factories is ignored, Tate and Lyle's share of the gross output of the trade may be estimated as 50–55 per cent. Thus, there can be no doubt that Tate and Lyle was by far the largest of the three largest units in the Sugar and Glucose Trade in 1935.

No other refining concern appears to qualify as one of the three largest units in the trade in 1935, for the two largest concerns among the beet-sugar manufacturers, the Anglo-Dutch and the Anglo-Scottish groups, would have enjoyed that distinction.

One of the principal features of the Sugar Industry (Reorganisation) Act of 1936 was the amalgamation of the eighteen beet-sugar factories into a single concern, the British Sugar Corporation. The reasons for this step need not detain us.[1] But its effect was an immediate increase in the degree of concentration in the industry. The magnitude of this increase in concentration can be assessed from the Census data for 1935 together with the above estimate of the share of Tate and Lyle in the refining section of the trade. The beet-sugar factories accounted for 24·5 per cent of the Trade's gross output in 1935: this would have been the British Sugar Corporation's share if it had been formed in 1935. To this must be added Tate and Lyle's share of 50–55 per cent as well as the estimated share, amounting to 4 per cent, of the now third largest concern—Westburn—to give a gross output concentration-ratio in the region of 80 per cent.

Thus, a large part of the increase in concentration between 1935 and 1951 occurred at the beginning of that period when the British Sugar Corporation was established. In 1938, however, Tate and Lyle purchased and closed the refinery of Macfie at Liverpool; its refining quota was transferred, of course, to Tate and Lyle. About the same time control of Sankey Sugar was acquired by Manbré and Garton, while Tate and Lyle and Westburn Sugar Refineries took joint control of Glebe Sugar Refining.

The transfer of quotas which these activities involved resulted in Tate and Lyle increasing its share of the refiners' total from 79·6 per cent to 85·1 per cent (or to 86·3 per cent if a half-interest in Glebe is included). When the refining quota of the British Sugar Corporation is taken into account, Tate and Lyle's share of the total refining trade was, after the

[1] For the background to the 1936 Act, see: *Report of the United Kingdom Sugar Industry Inquiry Committee*, Cmd. 4871 (1935); P. E. Hart, 'Competition and Control in the British Sugar Industry', *Oxford Economic Papers* (New Series), vol. 5, no. 3, September 1953, pp. 317–32; and 'The British Sugar Corporation—Private or Public Monopoly', *Cartel*, April 1952, pp. 153–8.

changes described above, increased from 59 per cent to 63 per cent, excluding its interest in Glebe.

From the Census data for 1951, the British Sugar Corporation's share of the trade's gross output can be assessed at 22·5 per cent—a slightly smaller proportion than it could have claimed in 1935 if it had been formed in that year. Given the Corporation's share and the gross output concentration-ratio for 1951, the two other largest units contributed another 65·5 per cent of the trade's gross output in that year. By far the larger part of that share must be represented by the output of Tate and Lyle. Indeed, if Westburn is taken to be the third largest unit, and it is assumed that its refining quota represents its share of all refinery products, then its share of the gross output of the trade does not amount to more than about 3·5 per cent. Thus, Tate and Lyle's share was in the region of 62 per cent in 1951, compared with 50–55 per cent in 1935.

Conclusion

The rise in concentration in the Sugar and Glucose trade between 1935 and 1951 is principally attributable to the amalgamation of the beet-sugar factories by Act of Parliament in 1936. In addition, the largest concern in the trade—Tate and Lyle—increased its share as a result of an acquisition which enabled it to add that concern's refining quota to its own. While the operation of the Refining Agreement has prevented expansion through aggressive competition, both sections of the trade—beet-sugar manufacture and sugar refining—have paid great attention to increasing productivity, and improvements in methods and techniques have been very marked. It is possible that the increase in concentration would have occurred if the industry had not become subject to regulation by the 1936 Act: the principal refiners might well have increased their share of the trade at the expense of the beet-sugar factories if the latter had not been protected to support domestic agriculture. As it is, State intervention was undoubtedly the principal factor in the increase in concentration in the Sugar and Glucose trade.

12. WROUGHT IRON AND STEEL TUBES

The Wrought Iron and Steel Tubes Trade has expanded almost continuously during the past thirty years. Between 1924 and 1934, production of tubes increased by more than half and, despite the difficulties of the war years and the post-war shortages of steel, output in 1955 was more than 75 per cent higher than twenty years earlier.

Tubes may vary greatly in their size—they can be so small that they have an outside diameter of 0·01 in. or so large that they have an internal diameter of a yard or more—and find their uses in a variety of trades, of which marine engineering, locomotive and other boiler manufacture, electrical engineering, bicycles, and oil refining and transportation are perhaps the most important. Basically, however, tubes are of two main types distinguished by their process of manufacture: (*a*) welded tubes, produced from plate and strip by bending to circular form and welding the edge, and (*b*) seamless tubes, produced from ingots, billets, etc. by piercing and elongating, or from discs by cupping and drawing.

The diversity of the production of the Wrought Iron and Steel Tubes Trade[1] is only partly revealed by the Census of Production, but a comparison of the total output of those principal products where quantity figures exist for both years shows an increase of 120 per cent between 1935 and 1951. The expansion of the trade is also indicated by the number of establishments, which at 156 in 1951 was double the 1930 total and two-thirds higher than in 1935. The number of business units also rose from sixty-two to eighty-one in the same period. Employment did not show quite as great an increase as the number of plants: a rise of 50 per cent from 27,650 to 42,400 in 1951. Most of the additional establishments were comparatively small; indeed, establishments employing more than 300 persons represented little more than one-fifth of the total number in 1951 compared with nearer one-quarter in 1935. On the other hand, these larger establishments accounted for almost precisely the same proportion of total employment (78 per cent) and net output (80 per cent) in both years.

The degree of concentration in this expanding trade increased between 1935 and 1951, though the fact that the 1951 data refer not to the share of the three largest but to the share of the four largest units makes precise comparison impossible. The share of the four largest units in 1951 was 77 per cent in terms of employment and 79 per cent in terms of net output, compared with 71 per cent and 70 per cent respectively for the three largest units in 1935. Though estimates of the share of the three largest units in 1935 make it almost certain that concentration has increased, the rise has not been large. Indeed, the more important point to note is that the trade was already highly concentrated in 1935, with 70 per cent or more of the trade controlled by the three largest units, and that it has remained so despite its expansion. The high degree of control in 1935 calls for some explanation in itself, particularly since the concentration-changes during the period of substantial expansion between 1935 and 1951 are largely attributable to the developments of the earlier period.

[1] The Trade was defined in 1951 as relating to 'establishments engaged wholly or mainly in the manufacture of tubes (including fittings) for boilers, cycles, bedsteads, etc.; metal conduits; gas cylinders and pressure vessels. Melting and rolling in integrated works and the manufacture of flexible tubes are included'. The main difference between 1935 and 1951 is that malleable cast fittings for wrought tubes were included as a principal product in 1935; the degree of comparability for the trade was, however, as high as 98 per cent.

Developments up to 1935

By 1935, two concerns dominated the tube trade—Stewarts and Lloyds and Tube Investments—and their separate interests had been built up over a number of years. The creation of Stewarts and Lloyds dates back to the early years of the century when the Lloyd tubemaking business of the Midlands joined forces with the Scottish tube combine of A. and J. Stewart and Clydesdale. The new concern began to operate a number of new plants, and by the outbreak of World War I its tube output was 50 per cent greater than in 1903, the year of the merger. Expansion continued during the early 1920's; at the beginning of the decade it acquired Alfred Hickman, thereby increasing its interests in steelmaking for conversion into tubes. Even so, it continued to face difficulties over the supply of suitable steel, and when its existing steel plants could no longer meet their full steel requirements, Stewarts and Lloyds decided to build an integrated steelmaking and tube plant at Corby.

The expansion at Corby enabled Stewarts and Lloyds to achieve a high degree of self-sufficiency as far as its raw materials were concerned. In 1938, its chairman reported that 'we are virtually independent of outside supplies of tube-making material and have control over the quality and suitability of material for our varied purposes: we have achieved the economies of an integrated plant from the ore to the finished tube...'.[1] But an integrated plant of the size of Corby depended for its successful operation on a number of factors. Thus, it was stated that 'in order to use the latest tube-making methods, involving mass production on a scale hitherto unknown in the British tube industry and giving economies impossible of achievement with small scattered works, concentration of production in large units was essential. Concentration of production could not take place without concentration of demand, and it therefore became necessary to attempt to consolidate the British demand for merchant pipe.'[2]

With this as its object, Stewarts and Lloyds made a number of acquisitions in the late 1920's and early 1930's. The two largest producers in England—John Russell and Company, and its subsidiary, James Russell and Sons—were acquired in 1929, and three years later, the largest producer in Scotland (with six works), the Scottish Tube Company, was taken over. There were, in addition, one or two smaller purchases, including John Spencer in 1935.

Meanwhile, Tube Investments (TI) was growing more important as a fabricator of tubes, and consequently as a customer for Stewarts and Lloyds' output. TI was formed in 1919 to merge the interests of Accles

[1] Chairman's Statement to the Annual Meeting of Stewarts and Lloyds Ltd, 18 May 1938.

[2] *Ibid.*

and Pollock, Simplex Conduits, Credenda Conduits Company and Tubes Ltd. After several purchases during the 1920's, it acquired the Chesterfield Tube Company (manufacturers of boiler tubes, steam pipes, etc.) in 1929, Talbot-Stead Tube Company in 1930, and the Stella Conduit Company in 1932. Its acquisitions brought it an important stake in the bicycle components and electrical goods trades as well as in tubes. Its total labour-force rose from under 3,000 in 1919 to 66,000 in 1936.

The interests of Stewarts and Lloyds and TI might have clashed during this period of common expansion. But that was effectively ruled out by a Working Agreement which the two concerns concluded in 1930, which implicitly recognized that Stewarts and Lloyds were mainly interested in the bulk production of tubes, while TI's interests were directed more to the finishing end of the business, that is, the production of precision or highly manipulated tubes. In that sense, they were complementary to each other. A merger would have recognised the complementary nature of the two businesses but, instead of consolidation, they chose to define their respective spheres of interest. The Working Agreement provided for the exchange of liaison shares, as well as a joint interest in some particular concerns. Thus, Stewarts and Lloyds took over a 50 per cent interest in the Bromford Tube Company and Howell and Company at the commencement of the Working Agreement. By 1935, therefore, the two concerns were linked together by a number of factors: liaison shares, interlocking directorships, jointly-owned subsidiaries as well as provisions for co-operation in research and technical development.

Despite the strength of these ties, Stewarts and Lloyds and TI were two distinct business units in 1935, and undoubtedly they would have accounted for the major part of the 70 per cent of the trade in the hands of the three largest units in that year.[1] It is difficult to be more precise concerning their respective shares of the trade, since TI do not publish production figures while Stewarts and Lloyds do not appear to have published their tube production in 1935. It must be noted, however, that the Corby plant was not in full production in 1935; its tube output then represented only 7 per cent of national output whereas by 1937 its share had risen to more than 20 per cent.

Probably the third most important producer was the British Mannesmann Tube Company (in which Mannesmannröhren-Werke of Düsseldorf was largely interested), with works at Landore and Newport. Two other tube concerns in 1935 were subsidiaries of the General Electric Company (G.E.C.) while two more were subsidiaries of Incledon and Lamberts but, for the rest, the manufacturers were relatively small.

[1] It is probable that the two jointly-owned subsidiaries mentioned above would have ranked as separate business units in 1935 and their output would not, therefore, have been attributed to either of their two parent concerns. However, it is unlikely that this would have made a substantial difference to the concentration-ratio in 1935.

Changes in the 1935–51 period

In 1936, Stewarts and Lloyds and TI acted jointly to acquire control of the British Mannesmann Tube Company (which was renamed the Newport and South Wales Tube Company) and again in 1938, when they formed the Jarrow Tube Works to manufacture high-grade tubes at this slump-ridden town on Tyneside. In the latter year, however, Stewarts and Lloyds transferred its 50 per cent interest in Howell and Company to TI, in return for the latter's 50 per cent interest in the former British Mannesmann concern.

By 1938, therefore, Stewarts and Lloyds were producing more than 420,000 tons of tubes, or nearly 65 per cent of the national output. Of Stewarts and Lloyds' total output, more than two-fifths came from the Corby plant in 1938, and in the following year Corby's share exceeded one-half. TI's acquisitions between 1935 and the outbreak of war were comparatively small, and its share of the trade probably did not alter very much either way. By the outbreak of war, it was generally reckoned that Stewarts and Lloyds and TI between them accounted for 75–80 per cent of tube production.

Production of tubes increased slightly in the first two years of World War II and remained around the 1938 level for the rest of the War. Again, except in 1947—the year of the fuel crisis—production rose steadily between 1946 and 1951, then remained stable between 1952 and 1954, but rose again to 1,260,000 tons in 1955.

Apart from another joint venture of Stewarts and Lloyds and TI—the formation of Tube Rolling Mills in 1940 with a plant at Wednesfield—there was little change in the structure or capacity of the industry during the War. At the end of the War, however, Stewarts and Lloyds surrendered their 50 per cent interest in both Jarrow Tube and Tube Rolling Mills to TI in return for its 50 per cent share of the Bromford Tube Company. This acquisition added considerably to Stewarts and Lloyds' seamless-tube capacity.

The 50 per cent increase in production between 1946 and 1951 was due to the expansion and modernisation schemes that were launched after the War. The tubemaking capacity at the Corby plant of Stewarts and Lloyds was increased by 125,000 tons per annum by the addition of a fourth continuous weld-mill, capable of making tubes from strip, while at its Clydesdale works, where tubes are rolled direct from ingots, a tube plant with a capacity of 60,000 tons per annum was installed to produce 16 in. outside-diameter line pipe for oil companies. There has also been a progressive modernisation at other tube plants, while the Phoenix works at Rutherglen has been equipped to produce large quantities of refinery pipework, etc.

The interests of TI in tube production have also been augmented by several acquisitions in the post-war period. Earlier it had acquired Alma and Cranmore Tube Company and the National Tube Company, while it purchased all the share capital of Buckleys (seamless steel tubes) in 1948, and Helliwells in 1949.

It is relevant to note that, according to the Minister of Supply, there were twenty-nine producers of tubes and pipes in March 1948, of which the British Iron and Steel Federation later stated that two—Stewarts and Lloyds, and Richard Thomas and Baldwins—were scheduled for nationalisation. Similarly, there were thirty-eight producers of wrought iron pipe fittings, of which three were scheduled for nationalisation.

There can be no doubt that Stewarts and Lloyds was the largest unit in the trade in 1951, for their production of tubes in that year amounted to virtually 800,000 tons, or just under three-quarters of the total output. Equally there can be no doubt that TI was the second largest unit, though the identity of the third (and fourth) largest units is less certain. Apart from G.E.C.'s continued interest in the trade, there have been one or two minor groupings between 1935 and 1951, such as Glynwed Tubes, formed in 1939 to acquire the Wednesbury Tube Company and Glynn Bros., which may perhaps fill the third and fourth places.

Since 1951, there have been one or two developments worthy of note. Perhaps the most important was the cancellation as from 14 February 1951 of the liaison shares of Stewarts and Lloyds and TI, with TI paying £650,000 to its former partner. In addition, TI has again extended its interests in tubemaking through the acquisition of W. H. A. Robertson and Company of Bedford in 1953. In the same year, TI acquired from the Iron and Steel Realisation Agency 'in order to safeguard as far as possible our supply lines for good quality tube steel' the whole of the share capital of the Round Oak Steel Works at a cost of £5·8 million. Finally, after installing £4 million of new equipment, TI has two new tube plants which came progressively into production during 1954–5. These modern plants have rendered redundant certain older and less economic equipment, involving some rearrangement in the manufacturing activities of a few of TI's subsidiaries.

Although Stewarts and Lloyds' tube production has risen continuously (except for a setback in 1954) between 1951 and 1955, its share of total national output has dropped from about 75 per cent to less than 70 per cent in the same period. It is unlikely, however, that the degree of concentration has fallen since 1951, since Stewarts and Lloyds' loss has almost certainly been TI's gain.

Conclusion

The foundations for the increased concentration in the Wrought Iron and Steel Tubes Trade between 1935 and 1951 were laid in the earlier part of the 1930's. The progressive rationalisation of the industry through mergers, acquisitions and concentration of production had already led to its domination by two concerns in 1935. That these two concerns have been able to increase their share of such a rapidly expanding industry since 1935 is sufficient testimony to their power and influence; a power and influence that has been forged and wielded in co-operation rather than competition. Although the number of concerns comprising the trade remains relatively high, most of them are either manufacturers of fittings or manipulators of purchased tubes. They are the pygmies that continue to live alongside the two giants, not least because they serve the giants well. Entry into the trade through such activities is not difficult. It is the mass production of tubes which requires expensive equipment, and it is here that Stewarts and Lloyds and Tube Investments have the financial resources, the specialised equipment, and the technical know-how which enable them to share the bulk of the trade between them.

13. BREAD AND FLOUR CONFECTIONERY

As the standard of living increases, so less bread but more cake is eaten. The long-term trend, therefore, is for bread consumption to fall, and cake consumption to rise. Yet the tendency for bread consumption to fall is interrupted when trade is depressed or the nation is at war. That is to say, when other foods are short or money scarce, people turn back to bread as a staple food. Thus, bread consumption rose during the slump of the 1930's, and again during World War II. Indeed, it reached its peak in 1948 with the failure of the potato crop, but by 1953 the *per capita* consumption of bread (in terms of flour usage) was down to 128 lb.; less than the pre-war average and 15 per cent below 1948.

Despite the resumption of the long-term decline in consumption, bread production was still substantially higher in 1951 than in 1935. So, too, was the production of cakes, sponges, puddings, trifles and other flour confectionery. This expansion in output is reflected in the Census data for the Bread and Flour Confectionery Trade, although changes in its product composition between 1935 and 1951 complicate comparison of the position in the two years.[1]

Using comparable data for the two years, it may be seen that the numbers employed in the larger establishments (those employing eleven and over) rose from 105,000 in 1935 to 132,000 in 1951, an increase of more than one-quarter. The number of larger establishments has, on the other hand, fallen by one-quarter, from nearly 2,650 to 1,900.

[1] The main difference was that ice cream, self-raising flour, mincemeat and rusks were included among the principal products of the Trade in 1935 but not in 1951. In 1935, these items accounted for nearly 10 per cent of the principal products of the trade. Moreover, the change in the Trade's definition reduces its 1935 employment from 110,600 to 105,100, and the number of its larger establishments from 2,644 to 2,590.

In this trade, however, a substantial proportion of the total activity is carried on in the small establishments employing ten or fewer persons. Here again the number of establishments has fallen during the period from 20,900 to 13,200, but in contrast with the larger establishments employment has also fallen, from 78,000 to less than 60,000. Even so, employment in large and small establishments together rose by more than 5 per cent between 1935 and 1951.

Although the concentration data refer only to that part of the trade covered by the larger establishments, it is important to note that the smaller establishments in 1951 still accounted for nearly one-third of the total employment, and for three-tenths of the total gross output.

The continued importance of the small establishments underlines the most striking feature of the structure of this trade: namely, the large differences that exist in the size of both productive and distributive concerns. These differences in size have been present for many years. They were observed by the Royal Commission on Food Prices in 1925 which declared:

> 'On the producing side, the trade ranges from the small master baker who produces a few hundred loaves a week to the loaf factory which produces hundreds of thousands. On its distributing side the range is from firms which restrict their deliveries to within a mile from their bakeries to firms which cover 100 miles daily in their deliveries.'[1]

At that time, however, it was by no means certain whether the balance of advantage lay with the small master baker or the large wholesale baker. But between then and World War II, the tide turned in favour of the plant bakery.

The economics of the plant bakery's operations are substantially different from those of the small bakery. The plant bakery is designed to produce large quantities of bread at much lower costs than can be achieved with the small output of the craft bakery. But those lower costs are dependent on the machinery of the plant bakery being fully used even though it may mean more widespread distribution than would otherwise be attempted. The lower production costs are at least partly offset by the higher distribution costs involved in delivering over a wide area, so that the competitive advantage of the plant bakery is limited to that extent.

Though the development of road transport and bakery machinery in the inter-war years favoured the plant bakery, their progress was slow and their importance limited. As late as 1937, the Committee on Night Baking reported that there were only thirty-five private firms which had plant bakeries, though they were responsible for one-ninth of the total

[1] Royal Commission on Food Prices, *First Report*, vol. I, Cmd. 2390 (London, H.M.S.O. 1925), par. 59.

bread output of Great Britain.[1] Certainly there was no immediate and dramatic reduction in the number of small bakers, even though the plant bakers could increase their trade only at the others' expense.

The survival of the small baker may perhaps be explained by three factors. First, the fact that many of them were family businesses enabled some to meet the competition of the plant bakers by exploiting themselves and their employees by long hours and low pay. In 1938, however, a Trade Board was established for England and Wales, and increase in wages followed. Improved labour conditions tended to work to the disadvantage of the small bakeries since their labour costs increased more than those of the plant bakeries. On the other hand, the small bakers were encouraged to employ machinery as labour became more expensive.

Secondly, the small bakers were able to provide bread which was preferred by many to the mass-produced loaves of the plant bakery, though to the quality difference was added a tendency for the small bakers to provide services 'for which the public generally had made no demand'.[2]

Thirdly, the small baker's survival was probably assisted by the attempts to regulate prices in some areas. At the time of the Royal Commission on Food Prices in 1925, local associations of bakers were fixing prices and persuading millers to refuse flour supplies to bakers who did not observe those prices. After the Food Council had established, in 1926, a scale of maximum bread prices (which were voluntary rather than statutory) for the London area, it was observed that there was a tendency for bakers in other areas to regard them as the minimum. So, in June 1936, in about two-thirds of the towns covered by an inquiry, the prices of bread were higher than in London, and in less than 5 per cent were they lower.[3]

During World War II, many conflicting influences were at work in the bread trade. It was government policy to maintain as many bakeries as possible in order to avoid the dislocation of supplies through air attack. On the other hand, the operation of the flour subsidy tended to reduce the number of bread producers and increase the importance of the plant bakeries.

The maximum price of the standard national bread was fixed by the Government, but at such a level that it was insufficient to cover costs and provide a margin of profit to the baker. Bakers received, therefore, a subsidy on the flour used in price-controlled bread. The controlled price and bread subsidy were calculated to give a margin of 5*s.* per sack, but in assessing this margin, the Ministry of Food was forced to treat the

[1] *Report of the Departmental Committee on Night Baking*, Cmd. 5525 (London, H.M.S.O. 1937), par. 46.

[2] Board of Trade, *Report by the Food Council for the year 1938* (London, H.M.S.O. 1939), p. 6.

[3] *Report by the Food Council for the year 1936* (London, H.M.S.O. 1937), p. 7.

baking trade as a homogeneous whole; an unrealistic assumption in view of the differing methods and scale of operations of the plant and craft bakers. The result was that the small baker only made about half the margin allowed, though the plant baker doubled it. Consequently, the number of small bakers began to dwindle; the number of applications for the flour subsidy fell from 20,000 in 1942 to 18,000 in 1945 and to 14,500 in 1952. Instead of baking bread, they bought their supplies from wholesale plant bakeries, and themselves concentrated on making cakes and pastries. Indeed, the proportion of bread sold wholesale rose from about one-third in 1945 to two-fifths in 1951.

The prohibition of wrapped bread during the War restricted the operations of the plant bakeries, but when the ban was lifted in 1949, they benefited greatly from the growing popularity of this product. In the first place, it is an uneconomic proposition for the small baker to install the costly automatic slicing and wrapping machines, so that the plant bakeries have this growing market to themselves. Secondly, wrapped bread is now finding a much wider range of retail outlets, to the obvious disadvantage of the specialist baker's trade.

Although the small and medium baker still exists in large number, there is no doubt that the larger bakeries are becoming increasingly important. There were some fifty concerns in England and Wales and five in Scotland which each used more than 1,000 sacks of flour a week in 1951, accounting for more than one-quarter and almost two-fifths of the bread supply respectively.[1] Altogether approximately one-third of Britain's bread trade was attributable to plant bakeries in 1951,[2] but by 1955 their share had increased to two-fifths. Similarly, the plant bakeries have probably become more important producers of flour confectionery, though here their advantages over the small baker are much less marked.

It is against this background of the growth in the size of the productive unit that the change in the trade's concentration between 1935 and 1951 must be viewed. In terms of the larger establishments only, the three largest units accounted for 6 per cent of employment and 10 per cent of net output in 1935; by 1951, they accounted for 15 per cent of employment and 17 per cent of net output.

Even though the three largest units were responsible for only 6 per cent of total employment in 1935, they were still quite large concerns since their combined labour-force came to more than 6,500 persons. It is important to note, however, that one of these three largest units in 1935 was Lever Bros., which presumably enjoyed that distinction not because of any baking interests but because of T. Wall and Son's ice cream interests.

[1] F. Garner, 'Baking Industry Changes, I', *Co-operative Review*, May 1953, p. 103.

[2] *Report of the Committee on Night Baking*, Cmd. 8378 (London, H.M.S.O. 1951), par. 30.

Whatever the identity of the other largest units in 1935, there is no doubt that in 1951 first place was taken by Allied Bakeries. This concern was formed by Mr W. Garfield Weston in 1935, to acquire control of six bakery businesses, in Manchester, Newcastle, Cardiff, Birmingham, Edinburgh and London, and to purchase the business and assets of another London bakery firm. It pursued a policy of acquiring old-established businesses of proved merit, until in 1937 it could already claim to be 'the largest of its kind in the country, with 2,786 employees, 17 modern bakeries, 86 shops and 494 bread delivery routes'.

By the outbreak of war, Allied Bakeries owned directly or through its subsidiaries twenty-eight bakeries and 217 shops, and a feature of its expansion was the geographical spread of its interests. In 1950, it claimed to have baked some 250 million loaves of bread (some 180,000 tons), and it is also significant that between 1948 and 1950 when the quantity of flour used nationally for bread and flour confectionery fell by 11 per cent, its own flour usage increased by 8 per cent.

Another concern which may well have been one of the three largest units in both 1935 and 1951 is J. Lyons and Company, which, besides having its catering interests, serves the general public through its own shops as well as acting as wholesaler to other retailers. The main production is carried on at Cadby Hall, where there were some 1,700 people employed in 1954 and over 3,000 sacks of flour a week were used in the making of bread, but it also has subsidiary bakeries in Lancashire, the Midlands, and West and South England.

Although co-operative societies produce a substantial proportion of the nation's bread—as much as 25 per cent in 1937 but nearer 20 per cent in 1953—their autonomous status makes them much less important as individual business units. On the other hand, parallel to the growth of larger units of production in the private sector of the trade, co-operative societies have tended to combine their baking interests in a federal bakery. Between 1948 and 1953 over eighty societies in England and Wales ceased baking national bread, taking their supplies from a federal bakery or from neighbouring societies, while in Scotland the United Co-operative Baking Society of Glasgow has been supplying an increasing number of retail societies. Indeed, the U.C.B.S. is in its own right one of the largest bakery concerns in Britain.[1]

There were, of course, several other concerns in the private sector which had reached some considerable size by 1951 and have continued to grow since then. Indeed, the process of concentration in this trade may well have continued at a faster rate after 1951 than between 1935 and 1951.

The continuing decline in the level of bread consumption has been the most important cause of this sustained process of concentration, since it

[1] F. Garner, 'Baking Industry Changes, II', *Co-operative Review*, July 1953, pp. 162–3.

has intensified the plant bakery's need to ensure that its trade is enough to keep its plant busy. There has been a marked tendency, therefore, for the largest units to increase the number of retail outlets under their control. Thus Allied Bakeries acquired about ten bakeries between 1953 and 1956, including Barrett and Pomeroy (Bakers), London and Provincial Bakeries, and the Aerated Bread Company (which owned 165 A.B.C. tea shops in London and the suburbs). Similarly, another important Greater London concern, A. B. Hemmings, has made a number of acquisitions since 1951, and probably doubled the number of its retail outlets in the process.

The bakers are not the only ones affected by the decline in bread consumption; so are the flour millers. But the acquisition of large baking interests by the two largest milling concerns, Ranks and Spillers, was as much directed at challenging Allied Bakeries' supremacy in the bakery trade as ensuring an outlet for their flour. The trouble started when Allied Bakeries held that it should, after the end of government control of the flour-milling industry in 1953, receive a special quantity discount from the millers. After the millers had refused the discount, Allied Bakeries imported flour from Canada and Australia and blended it with weaker English flour to their own requirements. Eventually they were importing about half their total needs.

When other bakery concerns began to follow suit, Ranks and Spillers decided to increase their existing, but relatively small, interests in the bakery trade, and their respective acquisitions were vested in British Bakeries and United Bakeries in 1955. Later in the same year, an agreement was reached whereby Allied Bakeries received a discount from the millers in return for an undertaking to take fixed quantities of flour on a quarterly basis.

As a result of these developments, it has been suggested that Ranks and Spillers have obtained control of 10 per cent and 5 per cent respectively of the bread trade, compared with Allied Bakeries' share of 18 per cent. On this basis, the degree of concentration in the Bread and Flour Confectionery Trade would now be substantially higher than in 1951.

Conclusion

Between 1935 and 1951 the changes in the structure and organization of the baking trade which had been proceeding already for many years were intensified. The mechanisation of baking encouraged the introduction of plant bakeries capable of supplying a large number of retail outlets over a wide area. The consequence was that production became separated from distribution, and the wholesale bakers became interested in developing new retail outlets, such as grocers and general stores, for their products.

The particular circumstances of the war and post-war period of control tended to favour the plant bakery, and many small bakers abandoned bread production and took their supplies instead from the large or medium-sized concerns. Yet the increase in the trade's concentration cannot be simply explained by the increasing importance of the plant bakery, though it has an obvious relevance to the emergence of the concerns with which the increased concentration is more directly associated.

Allied Bakeries, unlike most of the larger concerns in the trade, operates on a nation-wide scale, having acquired medium-sized bakery businesses, with existing goodwill or retail outlets, in different parts of the country. It has grown by acquisition rather than by new building, though where necessary acquired capacity has been modernised and expanded. It was certainly the largest unit in the trade in 1951, and it probably accounted for the greater part of the increase in the trade's concentration between 1935 and 1951.

The two milling concerns, Ranks and Spillers, have acquired their bakery interests in a similar fashion, until there is now little scope for further expansion by the larger units absorbing the medium-sized concerns. There still remains the major part of the trade in the hands of the small bakers, and as far as bread-baking is concerned, it is likely that their importance will continue to decline. But it is doubtful to what extent they will be taken over by the larger concerns.

The future of the small bakers lies more in the field of flour confectionery, to which many of them have already turned as the bread trade has become progressively more difficult. Unlike bread consumption, the demand for cakes and flour confectionery continues to rise, and the public's demand for variety and freshness in these lines provides an opportunity for the craft baker to succeed where it is harder for the plant bakery to compete.

14. SOAP

Soap manufacture is a trade that is centuries old, but its rise to the status of an important industry dates only from the early part of the nineteenth century. Even then another fifty or sixty years passed before the industry began to take on the characteristics of large-scale organisation and competitive selling that distinguish it today.

The period of rapid growth in the use of soap in this country was between 1861 and 1891, though consumption continued to increase slowly until 1921. Between 1924 and 1930 it was almost stationary, but in the 1930's demand revived strongly, and the decade showed a 27 per cent increase in sales. Although sales fell in the war and post-war years, because of raw material difficulties, home consumption was one-tenth higher in 1951 than in 1935. During the same period, the output of soap rose more than home consumption; in 1935 it was less than 10 million cwt., whereas in 1951 it was nearer 11·5 million cwt.

Nearly all this production was credited by the Census to the Soap, Candles and Glycerine Trade in 1951, and to the Soap, Candle and Perfumery Trade in 1935. The proportion outside the trades was slightly larger in 1951 than in 1935, because toilet preparations and perfumery had become a separate Trade in 1951. Most of the soap output classified to establishments in other Trades in 1951 consisted, in fact, of toilet and shaving soap.

It is not, however, with the whole Trade that we are concerned, but with a sub-division of it. In 1951, this Sub-Trade was described as 'the specialist producers of soap and glycerine'; in 1935, as 'soap boiling'.

For simplicity it may be assumed that the principal products characteristic of the sub-trade were soap, crude and distilled glycerine, and soap base, in both years. The total output of these products, wherever produced, came to £60·9 million in 1951, of which £55·7 million (or 92 per cent) was produced by establishments in the soap and glycerine subtrade. Similarly, for 1935 the total output of these products came to more than £17·5 million, but only £14·8 million (or less than 85 per cent) was produced by establishments classified to the soap boiling trade.

The number of establishments in the trade increased from sixty-five in 1935 to ninety-one in 1948, but then decreased slightly to eighty-eight in 1951. Paradoxically, the numbers employed fell between 1935 and 1948 but had risen again by 1951. Taking the period as a whole, employment increased by 5 per cent. There was also a very substantial rise in the number of business units, from thirty-nine in 1935 to seventy-four in 1951.

Despite the increase in the number of business units and the relatively small expansion in the trade, concentration rose between 1935 and 1951 in terms of both gross output (9 percentage points) and employment (2 percentage points), though net output showed a slight fall (1 percentage point). Moreover, the degree of concentration was already high in 1935—70 per cent in terms of employment and 81 per cent in terms of net output.

Two of the three largest units of 1935 have been identified by Leak and Maizels as Lever Bros. and the Co-operative Wholesale Society (C.W.S.). The other was almost certainly Thomas Hedley and Sons. The rise of the Lever business in the soap industry is well known and need only be briefly described.[1] From its entry into soap manufacture in 1885, Lever Bros. revolutionised the methods of selling soap, employing advertising and sales promotion to popularise its branded products. The first twenty

[1] For the fullest account, see C. Wilson, *The History of Unilever*, 2 vols. (London, Cassell, 1954).

years passed without a single acquisition at home, but in 1906 William Hesketh Lever was advocating the formation of a soap trust. The soap trust was killed by public opinion, led by the popular press. Lever realised that the combine could not be secured by the original ideal of an exchange of shares between a number of soapmakers. Instead, Lever Bros. began to acquire existing businesses for itself.

By 1914, Lever's companies made 60 per cent of all the soap consumed in Britain, and by 1921 there were thirty-nine soap manufacturing companies in which Lever Bros. had financial or other interests and for all but three of them Lever Bros. held control. In all, the Lever group controlled 70–75 per cent of the total British soap output in 1921.[1] Another 10–15 per cent was shared between some fifty concerns which were members of the U.K. Soap Manufacturers' Association. The rest of the trade was distributed between another 130 makers, but the only firm of any importance among them was the C.W.S.[2]

During the 1920's, when soap consumption was more or less stationary, Lever Bros. found it increasingly difficult to keep up such a high proportion of soap sales. Competition came from several distinct quarters. It came from the C.W.S., whose output, after running at a rate about two-thirds of that of Port Sunlight,[2] rose by about one-quarter between 1926 and 1929. It came from the Scottish Co-operative Wholesale Society (S.C.W.S.), whose sales jumped by 50 per cent between 1926 and 1929. It came also from the oil-milling concerns—principally the British Oil and Cake Mills (B.O.C.M.) and J. Bibby and Sons—which embarked upon soap manufacture for reasons of their own in the 1920's. In 1925, however, B.O.C.M. was amalgamated by an exchange of shares with Lever Bros. Thereafter sales of its 'New Pin' soap dropped from nearly 34,000 tons to 6,000 tons in 1928. Finally, competition came from across the Atlantic. 'After some abortive negotiations between Lever's and the Palmolive company for a union',[3] imported Palmolive soap began to appear in considerable quantities and by 1926 Palmolive was the biggest selling line in toilet soap on the British market.

By 1930, therefore, Lever Bros. had lost some ground in the British soap market. In that year, the sales of the Lever group probably amounted to about 60 per cent of the total soap consumption of the United Kingdom and Eire; its share of total production would have been somewhat higher, but certainly not so high as the 70–75 per cent with which it was credited in 1951.

In 1930 the leading American soap concern, Procter and Gamble, bought the old-established Newcastle firm of Thomas Hedley and Sons.

[1] Sub-Committee of the Standing Committee on Trusts, *Report on the Soap Industry*, Cmd. 1126 (London, H.M.S.O. 1921), p. 6.

[2] Wilson, *op. cit.* vol. 1, pp. 302–3.

[3] Wilson, *op. cit.* vol. 1, p. 280.

Hedley's had acquired a few smaller soap firms after World War I, but it was still only a minor producer: its Fairy soap could claim only some 2 per cent of the British market in 1930.[1] Procter and Gamble was, however, an old rival of Lever's in the United States market (for Lever's had been selling soap there since the middle of the 1890's), and with the powerful resources of Procter and Gamble behind it, Hedley's was destined for speedy development. A new Hedley factory was opened at Manchester in 1933 and subsequently extended four times, and the Newcastle plant was itself enlarged. One of Procter and Gamble's leading lines in the United States—Oxydol soap powder—was introduced to the British market through Hedley's, and by 1939 Hedley's was able to claim some 15 per cent of total United Kingdom soap consumption.[2]

Hedley's share was much smaller in 1935, and was almost certainly less than that of both Lever's and the C.W.S. The total sales of the Lever group, at home and for export, were about 290,000 tons in 1935, or roughly 58 per cent of the total soap production in that year. The C.W.S. output amounted to 49,800 tons (or just under 10 per cent of the total output in 1935). But while Lever's output of soap remained fairly constant after 1935, its share of the total production tended to decline. By 1938, its share was probably down to 53 per cent, while that of the C.W.S. also fell slightly. Only Hedley's among the largest concerns followed the upward trend in soap production, and its share of the industry increased as a result.

During the inter-war years, the product-structure of the soap trade also changed. Hard soap lost ground to soap powders and soap flakes, while toilet soap became more and more important. Since the War, however, the soap powders and flakes have had to compete with the synthetic detergents. Commercial production of synthetic detergents had already begun by 1930 in the United States, but their use was mainly confined to the textile industry until Procter and Gamble began to market a household detergent in hard-water areas (from 1933 onwards). But in 1938 this detergent still represented only about 1 per cent of the total sales of soap in the United States.

In Britain, the 'soap substitutes' began to make their appearance during the War, but they were not very popular with the housewife even though soap was rationed. Soap rationing continued after the end of the War, and as the quality of the synthetic detergents improved and they became more widely advertised, sales increased until they were accounting for about 10 per cent of total home consumption when soap was derationed in the late summer of 1950. The detergents continued to go ahead, doubling their share of the total soap and detergent consumption

[1] R. W. Evely, 'The Battle of the Detergents', *Cartel*, January 1954, p. 12.
[2] *Ibid.*

by 1952, and increasing it still further to 25–30 per cent at the end of 1953.

The production of synthetic detergents was treated by the Census of Production as part of the Soap, Candles and Glycerine Trade in 1951—they accounted for 15 per cent of the principal products of the Trade—but they do not fall within the scope of the soap and glycerine sub-trade. Before leaving the synthetic detergents on one side, however, it is relevant to note that both Hedley's and Unilever (as Lever Bros. is now known) are active producers of synthetic detergents, but that the C.W.S., though it markets a synthetic detergent, does not produce it for itself. In 1955 Hedley's was responsible for at least 60 per cent of the synthetic detergent sales in this country, compared with Unilever's 30 per cent or more.[1]

Returning to the soap trade proper, it is more difficult to assess the relative shares of the largest concerns in 1951 than in 1935. It can be stated, however, that the C.W.S. output from its three soapworks amounted to nearly 28,000 tons in 1951, or about 5 per cent of the total tonnage of soap produced. This marks a considerable fall in the relative importance of the C.W.S., not merely as compared with pre-war but also with 1948, for in that year the C.W.S. output amounted to more than 7 per cent of the total tonnage.

There is no question that the other two largest units in 1951 were Unilever and Hedley's. Although Unilever was still the biggest soap producer, its share was probably lower than before the War, for Hedley's opened a new plant at Purfleet in 1941 and has almost certainly continued its pre-war progress.[2] Thus, Unilever's share may have fallen below 50 per cent by 1951, and Hedley's has probably gained most of the trade lost by them and the C.W.S.

Conclusion

Although mergers and acquisitions played a considerable part in the concentration of soap production in the early part of this century, their importance has been small in the period after 1935.

The share of the largest unit in the trade—Unilever—has declined fairly steadily from its peak of 70–75 per cent after World War I to 50 per cent or under in 1951. Similarly, the C.W.S., after expanding its share of the trade in the 1920's, has tended to lose rather than to gain ground.

The loss to Unilever and the C.W.S. has been caused by the emergence of Thomas Hedley as a leading producer of soap and latterly as a still more important producer of synthetic detergents. Hedley's only assumed this importance after its acquisition by Procter and Gamble in 1930. Until then its share of the soap trade was modest. It was the financial re-

[1] W. J. Corlett, *The Economic Development of Detergents* (London, Duckworth, 1958), p. 56.

[2] See L. Hale, *Hedley of Newcastle* (Newcastle, Thomas Hedley & Co., 1955).

sources and the know-how of soap manufacture and marketing, made available to it by its American parent, that enabled Hedley's to expand both absolutely and relatively.

As a result, Hedley's has moved from third to second place among soap producers between 1935 and 1951, increasing its share from less than 10 per cent to more than 30 per cent in that period.

Although the number of soapmakers in the Sub-Trade was as high as seventy-four in 1951, and there were of course other producers outside the Sub-Trade, there are few that would come near to challenging even the C.W.S. for third place. Among the other more important soapmaking concerns are Bibby's, Colgate Palmolive-Peet, and the S.C.W.S., but for the rest the interests are small.

Finally, it must be observed that the structure of the soap trade is markedly oligopolistic and that competition frequently takes the form of sales promotion. Advertising expenditures are an important item in the costs of both Unilever and Thomas Hedley, though probably relatively less important for the C.W.S., Bibby's, and other soap makers. Moreover, the various brands of Unilever's soap products (let alone the synthetic detergents which compete with them) have been competitively advertised one against the other for years; there is, it has been claimed, a spirit of rivalry within the Unilever group as well as between it and other soap producers. For all that, the essential difference between the soap trade as it was before the War, and as it is today, is not the change in the degree of concentration, nor yet the growth of Thomas Hedley, but the increasing use and popularity of the synthetic detergents at the expense of the traditional soap products.

CHAPTER XV

TRADES WITH DECREASED CONCENTRATION, 1935–51

I. POLISHES AND CANVAS DRESSINGS

There are three main types of polishes which, together with canvas dressings, constitute the characteristic products of the Polishes and Canvas Dressings Sub-Trade of the Census of Production in 1951.[1] Most important of the three types were floor and furniture polishes (representing nearly 37 per cent of the total output of polishes and canvas dressings), followed by metal, stove and other polishes (31 per cent) and leather polishes (28 per cent). Compared with 1935, floor and furniture polishes have increased their relative importance, mainly at the expense of metal, stove and other polishes. At the same time, the output of all types of polishes increased during the 1935–51 period, the rise being as much as two-thirds for floor and furniture polishes, though less than 7 per cent for leather polishes.

Table 39. *Number of units and concentration-ratios for six case-study trades with decreased principal product concentration, 1935–51*

	Number of units*		Gross output concentration-ratios		Net output concentration-ratios		Employment concentration-ratios	
	1935	1951	1935 (%)	1951 (%)	1935 (%)	1951 (%)	1935 (%)	1951 (%)
Polishes and Canvas Dressings	38	38	75	54	81	43	74	52
Wallpaper	17	16	96	86†	98	86†	90	86†
Biscuit	71	92	34	26	37	31	37	34
Linoleum and Leathercloth	33	25	56	48	62	52	64	54
Grain Milling	308	240	42	35	39	33	34	31
Match	19	27	95	93‡	94	86‡	89	85‡

* Estimated in 1935; see footnote, p. 153.
† For four largest business units.
‡ For six largest business units.

Some part of the total output of polishes and canvas dressings is produced in establishments classified to other Census Trades, while there is also a certain amount of production which is classified to the Trade but not included in the Sub-Trade. Even so, the Polishes and Canvas Dressings Sub-Trade had a high degree of exclusiveness in both years, amounting to 89 per cent in 1951 and 95 per cent in 1935.

[1] This Sub-Trade belonged in 1951 to the Polishes Trade; in 1935, the comparable Sub-Trade was the Polishes sub-division of the Starch and Polishes Trade.

The number of larger establishments in the Census Sub-Trade fell from forty-four in 1935 to forty-one in 1951, while employment in these establishments fell by more than one-quarter.[1] The number of business units in the Sub-Trade was thirty-eight in 1951, the same as in 1935, but the degree of concentration was substantially lower. The fall in concentration was greatest by the net output indicator from 81 per cent in 1935 to 43 per cent in 1951, but in terms of employment it also fell from 74 to 52 per cent. To seek an explanation of this change in concentration it is convenient to examine each section of the Sub-Trade in turn, since there is an element of specialisation in the activities of many of the leading concerns.

Floor and furniture polishes

The most heavily populated section of the polishes trade consists of the producers of floor and furniture polishes, which are relatively easy to manufacture. This section of the trade has also shown the greatest expansion between 1935 and 1951, mainly as the result of the extensive house-building programme, the furnishing of these new houses and the introduction of new types of floor-tiling which require polishing. Exports have also increased, despite the fact that some of the principal pre-war markets have been closed to British firms through political and economic nationalism.

The number of firms selling on a nation-wide scale at home or on a large scale overseas is small. But the existence of local manufacturers tends to increase the degree of competition in both markets, and there appears to be strong pressure on manufacturers to ensure that new and improved types of polishes (such as the silicone polishes) are developed. It is significant also that advertising is extensively practised in this and other sections of the trade.

The most important concern in both 1935 and 1951 was Chiswick Products, which produces the several varieties of Mansion furniture polish, Min furniture cream and Cardinal tile polish. The development of this concern will be considered later. Among the other principal producers have been S. C. Johnson and Son (a subsidiary of an American company, which has been producing in this country since 1915), Ronuk, William Wren (makers of Lavendo) and O'Cedar (another concern with American associations).

Leather polishes

The leather polishes section of the trade was even more highly concentrated in 1935 than the Sub-Trade itself; the three largest units were

[1] In 1951, there were 107 small firms (that is, with ten or fewer persons) with a total employment of 510 persons in the Polishes Trade, and some of them might qualify as specialist producers of polishes and canvas dressings if they were larger.

responsible for 85 per cent of the total value of output.[1] Part of the reason for this high concentration was the limited number of producers, for boot and shoe polishes are difficult to manufacture. Though production in 1951 was slightly higher than in 1935, the quantities sold on the home market were 40 per cent lower. Indeed, supplies to the home market were curtailed during the post-war years in order to boost exports.

Chiswick Products was the leading concern in both 1935 and 1951, having been formed in 1929 by a merger between the Chiswick Polish Company and the Nugget Polish Company (producers of the well-known Cherry Blossom and Nugget boot polishes respectively).[2] Chiswick Polish was itself formed in 1913 jointly by Reckitt and Sons (which transferred to it two recent acquisitions, the Master Boot Polish Company, West Bromwich, and William Berry, London) and the Mason brothers of Chiswick, producers of Cherry Blossom boot and Mansion furniture polishes.[3] Reckitts have accordingly had a considerable financial stake in Chiswick Products since its formation.

Next in importance after Chiswick Products comes the Kiwi Polish Company, a subsidiary of the Australian concern. Third place in 1935 was probably claimed by Blyth and Platt which, however, sold its Cobra boot polish abroad. By 1951, Blyth and Platt's claim to this position was strengthened by its acquisition of another boot-polish manufacturer, William Wren, which had become of some importance in the home market. Production was rationalised by Blyth and Platt, and Wren became its selling agents.

Metal, stove and car polishes

In 1935, metal, stove and other polishes (including canvas dressings) accounted for the largest share of the output of polishes. By 1951, the total output of these polishes had increased, but their share had declined. There had, moreover, been a change in relative importance between the various types of polish: car polish had become more important and metal and stove polishes less important during the period.

The leading producer of metal and stove polishes in 1935 was undoubtedly Reckitt and Sons, which had maintained that position for a great many years. Reckitt's began manufacturing black lead more than a century ago, and in 1854 it represented some 28 per cent of its total business. First by expanding its own business and introducing new brands, and then in the 1890's and early 1900's by a process of acquiring rival concerns, Reckitt's established control over a large share of the trade. By

[1] Leak and Maizels, 'The Structure of British Industry', table 12, p. 161.

[2] B. N. Reckitt, *The History of Reckitt and Sons Ltd* (London, A. Brown and Sons, 1952), p. 76.

[3] After the Martindale business was purchased in 1917 by Reckitts, its boot-polish interests were merged in Chiswick Polish Company. In addition, a profit pooling arrangement between Chiswick and Nugget came into effect in 1916 (Reckitt, *op. cit.* p. 69).

the end of World War I, Reckitt's had reached the stage where 'about as much of the total Home Trade as could be won had been won and development must depend on increased consumption'.[1] Unfortunately that prospect was darkened by the fact that 'grates of the new type were tiled or finished in enamel; brass fittings were being replaced by oxydised metal of various kinds which did not need polishing'.[2] An attempt was made to stimulate demand whereby Reckitt's became interested in the selling of ornamental brassware through grocers' shops in the later 1920's, but it was the company's main endeavour to find new lines to offset the falling sales of the old. Most of these new lines lay outside the polishes trade, but two are relevant here: the introduction of Karpol car cleaner in 1927 and Windolene window polish three years earlier. In addition, Reckitt's made a number of selective acquisitions in the 1920's, including Hargreaves Bros. and Company (whose subsidiaries included the makers of Aladdin, Mitre and Midas metal polishes) in 1922 and the Glossit Company (Eze metal polish) in 1930. By 1935, the main brands marketed by Reckitt's were Brasso, Silvo, Shinio and Bluebell.

Among the other more important producers of stove and metal polishes during the 1935–51 period were J. Goddard and Sons, Town Talk Polish Company, and Duraglit; while in the car-polishes field, Reckitt's had to meet the competition of a large number of producers, including Simoniz (England), Lewis Berger and Sons (the paint manufacturers who produced the Lifeguard car polish) and S. C. Johnson and Son. Finally, the canvas dressings sections of the trade included such concerns as J. Pickering and Sons (Blanco), E. Brown and Son (Meltonian) and Propert.

Conclusion

There are many factors that have contributed to the fall in concentration in the polishes trade. Although it has been an expanding trade in terms of output if not employment, its growth has been uneven, centring mainly in the floor and furniture polishes section.

Two of the three largest units in 1935 were certainly Chiswick Products and Reckitt and Sons. While Chiswick Products is extensively interested in floor and furniture polishes, it might have failed to maintain its 1935 proportion of this section of the trade for two main reasons. First, it has been forced to open factories abroad in order to supply markets which otherwise would be lost to it, and to this extent the demand to be met by its factories in Britain has been reduced. Second, other firms may have been able to increase their home sales at Chiswick Products' expense because of the cramping effects of shortages of tinplate and imported raw materials on the latter's operation.

[1] Reckitt, *op. cit.* p. 71. [2] *Ibid.*

The long-term decline in the demand for metal and stove polishes (in which its interests are largely concentrated) has probably adversely affected Reckitt's sales of these lines, even though it may have benefited from the expanding sales of car polishes. But, on balance, it seems reasonable to expect that Reckitt's share of the polishes trade, though sufficient for it to retain second place, may be less than in 1935.

It is relevant to note that Reckitt's share would not have been increased by the merger in 1938 of its trading interests with those of J. and J. Colman, since Colman's were not interested in polishes. On the other hand, the merger of the entire interests of Reckitt's, Colman's and Chiswick Products, which might have had the effect of increasing concentration, did not occur until 1953.

The identity of the third largest unit in 1935 and 1951 is much less certain, particularly since the period saw the rise of some firms and the decline of others. The competitive nature of the trade, the emergence of new products, the growth of large-scale buying by institutions, offices and factories, etc., may all have combined to promote mobility in the ranking of the various concerns. But the third largest unit in both years was almost certainly one of three concerns: Kiwi Polish, S. C. Johnson and Son, and Blyth and Platt. Thus, the main explanation of the fall in concentration is not an increase in the number of concerns but the uneven growth of the different sections of the trade and the consequent effect on the fortunes of the largest concerns.

2. WALLPAPER

The development of wallpaper manufacture into an industry dates from the mechanisation of the printing process and the consequent increase in commercial production just over a hundred years ago. Up to the 1840's, wallpaper had to be printed by hand blocks on sheets of paper, but from then on, the rotary production of paper made it possible for reels of paper to be machine printed. Between 1851 and 1874, output was expanded by nearly 500 per cent, and many new concerns entered the trade. By the end of the century, however, the period of rapid expansion was over though production was still to fluctuate widely during the next fifty years.

By 1935, the output of the industry amounted to some 1·2 million cwt., which was some 40 per cent higher than in 1924 when the industry was suffering the effects of the post-war slump in house building. Between 1935 and 1951, however, output expanded only very slightly; it is difficult to be precise about the actual increase since the Census quantity data were given in hundredweights in 1935 but in thousands of rolls in 1951. It is relevant to note, however, that it was not until 1954 that it was reported that 'the demand is now rapidly approaching the pre-war figure of 100 million rolls a year'.[1]

The Wallpaper Trade of the Census of Production has high degrees of specialisation and exclusiveness. In 1935, the establishments classified to the Wallpaper Trade were responsible for virtually all of the wallpaper produced in Britain, while they also produced little else but wallpaper. In 1951, specialisation was a little lower than in 1935, but exclusiveness just as high.

Although output rose slightly between 1935 and 1951, employment fell by nearly 10 per cent. The number of establishments fell from thirty-seven in 1935 to thirty-two in 1951, and the number of business units from seventeen to sixteen. But concentration fell, too: in 1935 the three largest units in the trade accounted for 90 per cent of its employment and 98 per cent of its net output; but in 1951, the *four* largest units were responsible for 86 per cent of the trade by both indicators.

By far the largest unit in the industry is Wall Paper Manufacturers (W.P.M.) which was formed in 1899, by a voluntary combination of thirty-one firms. The preceding decade had been a very difficult one for the wallpaper industry: the 1900 prospectus of W.P.M. refers to 'the disabilities under which the individual firms and companies have suffered through the cutting of prices, irregularity of terms, long credits and unnecessary expenditure especially involved in obtaining orders'. The evidence suggests that the price-cutting was due to over-production. Not only had many leading firms in the trade entered into a gentlemen's agreement for the stabilisation of prices, but in the slump of 1893 more than one firm crashed. It is also known that some of the smaller firms in the industry were interested in forming a combine in 1898.

On its formation, W.P.M. claimed in its prospectus that it controlled 98 per cent of wallpaper manufacture in the United Kingdom. It was not to maintain such a high proportion for long, for between 1900 and 1910, many new concerns embarked upon wallpaper manufacture, some of them financially assisted by distributors and by the makers of wallpaper machinery. In addition, British manufacturers had to face the competition of cheap imports from Germany. It was the policy of W.P.M. to meet this competition wherever it was encountered. Special 'fighting lines' were marketed in the North of England, Scotland and Ireland from the Walker, Carver mill at Salford, while the same function was performed in the South by the Osborn and Shearman factory in Fulham.[2] Moreover, W.P.M. sought to strengthen its position by agreements with dealers whereby the latter undertook only to handle wallpaper made by

[1] 'Wallpaper Regains its Popularity,' *Times Review of Industry*, September 1954, p. 17.

[2] A. V. Sugden and J. L. Edmondson, *A History of English Wallpaper, 1509–1914* (London, Batsford, 1925), p. 236.

them, as well as by forming Wall Paper Stores in 1906 for selling wall-paper in its own retail shops.

In 1915, a number of the newcomers to the industry were acquired by W.P.M., including concerns with highly efficient modern plants. The concerns brought under W.P.M.'s control at this time were, however, comparatively small, and had been finding it increasingly difficult to obtain essential supplies, especially aniline dyes, which had been bought up in large quantities by W.P.M.[1] Once again, therefore, W.P.M. had secured a very large proportion of the wallpaper trade, while its position was strengthened both by the end of imports and by a 'friendly understanding as to general practice and conditions' which it had made with a group of outside manufacturers.[2]

The end of the War saw an immediate boom in the demand for wall-paper, followed by the slump of 1920 in which all the previous advantages gained by W.P.M. were lost. Once again, new concerns entered the industry, and between 1921 and 1933 there was a return of price-cutting competition, particularly in the depression of the early 1930's. Although W.P.M. reorganised its business, modernised several of its factories and succeeded in maintaining its 1921 volume of trade for the period up to 1933, it did not 'participate in the increase of consumption which took place as the outcome of general building and housing activity'.[3] It was the newcomers who enjoyed that distinction, and by 1934, W.P.M. admitted that 'the quality and range of their productions . . . pointed, in the interests of the Company's trade and of the wallpaper industry generally, to the advisability of approaching the principal firms amongst our competitors' with the object of acquiring them.[4]

Five concerns with valuable sales connections and a substantial turn-over were, therefore, acquired by W.P.M. in 1934, while two other small factories manufacturing specialities were bought a few months earlier to be closed shortly afterwards. Subsequently, the chairman of W.P.M. declared that 'as a result of these acquisitions, we propose in the interests of all concerned to adjust ourselves to changed conditions and to render it less easy for new competitors with machinery redundant to consumption to commence operations and also less easy for those already in existence to increase their share of the business obtainable'.[5]

By 1935, therefore, W.P.M. had once again increased its share of the trade to about 85–90 per cent, although it still had to face competition 'from the five or six manufacturers not included in the recent acquisi-

[1] A. V. Sugden and E. A. Entwisle, *Potters of Darwen, 1839–1939* (privately printed, 1939), p. 75.

[2] Wall Paper Manufacturers Ltd, Letter to the Stockholders, 8 September 1934.

[3] *Ibid.* [4] *Ibid.*

[5] Chairman's Speech to the Shareholders' Meeting of Wall Paper Manufacturers Ltd, 18 September 1934.

tions',[1] of which potentially the most important was Ashley United Industries with a factory at Gosport.

In the absence of further information, it is not possible to identify the two other largest units in 1935, but concentration fell so much in the 1935–51 period that the four largest units in 1951 probably did not possess as large a share of the trade as W.P.M. alone in 1935.

Between the wars, the channels through which wallpaper reached the public underwent a change. Traditionally, wallpaper was sold through the decorator's pattern book and the decorators obtained their requirements from merchants. Exclusive-dealing arrangements tended to tie merchants to particular groups of manufacturers. The members of the Wall Paper Manufacturers Employers' Association granted 'agreed discounts off the standard trade prices to distributors who can show a prescribed minimum level of turnover, in addition to undertaking to buy exclusively from members of the Association'.[2] Similar arrangements are also believed to have been operated by the National Wallpaper Council to which some of the manufacturers outside the W.P.M. group belong.

While the merchant remained the main channel of distribution for wallpaper during the inter-war years, there was a growing amount of over-the-counter sales in wallpaper or ironmongery and hardware shops. For a time W.P.M., despite its early entry into retailing through Wall Paper Stores, neglected this side of the trade, while others benefited as they gave it their attention. But during the 1930's, the number of shops operated by Wall Paper Stores increased from fifty-five in 1930 to around two hundred in 1938, partly by the acquisition of existing chains and partly by the opening of new branches.

The increased importance of direct sales to the general public has not only made the ownership of retail shops more desirable, but also placed a premium on attractive and distinctive designs. A manufacturer who is well served by his designers can, therefore, expect to increase his sales and exist alongside the largest concerns despite their relatively greater financial and manufacturing strength.

While W.P.M. still ranked as the largest unit in the trade, it probably accounted for only 70–75 per cent of wallpaper production in 1951 compared with 85–90 per cent in 1935. Its chief rival is Ashley United Industries whose share may have been as high as 10 per cent in 1951. Ashley United Industries, besides selling through merchants and independent retailers, also owns a chain of two hundred shops known as Brighter Homes Stores. Among the other wallpaper manufacturers are some well-known names, such as Shand Kydd, but their importance is not large compared with W.P.M.

[1] Report of Ordinary General Meeting of Wall Paper Manufacturers Ltd, 1934.

[2] Monopolies Commission, *Collective Discrimination* (1955), par. 104.

Conclusion

The wallpaper trade has been highly concentrated since the beginning of this century, though the share of the trade in the hands of the largest unit, W.P.M., has fluctuated from over 90 per cent to about 70 per cent at the present time. Despite periodic attempts to reduce the amount of competition—attempts which have varied from fighting lines to acquisition of rivals—newcomers have entered the trade and succeeded in establishing themselves without undue difficulty. Although the industry is highly capitalised, the technical know-how and capital required to enter the trade have not presented an insuperable obstacle. Perhaps greater difficulties have been encountered on the selling side, for independent manufacturers may have found it hard to secure outlets for their products because of the exclusive dealing arrangements. But as the proportion of total sales represented by direct retailing increased, so exclusive dealing became less important as an obstacle to the development of smaller concerns.

3. BISCUIT

The biscuit industry has been growing steadily for the greater part of this century, and the only major interruption in its expansion occurred during World War II. During the inter-war period, the production of biscuits doubled and employment in the industry increased by three-fifths. After 1942, however, production fell until in 1947 it was one-quarter below the level of 1938, but it recovered again as soon as supplies of raw materials improved. The demand for biscuits, despite the greater variety of food available, has remained high, encouraged by the excellent quality of the goods and the relatively small increase in their prices compared with pre-war. By 1951, the output of different kinds of biscuits was very much higher than in 1935: chocolate biscuits increased threefold, unsweetened biscuits doubled, and sweetened biscuits, other than chocolate, increased by three-fifths.

The Biscuit Trade was highly exclusive in both years—95 per cent of the total output of principal products was produced by establishments in the trade—while the degree of specialisation was about the same. Although some of the leading biscuit manufacturers have extensive interests in cakes and confectionery, these activities tend to be carried on in separate establishments, classified to the Bread and Flour Confectionery Trade.

The expansion of the biscuit industry between the wars is reflected in the employment of the Census Trade, which increased from 28,000 in 1924 to 44,000 in 1935. In 1951, however, employment was still 5 per cent below 1935 (though nearly 30 per cent higher than in 1949), so that the increase in output has been achieved by a substantial increase in productivity.

Although employment was slightly lower in 1951 than in 1935, the number of establishments rose from ninety-eight to 131 and the number of business units from seventy-one to ninety-two in the same period. There was also a decrease in concentration. The share of the trade controlled by the three largest units fell from 37 to 34 per cent in terms of employment, and from 37 to 31 per cent in terms of net output.

It has been suggested that concentration in the biscuit trade tended to decline during the inter-war years because the expansion of the trade increased the number of firms, and a proportionately higher number of the new workers found employment in the small and medium firms than in the large firms.[1] It is doubtful, however, whether the same explanation is valid for the fall in concentration between 1935 and 1951, particularly since there have been several developments, including mergers, which might have been expected to have increased rather than decreased concentration.

After World War I, the biscuit industry began to be rather set in its ways. Mechanisation and mass production had developed long before, so that new techniques aimed at perfecting rather than revolutionising the production process. There was also a tendency among the nationally known biscuit manufacturers to sell direct to the retailer, even though it meant high costs of distribution. But during the 1930's there were signs that changes were on the way.

In the first place, a considerable quantity of low-priced biscuit flour was imported from the continent during the depression years and used for the manufacture of cheap lines of biscuits by new firms which entered the market at that time. Secondly, other firms began to distribute through wholesalers (instead of direct to the retailer), and consequently were able to provide biscuits, comparable in quality to those of the national firms, at lower prices. As a result, there was not only an extension of the market, but new firms began to emerge among the leaders of the trade.

Probably the most successful of these new enterprises was the Weston concern, for by concentrating on the production of a good-quality but cheap biscuit, Mr W. Garfield Weston captured an immense new market. At first the Weston companies met little competition since the greater part of their output was retailed at 6*d.* per lb. and distributed mainly through low-price chain stores and equivalent retail outlets.[2] Production increased from 7 million biscuits per day in 1937 to 11 million per day in 1938.[3]

[1] Rostas, *Productivity, Prices and Distribution in Selected British Industries*, p. 130.

[2] *Food Industries Weekly*, 27 January 1939, p. 3. [3] *Ibid.* 30 December 1938, p. 5.

In 1935, however, there was only one Weston biscuit factory in operation, so that for the identity of the three largest business units in that year we must look elsewhere. Undoubtedly one of them, and probably the largest of the three, was Associated Biscuit Manufacturers, which in 1921 amalgamated the old-established firms of Huntley and Palmer and Peek, Frean and Company. The identity of the other two largest units is less certain, but among the candidates were Macfarlane, Lang, and Company, McVitie and Price, George Kemp, and Carr and Company.

The principal feature of the 1935–9 period was the development of this low-price market. Encouraged by the success of the Weston concern, other firms began to enter this field. In particular, Kemp established a flourishing trade which took them below the prices of other leading makers, though even Kemp did not sell at the Weston price of 6*d.* a lb.

By 1938, the situation had changed. The low-priced biscuit had attracted new consumers, but now it was beginning to cut into the established trade, leading to some price-cutting and lower profits. As a consequence, some firms announced plans to lower production costs by installing new machinery, but the anticipated battle in the 7*d.*–8*d.* a lb. range was halted by the outbreak of World War II.

War-time control of the industry was exercised through the Cake and Biscuit Alliance, established in 1939 by the main trade associations and co-operative organisations with Ministry of Food representation.[1] Membership was obligatory during the war years for matters of allocation of raw materials and price control. Retail distribution was restricted by zoning and the consumer was rationed by a points scheme. Zoning was discontinued in 1946. Unsweetened biscuits were derationed in 1949, but retail price controls were not lifted until 1952. During the same year the restriction on the packing of assortments was removed.

Improvement in the supply of raw materials was sporadic; for example, a substantial increase in the fats ration in 1949 was accompanied by a reduction in sugar, permitting increased production of plain biscuits but not of sweetened. The industry suffered a further setback in 1951, when production was curtailed by a sudden reduction in fat supplies. These unpredictable changes in the allocation of ingredients posed serious problems in planning output. It was not until 1953 that manufacturers were able to bake with grades of flour and sugar of their own choosing, while fats came into free supply early in 1954.

In spite of rigid control there was a considerable increase in the number of biscuit makers. New entrants were allocated a share of the com-

[1] There are also two trade organisations (constituents of the Cake and Biscuit Alliance)—the National Association of Biscuit Manufacturers, with a membership of seven firms all of whom are among the largest in the industry, and the British Cake and Biscuit Association whose membership of some 150 firms includes both cake and biscuit manufacturers ranging from the very small to the very largest.

mon pool of raw materials. But it was also possible to import unrationed ingredients at market prices, and many firms supplemented their allocations in this way.

While new firms entering the trade to meet the increased demand for biscuits were able, during the control period, to produce from unrationed ingredients lines which sold under conditions of shortage, the largest firms were unable to expand their production at the same rate without jeopardising the good name of their products. This is possibly the reason for the fall in concentration.

On the other hand, some of the leading concerns in the trade have grown since the end of the War. In particular, the Weston biscuit interests, controlled since 1938 by Weston Foods, a subsidiary of Allied Bakeries, have developed rapidly. At the time of its formation, Weston Foods controlled four biscuit factories and a number of bakers and confectioners. In 1948 the company gained control of Burton's Gold Medal Biscuits and in 1953 of the Caledonian Oat Cake Baking Company. Then in 1954, Allied Bakeries succeeded in buying practically all the shares of Meredith and Drew in the hands of the public, although control of the business still rests with the families of its founders.

Another event of significance to the degree of concentration in the biscuit industry was the formation of United Biscuits in 1948, which amalgamated the well-known firms of Macfarlane, Lang and Company, and McVitie and Price. The purpose of the amalgamation was to facilitate the realisation of the family interests in the two concerns, rendered necessary by taxation, and to continue the successful co-operation that had developed between them during the War. In 1948, the new concern operated six factories, with a total labour-force of approximately 3,350, or roughly 8 per cent of the employment in the trade. Since 1948, sales have continued to increase, and it is possible that its share of the total turnover of the industry was between one-tenth and one-eighth in 1954.

It is, however, very difficult to establish the relative sizes of the leading biscuit producers. Peek, Frean's London factory employed some 3,700 workers in 1954, while Huntley and Palmer's employed 3,000 in 1954. Therefore the labour-force of Associated Biscuit would probably represent some 16 per cent of the trade's total employment, indicating that Associated Biscuit retained a place among the three largest units in 1951.

If it is accepted that Associated, United and Weston's were the three largest units in 1951, this would indicate that there has been a substantial change in the identity of the leaders compared with 1935. One of the newcomers is, it is true, an amalgamation of two firms, and either or both may have been among the three largest in 1935. But equally another newcomer is a firm which had barely started on its expansion in 1935, and in its case, growth has been associated with breaking new ground rather than by directly challenging established firms.

The biscuit industry was still subject to a substantial degree of control in 1951, and since decontrol in 1953 many features of the trade, including its degree of concentration, may have changed. The prosperity of the trade has not been shared equally by all its members, for the public tends to buy the better known, that is, highly advertised, brands of biscuits to the detriment of the smaller concerns. The firms which maintained a high standard of quality and kept their names before the public by advertisement during the period of control can consequently sell all they produce, whereas the small firms are finding it more difficult. Although quality is important, prices must also be right, and many of the smaller firms are not able to undertake the extensive reorganisation needed to keep costs down. It is possible, therefore, that concentration might have risen since 1951 to nearer the level of 1935.

Conclusion

The decrease in concentration in the biscuit trade between 1935 and 1951 can be attributed in part to the development of a new low-price biscuit industry, in which the older firms had little or no part. Although circumstances forced some of the older firms to produce cheaper lines, the War intervened and, for the next fourteen years, raw materials were no longer freely available. The growing demand for biscuits, coupled with zoning schemes, provided an opportunity for smaller concerns to increase their business at the expense of the share of the largest producers.

Since the lifting of controls, the situation has changed again. Although the demand for biscuits remains high, the public prefer well-known brands, and since this favours the larger producers, it is possible that concentration has risen again.

4. LINOLEUM AND LEATHERCLOTH

Linoleum and leathercloth are distinct products and not competitive with each other in use. Linoleum is 'a hard-surfaced, pliable floor covering, made by pressing or calendering a plastic mass in a smooth sheet on to jute canvas' or bituminised paper felt.[1] Leathercloth is used principally as an upholstery material in the furniture and motor-car trades, and generally as a substitute for leather.

Although linoleum and leathercloth are not close-substitutes, there are points of similarity in their manufacturing processes; this presumably accounts for their conjunction in the Census of Production as the Linoleum, Leathercloth and Allied Trades. It is not, however, generally the

[1] Board of Trade, *Linoleum and Felt Base*, Working Party Reports (H.M.S.O. 1947), p. 1.

case that linoleum firms are also manufacturers of leathercloth. More of the linoleum manufacturers are also producers of felt-base floor-coverings which, consisting of bituminised paper felt overprinted with a flexible glossy paint in multi-coloured patterns, are directly competitive with linoleum.

The relative importance of these three principal products of the Census Trade is indicated by the fact that linoleum accounted for 42 per cent of the value of total sales in 1951, while another 19 per cent was contributed by felt-base floor-coverings, and 29 per cent by leathercloth. The most important of the remaining principal products are oil baize and fabric-backed oilcloth. Compared with 1935, however, both linoleum and leathercloth have declined relatively to felt-base floor-coverings. Indeed, the sales of felt base were 80 per cent higher by volume in 1951, whereas linoleum sales were 16 per cent lower and leathercloth 25 per cent lower. For the whole Trade, it is estimated that its volume of production was slightly lower in 1951 than in 1935.

This fall in output is paralleled by a reduction (from thirty-eight to thirty-three) in the number of establishments comprising the Trade, although the 1951 total shows an increase compared with 1948. Employment, on the other hand, was considerably higher in 1951 than in 1935, rising from less than 12,500 to more than 14,500.

The decrease in the number of plants has been matched by a fall in the number of business units from thirty-three in 1935 to twenty-five in 1951. Concentration also fell during the same period, from 64 to 54 per cent by employment and from 62 to 52 per cent by net output. To explain this change in concentration and the factors contributing towards it, it is necessary to examine separately the various sections of the Census Trade.

Linoleum

The manufacture of linoleum constitutes the largest section of the Trade, although its share fell between 1935 and 1951. Inlaid linoleum became relatively more important during the same period, for its output increased by nearly 20 per cent while the cheaper types of linoleum (which were more affected by the competition of felt bases) suffered a 40 per cent fall in output.

There have been very few manufacturers of linoleum for the whole of the period under consideration. By 1951, the trade consisted of only nine manufacturing companies, but since one was a subsidiary of another, the number of business units was only eight. The position was not greatly different in 1935, when there were twelve manufacturing companies but eleven business units. Of the three manufacturing companies that went out of business between 1935 and 1951, two were pre-war casualties while the other went into liquidation in 1949. In each case, the premises were acquired by one or a group of linoleum manufacturers but subsequently disposed of, subject in the first two cases to restrictive covenants.[1]

During World War II, the factories of four linoleum manufacturers were closed under the policy of concentrating production. Until normal trading was resumed, the linoleum interests of these manufacturers were looked after by the 'nucleus' firms that remained in production, though even the latter concerns devoted a great deal of space to war production. Three of the four firms subsequently resumed production; the other was the concern liquidated in 1949.[2] No newcomers entered the industry after 1935.

All but two of the linoleum manufacturing concerns in the British industry have been members of the Linoleum Manufacturers' Association (L.M.A.) since its formation in 1934. The L.M.A. has operated a common-price system for its members, accompanied by a number of common trade practices affecting both the production and distribution of linoleum.[3] It has been reported that in 1953 and 1954, the sales of linoleum by L.M.A. members represented about 80 per cent of the total home trade and over 92 per cent of the export trade. Thus, it would appear that the six business units that make up the L.M.A. were together responsible for some 82 per cent of the total sales of the United Kingdom industry in 1953.

The identity of the three largest units in the linoleum industry is also evident, since the Monopolies Commission has reported that the two largest are Barry and Staines Linoleum (controlling two manufacturing subsidiaries, Barry, Ostlere and Shepherd, and the Linoleum Manufacturing Company) and Michael Nairn and Greenwich. Both these concerns are responsible for nearly one-third of the home supply of linoleum and the third largest unit is the larger of the two non-members of the L.M.A., the Tayside Floorcloth Company.[4]

Felt base

The production of felt-base floor-coverings has shown an 80 per cent increase between 1935 and 1951 and has been largely responsible for the declining importance of the cheaper types of linoleum. Once again, the number of producers is small. In 1947, there were eleven manufacturers in all, seven of which also produced linoleum.

By 1951, it would appear that one of the specialist felt producers had ceased production, since the number of business units in the Floor-Coverings Sub-Trade, including the one concern which produces only linoleum, was put at eleven. The L.M.A. does not include felt base within

[1] Monopolies and Restrictive Practices Commission, *Report on the Supply of Linoleum* (H.M.S.O. 1956), pars. 14 and 23.

[2] *Ibid.* par. 48. [3] *Ibid.* ch. 7. [4] *Ibid.* par. 184.

the scope of its activities, but five of the six business units that comprise the L.M.A., and both the outsiders, are also manufacturers of felt base. Indeed, one of the two outsiders, Thomas Witter and Company, is mainly interested in felt base.

Since felt base and linoleum are so much associated with each other, and to a considerable degree are competing floor-coverings, it is proper that they should together comprise the Floor-Coverings Sub-Trade of the Census of Production Trade. The three largest units in the Sub-Trade were responsible for 76 per cent of its net output and 75 per cent of its employment in 1951. Although a comparable Sub-Trade was not distinguished for 1935, the four largest firms (which would in fact represent the three largest units in the trade) were responsible in that year for 75 per cent of the total employment in all firms producing linoleum and felt base and for 73 per cent of their net output.[1] Thus it would appear that there was little change in the degree of concentration between 1935 and 1951 as far as floor-coverings are concerned.

Leathercloth

The manufacture of leathercloth dates back to the end of the nineteenth century, when nitro-cellulose dope was applied to fabrics to produce an artificial leather. By the end of World War I, three firms—the British Pluviusin Company, New Pegamoid, and the British Leather Cloth Manufacturing Company—had established themselves as the leading leathercloth concerns. Each of these producers obtained its supplies of nitro-cellulose from Nobel's Explosives, and between 1920 and 1925 Nobel's acquired them to make Imperial Chemical Industries (I.C.I.) the principal producer of leathercloth from its formation in 1926. Subsequently, I.C.I. acquired Levvarex of Hainault, Essex, and concentrated the manufacture of leathercloth into two plants.[2]

By 1935, I.C.I. was responsible for some 45 per cent of the total production of leathercloth,[3] equivalent to a 14 per cent share of the whole Census Trade. At that time, I.C.I.'s production consisted entirely of nitro-cellulose coated fabric, marketed under the trade-name of Rexine. Since then, I.C.I. has also developed leathercloth with a polyvinyl chloride coating, sold as Vynide, which has expanded at the expense of Rexine's share of I.C.I.'s leathercloth business.

The production of leathercloth in 1951 was one-quarter less than in 1935, and the total value of production in 1951 was fairly equally divided between the nitro-cellulose and the polyvinyl chloride types. As stated above, linoleum manufacturers are not generally interested in leather-

[1] *Linoleum*, Working Party Report, p. 4.

[2] *Imperial Chemical Industries Ltd and its Founding Companies*, vol. I, *The History of Nobel's Explosives Company Ltd and Nobel Industries Ltd, 1871–1926* (London, I.C.I., 1938), pp. 206–12.

[3] *United States v. I.C.I.*, Civil 24–13, S.D.N.Y., Defendant's Exhibit D-2233, p. 25.

cloth production. The sole exception is Jas. Williamson and Son, which has been engaged in leathercloth manufacture for many years and in 1955 acquired the Leather Cloth Company, whose products were largely complementary to its own range of manufacture. There are in addition a number of other makers of leathercloth, including British Geon, Ioco, and Bernard Wardle and Company.

Although precise information is not available, it is doubtful whether I.C.I. has increased its share of leathercloth production since 1935, although it has certainly retained its predominant position. In any case, I.C.I.'s interest in this field is not sufficiently great for it to rank as one of the three largest units in the Census Trade for either 1935 or 1951.

Conclusion

It has been stated above that the degree of concentration for floor-coverings (that is, linoleum and felt base) was probably not greatly different in 1951 from what it was in 1935. It can also be established that the three largest units in the Floor-Coverings Sub-Trade were the same as the three largest units in the whole Trade. Thus, the explanation of the Trade's decrease in concentration must rest with the changes in the internal product-structure of the Trade, which has reduced the relative importance of floor-coverings from 65 per cent of total sales in 1935 to 61 per cent in 1951.

The conclusion, therefore, must be that the fall in the Trade concentration does not reflect any significant change in the share of the three largest units as far as their main activity is concerned. Indeed, the fact that concentration in the floor-coverings section of the Trade was maintained between 1935 and 1951, despite the increased popularity of felt-base coverings produced by a number of concerns which are not linoleum producers, is an indication of strength rather than weakness.

Although there have been no newcomers to linoleum manufacture since 1934, for it is a costly trade to enter, linoleum producers are subject to a substantial measure of competition from alternative flooring materials, such as carpets and the many varieties of tiling and sheet flooring. On the other hand, linoleum manufacturers have embarked upon the manufacture of many of these alternative types of flooring themselves. It seems, therefore, that the floor-coverings section of the Trade is likely to remain highly concentrated, but that the level in the Trade will depend substantially on the future development of its heterogeneous content.

5. GRAIN MILLING

Grain milling as a Census Trade covers a variety of products obtained from the treatment of wheat, oats, barley, maize and rice, as well as the animal feedingstuffs in which grain is the main ingredient. In addition, the Trade includes establishments engaged in splitting and grinding peas, beans and lentils, soya beans, sago and tapioca, and in 1951, though not in 1935, in the manufacture of ready-to-eat breakfast cereals.

Although the Census Trade is markedly heterogeneous, nearly two-thirds of the total output of its principal products in 1951 (and more than seven-tenths in 1935) consisted of wheat products. Another 17 per cent of the 1951 output was represented by animal and poultry feedingstuffs (compared with 8 per cent in 1935), for which production increased by nearly half between 1935 and 1951. The production of oat products also increased during the same period, thereby increasing their relative importance among the principal products of the trade. This was attributable initially to war-time shortages of feedingstuffs, and after the War to balance-of-payments difficulties.

Among the wheat products, flour is by far the most important. Indeed, flour and meal accounted for more than 81 per cent of the total tonnage of wheat products in 1951, compared with less than 72 per cent in 1935. The production of flour from wheat is, of course, connected with the rate of extraction, which was raised from a pre-war 70 per cent to as high as 90 per cent in 1946, though it was thereafter reduced by stages to 81 per cent in August 1950. The milling of white flour at 70 per cent was not recommenced until the decontrol of the industry in 1953, but the output of 'national' flour at the old extraction rate has continued since bread made from this flour remained subsidised up to the autumn of 1956.

Despite its heterogeneity, the Grain Milling Trade has a high degree of specialisation (around 99 per cent in both 1935 and 1951) and exclusiveness (around 98 per cent in both years). On the other hand, the various sub-divisions of the Trade are far less specialised. The specialist millers of wheat were, it is true, responsible for well over 90 per cent of all the wheat products in 1951, but they also accounted for over 40 per cent of the remainder of the gross output of the entire Trade. The specialist oat millers were responsible for only three-fifths of the total output of oat products in 1951, and their degree of specialisation was 86 per cent.

The number of establishments in the Trade has been steadily declining since the end of the nineteenth century, and in 1951 the larger establishments numbered 355 compared with 502 in 1935. There were, in addition, no less than 2,145 small establishments in 1935, but by 1951 the total had fallen to 771. Moreover, the numbers employed in the small establishments represented less than 10 per cent of the total employment in all establishments in 1951, compared with more than 22 per cent in 1935.

The decline in the number of establishments in the Trade is seen in the number of wheat mills in 1935 and 1951. From the 277 wheat mills of 1935, the total fell by nearly one-fifth to 228 by 1951, but the numbers employed in these mills rose from less than 22,900 to nearly 23,800 during the same period. The number of specialist oat mills increased, on the other hand, from twenty-two in 1935 to twenty-six in 1951, with their employment rising from 900 to more than 1,350. For the Trade as a whole, employment in the larger establishments increased slightly between 1935 and 1951, though there was a considerable decrease (nearly 10 per cent) in total employment when the smaller establishments are also taken into account.

The long-term decline in the number of mills has been associated with the surplus capacity that has bothered the industry for most of the present century. Milling capacity began to increase at a faster rate than flour consumption after 1908, particularly as large port mills were established 'without the actual extinction of an equivalent amount of milling capacity in other less economic situations throughout the country'.[1] The events of World War I aggravated the complaint. Some mills found part of their market denied as the result of transport restrictions; some found it possible to enlarge their capacity; others entered the industry for the first time. But when government control ended in 1921, surplus capacity emerged with a vengeance. Even if there had been no import of flour, total capacity still exceeded requirements by as much as 25 per cent. Throughout the 1920's competition was severe; there was 'a bitter struggle between the individualism of the small firms and the programme of control which the larger millers felt necessary for the preservation of the industry'.[2]

The clash of interests within the trade prevented a concerted attack on the problem until 1929, though the year before the two principal milling concerns—Ranks and Spillers—had jointly acquired a group of flour mills in Yorkshire and Durham which had been 'more or less available in the market for a number of years'.[3] The situation was too serious to be solved by the action of the largest firms alone, though it is significant that the Chairman of Spillers commented later that if the 1928 transaction had not occurred 'there would have been no chance of bringing about any scheme for reorganisation in the flour-milling industry'.

The scheme for the industry's reorganisation came from the Millers' Mutual Association, established in August 1929 by the private millers and representing about 90 per cent of the total flour production outside the Co-operative mills. The details of the workings of the Millers' Mutual Association were not disclosed but they appear to follow closely the recommendations of the Trade Organisation Committee set up by the

[1] Royal Commission on Food Prices, *First Report*, vol. I (1925), par. 110.

[2] A. F. Lucas, *Industrial Reconstruction and the Control of Competition* (London, Longmans, 1937) p. 138.

[3] Chairman's Speech to the Ordinary General Meeting of Spillers Ltd, 1929.

Incorporated National Association of British and Irish Millers in 1924.[1] Under this scheme output was to be regulated by means of quotas based on production in a given period, excess deliveries being penalised and under-deliveries compensated. The organisation was to be financed by a levy on capacity and no new mills were to be built except by purchasing quotas from existing establishments.

The elimination of the excess capacity—by the purchase and closure of redundant mills—was undertaken by the Association's subsidiary, the Purchase Finance Company. This company was controlled by the seven most important firms in the industry, each of whom held one of the seven sole issued shares. No figures are available as to the number of mills closed down as a result of Millers' Mutual Association policy, but generous compensation was paid to both workers and dispossessed owners. Also, a number of the millers who were bought out turned to provender milling.

It is doubtful if the net reduction in capacity achieved was very great, since the building and modernisation of mills continued. The success of the Millers' Mutual in increasing the profitability of milling was due rather to the regulation of production, which reduced the temptation to millers to increase their own sales by selling below the recommended price. On the other hand, it is equally certain that the activities of the Millers' Mutual, coupled with the continued expansion of the two leading private concerns, caused a substantial change in the industry's structure.

Changes in concentration, 1935–51

For the whole Trade, concentration fell from 34 to 31 per cent by employment and from 39 to 33 per cent by net output between 1935 and 1951. Concentration has also fallen in the wheat-milling section of the Trade in the same period, although it was markedly higher among the port wheat mills than the inland mills in 1935. Similarly, concentration in the wheat-milling section of the Trade was higher than for its other sections in both years.

The Co-operative Wholesale Society (C.W.S.) was cited by Leak and Maizels as one of the three largest units among the port wheat mills in 1935, and there is little doubt that it was also one of the three largest units in the Grain Milling Trade in that year. The C.W.S. embarked on flour

[1] The National Association, which embraced some 225 millers with 90 per cent of the national flour output in 1937, represents the industry in all its dealings with the Government. There are also twenty or so local associations, affiliated to the National Association, which recommended regional flour prices before the War: the recommended price was largely the responsibility of the port association in the region, with area prices varying according to distance from the port. The practice of recommended prices was resumed when the industry was decontrolled.

milling as long ago as 1891, though several retail co-operative societies had been owners of small local mills for many years previously. By 1920, the C.W.S. was responsible for somewhat less than 10 per cent of the national output, and in 1935 it was operating nine flour and provender mills (four of them at the ports) which probably accounted for about 12 per cent of the activity of the Trade.

The other two largest concerns are also easily identified: they are Ranks and Spillers. In 1885 Joseph Rank opened his first roller mills, and when the business was converted into a limited company in 1899, it owned three mills with a total capacity approaching 100 sacks per hour.[1] From the beginning, Ranks milled imported wheat, finding a ready market for its higher-grade flour in Hull, and for its lower grades in London, where the bakers were accustomed to blend strong American flour with English flour sent in from East Anglia. Agencies were set up in Cardiff and London, to be followed by mills—the Premier Mill at Silvertown and the Atlantic Mill at Barry Docks.

After 1905, London rather than Hull became the company headquarters. In 1912 the Ocean Mill at Birkenhead was opened, and by the end of the First World War a total capacity of 540 sacks per hour had been reached, but the company lost about half of its business during the period of government control. In the following year the company branched out in Scotland with the acquisition and reorganisation of the Riverside Milling Company and John Ure and Sons of Glasgow. By 1924 Ranks controlled at least eight other sizeable companies.

Apart from the joint acquisition with Spillers in 1928, already mentioned above, the Associated London Flour Millers, with their famous Blue Cross trade-mark for animal feedingstuffs, were acquired by Ranks in 1932,[2] and it was this acquisition which established Ranks as the biggest millers in the United Kingdom.[3] Consequently, when Ranks became a public company in 1933,[4] it could claim an aggregate capacity of over 1,200 sacks per running hour. Modernisation continued with the building in 1935 of the new Empire Mill in London to replace some of the older plants worked by its subsidiaries. Indeed, by 1938 Ranks was claiming that its aggregate mill capacity had reached 1,550 sacks per running hour 'by the inclusion of additional companies'. It was also stated that the 'normal output' of the Group had risen from seven million

[1] See Joseph Rank Ltd, *The Master Millers: the Story of the House of Rank, 1875–1955* (London, Harley, 1955), pp. 39–40.

[2] This company had been formed in 1921 by seven London milling firms in an attempt to combat the menace from the North in the shape of Joseph Rank of Hull and William Vernon and Sons. Both these companies had dock mills in London. It was not until the London Millers decided to build a dock mill of their own that Ranks showed any interest, and employed a broker to negotiate purchase.

[3] Joseph Rank Ltd, *op. cit.* pp. 62–3.

[4] A holding company, Ranks Ltd, was formed to acquire all the capital of Joseph Rank Ltd.

sacks (or 875,000 tons) in 1933 to nine million sacks (or 1,125,000 tons) in 1938, an increase of nearly 30 per cent. From this it appears that in terms of quantity, Ranks was responsible for more than one-fifth of the wheat products produced in 1938, compared with about one-sixth in 1933.

The Spillers business can trace its ancestry back to a flour merchant in Bridgwater active before 1830, but it was in 1887 that it became registered as a public company. In 1891, it made its first acquisitions which brought with it a new line of manufacture—ship and dog biscuits. Five years later, it acquired a mill at Newcastle, and in 1903 a mill adjacent to its own at Cardiff. The process of expansion by building new mills and buying old ones continued throughout World War I, but it was said that a new policy had been adopted whereby amalgamation was not pursued 'for amalgamation's sake, but in order to avoid unnecessary overlapping, and to ensure economic distribution'.[1] In 1921, five important concerns were acquired, including William Vernon and Sons (with a port mill in London) and the Swan Mill at Hull,[2] but the pace of acquisition was slowed down as the effects of surplus capacity made themselves felt.

In 1927, thirteen subsidiary companies were eliminated and production concentrated in the main company, though in the following year (with Ranks) and again in the early 1930's new acquisitions were made. As in the case of Ranks it is difficult to assess Spillers' share of the Grain Milling Trade in 1935, particularly since many of its interests were, and still are, in animal feedingstuffs rather than grain milling. However, it was generally asserted that its flour-milling interests were smaller than Ranks', and closer to those of the C.W.S.

Among the other more important grain-milling concerns in 1935 were Hovis and the Scottish Co-operative Wholesale Society (S.C.W.S.). Hovis took on a national significance when it acquired Marriage, Neave and Company of Battersea in 1920, and after further mills at Lincoln and Bristol had been acquired, it became responsible for 7–8 per cent of flour output in 1939.[3]

Like the C.W.S., the S.C.W.S. embarked on flour production in the 1890's, and by 1918 it was responsible for some 2 per cent of the national output. By 1939 there were five flour and meal mills operated by the S.C.W.S., but its share of the total output was still comparatively small.

[1] 'Spillers: a Giant of the Milling Trade', *Financial News*, 7 June 1934.

[2] This mill had been built by three Yorkshire milling families operating between them eleven mills. In 1898 they decided to amalgamate in order to build a port mill. The Swan Mill was started in 1900 and capacity was doubled before the First World War. A serious shortage of skilled workpeople at the end of the War made continued production difficult and in 1921, the year of decontrol, the decision to join Spillers was made.

[3] Mrs H. V. Edwards, 'Flour-Milling', in *Further Studies in Industrial Organisation*, ed. by M. P. Fogarty (London, Methuen, 1948), p. 46.

Between 1935 and the outbreak of war, both Ranks and Spillers continued their process of expansion. Spillers built new mills and animal foods factories at Bristol in 1935 and Newcastle in 1938, as well as acquiring the important West Country firm, Hosegood Industries, in 1938. Similarly, Ranks acquired John Greenwood Millers in 1939, thereby raising its share of the total United Kingdom flour-milling capacity from 28 to 30 per cent.

It was estimated in 1944 that the three largest concerns controlled some two-thirds of the total United Kingdom flour output in 1939, divided between them as follows: Ranks 30 per cent, Spillers 20 per cent, and the Co-operative Wholesale Society 17 per cent.[1] Sources within the trade claim, however, that this overestimated the importance of the three largest units at that time, but there is no dispute that these three concerns were by far the most important in the flour industry and that the gap between them and the fourth largest concern, Hovis, was substantial.

On the outbreak of war in 1939, the industry entered another period of control which was to last until August 1953. Financial arrangements were negotiated between the Ministry of Food and the British Millers' Mutual Pool,[2] which then had a membership of some 300 firms, that is, almost all the millers in the country. Millers outside the Pool were in fact aided on the basis of the agreement with the Pool.

The outbreak of war found the major concerns in a vulnerable position since their main productive capacity (indeed, almost 75 per cent of the national capacity) was concentrated at the ports in the first line of air attack. The mills of both Ranks and Spillers suffered considerable damage, although Spillers claimed in 1945 that despite the destruction of mills at London and Hull, its output of flour throughout the War had been consistently maintained at above the pre-war level.

Similarly, the Manchester mill of Hovis was destroyed by enemy action in 1940, and was not restored until 1955. The C.W.S. was more fortunate, though its new mill at Royal Victoria Dock, London, did not open until 1945 whereas, but for the War, it would have commenced operations in 1940.

Post-war reconstruction in the milling industry was hampered by rigid

[1] Edwards, 'Flour-Milling', pp. 45–6.

[2] The millers were guaranteed a standard profit based on their average pre-war profits. All payments were made through the Mutual Pool Company. If a miller made a profit he retained it up to his standard profit, and paid any excess to the Pool for the credit of the Ministry of Food. If he made a loss the amount of the loss was paid by the Ministry of Food and his standard profit by the Pool. Any profit less than the standard was made up by the Pool. In 1945 a supplementary agreement was reached by which if the industry as a whole dealt with more than the standard in any one year, payment at a considerably lower rate per ton was made by the Ministry to the firms who had earned it. In 1949 production was running at about 25–30 per cent above the pre-war level. (Select Committee on Estimates (House of Commons), *Thirteenth Report*, Session 1949–50, H.M.S.O. December 1949.)

licensing and shortages of raw materials. Ranks' first new mill was completed at Gateshead-on-Tyne in 1949. The rebuilt Solent Mill at Southampton was in operation in 1951, the Clarence Mill at Hull in 1952, and the Premier Mill in London in 1955. The Caledonian Mill at Leith was also opened in 1955, and in the same year three new mills for animal feedingstuffs were being erected. But it was not until April 1954 that 'so far as quantity is concerned, the reconstructed mills following the war damage have restored the company to full capacity'. By 1955 the company owned twenty-seven flour and provender mills.[1]

Spillers too had difficulty in replacing destroyed capacity. The Swan Mill at Hull did not start running until 1953 although reconstruction began in 1948. In September 1953 the Millennium Mill in London came into operation and a mill at Silvertown was returned to the Co-operative Wholesale Society. This mill had been leased in 1946 after the C.W.S. had transferred production to its new mill at Victoria Dock, London, in April 1945. Since the end of the War Spillers has acquired a controlling interest in A. H. Allen and Company of Croydon and Charles Brown, which together were stated to control 2 per cent of the United Kingdom flour output.

By 1951, the process of reconstruction of the port mills was far from complete, and whereas the evidence of Spillers suggests that its output was greater than pre-war, the experience of Ranks appears to be the opposite. Indeed, it is possible that, as far as the wheat-milling section is concerned, the combined share of Ranks and Spillers did not change substantially between 1935 and 1951 (though it was considerably lower in 1951 than in 1939), though the share of the C.W.S. almost certainly fell.

The fall in the Trade's degree of concentration may be explained, therefore, by the fact that not only did the three largest units have a slightly smaller share of wheat milling in 1951 than in 1935, but that wheat milling was itself accounting for a smaller proportion of the whole Trade. In particular, the inland and country millers were strong in the animal feedingstuffs section of the Trade, which increased its relative importance during the 1935–51 period.

It seems probable, however, that with the replacement of port mill capacity since 1951, concentration in wheat milling may have regained or surpassed the 1935 level. On the other hand, there have been several factors which have tended to favour the inland and country millers in more recent years. They may have benefited in increased business from governmental policy, which has aimed at maintaining domestic wheat production, although the price competition following decontrol in 1953 is reported to have caused them many difficulties. Even the demand of Allied Bakeries for English flour during their struggle with Ranks and

[1] *Milling*, 12 November 1955, p. 604.

Spillers[1] provided them with only a temporary respite, so that it seems unlikely that they will improve their position permanently.

Conclusion

The fall in the concentration of the Grain Milling trade between 1935 and 1951 was primarily due to the circumstances of war, which destroyed or severely damaged many of the largest port mills owned by the three largest units in the Trade. Two of those three largest units—Ranks and Spillers—have subsequently rebuilt and re-equipped many of these mills, so that it may well be that the degree of concentration has now become as high as it was in 1935, as it almost certainly is for wheat milling.

The growth of Ranks and Spillers was largely due to the acquisitions they made both before and after World War I. Particularly in the inter-war years, these acquisitions were designed, at least in part, to alleviate the problems of severe competition arising from the surplus capacity in the industry.

Finally, it must be stated that the main problem facing the flour-milling industry is the long-term tendency for flour consumption to decline. The fall in demand may be, to some extent, compensated by increasing interests in other fields. It is difficult, however, to forecast what the effect will be on concentration in the Grain Milling Trade with its heterogeneity of products and its large number of units.

6. MATCHES

The Match Trade consisted in 1951 of 'establishments engaged wholly or mainly in the manufacture of matches and firelighters'. Matches, however, represented by far the larger part of the Trade's activity, though their share of total sales fell from nearly 99 per cent in 1935 to 95 per cent in 1951. For this Trade, the small establishments with ten or fewer persons were numerically important (outnumbering the larger establishments by more than three to one), and their employment represented around 15 per cent of the labour-force in the larger establishments in both years. There is no doubt, however, that these small establishments are exclusively engaged in the firelighters side of the Trade.

Confining attention to the larger establishments, there has been a slight increase in numbers (from thirty to thirty-four) between 1935 and 1951, while employment has risen by 8 per cent over the period. The volume of the Trade's output has likewise risen; after adjustment for price-changes, it is estimated that sales of the Trade's principal products have increased by 16 per cent between 1935 and 1951. At the same time,

[1] See Chapter XIV, Section 13, Bread and Flour Confectionery, for an account of this struggle.

the increase has been relatively much greater for firelighters than for matches.

The concentration data for the Match Trade suggest that concentration fell between 1935 and 1951. The level of concentration was very high in 1935. The three largest units were responsible for 89 per cent of employment and 94 per cent of net output in that year, leaving a comparatively small portion of the Trade to be shared among sixteen other units. Since firelighters were so unimportant in 1935, these percentages can also be taken as reflecting the division of the match industry proper.

In 1951, the *six* largest units did not account for as high a proportion of the Trade as the three largest units in 1951, for their share was 85 per cent of employment and 86 per cent of net output. Moreover, the number of business units in 1951 was twenty-seven, an increase of eight compared with 1935. But in 1951, the importance of firelighters was much greater than in 1935, so that it is necessary to examine very closely the reasons for the fall in concentration between 1935 and 1951.

Since the match industry has been the subject of a Monopolies Commission report, there is ample information on the early history of the industry.[1] It is sufficient to state that by the early 1920's, the British industry was divided between two groups—one centred in J. John Masters and Company (representing the interests of the Swedish Match Company of Jönköping) and the other in Bryant and May.[2] To meet the threat of growing competition from foreign imports, Bryant and May entered into a series of agreements with Masters (and through Masters with Swedish Match and its interests in Belgium, Denmark, Holland and Norway) which embodied a division of the home market, the fixing of minimum prices, as well as compensation and penalty arrangements of the usual type. These agreements were due to expire in 1927, but in that year collaboration became closer still. A new agreement on markets was negotiated, but, more relevant for our present purposes, the British Match Corporation (B.M.C.) was formed to acquire all the ordinary shares of Bryant and May and all the shares of Masters. By this move, twelve match manufacturing concerns came under the control of B.M.C.

Between 1927 and 1935, a number of other match manufacturers were acquired by B.M.C.: the Monopolies Commission states that there were six concerns 'whose assets or businesses were purchased by B.M.C. between 1929 and 1939'. In almost every case, however, the concern ceased to operate after control had passed to B.M.C.

By 1935, B.M.C. was responsible for about 95 per cent of the total number of matches produced for the home market. Exports account in that year for only 3 per cent of home production, so that B.M.C.'s share of

[1] Monopolies Commission, *Supply and Export of Matches* (1953).

[2] For a brief description of the emergence of these two concerns, see Chapter VII, p. 119.

total production was not less than 94 per cent and might have been as high as 97 per cent. On this basis, B.M.C.'s share of the trade in 1935 was probably well over 90 per cent, leaving only a small proportion in the hands of the other two largest units.

Apart from B.M.C. there was only a handful of match concerns in 1935. Probably the two most important were the United Match Industries, formed in 1928 to take over the assets of an earlier concern at Bishop's Stortford, and Maguire and Paterson (Belfast) which was a subsidiary of Maguire (Dublin). The remaining concerns—such as the Anglia Match Company and the North of England Match Company—were relatively small.

In 1938, Bryant and May entered into an agreement with the two Irish concerns, whereby *inter alia* it acquired a minority interest in both of them, subsequently increased to give it 49 per cent of the voting power in Maguire and Paterson (N.I.). Similar agreements in 1937 gave it about 49 per cent of the voting power in United Match Industries, so that both these formerly independent concerns became financially associated with (though not subsidiaries of) B.M.C.

Apart from abortive attempts by the Co-operative Wholesale Society and 'another concern [which] from time to time since 1929 endeavoured to start manufacture on a commercial scale',[1] the only new entrant to the trade which has survived for any time is the Magnet Match Works which began operations as a manufacturer of book matches early in the War. Its factory was, however, badly damaged by fire in 1950, and at the time of the Monopolies Commission's report (October 1952) it had not resumed full production. During the War, one of Bryant and May's factories, indeed its largest, was destoyed by enemy action, while one of the other concerns in the B.M.C. group—the Midland Match Works—also ceased manufacture.

According to the Monopolies Commission's report the B.M.C. group was responsible for more than 87 per cent of the total sales of home-produced matches (that is, to the home market and for export combined) in the year ending 31 March 1950. The two firms associated with B.M.C.—United Match Industries and Maguire and Paterson (N.I.)—were responsible for another 7 per cent, leaving less than 6 per cent to be shared among the three independent producers: Anglia, North of England, and Magnet.

Furthermore, the report gives details of the production of B.M.C. companies for each of the three years (ending 31 March) 1950, 1951 and 1952. If the 1952 figures are taken as those which conform most closely to the Census year of 1951, the total production of B.M.C. companies amounted to 11,471,000 gross containers (each container being the equivalent of

[1] Monopolies Commission, *Supply and Export of Matches*, pars. 143–5.

50 matches), compared with the Census total sales of 12,426,000 gross containers. On this basis, B.M.C.'s share was 91–92 per cent in 1951, compared with 94–97 per cent in 1935. Thus, there would appear to have been some slight fall in the relative importance of B.M.C. as a match producer during this period. On the other hand, when the output of its two associates—U.M.I. and Maguire—which are almost certainly the second and third largest units in the trade are taken into account, their combined share of match production was probably not substantially different from 1935.

The fact remains, however, that the Census Trade showed a decrease in concentration between 1935 and 1951, and the explanation rests in the increased relative importance of the firelighters section of the Trade during this period. Since the interests of the match manufacturers in this section are very limited, its growth has meant that their share of the whole Trade has fallen without a comparable fall in their share of match production.

Conclusion

Although the concentration of the Match Trade has decreased, there has been no important corresponding change in the structure of the match industry proper. The match industry continued to be dominated in 1951 as in 1935 by B.M.C., though its own share of production had fallen slightly. Its position as a manufacturer has, moreover, been strengthened by its interests as a match importer, for imports accounted for more than a third of home consumption in 1951. By virtue of its arrangements with Swedish Match, whereby all the imports from that company and its associates were marketed through B.M.C., it was able to supply 87 per cent of all the matches on the United Kingdom market.

All in all, the leading match concerns held their very substantial own between 1935 and 1951, thanks in no small measure, as the Monopolies Commission found, to the elaborate system of restrictive controls they have exercised over matchmaking machinery and raw materials. The decline in concentration for the Match Trade is, therefore, rather misleading though it can be explained by a careful examination of the Census data.

APPENDIX A

GLOSSARY

The basic data for this inquiry relate to Census of Production trades, so that many of the terms used are defined by the Census. But there are also concepts and classifications introduced into the analysis which are peculiar to this study. These terms are, for convenience, set out below.

I. CENSUS OF PRODUCTION DEFINITIONS

An establishment (*or plant*) is the basic unit for the collection of Census of Production data; in most cases, it comprises the whole of the premises under the same ownership or management at a particular address (for example, a factory). Offices, warehouses and other ancillary places of business situated apart from the producing works are included in the return for the works.

Larger establishments (*or plants*) are those which employed more than ten persons on the average during the year; except where otherwise stated, this study is concerned only with the larger establishments.

Small firms are those employing, on the average, during the year ten or fewer persons; they are generally excluded from this study.

Principal products are those identified as characteristic of the production of individual trades, and which for a given trade are generally either of a similar nature or commonly associated in production.

Census Trade consists of those establishments whose output of the principal products of that trade accounted for a greater proportion of the value of their total output than did their output of the principal products of any other trade.

Census Sub-Trades are those sub-divisions of Census Trades described as 'the specialist producers' of a particular group of principal products; the specialist producers are those establishments 50 per cent or more of whose total output by value consists of the 'characteristic' principal products specified.

Gross output is the total value of goods made and other work done during the year: this means the value of sales and work done during the year, adjusted for changes in the value of stocks.

Net output is the amount left after deducting from the value of gross output the aggregate of the cost of materials and fuel used, the amount paid for work given out and any transport payments included in firms' returns. Net output represents, therefore, the value added to materials by the process of production, and constitutes the fund from which wages, salaries, rents, rates and taxes, advertising and other selling expenses and all other charges have to be met, as well as depreciation and profits.

Employment is the total number employed including administrative employees as well as operatives.

2. CONCEPTS

Business unit is a single firm, or aggregate of firms owned or controlled by a single parent company, control being defined as ownership of more than half the capital (or voting power) of each firm. The largest units in a trade are determined by ranking the business units by their employment in that trade alone.

Concentration-ratio (or *degree of concentration*) is the percentage share of Census Trades or Sub-Trades—expressed in terms of gross output, net output, employment or principal products—represented by the three (or otherwise specified number) largest business units.

Degree of specialisation is the value of the Trade's principal (or Sub-Trade's characteristic) products produced by establishments classified to that Trade (or Sub-Trade), expressed as a percentage of the Trade's (or Sub-Trade's) gross output.

Degree of exclusiveness is the value of the Trade's principal (or Sub-Trade's characteristic) products produced by establishments classified to that Trade (or Sub-Trade), expressed as a percentage of the total output of those principal or characteristic products wherever produced.

Degree of comparability is the value for 1935 of a Trade's principal (or Sub-Trade's characteristic) products sold by establishments classified to that Trade (or Sub-Trade) according to the 1948 Census of Production, expressed as a ratio of the same data for 1935 according to the 1935 Census of Production.

Size-ratio of units (W) is the average employment of the three largest units divided by the average employment of the *other* units. Alternatively, the size-ratio of units (X) is the average employment of the three largest units divided by the average employment of *all* units.

Number-ratio of plants (R) is the average number of establishments of the three largest units divided by the average number of establishments of the other units.

Size-ratio of plants (S) is the average employment per establishment of the three largest units divided by the average employment per establishment of the *other* units. Alternatively, the size-ratio of plants (*T*) is the average employment per establishment of the three largest units divided by the average employment per establishment of *all* units.

Giant concern refers to those largest units whose average employment in a specific trade is more than 2,500.

3. CLASSIFICATIONS

Concentration categories. Three categories of concentration are distinguished according to whether a trade's employment and/or net output concentration-ratio is *High* (67 per cent and over); *Medium* (34–66 per cent); or *Low* (33 per cent and under).

Number of units (*U*). The number of units in a trade is said to be *Many*, when there are more than thirty, or *Few*, when there are thirty or under.

Size-ratio of units. The size-ratio of units (*W*) is said to be *Large*, when it is 16 and over, or *Small*, when it is 15 or under.

Average unit size (*V*). The average size of units (that is, total employment divided by number of units) is said to be *Large*, when it is more than 750 persons; *Medium*, when it is between 250 and 749 persons; or *Small*, when it is less than 250 persons.

Average plant size (*Q*). The average size of plants (that is, total employment divided by number of establishments) is said to be *Large*, when it is more than 500 persons; *Medium*, when it is between 250 and 499 persons; or *Small*, when it is less than 250 persons.

Number-ratio of plants (*R*). The number-ratio of plants is said to be *Large*, when it is over five, or *Small*, when it is five or under.

Size-ratio of plants (*S*). The size-ratio of plants is said to be *Large*, when it is over five, or *Small*, when it is five or under.

APPENDIX B

Concentration of output and employment in Census of Production Trades, 1951

Group and code no.	Group, Trade or Sub-Trade	Total no. of business units	Concentration data for the largest business units*: No. of units	No. of establish-ments	Gross output (£000)	Net output (£000)	Nos. em-ployed
A.	MINING AND QUARRYING AND TREATMENT OF NON-METALLIFEROUS MINING PRODUCTS						
1	Cement	12	4	35	39,589	16,338	10,701
				73	*86*	*89*	*87*
2	Non-Metalliferous Mines and Quarries (other than Coal, Salt and Slate)	709	3	67	10,844	6,213	6,452
				6	*16*	*17*	*14*
3	Stone	419	3	35	5,818	2,918	2,966
				6	*18*	*18*	*13*
4	Clay, sand, gravel and chalk	277	4	51	6,052	3,504	4,205
				13	*25*	*26*	*29*
5	Salt Mines, Brine Pits and Salt Works	12	3	13	9,242	3,955	4,605
				59	*87*	*87*	*83*
6	Slate Quarries and Mines	21	3	4	1,450	1,314	3,101
				15	*62*	*64*	*65*
7	Brick and Fireclay	660	3	115	15,374	8,450	12,878
				11	*18*	*18*	*17*
8	Building bricks (including flooring and wall partition blocks)	397	3	94	12,990	7,503	11,586
				15	*33*	*32*	*30*
9	Roofing tiles of clay	40	3	13	1,190	761	1,238
				22	*39*	*39*	*34*
10	Refractory goods (other than plumbago and other crucibles)	123	3	22	7,885	3,462	4,908
				12	*32*	*30*	*27*
11	Sanitary ware (other than cement, concrete or earthenware)	83	3	7	1,609	931	1,782
				7	*14*	*14*	*16*
12	Building Materials	724	3	39	19,856	7,975	9,383
				4	*25*	*22*	*18*
13	Pre-cast concrete goods	326	3	15	5,456	2,028	2,809
				3	*18*	*14*	*12*
14	Asbestos cement goods	9	4	15	12,464	5,485	6,773
				75	*92*	*92*	*92*
15	Lime and whiting	83	3	7	1,227	489	779
				7	*20*	*17*	*18*
16	Roofing Felts	13	3	7	5,539	1,684	1,103
				28	*68*	*65*	*58*
17	Abrasives	37	3	4	7,658	4,232	4,282
				10	*45*	*53*	*56*

* Figures in italics give the percentage shares of the specified number of largest units.

Group and code no.	Group, Trade or Sub-Trade	Total no. of business units	Concentration data for the largest business units* No. of units	No. of establish-ments	Gross output (£000)	Net output (£000)	Nos. em-ployed
18	Abrasive wheels, discs, segments, sharpening stones and other shapes or forms	19	3	4	7,382	4,375	4,133
				20	*76*	*79*	*76*
19	China and Earthenware	269	3	19	4,998	3,325	7,053
				6	*10*	*10*	*10*
20	Glazed tiles (not of brick earth)	39	3	6	3,585	2,075	3,258
				13	*37*	*37*	*32*
21	Sanitary earthenware (including vitreous ware)	19	3	4	1,960	1,279	1,570
				17	*45*	*47*	*38*
22	China and porcelain, other than electrical ware	44	3	7	2,891	2,078	4,041
				13	*35*	*35*	*30*
23	Electrical ware	15	3	7	3,212	2,168	3,770
				33	*63*	*60*	*54*
24	Other earthenware and stoneware	126	3	6	3,215	2,194	5,167
				4	*15*	*15*	*14*
25	Glass Containers	48	3	9	14,143	7,357	11,660
				14	*45*	*45*	*47*
26	Glass (other than containers)	249	3	17	24,707	13,799	19,422
				6	*50*	*51*	*46*
27	Domestic and fancy glassware including heat-resisting glassware	37	3	5	3,398	2,122	3,341
				15	*57*	*56*	*49*
B.	CHEMICALS AND ALLIED TRADES						
1	Chemicals (General)	307	4	75	106,626	46,454	42,777
				15	*41*	*48*	*49*
2	Dyes and Dyestuffs	28	4	10	47,787	21,119	18,369
				28	*85*	*89*	*89*
3	Coal Tar Products	33	3	23	7,974	1,972	2,240
				32	*34*	*34*	*36*
4	Plastics Materials	51	3	13	29,202	11,237	10,898
				19	*50*	*51*	*53*
5	Coke Ovens and By-Products	24	3	60	56,312	10,583	11,766
				71	*60*	*63*	*63*
6	Fertiliser, Disinfectant, Insecticide and Allied Trades	113	3	48	36,196	11,916	12,064
				28	*59*	*58*	*56*
7	Fertilisers	68	3	48	36,196	11,916	12,064
				40	*73*	*75*	*73*
8	Disinfectants, antiseptics, insecticides, weedkillers, sheep and cattle dips, and like products	47	3	6	4,081	1,620	1,661
				11	*34*	*35*	*33*
9	Drugs and Pharmaceutical Preparations	232	3	12	30,439	12,007	13,695
				4	*27*	*24*	*27*
10	Pharmaceutical chemicals	18	3	5	6,105	2,743	2,176
				24	*66*	*66*	*64*
11	Pharmaceutical preparations	192	3	6	14,562	6,184	7,564
				3	*21*	*19*	*23*

* Figures in italics give the percentage shares of the specified number of largest units.

Group and code no.	Group, Trade or Sub-Trade	Total no. of business units	Concentration data for the largest business units* No. of units	No. of establishments	Gross output (£000)	Net output (£000)	Nos. employed
12	Toilet Preparations and Perfumery	77	3	4	9,460	4,926	3,561
				5	*38*	*41*	*35*
13	Paint and Varnish	296	3	20	21,962	7,994	6,968
				6	*20*	*20*	*19*
14	Oils and Greases	138	3	10	14,489	2,846	2,551
				6	*30*	*24*	*25*
15	Lubricating oils and greases	78	3	11	12,852	2,786	2,429
				10	*36*	*32*	*34*
16	Mineral Oil Refining	8	3	9	169,305	1,289	10,178
				60	*93*	*35*	*84*
17	Seed Crushing and Oil Refining	26	3	20	31,854	6,346	7,410
				43	*73*	*79*	*81*
18	Soap, Candles, and Glycerine	113	3	15	66,172	14,077	14,645
				11	*75*	*71*	*63*
19	Soap and glycerine	74	3	15	60,674	12,564	13,621
				17	*85*	*80*	*72*
20	Polishes	66	3	5	6,250	1,746	2,409
				7	*39*	*33*	*41*
21	Polishes and canvas dressings	38	3	5	6,250	1,746	2,409
				12	*54*	*43*	*52*
22	Glue, Gum, Paste and Allied Trades	53	3	9	6,154	2,262	2,104
				14	*39*	*41*	*39*
23	Explosives and Fireworks	29	6	35	29,657	13,457	28,242
				59	*93*	*91*	*93*
24	Match	27	6	12	12,048	1,933	3,439
				35	*93*	*86*	*85*
25	Ink	37	3	12	5,027	2,177	1,679
				22	*47*	*45*	*40*
C.	IRON AND STEEL AND NON-FERROUS METALS						
1	Blast Furnaces	35	3	11	49,607	10,000	12,418
				24	*41*	*47*	*45*
2	Iron and Steel (Melting and Rolling)	282	3	24	119,176	43,909	49,974
				6	*22*	*25*	*24*
3	Steel manufactures (with melting) other than alloy steel	76	3	13	112,069	34,083	38,096
				11	*35*	*35*	*33*
4	Steel manufactures (with melting) of alloy steel	49	3	14	36,108	17,211	23,666
				20	*44*	*46*	*50*
5	Steel manufacture (without melting)	108	3	9	28,377	7,582	8,697
				7	*27*	*29*	*29*
6	Steel forgings (other than drop forgings)	30	3	4	1,992	878	1,198
				13	*31*	*30*	*34*
7	Iron puddling and wrought iron, etc.	11	3	4	1,478	626	1,149
				33	*37*	*50*	*61*
8	Iron Foundries	797	3	30	27,379	12,681	15,794
				3	*18*	*16*	*13*
9	Cast iron stoves, grates, etc. for coal and other solid fuel	36	3	13	9,298	5,019	6,564
				27	*57*	*56*	*54*

* Figures in italics give the percentage shares of the specified number of largest units.

Group and code no.	Group, Trade or Sub-Trade	Total no. of business units	Concentration data for the largest business units* No. of units	No. of establish-ments	Gross output (£000)	Net output (£000)	Nos. em-ployed
10	Other cast iron stoves, grates, etc.	15	3	6	10,297	4,790	6,811
				32	*70*	*69*	*68*
11	Cast iron pipes and fittings therefor	31	3	15	17,283	6,309	9,212
				33	*77*	*68*	*66*
12	Iron engineering castings	613	3	11	11,974	6,865	9,267
				2	*17*	*17*	*15*
13	Steel Sheets	21	3	11	51,354	11,758	11,655
				35	*69*	*65*	*59*
14	Tinplate	18	3	27	39,098	11,478	11,979
				61	*74*	*72*	*71*
15	Wrought Iron and Steel Tubes	81	4	40	81,710	26,465	32,649
				26	*84*	*79*	*77*
16	Metalliferous Mines and Quarries	33	3	21	4,105	1,963	3,981
				33	*46*	*41*	*50*
17	Iron ore and ironstone	26	3	21	4,105	1,963	3,981
				41	*55*	*55*	*58*
18	Non-Ferrous Metals (Smelting, Rolling, etc.)	374	3	20	72,307	19,806	28,525
				4	*17*	*20*	*27*
19	Copper and copper alloys	104	3	13	47,628	11,167	16,664
				10	*29*	*35*	*51*
20	Aluminium and magnesium, and alloys	138	3	17	46,910	15,547	21,402
				10	*43*	*43*	*44*
21	Lead	40	3	7	27,681	3,856	1,682
				15	*69*	*69*	*53*
22	Zinc	42	5	9	26,044	8,038	5,500
				17	*85*	*82*	*68*
23	Tin	13	3	5	32,809	2,510	1,482
				33	*83*	*80*	*75*
D.	SHIPBUILDING AND NON-ELECTRICAL ENGINEERING						
1	Shipbuilding and Ship Repairing	513	3	27	47,314	25,744	51,409
				4	*19*	*23*	*25*
2	Marine Engineering	79	3	9	17,955	8,615	15,293
				9	*26*	*27*	*27*
3	Machine Tools	590	3	19	16,168	9,459	11,725
				3	*14*	*15*	*13*
4	Textile Machinery and Accessories	375	3	22	28,842	16,326	26,786
				5	*35*	*36*	*36*
5	Constructional Engineering	363	3	10	18,620	7,279	10,188
				2	*18*	*17*	*16*
6	Mechanical Engineering (General)	2,400	3	34	65,034	33,471	58,910
				1	*9*	*9*	*11*
7	Agricultural machinery (except tractors)	134	3	7	18,749	6,172	6,450
				5	*48*	*40*	*32*
8	Boilers and boiler-house plant	40	3	6	19,055	11,631	17,844
				12	*55*	*62*	*67*
9	Prime movers (stationary): internal combustion	25	3	20	37,705	15,891	21,715
				44	*80*	*80*	*77*

* Figures in italics give the percentage shares of the specified number of largest units.

Group and code no.	Group, Trade or Sub-Trade	Total no. of business units	Concentration data for the largest business units*: No. of units	No. of establish-ments	Gross output (£000)	Net output (£000)	Nos. em-ployed
10	Prime movers (stationary): other	8	3	3	6,582	3,177	4,947
				38	*86*	*82*	*83*
11	Ordnance (except small arms)	35	5	25	38,167	17,717	35,143
				43	*92*	*92*	*93*
12	Office machinery	51	3	7	8,278	5,052	6,140
				9	*34*	*34*	*29*
13	Ball and roller bearings	15	3	11	17,161	9,635	16,215
				44	*73*	*70*	*75*
14	Mining machinery	41	3	7	5,191	2,427	3,592
				15	*30*	*32*	*33*
15	Heating and ventilating apparatus	143	3	9	6,405	2,707	3,684
				6	*33*	*29*	*26*
16	Gas meters	20	3	28	5,617	3,119	4,588
				47	*60*	*63*	*60*
17	Scales and weighing machinery	23	6	54	5,473	3,649	5,105
				74	*80*	*83*	*85*
18	Refrigerating machinery	35	3	6	15,285	7,136	7,265
				13	*48*	*55*	*47*
19	Pumps and pumping machinery	56	3	4	8,520	4,296	6,471
				7	*36*	*37*	*40*
20	Transmission chains	5	5	6	6,140	3,936	6,100
				100	*100*	*100*	*100*
21	Small Arms	15	3	5	3,277	2,482	4,238
				25	*82*	*85*	*82*
22	Mechanical Handling Equipment	152	3	17	8,925	4,622	7,159
				9	*20*	*21*	*23*
23	Printing and Bookbinding Machinery	104	3	4	6,491	4,629	5,847
				3	*29*	*33*	*31*
24	Mechanical Engineering (Repairing)	679	3	34	2,881	2,015	4,907
				4	*10*	*11*	*15*
E.	ELECTRICAL ENGINEERING AND ELECTRICAL GOODS						
1	Electrical Engineering (General)	731	3	49	117,401	61,103	94,765
				5	*32*	*33*	*32*
2	Electrical machinery	212	3	32	86,184	44,376	74,653
				11	*44*	*46*	*48*
3	Electrical equipment for motor vehicles, cycles and aircraft	24	5	17	33,413	15,243	24,164
				34	*96*	*96*	*95*
4	Electrical cooking and heating apparatus	65	3	6	8,461	2,972	6,210
				8	*52*	*45*	*49*
5	Electrical contract and other work	135	3	14	2,618	1,986	2,888
				8	*37*	*42*	*33*
6	Electric Wires and Cables	46	3	15	61,753	17,417	25,141
				19	*48*	*48*	*50*
7	Radio and Telecommunications	273	4	50	97,726	61,723	115,897
				11	*41*	*48*	*48*

* Figures in italics give the percentage shares of the specified number of largest units.

Group and code no.	Group, Trade or Sub-Trade	Total no. of business units	Concentration data for the largest business units* No. of units	No. of establish-ments	Gross output (£000)	Net output (£000)	Nos. em-ployed
8	Telegraph and telephone apparatus†	30	3	16	33,520	20,211	33,300
				26	*75*	*74*	*72*
9	Radio apparatus (except valves) and gramophones	180	3	21	21,872	11,481	23,806
				8	*21*	*27*	*30*
10	Valves and cathode ray tubes	9	3	15	10,327	5,752	12,337
				63	*82*	*82*	*85*
11	Electric lamps	41	3	14	7,558	3,374	7,118
				23	*57*	*56*	*55*
12	Batteries and Accumulators	28	3	24	23,916	8,636	12,826
				45	*74*	*78*	*78*
13	Primary batteries and cells, and parts thereof other than carbons	8	8	22	11,535	4,382	9,036
				100	*100*	*100*	*100*
14	Accumulators and parts and accessories	20	4	12	17,851	5,998	6,405
				39	*85*	*89*	*86*
15	Electric Lighting Accessories and Fittings	122	3	10	4,550	2,489	3,828
				7	*26*	*29*	*26*
F.	VEHICLES						
1	Motor Vehicles and Cycles (Manufacturing)	807	3	19	207,586	58,090	59,491
				2	*27*	*22*	*16*
2	Cars and taxis, and chassis with engines therefor	21	3	7	129,156	33,871	34,395
				21	*82*	*80*	*69*
3	Commercial vehicles and chassis with engines therefor; tractors, industrial and works trucks and works tractors	77	3	17	64,112	20,541	30,319
				15	*46*	*51*	*49*
4	Motor cycles (complete); three-wheeled vehicles and chassis with engines therefor	17	4	11	19,781	9,025	12,870
				42	*82*	*87*	*86*
5	Motor bodies; sidecars and sidecar chassis and bodies; trailers (motor drawn) and caravans	244	3	9	47,426	17,868	26,181
				3	*51*	*48*	*45*
6	Bicycles and tricycles (not mechanically propelled) and parts thereof	99	3	12	30,578	12,913	16,967
				10	*68*	*69*	*64*
7	Other parts and accessories of motor vehicles and motor cycles	303	3	10	28,092	10,730	15,754
				3	*20*	*17*	*18*
8	Motor Vehicles and Cycles (Repairing)	726	3	15	1,971	1,384	3,137
				1	*3*	*4*	*4*
9	Aircraft Manufacture and Repair	117	3	44	98,881	46,837	71,918
				20	*52*	*47*	*46*
10	Complete aircraft and air-frames	7	3	8	34,585	11,874	16,570
				42	*70*	*59*	*58*
11	Other parts and accessories of aircraft	52	3	7	11,467	6,318	9,411
				11	*47*	*45*	*43*

* Figures in italics give the percentage shares of the specified number of largest units.

† Private firms only. No specialisation within Government Departments was distinguished.

Group and code no.	Group, Trade or Sub-Trade	Total no. of business units	Concentration data for the largest business units*				
			No. of units	No. of establishments	Gross output (£000)	Net output (£000)	Nos. employed
12	Locomotive Manufacturing (excluding railway locomotive shops)	28	3	10	13,868	6,282	12,949
				28	*54*	*53*	*61*
13	Railway Carriages and Wagons and Trams (excluding railway establishments)	107	3	116	10,177	5,022	8,073
				38	*21*	*25*	*25*
14	Carts, Perambulators, etc.	89	3	3	2,174	938	1,464
				3	*29*	*29*	*23*
G.	OTHER METAL INDUSTRIES						
1	Tool and Implement	287	3	5	3,688	2,152	3,337
				2	*11*	*12*	*11*
2	Edge and similar tools	94	3	4	3,008	1,684	2,623
				4	*30*	*31*	*27*
3	Cutlery	153	4	5	10,473	7,515	4,518
				3	*54*	*60*	*33*
4	Razors (excl. electric)	11	4	6	10,176	7,299	3,626
				46	*98*	*99*	*94*
5	Knives (other than machine and surgical knives) and scissors (including tailors' shears), and parts	99	3	3	1,137	734	1,587
				3	*18*	*21*	*22*
6	Chain, Nail, Screw and Miscellaneous Forgings	591	4	15	26,573	11,226	17,409
				2	*23*	*20*	*21*
7	Bolts, nuts, screws, rivets, nails, etc.	244	3	9	15,353	6,857	11,577
				3	*27*	*25*	*28*
8	Steel drop forgings	70	3	6	11,057	4,219	5,531
				8	*39*	*35*	*36*
9	Anchors and chains	49	3	9	2,223	924	1,468
				15	*40*	*35*	*36*
10	Springs, other than laminated	104	3	5	2,172	1,089	2,063
				4	*23*	*20*	*20*
11	Hardware, Hollow-ware, Metal Furniture and Sheet Metal	1,842	3	28	36,326	11,599	20,837
				1	*15*	*11*	*12*
12	Domestic hollow-ware (excl. hollow-ware of cast iron)	119	3	7	4,829	2,835	3,161
				5	*25*	*31*	*22*
13	Metal boxes and containers (excl. composite containers partly of metal)	83	4	23	29,688	8,251	15,558
				20	*68*	*61*	*60*
14	Other hollow-ware (excl. hollow-ware of cast iron)	87	3	8	3,311	1,226	1,800
				8	*21*	*19*	*19*
15	Metal furniture, other than aseptic hospital furniture	136	3	6	2,854	1,526	2,013
				4	*18*	*21*	*18*
16	Metal door and window frames and casements	37	3	9	10,603	5,135	8,227
				17	*67*	*67*	*68*
17	Safes, locks, latches and keys, and cash and deed boxes	68	3	4	3,181	1,895	3,027
				5	*41*	*40*	*36*
18	Specialists in the finishing of metal goods	363	3	3	1,279	900	929
				1	*8*	*9*	*6*

* Figures in italics give the percentage shares of the specified number of largest units.

Group and code no.	Group, Trade or Sub-Trade	Total no. of business units	Concentration data for the largest business units*: No. of units	No. of establish-ments	Gross output (£000)	Net output (£000)	Nos. em-ployed
19	Needles, Pins, Fish-Hooks and Metal Smallwares	145	3	16	4,904	2,680	4,571
				8	*23*	*22*	*20*
20	Needles (excluding surgeons' suture needles and hypodermic needles), pins, hair grips and curlers, and fish hooks	43	3	14	2,000	1,398	2,744
				23	*37*	*41*	*42*
21	Wire and Wire Manufactures	227	3	24	26,664	6,507	7,944
				8	*28*	*23*	*22*
22	Establishments specialising in the drawing of wire	71	3	12	19,002	3,763	3,953
				14	*37*	*30*	*28*
23	Establishments specialising in the working of wire	139	3	7	3,301	1,330	1,880
				4	*17*	*17*	*16*
24	Establishments engaged in the drawing and working of wire	28	3	15	15,791	4,329	5,666
				36	*63*	*55*	*58*
25	Brass Manufacture	533	3	6	7,340	3,183	3,658
				1	*10*	*10*	*8*
26	Scrap Metal Processing	156	3	42	8,904	2,655	3,240
				19	*22*	*37*	*34*
27	Precious Metals Refining	13	3	17	49,622	6,576	4,754
				59	*80*	*84*	*83*
28	Musical Instruments	92	3	5	4,163	1,330	2,229
				5	*46*	*28*	*32*
29	Jewellery and Plate	333	3	6	1,711	1,100	1,983
				2	*8*	*10*	*10*
30	Watch and Clock	61	3	14	6,912	3,940	6,613
				17	*60*	*62*	*60*
31	Scientific, Surgical and Photographic Instruments, etc.	567	3	14	20,752	9,587	12,132
				2	*25*	*21*	*16*
32	Ophthalmic instruments and appliances (including prescription and repair work)	147	3	27	2,972	1,700	3,230
				13	*31*	*31*	*26*
33	Other optical instruments and appliances, and parts thereof	27	3	7	2,882	1,956	3,503
				19	*58*	*58*	*57*
34	Medical, surgical, veterinary and dissecting instruments, appliances and equipment (including repair work on surgical instruments)	125	4	12	1,449	1,002	2,575
				8	*18*	*20*	*29*
35	Photographic and cinematograph apparatus and appliances	34	3	3	958	602	1,205
				8	*34*	*38*	*44*
36	Sensitised photographic plates and films, and photographic paper and cloth	14	4	11	18,587	8,044	9,152
				46	*90*	*91*	*90*
37	Scientific, engineering, industrial, etc. instruments and apparatus, not elsewhere specified (except optical)	171	3	9	9,574	5,433	8,324
				4	*33*	*30*	*28*

* Figures in italics give the percentage shares of the specified number of largest units.

Group and code no.	Group, Trade or Sub-Trade	Total no. of business units	Concentration data for the largest business units*				
			No. of units	No. of establish-ments	Gross output (£000)	Net output (£000)	Nos. em-ployed
H.	COTTON						
1	Cotton Spinning and Doubling	442	3	111	102,457	22,509	41,429
				15	*22*	*20*	*24*
	Cotton and spun rayon, nylon, etc. yarn						
2	Spinners and spinner-doublers	212	3	97	90,624	21,566	35,078
				23	*27*	*25*	*27*
3	Doublers only	97	3	22	16,705	2,207	5,684
				17	*25*	*23*	*30*
4	Cotton waste yarn (single or doubled)	76	3	10	4,106	1,039	1,139
				10	*18*	*17*	*17*
5	Finished thread of cotton for sewing, embroidery, etc.	27	8	13	23,153	6,067	11,879
				38	*90*	*91*	*94*
6	Cotton Weaving	597	3	12	10,745	3,102	6,506
				1	*3*	*4*	*6*
7	Woven cotton cloth	539	3	20	13,169	2,887	5,104
				3	*4*	*4*	*5*
8	Surgical and medical dressings	16	3	6	5,386	1,229	1,716
				26	*55*	*52*	*57*
9	Sanitary towels and tampons	13	3	7	3,456	1,348	1,943
				39	*67*	*73*	*64*
I.	WOOLLEN AND WORSTED						
1	Woollen and Worsted	1,040	3	39	38,519	10,036	15,144
				3	*6*	*8*	*8*
	Tops						
2	Commission combers	39	3	21	3,276	2,266	3,355
				36	*47*	*47*	*44*
3	Other combers	16	3	4	24,686	1,761	2,970
				22	*55*	*63*	*70*
4	Woollen yarns	80	3	6	7,221	784	1,807
				7	*17*	*12*	*21*
5	Worsted yarns	199	3	22	37,547	8,539	11,812
				8	*20*	*27*	*22*
6	Woven woollen fabrics other than damasks, tapestries, brocades and the like	278	3	8	8,581	2,048	4,391
				2	*7*	*6*	*8*
7	Woven worsted fabrics other than damasks, tapestries, brocades and the like	238	3	27	17,671	3,883	6,842
				8	*16*	*17*	*18*
8	Blankets, shawls (other than knitted), travelling rugs, etc.	52	5	14	6,882	1,090	2,956
				21	*41*	*35*	*45*
9	Mechanical cloth and wool felts	23	3	12	7,879	2,009	2,146
				36	*54*	*50*	*48*
J.	OTHER TEXTILES						
1	Hosiery and Other Knitted Goods	865	3	16	25,414	7,536	9,452
				2	*13*	*12*	*8*

* Figures in italics give the percentage shares of the specified number of largest units.

Group and code no.	Group, Trade or Sub-Trade	Total no. of business units	Concentration data for the largest business units*: No. of units	No. of establish-ments	Gross output (£000)	Net output (£000)	Nos. em-ployed
2	Rayon, Nylon, etc. and Silk	286	3	24	86,834	41,407	33,928
				6	*43*	*52*	*37*
3	Rayon, nylon, etc. single continuous filament yarn, and staple fibre	10	3	10	77,364	38,957	28,816
				50	*81*	*82*	*72*
4	Woven cloth of rayon, nylon, etc. and of rayon, nylon, etc. mixed with cotton	175	3	14	9,889	3,389	6,178
				6	*13*	*14*	*17*
5	Carpets	88	3	16	13,175	3,594	7,496
				12	*20*	*24*	*26*
6	Carpets, carpeting and floor rugs of wool, including carpets and rugs on a wool or jute base, other than printed tapestry and tapestry velvet	59	3	16	13,175	3,594	7,496
				16	*21*	*26*	*28*
7	Textile Finishing	538	3	65	22,794	13,460	19,578
				9	*24*	*24*	*22*
8	Cotton yarn (including sewing cotton), bleached, dyed, finished (including warp printed), etc.	57	3	15	2,863	1,467	2,682
				20	*38*	*36*	*34*
	Woven cotton, rayon, nylon, etc. fabrics						
9	Bleached, but not dyed or printed	15	4	20	3,461	2,326	3,969
				6	*77*	*77*	*78*
10	Dyed, but not printed	79	3	19	6,214	3,965	5,839
				18	*30*	*32*	*32*
11	Printed, whether dyed or not	52	3	18	12,333	6,710	9,514
				23	*51*	*50*	*51*
12	Woven woollen and worsted fabrics, bleached, dyed, printed, etc.	76	3	5	2,363	1,526	1,908
				6	*32*	*33*	*31*
13	Hosiery and knitted fabrics, bleached, dyed, finished, etc.	64	3	4	1,214	889	1,744
				6	*20*	*20*	*22*
14	Textile Packing	42	3	17	1,359	778	1,254
				27	*47*	*48*	*46*
15	Linen and Soft Hemp (Great Britain)	62	3	5	5,318	1,622	3,211
				6	*26*	*27*	*27*
16	Rope, Twine and Net	118	3	14	12,592	3,760	3,556
				10	*34*	*36*	*24*
17	Cordage, cables, ropes and twine (including hard hemp yarn)	86	3	9	12,353	3,653	3,292
				9	*37*	*40*	*27*
18	Jute	49	3	16	14,893	3,167	6,724
				22	*38*	*38*	*38*
19	Canvas Goods and Sack	211	3	13	4,881	593	1,422
				4	*12*	*8*	*10*
20	Lace	179	3	12	1,938	769	1,491
				5	*8*	*8*	*12*

* Figures in italics give the percentage shares of the specified number of largest units.

Group and code no.	Group, Trade or Sub-Trade	Total no. of business units	Concentration data for the largest business units*				
			No. of units	No. of establish-ments	Gross output (£000)	Net output (£000)	Nos. em-ployed
21	Lace finishers	34	3	5	1,635	474	695
				13	*30*	*30*	*35*
22	Narrow Fabrics	165	3	14	4,955	1,774	3,056
				7	*17*	*16*	*15*
23	Elastic goods	28	3	11	4,508	1,590	2,461
				28	*51*	*47*	*44*
24	Made-up Household Textiles	119	3	10	5,617	902	942
				5	*26*	*20*	*9*
25	Asbestos	52	3	8	17,794	9,484	8,876
				12	*59*	*60*	*53*
26	Asbestos manufactures and pastes and compositions for coverings	31	3	11	17,710	9,280	8,724
				26	*70*	*70*	*65*
27	Flock and Rag	170	3	6	5,429	960	907
				3	*13*	*13*	*11*
28	Hair, Fibre and Kindred Trades	94	3	10	2,199	852	1,310
				9	*16*	*20*	*22*
K.	CLOTHING						
1	Tailoring, Dressmaking, etc.	4,896	3	47	27,807	8,087	27,011
				1	*6*	*5*	*7*
2	Retail bespoke tailored and dressmade garments	475	3	11	811	388	841
				2	*7*	*6*	*6*
3	Wholesale tailored garments, men's, youths' and boys'	424	3	28	23,739	6,959	23,144
				5	*22*	*20*	*24*
4	Wholesale tailored garments, women's, maids' and girls'	457	3	12	5,883	2,012	5,029
				2	*9*	*9*	*12*
5	Battledress, service and other uniforms, including liveries for men and women	31	3	11	4,547	1,607	3,953
				22	*41*	*48*	*45*
6	Wholesale dressmade garments	700	3	13	3,009	995	2,813
				2	*6*	*6*	*6*
7	Proofed, etc. garments	244	3	11	5,215	1,604	3,361
				4	*13*	*14*	*13*
8	Men's and boys' shirts, underwear and nightwear	228	3	10	3,318	831	2,619
				3	*8*	*7*	*8*
	Lingerie and infants' wear						
9	Women's and girls' nightwear and underwear	202	3	8	4,427	1,258	3,091
				3	*23*	*23*	*21*
10	Infants' wear	144	3	8	747	273	996
				5	*7*	*7*	*10*
11	Corsets and brassières	76	3	12	3,778	1,597	3,923
				10	*24*	*25*	*29*
12	Heavy overalls and aprons, other than of rubber	115	3	3	1,926	528	1,643
				2	*13*	*13*	*15*
13	Alteration, etc., of goods (in workrooms of drapers, dressmakers, tailors and milliners for their selling departments)	126	3	41	419	350	1,886
				21	*33*	*32*	*31*

* Figures in italics give the percentage shares of the specified number of largest units.

Group and code no.	Group, Trade or Sub-Trade	Total no. of business units	Concentration data for the largest business units* No. of units	No. of establish-ments	Gross output (£000)	Net output (£000)	Nos. em-ployed
	Work done for the trade or on private customers' materials or goods						
14	Making up of Tailored garments	700	3	16	1,392	967	3,184
				2	*10*	*9*	*11*
15	Dressmade garments	370	3	3	285	234	718
				1	*6*	*6*	*6*
16	Hats, Caps and Millinery	275	3	6	2,753	881	2,238
				2	*15*	*12*	*13*
	Hoods, capelines, hats and millinery (excluding shapes and children's hats)						
17	Of wool felt	79	3	6	2,396	427	1,507
				7	*36*	*23*	*30*
18	Of fur felt	63	3	3	1,789	897	1,895
				4	*31*	*32*	*30*
19	Glove	153	3	21	1,265	459	1,395
				10	*10*	*10*	*13*
20	Gloves and mittens, wholly or partly of leather (other than sports' gloves and gloves of leather and astrakhan)	123	3	21	1,415	458	1,264
				13	*15*	*13*	*15*
21	Umbrella and Walking Stick	48	3	4	501	165	345
				7	*19*	*16*	*14*
22	Boot and Shoe	781	3	42	13,302	4,515	9,675
				4	*8*	*8*	*8*
23	Boots, shoes, sandals, slippers, clogs and parts thereof	649	3	28	11,958	4,745	9,421
				3	*7*	*8*	*8*
24	Repairs for the trade	105	3	25	880	514	936
				19	*27*	*30*	*24*
L.	FOOD						
1	Grain Milling	240	3	36	70,864	9,919	10,015
				10	*35*	*33*	*31*
2	Milled wheat	164	3	35	69,613	9,788	9,801
				15	*47*	*46*	*41*
3	Bread and Flour Confectionery	1,512	3	82	32,673	12,519	20,266
				4	*18*	*17*	*15*
4	Biscuit	92	3	9	19,371	7,404	14,158
				7	*26*	*31*	*34*
5	Sugar and Glucose	25	3	26	155,635	15,124	15,749
				52	*88*	*82*	*84*
6	Beet sugar	1	1	18	39,767	5,030	5,910
				100	*100*	*100*	*100*
7	Cocoa, Chocolate and Sugar Confectionery	328	3	13	64,107	17,966	24,984
				4	*39*	*38*	*34*
8	Cocoa and chocolate	85	3	12	63,990	17,923	24,869
				12	*59*	*61*	*57*

* Figures in italics give the percentage shares of the specified number of largest units.

Group and code no.	Group, Trade or Sub-Trade	Total no. of business units	Concentration data for the largest business units* No. of units	No. of establish-ments	Gross output (£000)	Net output (£000)	Nos. em-ployed
9	Sugar confectionery	225		33	5,129	1,841	3,811
				1	*11*	*12*	*15*
10	Preserved Fruit and Vegetables	287	3	13	24,873	6,597	8,524
				7	*23*	*21*	*17*
11	Jams, marmalade and mince-meat	74	3	14	14,855	3,481	5,833
				14	*35*	*35*	*31*
12	Pickles, sauces and relishes	68	3	7	5,052	1,897	2,194
				10	*52*	*50*	*40*
13	Cattle, Dog and Poultry Foods	160	3	14	58,292	6,953	5,830
				7	*53*	*45*	*36*
14	Feedingstuffs for animals, poultry, etc. (except dog foods)	134	3	14	58,292	6,953	5,830
				8	*56*	*55*	*43*
15	Bacon Curing and Sausage	320	3	16	15,345	2,578	4,479
				4	*17*	*17*	*19*
16	Bacon and ham curing, including smoking if carried on at the same establishment	65	3	11	10,649	1,517	1,960
				12	*26*	*29*	*28*
17	Sausages, including sausage meat	79	3	6	2,336	635	1,285
				7	*23*	*24*	*29*
18	Starch	11	3	9	5,570	2,036	2,143
				47	*82*	*89*	*83*
19	Fish Curing	129	4	20	3,330	745	1,741
				12	*25*	*28*	*30*
20	Milk Products	364	3	97	80,512	7,334	11,192
				15	*28*	*21*	*21*
21	Whole milk (bottled or processed)	334	3	81	71,524	6,054	9,964
				14	*28*	*22*	*23*
22	Ice Cream	65	3	6	12,360	4,892	3,913
				8	*77*	*76*	*65*
23	Margarine	27	4	7	10,193	4,564	4,060
				23	*79*	*85*	*77*
24	Miscellaneous Preserved Foods	171	3	5	8,642	3,239	2,687
				2	*17*	*22*	*13*
25	Preserved Meat	21	3	5	5,317	1,456	2,737
				21	*40*	*32*	*48*
26	Vinegar and Other Condiments	21	4	10	3,775	1,779	1,449
				33	*62*	*80*	*75*
27	Ice	14	3	4	399	303	278
				25	*53*	*57*	*46*
28	Tea Blending and Coffee Roasting	82	3	11	32,568	2,577	3,025
				10	*52*	*43*	*41*
29	Tea blending	76	3	10	32,369	2,542	2,997
				10	*53*	*45*	*43*
M.	DRINK AND TOBACCO						
1	Brewing and Malting	283	3	34	60,433	9,481	8,964
				5	*14*	*11*	*13*
2	Brewing but not malting	187	3	8	24,102	5,463	4,536
				3	*11*	*12*	*14*

* Figures in italics give the percentage shares of the specified number of largest units.

Group and code no.	Group, Trade or Sub-Trade	Total no. of business units	Concentration data for the largest business units*				
			No. of units	No. of establish-ments	Gross output (£000)	Net output (£000)	Nos. em-ployed
3	Brewing and malting	118	3	30	51,713	6,793	7,700
				15	*26*	*19*	*23*
4	Malting only	74	3	41	7,246	1,314	1,586
				23	*32*	*31*	*30*
5	Wholesale Bottling	338	4	68	67,845	19,565	9,684
				14	*42*	*53*	*34*
6	Of beer (including ale, stout, porter, etc.)	220	3	52	23,211	5,010	5,349
				16	*31*	*36*	*30*
7	Of wines and/or spirits	112	7	25	49,694	16,076	4,206
				17	*61*	*74*	*58*
8	Spirit Distilling	38	6	59	27,373	5,214	4,206
				59	*85*	*73*	*80*
9	Spirit Rectifying and Compounding	10	3	6	30,648	3,303	1,208
				43	*85*	*83*	*75*
10	Soft Drinks, British Wines and Cider	381	3	76	7,225	3,295	4,705
				14	*18*	*18*	*19*
11	Soft drinks, including fruit juices	357	3	76	7,225	3,295	4,705
				14	*24*	*23*	*22*
12	Tobacco	60	3	24	605,335	47,051	32,054
				24	*79*	*74*	*70*
N.	PAPER AND PRINTING						
1	Paper and Board	193	3	36	68,277	20,315	15,535
				13	*22*	*19*	*21*
2	Other uncoated printing paper	16	3	7	16,347	5,451	3,462
				32	*47*	*49*	*45*
3	Writing paper	11	3	9	14,315	5,127	3,775
				53	*80*	*83*	*72*
4	Other packings and wrappings	39	4	7	31,475	10,537	4,712
				14	*54*	*53*	*46*
5	Board, other than coated	39	3	4	17,655	7,283	4,697
				9	*57*	*58*	*51*
6	Wallpaper	16	4	19	7,753	3,215	4,779
				59	*86*	*86*	*86*
7	Cardboard Box, Carton and Fibreboard Packing Case	386	3	14	17,538	6,608	9,278
				3	*18*	*17*	*18*
8	Rigid boxes	273	3	8	2,569	1,339	2,498
				2	*13*	*14*	*13*
9	Cartons	64	3	7	11,944	4,595	7,113
				9	*35*	*35*	*42*
10	Fibreboard packing cases	29	3	8	13,754	4,832	2,906
				19	*42*	*43*	*37*
11	Manufactured Stationery, Paper Bag and Kindred Trades	324	3	15	25,889	9,502	10,307
				4	*24*	*24*	*20*
12	Notepaper, pads, envelopes and boxed stationery	30	3	8	13,279	5,064	6,665
				20	*71*	*68*	*66*
13	Paper bags	72	3	7	20,062	4,990	3,354
				9	*54*	*51*	*40*
14	Newspaper and Periodical Printing and Publishing	460	3	30	40,570	22,079	24,346
				5	*25*	*24*	*25*

* Figures in italics give the percentage shares of the specified number of largest units.

Group and code no.	Group, Trade or Sub-Trade	Total no. of business units	Concentration data for the largest business units*				
			No. of units	No. of establishments	Gross output (£000)	Net output (£000)	Nos. employed
15	Newspapers	351	3	28	35,417	21,366	22,466
				6	*32*	*32*	*30*
16	Magazines and periodicals	86	3	21	25,774	11,635	9,987
				19	*56*	*53*	*54*
17	Printing and Publishing, Book-binding, Engraving, etc. Trades	2,664	3	27	18,667	9,709	12,865
				1	*9*	*8*	*7*
	Printed books, music and diaries						
18	Non-printers	111	3	3	3,769	1,516	1,376
				3	*14*	*17*	*20*
19	Printers	65	3	4	6,641	2,717	4,465
				6	*37*	*27*	*27*
20	Christmas cards, greeting cards, calendars and picture postcards						
	Printers	59	3	6	2,351	1,216	2,157
				9	*40*	*39*	*37*
21	Machine ruling, bookbinding, stitching and finishing	154	3	4	866	602	1,252
				3	*15*	*15*	*15*
22	Stereotyping, electrotyping, engraving, photo-litho off-set plates, die sinking and relief stamping, and type-setting	220		10	1,975	1,562	1,981
				4	*19*	*20*	*18*
O.	OTHER MANUFACTURING AND SERVICE TRADES						
1	Rubber	252	3	27	105,496	25,555	36,278
				8	*41*	*33*	*36*
2	Rubber tyres and tubes	11	3	6	103,861	20,626	26,222
				32	*76*	*73*	*75*
3	Machinery belting	14	3	4	16,092	5,356	3,423
				27	*78*	*75*	*65*
4	Timber	1,440	3	30	4,907	1,529	3,254
				2	*3*	*3*	*4*
5	Saw mill products	789	3	41	5,131	1,437	3,044
				4	*6*	*5*	*6*
6	Other woodwork for buildings	248	3	10	3,460	1,238	2,022
				4	*13*	*13*	*12*
7	Shop and Office Fittings	255	3	12	3,284	1,606	2,980
				4	*17*	*15*	*17*
8	Wooden Containers and Baskets	479	3	20	2,150	778	1,629
				4	*5*	*5*	*6*
9	Wooden boxes, packing cases and similar containers	335	3	6	1,670	595	1,111
				2	*5*	*5*	*5*
10	Furniture and Upholstery	1,191	3	20	10,583	4,811	7,095
				1	*8*	*9*	*7*
11	Furniture, not upholstered, mainly of wood	654	3	14	9,094	4,380	6,119
				2	*11*	*12*	*10*

* Figures in italics give the percentage shares of the specified number of largest units.

Group and code no.	Group, Trade or Sub-Trade	Total no. of business units	Concentration data for the largest business units* No. of units	No. of establishments	Gross output (£000)	Net output (£000)	Nos. employed
12	Upholstered furniture	317	3	8	4,051	1,784	2,650
				2	*12*	*15*	*12*
13	Soft Furnishings	251	3	12	6,170	1,926	3,090
				4	*21*	*22*	*18*
14	Bedding	181	3	12	3,838	1,126	2,049
				5	*16*	*17*	*16*
15	Fellmongery	41	3	5	2,464	—	477
				12	*40*	*26*	*29*
16	Leather (Tanning and Dressing)	393	3	20	14,729	1,702	3,528
				4	*12*	*7*	*11*
17	Tanning of cattle hides	63	3	6	8,779	873	1,754
				8	*22*	*13*	*24*
18	Tanning and dressing	84	3	4	9,203	1,586	2,589
				4	*22*	*19*	*20*
19	Dressing only	181	3	4	5,612	1,139	811
				2	*16*	*15*	*8*
20	Leather Goods	315	4	13	1,633	611	1,811
				4	*10*	*9*	*10*
21	Fur	187	3	5	992	590	1,045
				3	*9*	*13*	*14*
22	Linoleum, Leathercloth and Allied Trades	25	3	4	19,658	5,976	7,879
				12	*48*	*52*	*54*
23	Floor coverings	11	3	4	19,658	5,976	7,879
				27	*72*	*76*	*75*
24	Plastic Goods and Fancy Articles	435	3	9	5,077	2,003	3,698
				2	*15*	*12*	*11*
25	Plastic goods	252	3	9	4,858	1,944	3,677
				3	*19*	*16*	*16*
26	Sports Requisites	104	3	6	1,962	838	2,211
				5	*29*	*26*	*29*
27	Toys and Games	163	3	8	9,610	4,640	9,102
				4	*40*	*42*	*38*
28	Brushes and Brooms	195	3	5	2,951	1,351	1,846
				2	*16*	*18*	*13*
29	Paint, paste, distemper, whitewash and similar brushes	31	3	5	2,696	1,090	1,678
				14	*45*	*50*	*49*
30	Miscellaneous Stationers' Goods	97	3	9	3,802	1,986	3,365
				8	*23*	*26*	*26*
31	Pens, pencils, crayons, etc.	57	3	8	2,925	1,501	2,405
				13	*32*	*35*	*32*
32	Office machinery requisites	18	3	5	2,815	1,363	2,273
				21	*44*	*46*	*52*
33	Incandescent Mantles	5	5	6	709	424	769
				100	*100*	*100*	*100*
34	Cinematograph Film Production	54	3	9	4,933	3,286	2,742
				14	*41*	*40*	*45*
35	Cinematograph Film Printing	18	3	3	4,146	1,744	1,464
				16	*66*	*70*	*61*
36	Laundry, Cleaning, Job Dyeing and Carpet Beating	1,854	3	48	7,395	5,305	14,235
				2	*10*	*9*	*8*

* Figures in italics give the percentage shares of the specified number of largest units.

Group and code no.	Group, Trade or Sub-Trade	Total no. of business units	Concentration data for the largest business units*: No. of units	No. of establish-ments	Gross output (£000)	Net output (£000)	Nos. em-ployed
37	Laundry work	1,500	3	51	3,235	2,380	8,145
				3	*6*	*6*	*6*
38	Dry cleaning, valeting, dyeing, carpet beating, etc.	310	3	14	6,122	4,912	11,835
				4	*32*	*34*	*34*
P.	BUILDING AND CONTRACTING AND CIVIL ENGINEERING						
1	Building and Contracting Trade (Private firms only)	18,536	3	3	56,510	17,203	35,944
				0	*5*	*3*	*4*
2	New building construction	5,312	3	3	56,510	17,203	35,944
				0	*10*	*8*	*8*
3	Repairs, maintenance and conversion of existing buildings	8,129	3	3	1,697	852	1,804
				0	*1*	*1*	*1*
4	Work on highways and sewers†	131	3	3	3,162	1,281	2,247
				2	*16*	*15*	*15*
5	Other civil engineering†	318	3	3	15,321	7,005	12,510
				1	*18*	*16*	*18*
6	Opencast coal mining†	24	3	4	5,076	2,256	3,028
				16	*54*	*54*	*55*
	Specialist work†						
7	Electrical work	369	3	3	6,318	3,943	6,634
				1	*17*	*22*	*18*
8	Heating and ventilating contracting	154	3	4	7,861	3,327	5,627
				3	*27*	*27*	*29*
9	Other specialist work	1,331	3	4	13,029	5,938	8,071
				0	*10*	*8*	*7*
10	Tramway, Trolley Bus and Omnibus Undertakings (Civil Engineering)	11	3	6	2,040	1,252	3,371
				32	*73*	*74*	*75*
11	Canal, Dock and Harbour Undertakings (Civil Engineering)	51	3	57	8,180	5,767	14,449
				47	*58*	*58*	*58*

* Figures in italics give the percentage shares of the specified number of largest units.
† Relates to firms employing twenty-five or more persons.

APPENDIX C

*Frequency distribution of 147 Census Trades and 167 Sub-Trades according to degrees of specialisation and exclusiveness, 1951**

Degree of specialisation or exclusiveness	Specialisation				Exclusiveness			
	Trades		Sub-Trades		Trades		Sub-Trades	
%	Number	Per cent of total	Number	Per cent of total	Number	Per cent of total	Number	Per cent of total
100	5	3·4	—	—	18	12·2	5	3·0
95–99	31	21·1	8	4·8	50	34·0	26	15·5
90–94	50	34·0	35	20·9	30	20·4	24	14·4
85–89	27	18·4	42	25·1	18	12·2	32	19·1
80–84	21	14·3	30	18·0	17	11·6	22	13·2
75–79	7	4·7	27	16·2	5	3·4	13	7·8
70–74	4	2·7	11	6·6	4	2·7	14	8·4
65–69	1	0·7	10	6·0	1	0·7	5	3·0
60–64	1	0·7	1	0·6	1	0·7	17	10·2
59 and under	—	—	3	1·8	3	2·1	9	5·4
Total	147	100·0	167	100·0	147	100·0	167	100·0

* There are thirty-three Sub-Trades that have been omitted because of lack of data on which to base specialisation and exclusiveness.

APPENDIX D

FORMULAE FOR THE ESTIMATION OF PRINCIPAL PRODUCT CONCENTRATION

Symbols and definitions

For trades:

T is the gross output of the trade
T_3 is the gross output of the three largest units
T_0 is the gross output of the units other than the three largest
P is the total principal products of the trade wherever produced
O_t is the total of other than principal products produced by the trade
P_t is the total principal products by the trade produced by establishments in the trade
P_3 is the principal products produced by the establishments in the trade of the three largest units
P_0 is the principal products produced by the establishments in the trade of the units other than the three largest.

For sub-trades:

D is the gross output of the sub-trade
D_3 is the gross output of the three largest units
D_0 is the gross output of the units other than the three largest
C is the total principal products, characteristic of the sub-trade, wherever produced
C_3 is the total principal products, characteristic of the sub-trade, produced by the establishments of the three largest units in the sub-trade
C_t is the total principal products, characteristic of the sub-trade, produced by establishments classified to the trade
C_{st} is the total principal products, characteristic of the sub-trade, produced by establishments classified to the sub-trade.

For trades or sub-trades:

Cr is the Board of Trade gross output concentration-ratio for a trade or sub-trade: that is, the proportion of the trade's (or sub-trade's) gross output controlled by the three largest units
CR is the estimated principal product concentration-ratio: that is, the proportion of the total principal products appropriate to the trade (or sub-trade) produced by the establishments in the trade (or sub-trade)

S_t, S_s are the degrees of specialisation of a trade and a sub-trade respectively: that is, the proportion of the gross output of a trade or sub-trade represented by the output of principal products by establishments classified to it

e_t, e_s are the degrees of exclusiveness of a trade and a sub-trade respectively: that is, the proportion of the total principal products appropriate to the trade or sub-trade produced by establishments classified to it.

Identities:

The following identities held by virtue of the definitions:

$$Cr \equiv \frac{T_3}{T} \quad \ldots\ldots (1)$$

$$CR \equiv \frac{P_3}{P} \quad \ldots\ldots (2)$$

$$S_t \equiv \frac{P_t}{T} \quad \ldots\ldots (3)$$

$$S_s \equiv \frac{C_{st}}{D} \quad \ldots\ldots (4)$$

$$e_t \equiv \frac{P_t}{P} \quad \ldots\ldots (5)$$

$$e_s \equiv \frac{C_{st}}{C} \quad \ldots\ldots (6)$$

I. ESTIMATING PRINCIPAL PRODUCT CONCENTRATION

In order to estimate the principal product concentration-ratio, CR, it is necessary to make certain assumptions about the principal product content of T_3.

Maximum principal product concentration

This occurs when P_3 is greatest, that is, when $T_3 = P_3$.

Since $CR = \frac{P_3}{P}$ it follows from this that

$$CR\text{max.} = \frac{T_3}{P} = \frac{T_3}{T} \times \frac{T}{P} = Cr \times \frac{P_c}{s_t} \times \frac{e_t}{P_t} = \frac{Cr.e_t}{s_t} \quad \ldots\ldots (\text{I})$$

There is, however, a limit set to the extent to which T_3 may consist of principal products, since the other units need to have sufficient principal products to justify their establishments being classified to the trade.

The minimum degree of specialisation is assumed to be 50 per cent, so that the principal product output of the other largest units must equal at least half their gross output.

Thus, since $$P_0 \geq \frac{T_0}{2} \geq \frac{T-T_3}{2}$$

and $$P_3 = P_t - P_0.$$

Then, in the limiting case where $P_0 = \dfrac{T-T_3}{2}$

$$P_3 = P_t - \frac{(T-T_3)}{2}.$$

Thus, $$CR\text{max.} = \frac{P_3\text{max.}}{P} = \frac{2P_t - (T-T_3)}{2P}$$

$$= \frac{P_t}{P} - \frac{T}{2P} + \left[\frac{T_3}{T} \times \frac{T}{2P}\right]$$

After substitution we have,

$$CR\text{max.} = e_t\left[1 - \frac{1}{2s_t}(1 - Cr)\right] \quad \ldots\ldots\ldots\ldots\ldots \text{(II)}$$

Thus, the maximum principal product concentration-ratio (CRmax.) is the *lower* of (I) or (II).

Minimum principal product concentration

This occurs when P_3 is least, that is when T_3 consists of only sufficient principal products to satisfy the minimum specialisation requirement.

Thus, $$P_3\text{min.} = \frac{T_3}{2}.$$

Then, $$CR\text{min.} = \frac{P_3\text{min.}}{P} = \frac{T_3}{2P} = \frac{T_3}{T} \times \frac{T}{2P}.$$

Whence, after substitution, we have

$$CR\text{min.} = \frac{Cr.e_t}{2s_t} \quad \ldots\ldots\ldots\ldots\ldots\ldots\ldots \text{(III)}$$

But there is another factor, apart from the minimum degree of specialisation, which may determine the minimum principal product concentration. This is that the principal products of the other units cannot be greater than their gross output, that is

$$P_0 \leqq T_0.$$

Whence $$P_t - P_3 \leqq T - T_3$$

and, in the limiting case, $P_3\text{min.} = P_t - (T - T_3)$

Thus, $$CR\text{min.} = \frac{P_3\text{min.}}{P} = \frac{P_t}{P} - \frac{(T-T_3)}{P}$$

$$= e_t - \left[\frac{T}{P} - \frac{T_3}{T} \times \frac{T}{P}\right]$$

$$= e_t - \left[\frac{e_t}{s_t} - \frac{e_t Cr}{s_t}\right]$$

$$= e_t \left[1 - \frac{1 - Cr}{s_t}\right] \text{.............. (IV)}$$

Thus, the minimum principal product concentration-ratio CR is determined by the *higher* of (III) or (IV).

2. ESTIMATING PRINCIPAL PRODUCT CONCENTRATION-RATIOS FOR SUB-TRADES

For sub-trades:

Board of Trade concentration-ratio $= Cr = \frac{D_3}{D}$

Degree of specialisation $= s_s = \frac{C_{st}}{D}$

Degree of exclusiveness $= e_s = \frac{C_{st}}{C}$

Principal product concentration-ratios $= CR = \frac{C_3}{C}$

By the same reasoning as applied in the case of trades, it may be shown that maximum CR occurs when

$$C_3 = D_3 \quad \text{or} \quad C_3 = \frac{2C_{st} - (D - D_3)}{2}$$

Thus, formulae (I) and (II) may be applied with appropriate change of symbols to sub-trades as well as trades to give the alternative maximum values of the principal product concentration-ratio.

Similarly, it may be shown that minimum *CR* occurs when

$$C_3=\frac{D_3}{2} \quad \text{or} \quad C_3=C_{st}-(D-D_3)$$

Thus, formulae (III) and (IV) may be applied with appropriate change of symbols to sub-trades as well as trades to give the alternative minimum values of the principal product concentration-ratios.

3. REVISION OF PRINCIPAL PRODUCT CONCENTRATION DUE TO CHANGES IN THE DEFINITIONS OF CENSUS TRADES

In what follows, dashed symbols refer to the redefined, and undashed symbols to the original, trades.

Changes in the definitions of Census trades may occur in two directions:

(*a*) Additional establishments may be classified to the trade by adding new principal products to the trade (in such instances, $P'_t>P_t$)

(*b*) Establishments may be classified to other trades by withdrawing principal products from the trade (in such instances $P_t>'_t$).

(*a*) *Revision of principal product concentration where* $P'>P$

In the original trade, $CR\text{max.}=\frac{T_3}{P}$ or $\frac{2P_t-(T-T_3)}{2P}$ whichever is the lower.

For maximum *CR* in the redefined trade, assume that the additional establishments are all owned by the three largest units.

Whichever formula was operative the entire extra output of principal products can thus be added to the top three.

Thus the revised formulae are

$$\frac{T_3+P'_t-P_t}{P'} \quad \ldots\ldots\ldots\ldots\ldots\ldots\ldots\ldots \text{(V)}$$

and

$$\frac{2P'_t-(T-T_3)}{2P'} \quad \ldots\ldots\ldots\ldots\ldots\ldots\ldots \text{(VI)}$$

For minimum *CR* in the redefined trade assume that none of the new establishments classified to the trade are owned by the top three.

If $\frac{T_3}{2P}$ was the operative formula for the original trade, then since the output of principal products by the top three is unaffected, the revised formula is

$$CR\text{min.} = \frac{T_3}{2P'} \quad \ldots\ldots\ldots\ldots\ldots\ldots\ldots \text{(VII)}$$

If $\frac{P_t - (T - T_3)}{P}$ was the operative formula, then, since the estimated minimum output of the top three (the denominator) cannot be altered by the addition of establishments to other units, the revised formula is

$$CR\text{min.} = \frac{P_t - (T - T_3)}{P'} \quad \ldots\ldots\ldots\ldots\ldots \text{(VIII)}$$

Thus, the revised minimum principal product concentration-ratio, *CR*, is determined by the *higher* of (VII) and (VIII).

(*b*) *Revision of principal product concentration where* $P > P'$

For maximum *CR*, assume that the loss of establishments to the trade did not affect the three largest units but was wholly reflected in a loss by the other units.

If in the original trade the formula $\frac{T_3}{P}$ held, then since the removal of establishments is assumed not to affect the top three units, the revised formula is

$$CR\text{max.} = \frac{T_3}{P'} \quad \ldots\ldots\ldots\ldots\ldots\ldots\ldots\ldots \text{(IX)}$$

If the formula $\frac{2P_t - (T - T_3)}{2P}$ held, then, for the same reason, the revised formula is

$$CR\text{max.} = \frac{2P_t - (T - T_3)}{2P'} \quad \ldots\ldots\ldots\ldots\ldots\ldots \text{(X)}$$

Thus, the revised maximum principal product concentration-ratio, *CR*, is determined by the lower of (IX) and (X).

For minimum *CR*, assume that the loss of establishments to the trade is wholly borne by the three largest units.

If in the original trade the formula $\frac{T_3}{2P}$ held, then, since each establishment removed must have been only half specialised, the revised formula is

$$CR\text{min.}=\frac{T_3-(T-T')}{2P'} \qquad \ldots\ldots\ldots\ldots\ldots (\text{XI})$$

If the formula $\frac{P_t-(T-T_3)}{P}$ was operative, the whole of the reduction in principal products in the trade (that is, $P_t-P'_t$) may be attributed to the top three (unless formula (XI) becomes operative). Thus we have:

$$CR\text{min.}=\frac{P'_t-(T-T_3)}{P'} \qquad \ldots\ldots\ldots\ldots\ldots (\text{XII})$$

Thus, the revised minimum principal product concentration-ratio, *CR*, is determined by the higher of (XI) and (XII).

It should be noted, however, that if the redefinition of the trade is large, these formulae may be unrealistic in that the hypothetical removal of establishments from the top three might be inconsistent with their remaining the top three.

4. REVISION OF PRINCIPAL PRODUCT CONCENTRATION DUE TO CHANGES IN THE DEFINITIONS OF CENSUS SUB-TRADES

For re-defined Sub-Trades, as distinct from Trades, no Census data are available for the total characteristic products in the redefined sub-trade (C'_{st}), or the total gross output of the undefined Sub-Trade (D'). This means that the change in definition can be identified only by the change in the characteristic products of the sub-trade classified to establishments in the trade (C'_t-C_t).

(a) *Revision of principal product concentration where* $C'_t>C_t$

In this case, the total of the products characteristic of the sub-trade produced by establishments classified to the trade increases as the result of redefinition—a condition analogous to that of redefined Trades where $P'>P$.

Thus, formulae (V) and (VI) can be modified to apply to Sub-Trades, so that

$$CR\text{max.}=\frac{D_3+C'_{st}-C_{st}}{C'} \quad \text{or} \quad \frac{2C'_{st}-(D-D_3)}{2C'}$$

whichever is the lower.

C'_{st} is unknown, but is clearly maximised when the whole of the increase in characteristic products (that is, $C'_t - C_t$) is attributed to the sub-trade;

and then $$C'_{st} = C_{st} + C'_t - C_t$$

Substituting for C' above,

$$\text{Revised } CR\text{max.} = \frac{D_3 + C'_t - C_t}{C'} \quad \ldots\ldots\ldots\ldots\ldots\ldots \text{(XIII)}$$

or $$\text{Revised } CR\text{max.} = \frac{2(C_{st} + C'_t - C_t) - (D - D_3)}{2C'} \quad \ldots\ldots \text{(XIV)}$$

Thus, the revised maximum principal product concentration-ratio, *CR*, is determined by the lower of (XIII) or (XIV).

For minimum *CR*, formulae (VII) and (VIII) may be modified to apply to Sub-Trades, so that:

$$CR\text{min.} \equiv \frac{D_3}{2C'}$$

or $$CR\text{min.} = \frac{C_{st} - (D - D_3)}{C'}$$

whichever is the higher.

Thus the two formulae for minimum *CR* in Sub-Trades are:

$$\text{Revised } CR\text{min.} = \frac{D_3}{2C'} \quad \ldots\ldots\ldots\ldots\ldots\ldots\ldots \text{(XV)}$$

or $$\text{Revised } CR\text{min.} = \frac{C_{st} - (D - D_3)}{C'} \quad \ldots\ldots\ldots\ldots \text{(XVI)}$$

As before, whichever is the higher applies.

(*b*) *Revision of principal product concentration where* $ct > ct'$

In this case, the total of the products characteristic of the Sub-Trade produced by establishments classified to the trade decreases as the result of re-definition—a condition analogous to that of redefined Trades where $P > P'$.

For maximum concentration, the relevant Trade formulae (IX) and (X) are, after modification for application to sub-trades:

$$\text{Revised } CR\text{max.} = \frac{D_3}{C'} \quad \ldots\ldots\ldots\ldots\ldots\ldots \text{(XVII)}$$

or $$\text{Revised } CR\text{max.} = \frac{2C_{st} - (D - D_3)}{2C'} \quad \ldots\ldots\ldots\ldots\ldots\ldots (\text{XVIII})$$

whichever is the lower.[1]

For minimum concentration, the relevant Trade formulae (XI) and (XII) are, after modification for application to sub-trades:

$$CR\text{min.} = \frac{D_3 - (D - D')}{2C'}$$

or $$CR\text{min.} = \frac{C'_{st} - (D - D_3)}{C'}$$

whichever is the higher.

But C'_{st} and D' are unknown.

Consider the second formula, which applies when the top three had initially more than minimum specialisation. Characteristic products can be removed until minimum specialisation is reached, when the other formula applies, or until the whole reduction is accounted for. Thus, C'_{st} must be minimised, which occurs when $C'_{st} = C_{st} - (C_t - C'_t)$.
Thus,

$$\text{Revised } CR\text{min.} = \frac{C_{st} - (C_t - C'_t) - (D - D_3)}{C'} \quad \ldots\ldots (\text{XIX})$$

Considering the first formula, in which it is necessary to minimise D′. When this formula applies, the removal of every unit of characteristic products entails the removal of a unit of other products. The maximum removal of characteristic products is $(C_t - C'_t)$,[2] which required a total removal of $2(C_t - C'_t)$ from the output of the top three and hence the trade. This amount obviously cannot be removed if $T - T'$ is not equal to or greater than $2(C_t - C'_t)$.[3]

[1] There is an exception to these formulae which occurs when redefinition is so extensive as to require the removal of establishments from the three largest units. Suppose, first, that the top three are 100 per cent specialised. Then, the total trade production of characteristic products outside the top three of the sub-trade $= (C_t - D_3)$. Thus, if $C_t - C'_t \leqq C_t - D_3$, that is, if $C'_t \geqq D_3$, there is no need to withdraw characteristic products from the top three. Suppose, secondly, that the top three cannot be 100 per cent specialised. Then the total trade production of characteristic products outside the top three of the sub-trade $= C_t - C_{st} + \frac{1}{2}(D - D_3)$. Thus if $C_t - C_{st} + \frac{1}{2}(D - D_3) \geqq C_t - C'_t$, that is, if $C'_t \geqq C_t - \frac{1}{2}(D - D_3)$, there is no need to withdraw characteristic products from the top three.

[2] This might not be true if the sub-trade in question had lost characteristic products to another sub-trade in the Trade. As before, this possibility is ignored.

[3] Again it might be possible for the sub-trade in question to lose $2(C_t - C'_t)$ of output without the trade losing as much if another sub-trade gained. Once again, this possibility is ignored.

Thus, the minimum value of $D'=D-(T-T')$, so that the

$$\text{Revised } CR\text{min.} = \frac{D_3-(T-T')}{2C'} \qquad \ldots\ldots\ldots\ldots (XX)$$

These minimum *CR*'s, it should be noted, may be unreal if $(C_t - C_t')$ is large, since the assumption that the identity of the top three is unchanged may easily be invalidated.

APPENDIX E

IMPORTANCE OF SMALL FIRMS

Table 1. *Frequency distribution of 147 Census Trades, by (a) the total employment of small firms, and (b) small firms as a percentage of total business units (including small firms), 1951*

Number of persons employed by small firms	Number of Trades	Small firms as percentage of total business units (including smaller firms) %	Number of Trades
Nil	4	Nil	4
Less than 10	3	Less than 10	10
10–100	24	10–20	9
100–250	17	20–30	29
250–500	19	30–40	18
500–1,000	16	40–50	17
1,000–2,000	26	50–60	24
2,000–5,000	24	60–70	18
5,000–10,000	6	70–80	9
10,000 and over	8	80–90	9
Total	147	Total	147

Table 2. *Frequency distribution of 147 Census Trades, according to the percentage points decrease in the employment concentration-ratio due to the inclusion of small firms, 1951*

Percentage points decrease in employment concentration-ratio	Number of Trades
No change	60
1% point	46
2% points	16
3% points	8
4% points	5
5% points	3
6% points	1
7% points	4
8% points	–
9% points	1
10% points	1
11% points and over	2
Total	147

APPENDIX F

THE RELATION BETWEEN CONCENTRATION, SIZE-RATIO OF UNITS AND THE NUMBER- AND SIZE-RATIOS OF ESTABLISHMENTS

(1) *The relation between concentration-ratio and size-ratio of units*

Symbols: C = employment concentration-ratio
E = total employment of the trade
E_3 = employment of three largest units
U = total number of business units
W = size-ratio of units (average size of three largest divided by average size of *other* units)
X = size-ratio of units (alternative definition: average size of three largest divided by average size of *all* units).

By definition,

$$C = \frac{E_3}{E} \qquad (1)$$

$$W = \frac{E_3}{3} \div \frac{E - E_3}{U - 3} \qquad (2)$$

Multiplying both fractions on the right-hand side of (2) by E, and substituting EC for E_3, then

$$W = \frac{C}{3} \div \frac{1 - C}{U - 3}$$

$$= \frac{CU/3 - C}{1 - C} \qquad (3)$$

Also, by definition,

$$X = \frac{E_3}{3} \div \frac{E}{U} = \frac{CU}{3} \qquad (4)$$

Thus, from (3) and (4),

$$W = \frac{X - C}{1 - C} \qquad (5)$$

(2) *The relation between size-ratio of units and number- and size-ratio of establishments*

Symbols: P = total number of establishments in the trade
P_3 = number of establishments of the three largest units

R =number-ratio of establishments (that is, average number of establishments of three largest units divided by average number of establishments of other units)

S =size-ratio of establishments (that is, average numbers employed per establishments of three largest units divided by average numbers employed per establishment of other units).

By definition, $$R=\frac{P_3}{3}\div\frac{P-P_3}{U-3}=\frac{P_3(U-3)}{3(P-P_3)} \qquad (6)$$

and $$S=\frac{E_3}{P_3}\div\frac{E-E_3}{P-P_3}=\frac{E_3(P-P_3)}{P_3(E-E_3)} \qquad (7)$$

Then, $$R\times S=\frac{P_3(U-3)}{3(P-P_3)}\times\frac{E_3(P-P_3)}{P_3(E-E_3)}=\frac{E_3(U-3)}{3(E-E_3)} \qquad (8)$$

Therefore $R\times S=W$ (see equation (2) above).

APPENDIX G

THE SELECTION OF TRADES FOR THE ANALYSIS OF 1951 CONCENTRATION

(1) The principles guiding the selection of the trades for the analysis of 1951 concentration may be summarised as follows:

(*a*) where data are available for both a Trade and its constituent Sub-Trades, the Sub-Trades have been selected except:

(i) where its degree of specialisation or exclusiveness is either not available or less than 67 per cent;

(ii) where employment in the Sub-Trades eligible for selection on the basis of (i) represents less than one-third of the total employment of the Trade itself;

(iii) where there are special reasons why the Trade should be preferred to any eligible Sub-Trade.

(*b*) where data are available for a Trade but not for any Sub-Trades, the Trade is selected except:

(i) where its degree of specialisation or exclusiveness is less than 67 per cent;

(ii) where the concentration data available are not complete in terms of gross output, net output and employment.

(2) The trades selected for the 1951 analysis are indicated in Appendix H. The Trades or Sub-Trades rejected and the reasons for their rejection are shown in the following table, where Trades are denoted by block capitals:

Reason for rejection	Trade	
Low exclusiveness or specialisation (less than 67 per cent)	Domestic Glassware DYES AND DYESTUFFS Disinfectants, etc. COAL TAR PRODUCTS Ordnance (excl. Small Arms) Prime Movers: other than I.C. Pumps and Pumping Machinery Telegraph and Telephone Apparatus Electrical Contract Work ELECTRIC LIGHT ACCESSORIES Motor Vehicles CARTS, PERAMBULATORS, ETC. Cars and Taxis Other Motor Vehicle Parts Metal Door and Window Frames Cotton Yarn: Doublers only	Sanitary Towels and Tampons Surgical and Medical Dressings Rayon, Nylon, etc., Woven Cloth Cotton, Rayon, etc.: Bleaching Battledress and Other Uniforms MADE-UP HOUSEHOLD TEXTILES Alteration of Goods, etc. Infants' wear Sausages MISCELLANEOUS PRESERVED FOODS Uncoated Board Uncoated Printing Paper Greeting Cards: Printers Rubber Machinery Belting Highways and Sewers Repairs, Maintenance and Conversion
Specialisation or exclusiveness not available	Pharmaceutical Chemicals Pharmaceutical Preparations Iron Puddling Steel Manufactures—Alloy Steel Manufactures—Non-Alloy Steel Forgings Steel Manufactures (without Melting) Complete Aircraft and Airframes Wire Drawing and Working Wire Drawing only Wire Working only Cotton Waste Yarn Tops—Commission Combers Tops—Other Combers	Bacon and Ham Curing Brewing and Malting Brewing but not Malting Malting Other Packing and Wrappings Books, etc.: Printers Books, etc.: Non-printers Machine-ruling, etc. Tanning and Dressing Dressing only Other Woodwork for Buildings Heating and Ventilating Specialists Electrical Specialists Other Specialist Contractors
Employment inadequate	Needles, Pins, Fish Hooks, etc. Elastic Goods Lace Finishers	Stereotyping, etc. Paint Brushes, etc. Tanning of Cattle Hides
Inadequate data or special reasons		Beet-Sugar

APPENDIX H

Average size of units and plants, size-ratio of units and number- and size-ratios of plants for 219 trades, 1951*

	Average size of units (V) (000's)	Average size of plants (Q) (000's)	Size-ratio of units (W)	Number-ratio of plants (R)	Size-ratio of plants (S)
A. HIGH CONCENTRATION TRADES					
Rayon, Nylon, etc., C.F. Yarn and Staple Fibre	4·03	2·01	6	2·4	2·5
Spirit Rectifying	0·16	0·11	7	1·8	4·0
Floor Coverings	0·95	0·70	8	1·0	8·4
Rubber Tyres and Tubes	3·19	1·85	8	1·2	6·4
Tramway, Trolley Bus and Omnibus Undertakings (Civil Engineering)	0·41	0·24	8	1·2	6·3
Cinematograph Film Printing	0·13	0·13	8	0·9	8·5
Mineral Oil Refining	1·52	0·81	8	2·5	3·5
Cast Iron Stoves: Other	0·66	0·52	9	1·9	4·7
Tin	0·15	0·13	10	1·7	6·0
Valves and Cathode Ray Tubes	1·62	0·61	11	3·3	3·4
Ball and Roller Bearings	1·44	0·86	12	3·2	3·9
Tinplate	0·94	0·38	12	8·0	1·5
Starch	0·23	0·14	13	2·3	5·5
Asbestos Cement Goods	0·82	0·37	14	3·7	3·9
Salt Mines and Quarries	0·47	0·25	14	4·3	3·3
Lead	0·80	0·07	14	2·1	6·5
Cement	1·03	0·26	15	6·6	2·2
Vinegar and Other Condiments	0·09	0·06	15	2·6	5·9
Wallpaper	0·35	0·17	16	5·5	2·9
Transmission Chains	1·22	1·02	17	1·3	12·6
Precious Metals Refining	0·44	0·20	17	4·7	3·6
Abrasive Wheels, etc.	0·29	0·28	17	1·3	12·7
Incandescent Mantles	0·15	0·13	17	1·3	12·8
Asbestos Manufactures	0·43	0·31	17	3·2	5·4
Notepaper, Pads, Envelopes	0·34	0·25	17	2·2	7·7
Small Arms	0·35	0·26	18	1·3	13·3
Cast Iron Pipes and Fittings	0·45	0·30	19	4·5	4·1
Motor Cycles, etc.	0·88	0·58	22	2·9	7·4
Margarine	0·20	0·18	22	2·0	11·2
Photographic Plates and Films	0·73	0·42	23	2·6	8·7
Razors (excl. Electric)	0·35	0·30	24	1·7	14·5
Prime Movers: internal combustion	1·13	0·63	24	5·9	4·1
Zinc	0·19	0·16	24	2·0	11·8
Boilers and Boiler-house Plant	0·66	0·53	26	1·7	15·2
Accumulators and Parts	0·37	0·24	26	3·1	8·4
Scales and Weighing Machinery	0·26	0·08	28	14·5	1·9
Match	0·15	0·12	33	2·8	11·6
Seed Crushing	0·35	0·19	34	5·6	6·0

* The trades in italics are those for which the concentration-ratios closely approximate to the degree of control over the production of the specific products; see p. 50.

	Average size of units (*V*) (000's)	Average size of plants (*Q*) (000's)	Size-ratio of units (*W*)	Number-ratio of plants (*R*)	Size-ratio of plants (*S*)
Sugar and Glucose	0·75	0·38	38	8·0	4·7
Spirit Distilling	0·14	0·05	38	14·9	2·6
Ice Cream	0·09	0·09	39	1·9	19·8
Primary Batteries	1·13	0·41	42	5·7	7·4
Tobacco	0·77	0·45	44	5·8	7·5
Wholesale Bottling of Wines and Spirits	0·08	0·06	46	7·0	6·5
Bicycles and Tricycles	0·27	0·23	58	3·7	15·6
Fertilisers	0·24	0·14	59	14·3	4·1
Soap and Glycerine	0·25	0·21	62	4·9	12·7
Explosives and Fireworks	1·05	0·52	70	10·3	6·8
Cotton Thread	0·47	0·37	70	3·3	21·0
Wrought Iron and Steel Tubes	0·52	0·27	74	8·4	8·8
B. MEDIUM CONCENTRATION TRADES					
Ice	0·04	0·04	3	1·2	2·6
Sanitary Earthenware	0·22	0·17	3	1·0	3·1
Roofing Felts	0·15	0·16	5	1·3	3·5
Electrical Ware	0·47	0·33	5	2·0	2·3
Office Machinery Requisites	0·24	0·18	5	1·3	4·1
Fibreboard Packing Cases	0·27	0·19	5	2·0	2·5
Preserved Meat	0·27	0·24	6	1·6	3·5
Mechanical Cloth and Wool Felts	0·20	0·14	6	3·8	1·6
Glazed Tiles	0·26	0·21	6	1·7	3·3
China and Porcelain	0·30	0·26	6	2·1	2·8
Clay Roofing Tiles	0·09	0·06	6	3·6	1·8
Office Machinery	0·42	0·28	7	1·6	4·1
Ink	0·11	0·08	8	3·2	2·4
Photographic and Cine Apparatus	0·08	0·07	8	0·9	8·8
Pens, Pencils, Crayons	0·13	0·12	8	2·7	3·1
Gas Meters	0·38	0·13	9	5·0	1·7
Steel Sheets	0·94	0·63	9	3·3	2·7
Blast Furnaces	0·79	0·60	9	3·3	2·6
Anchors and Chains	0·08	0·07	9	2·7	3·2
Cotton Yarn—Finishing	0·14	0·10	9	4·4	2·1
Jute	0·38	0·24	10	4·3	2·2
Refrigerating Machinery	0·44	0·33	10	1·6	6·1
Cordage, Cables, Ropes	0·14	0·12	10	2·7	3·7
Glue, Gum, Paste, etc.	0·10	0·09	10	2·7	3·8
Other Optical Instruments	0·23	0·17	11	1·9	5·5
Iron Ore and Ironstone	0·26	0·13	11	5·4	2·0
Slate Quarries and Mines	0·23	0·18	11	1·0	10·7
Cinematograph Film Production	0·11	0·10	11	2·8	3·9
Textile Packing	0·07	0·04	11	4·7	2·4
Coke Ovens and By-Products	0·78	0·22	12	16·8	0·7
Blankets, Shawls, etc.	0·13	0·10	12	3·6	3·3
Steel Drop Forgings	0·22	0·20	12	1·9	6·6
Safes, Locks, Latches, etc.	0·12	0·11	12	1·3	9·9
Locomotive Manufacturing	0·76	0·59	13	3·2	4·0
Cast Iron Stoves, etc.: Solid Fuel	0·34	0·26	13	4·1	3·1

* The trades in italics are those for which the concentration-ratios closely approximate to the degree of control over the production of the specific products; see p. 50.

	Average size of units (*V*) (000's)	Average size of plants (*Q*) (000's)	Size-ratio of units (*W*)	Number-ratio of plants (*R*)	Size-ratio of plants (*S*)
Lubricating Oils and Greases	0·09	0·07	13	2·8	4·6
Toilet Preparations and Perfumery	0·13	0·13	13	1·3	10·3
Glass Containers	0·52	0·39	13	2·5	5·4
Polishes and Canvas Dressings	0·12	0·11	13	1·6	7·8
Electric Wires and Cables	1·09	0·65	15	3·5	4·2
Cartons	0·26	0·21	15	2·0	7·6
Biscuit	0·46	0·32	15	2·2	6·9
Electric Lamps	0·32	0·22	15	3·9	4·0
Paper Bags	0·12	0·10	15	2·2	7·1
Woven Cotton Fabrics—Printing	0·36	0·24	17	4·8	3·5
Tea Blending	0·09	0·07	18	2·8	6·5
Plastics Materials	0·40	0·30	18	3·8	4·8
Electric Cookers and Heaters	0·19	0·17	20	1·8	11·0
Agricultural Machinery	0·15	0·14	21	2·2	9·5
Canal, Dock and Harbour Undertakings (Civil Engineering)	0·49	0·20	22	13·5	1·6
Commercial Vehicles	0·80	0·53	24	4·2	5·7
Scrap Metal Processing	0·06	0·04	27	12·1	2·2
Watch and Clock	0·18	0·14	28	4·0	7·1
Wholesale Bottling of Beer	0·08	0·05	32	13·7	2·3
Aircraft Manufacture	1·35	0·73	32	9·8	3·3
Animal Feedingstuffs	0·10	0·08	33	3·8	8·7
Toys and Games	0·15	0·12	33	2·3	14·5
Magazines and Periodicals	0·22	0·17	33	6·5	5·0
Aluminium and Magnesium	0·35	0·28	35	4·8	7·3
Copper and Copper Alloys	0·31	0·25	35	3·7	9·5
Cocoa and Chocolate	0·52	0·42	36	3·6	9·9
Metal Boxes and Containers	0·31	0·23	36	6·1	5·9
Milled Wheat	0·15	0·10	38	9·7	3·9
Dry Cleaning, Valeting, Dyeing	0·11	0·09	53	3·9	13·7
Motor-Bodies, Sidecars, etc.	0·24	0·20	65	2·5	25·3
Electrical Machinery	0·73	0·52	65	8·4	7·8
Glass (Other than Containers)	0·17	0·14	70	4·9	14·4
Textile Machinery and Accessories	0·20	0·16	71	6·2	11·4
Chemicals (General)	0·28	0·18	90	16·7	5·4
C. LOW CONCENTRATION TRADES					
Umbrella and Walking Stick	0·05	0·04	2	1·1	2·1
Fellmongery	0·04	0·04	5	1·7	3·1
Sanitary Ware	0·13	0·12	5	2·1	2·4
Lime and Whiting	0·05	0·04	6	1·9	3·1
Hosiery and Knitted Fabrics—Finishing	0·12	0·11	6	1·2	4·7
Wooden Boxes and Containers	0·06	0·06	6	1·8	3·4
Mining Machinery	0·27	0·23	6	2·2	2·8
Men's and Boys' Shirts, Underwear, etc.	0·15	0·11	6	2·4	2·6
Heavy Overalls and Aprons	0·10	0·08	6	0·8	7·9
Other Hollow-ware	0·11	0·10	7	2·5	2·6
Woollen Yarns	0·11	0·10	7	1·8	3·7
Flock and Rag	0·05	0·04	7	1·8	3·9

* The trades in italics are those for which the concentration-ratios closely approximate to the degree of control over the production of the specific products, see p. 50.

	Average size of units (V) (000's)	Average size of plants (Q) (000's)	Size-ratio of units (W)	Number-ratio of plants (R)	Size-ratio of plants (S)
Other Earthenware and Stoneware	0·29	0·23	7	1·6	4·2
Gloves and Mittens	0·07	0·05	7	6·0	1·2
Carpets, Rugs of Wool	0·46	0·28	7	3·7	2·0
Linen and Soft Hemp	0·19	0·15	7	5·3	1·4
Canvas Goods and Sack	0·07	0·05	8	3·3	2·4
Specialist Metal Finishers	0·04	0·04	8	0·9	8·5
Lace	0·07	0·05	8	3·1	2·7
Woven Woollen Fabrics	0·19	0·15	8	2·2	3·8
Work Done—Dressmade Garments	0·03	0·03	8	0·9	8·6
Springs, other than laminated	0·10	0·09	9	1·5	5·8
Hair, Fibre and Kindred Trades	0·06	0·05	9	3·1	2·8
Hats, Hoods of Fur Felt	0·10	0·09	9	1·0	9·3
Knives	0·07	0·07	9	0·9	9·7
Marine Engineering	0·72	0·59	9	2·6	3·5
Woven Cotton Cloth	0·19	0·14	9	5·1	1·8
Corsets and Brassières	0·18	0·12	10	2·8	3·5
Brushes and Brooms	0·07	0·06	10	1·5	6·5
Metal Furniture	0·08	0·08	10	1·9	5·1
Narrow Fabrics	0·12	0·09	10	3·9	2·5
Fur	0·04	0·04	10	1·6	6·2
Retail Tailoring and Dressmaking	0·03	0·03	10	3·4	3·0
Boot and Shoe Repairs for the Trade	0·04	0·03	10	7·9	1·3
Domestic Hollow-ware	0·12	0·11	11	2·1	5·1
Hats, Hoods of Wool Felt	0·06	0·06	11	2·0	5·5
Woven, Woollen and Worsted Fabrics—Finishing	0·08	0·07	11	1·5	7·3
Leather Goods	0·06	0·05	11	4·0	2·7
Motor Vehicles and Cycles (Repairing)	0·10	0·06	11	3·0	3·7
Edge Tools	0·10	0·10	11	1·2	4·1
Railway Carriages, Wagons and Trams	0·30	0·11	11	21·6	0·5
Bedding	0·07	0·06	12	3·4	3·4
Upholstered Furniture	0·07	0·06	12	2·4	4·9
Proofed Garments	0·11	0·09	12	3·1	3·8
Needles, Pins, Fish Hooks	0·16	0·12	12	4·3	2·7
Woven Cotton Fabrics (Dyeing)	0·23	0·17	12	5·6	2·2
Sugar Confectionery	0·12	0·11	13	0·9	13·4
Jewellery and Plate	0·06	0·05	13	1·9	6·8
Rigid Boxes	0·07	0·06	13	2·3	5·6
Brewing and Malting	0·25	0·11	14	5·4	2·5
Sports Requisites	0·07	0·06	14	1·7	8·2
Musical Instruments	0·08	0·06	14	1·4	9·8
Pre-cast Concrete Goods	0·07	0·05	14	3·8	3·8
Mechanical Handling Equipment	0·21	0·17	15	5·0	2·9
Printing and Bookbinding Machinery	0·18	0·16	15	1·2	12·7
Refractory Goods	0·15	0·10	15	5·4	2·8
Plastic Goods	0·09	0·08	15	2·7	5·6
Brass Manufacture	0·09	0·08	15	1·8	8·3
Wholesale Dressmade Garments	0·07	0·06	15	3·8	4·0
Leather (Tanning and Dressing)	0·09	0·07	15	6·0	2·5

* The trades in italics are those for which the concentration-ratios closely approximate to the degree of control over the production of the specific products; see p. 50.

	Average size of units (*V*) (000's)	Average size of plants (*Q*) (000's)	Size-ratio of units (*W*)	Number-ratio of plants (*R*)	Size-ratio of plants (*S*)
Medical, Surgical, etc. Instruments	0·07	0·06	16	3·2	4·9
Heating and Ventilating Apparatus	0·10	0·09	16	2·8	5·8
Fish Curing	0·04	0·03	17	5·4	3·1
Paper and Board	0·38	0·26	17	9·3	1·8
Ophthalmic Instruments	0·08	0·06	17	6·9	2·5
Woven Worsted Fabrics	0·16	0·12	17	7·1	2·4
Shop and Office Fittings	0·07	0·06	17	3·7	4·7
Saw Mill Products	0·06	0·05	18	10·5	1·7
Women's and Girls' Nightwear, etc.	0·07	0·06	18	2·3	7·6
Worsted Yarns	0·27	0·19	18	5·6	3·3
Preserved Fruit and Vegetables	0·18	0·13	19	3·4	5·7
Boots, Shoes, Sandals, etc.	0·18	0·13	19	7·2	2·7
Stone	0·06	0·04	21	9·1	2·3
Wholesale Tailoring—Women's and Girls'	0·09	0·08	21	3·4	6·1
Wire and Wire Manufactures	0·16	0·12	22	6·7	3·2
Scientific, Engineering, Industrial Instruments	0·17	0·14	22	2·6	8·6
Paint and Varnish	0·12	0·10	23	5·7	4·1
Constructional Engineering	0·17	0·15	24	3·0	8·0
Wooden Furniture	0·09	0·08	24	4·0	6·1
Radio Apparatus and Gramophone	0·45	0·31	25	5·2	4·8
Bacon Curing and Sausage	0·07	0·06	25	4·4	5·7
Hosiery and Knitted Goods	0·14	0·11	25	4·3	5·9
Cotton Spinners and Doublers	0·61	0·31	26	21·0	1·2
Drugs and Pharmaceutical Preparations	0·22	0·18	28	3·3	8·5
Making-up of Tailored Garments	0·04	0·04	28	5·2	5·5
Iron and Steel (Melting and Rolling)	0·73	0·51	30	6·0	5·0
Machine Tools	0·15	0·13	30	5·6	6·0
Bolts, Nuts, Screws, Rivets	0·17	0·15	31	2·7	11·7
Whole Milk (Bottled or Processed)	0·13	0·08	32	18·5	1·7
Soft Drinks	0·06	0·04	33	19·7	1·7
Laundry Work	0·09	0·07	34	14·5	2·4
Clay, Sand, Gravel, Chalk	0·05	0·04	36	12·8	2·8
Iron Engineering Castings	0·10	0·10	36	3·5	10·2
Mechanical Engineering (Repairing)	0·05	0·04	39	9·9	3·9
Wholesale Tailoring—Men's and Boys'	0·23	0·16	45	6·9	6·5
Newspapers	0·21	0·17	50	7·9	6·4
Building Bricks	0·10	0·06	55	22·4	2·5
Shipbuilding and Ship Repairing	0·41	0·30	56	7·0	8·0
Printing and Publishing, Bookbinding, Engraving	0·07	0·06	66	8·3	7·9
Bread and Flour Confectionery	0·09	0·07	91	22·6	4·0

* The trades in italics are those for which the concentration-ratios closely approximate to the degree of control over the production of the specific products; see p. 50.

APPENDIX I

REGRESSION AND CORRELATION COEFFICIENTS FOR VARIABLES IN ANALYSIS OF CHAPTER VII

(1) *Concentration and other variables*

$r_{cu} = -0{\cdot}83$ $\quad b_{cu} = -0{\cdot}50(\pm 0{\cdot}02)$ $\quad b_{uc} = -1{\cdot}39(\pm 0{\cdot}06)$

$r_{cx} = -0{\cdot}40$ $\quad b_{cx} = -0{\cdot}40(\pm 0{\cdot}06)$ $\quad b_{xc} = -0{\cdot}40(\pm 0{\cdot}06)$

$r_{cv} = 0{\cdot}63$ $\quad b_{cv} = 0{\cdot}50(\pm 0{\cdot}04)$ $\quad b_{vc} = 0{\cdot}81(\pm 0{\cdot}07)$

$r_{ce} = -0{\cdot}42$ $\quad b_{ce} = -0{\cdot}29(\pm 0{\cdot}04)$ $\quad b_{ec} = -0{\cdot}57(\pm 0{\cdot}09)$

$r_{cq} = 0{\cdot}60$ $\quad b_{cq} = 0{\cdot}53(\pm 0{\cdot}05)$ $\quad b_{qc} = 0{\cdot}67(\pm 0{\cdot}06)$

$r_{cp_3} = -0{\cdot}02$ $\quad b_{cp_3} = -0{\cdot}02(\pm 0{\cdot}06)$ $\quad b_{p_3c} = -0{\cdot}02(\pm 0{\cdot}07)$

(2) *Relation between variables other than concentration*

$r_{ux} = 0{\cdot}84$ $\quad b_{ux} = 1{\cdot}40(\pm 0{\cdot}06)$ $\quad b_{xu} = 0{\cdot}50(\pm 0{\cdot}02)$

$r_{ue} = 0{\cdot}66$ $\quad b_{ue} = 0{\cdot}79(\pm 0{\cdot}06)$ $\quad b_{eu} = 0{\cdot}55(\pm 0{\cdot}04)$

$r_{vx} = -0{\cdot}30$ $\quad b_{vx} = -0{\cdot}38(\pm 0{\cdot}08)$ $\quad b_{xv} = -0{\cdot}23(\pm 0{\cdot}05)$

$r_{vu} = -0{\cdot}55$ $\quad b_{vu} = -0{\cdot}42(\pm 0{\cdot}04)$ $\quad b_{uv} = -0{\cdot}72(\pm 0{\cdot}07)$

$r_{ve} = 0{\cdot}24$ $\quad b_{ve} = 0{\cdot}21(\pm 0{\cdot}06)$ $\quad b_{ev} = 0{\cdot}26(\pm 0{\cdot}07)$

$r_{xe} = 0{\cdot}70$ $\quad b_{xe} = 0{\cdot}49(\pm 0{\cdot}03)$ $\quad b_{ex} = 0{\cdot}99(\pm 0{\cdot}07)$

$r_{mq} = 0{\cdot}34$ $\quad b_{mq} = 0{\cdot}10(\pm 0{\cdot}01)$ $\quad b_{qm} = 1{\cdot}21(\pm 0{\cdot}22)$

$r_{qv} = 0{\cdot}97$ $\quad b_{qv} = 0{\cdot}86(\pm 0{\cdot}01)$ $\quad b_{vq} = 1{\cdot}09(\pm 0{\cdot}07)$

$r_{mv} = 0{\cdot}56$ $\quad b_{mv} = 0{\cdot}14(\pm 0{\cdot}01)$ $\quad b_{vm} = 2{\cdot}22(\pm 0{\cdot}22)$

(3) *Multiple regression equations*

$$c = -0{\cdot}41(\pm 0{\cdot}03)e + 0{\cdot}61(\pm 0{\cdot}03)v + 1{\cdot}83;\ R^2 = 0{\cdot}72$$

$$c = -0{\cdot}41(\pm 0{\cdot}03)e + 0{\cdot}66(\pm 0{\cdot}04)q + 1{\cdot}81;\ R^2 = 0{\cdot}675$$

$$c = -0{\cdot}41(\pm 0{\cdot}03)e + 0{\cdot}65(\pm 0{\cdot}04)q - 0{\cdot}006(\pm 0{\cdot}06)t + 1{\cdot}82;\ R^2 = 0{\cdot}675$$

$$c = -0{\cdot}54(\pm 0{\cdot}03)e + 0{\cdot}70(\pm 0{\cdot}03)q + 0{\cdot}33(\pm 0{\cdot}04)p_3 + 1{\cdot}91;\ R^2 = 0{\cdot}765$$

APPENDIX J

*Degree of comparability, gross output and estimated principal products concentration for 185 Trades, 1935 and 1951**

	Degree of comparability	Gross output concentration-ratio		Estimated principal products concentration-ratio		
		1935	1951	1935 original	1935 revised	1951
CEMENT	0·96	72	86†	71–75	68–79	79–89
SALT MINES, ETC.	1·20	62	87	48	51–69	83–90
SLATE QUARRIES	1·00	58	62	57–59	57–59	59–67
ROOFING FELTS	1·10	60	68	48–73	43–75	64–76
ABRASIVES	1·00	47	45	45–48	45–49	41–46
GLASS CONTAINERS	1·03	38	45	33–40	19–22	40–48
Domestic and Fancy Glassware	0·79	44	57	22–37	5–38	28–45
BUILDING MATERIALS	0·92	15	25	12–13	14–15	14–24
BRICK AND FIRECLAY	1·03	11	18	7–11	7–14	17–18
Building Bricks	0·97	18	33	11–19	9–18	29–34
Refractory Goods	1·26	25	32	14–28	13–34	21–32
Clay Sanitary Ware	0·99	20	14	11–21	15–29	8–15
NON-METALLIFEROUS MINES AND QUARRIES	0·91	12	16	6–11	4–13	11–22
CHINA AND EARTHENWARE	1·02	8	10	4–8	4–10	8–10
Electrical Ware	1·00	64	63	54–64	54–62	52–56
Sanitary Earthenware	1·00	49	45	29–42	31–44	38–42
Glazed Tiles	1·03	30	37	15–30	21–31	18–35
China and Porcelain	1·00	16	35	7–14	7–14	18–36
Other Earthenware, etc.	0·98	17	15	9–18	8–18	8–16
EXPLOSIVES AND FIREWORKS	1·28	86	93†	71–77	56–79	74–84
DYES AND DYESTUFFS	1·07	77	85†	70–83	66–86	63–83
MINERAL OIL REFINING	1·00	78	93	66–75	65–75	93–96
SEED CRUSHING AND OIL REFINING	1·54	78	73	69–73	44–88	66–69
MATCH	1·00	95	93‡	95	95	88–89
COKE-OVENS AND BY-PRODUCTS	1·04	21	60	12–23	14–30	51–74
SOAP, CANDLES AND GLYCERINE	0·77	48	75	42–47	27–63	68–79
Soap and Glycerine	1·02	76	85	66–77	64–74	74–84
FERTILISER, DISINFECTANT, ETC.	0·77	21	59	8–15	0–20	46–54
Fertilisers	0·96	34	73	15–19	16–23	64–74
Polishes and Canvas Dressings	0·99	75	54	65–81	65–81	42–54
COAL TAR PRODUCTS	1·60	30	34	10–14	7–30	16–20
TOILET PREPARATIONS	1·00	19	38	8–16	8–16	21–31
DRUGS AND PHARMACEUTICALS	0·94	18	27	10–19	10–14	15–29
PAINT AND VARNISH	0·86	20	20	16–19	18–23	11–21
WROUGHT IRON AND STEEL TUBES	0·98	71	84†	65–69	66–72	75–88
TINPLATE	1·02	59	74	53–60	52–61	71–77

* Capitals are used to distinguish Trades from Sub-Trades, while italics are used to indicate the forty-one trades on which the analysis of concentration changes between 1935 and 1951 is based. † Four largest units. ‡ Six largest units.

	Degree of comparability	Gross output concentration-ratio 1935	Gross output concentration-ratio 1951	Estimated principal products concentration-ratio 1935 original	Estimated principal products concentration-ratio 1935 revised	Estimated principal products concentration-ratio 1951
METALLIFEROUS MINES AND QUARRIES	1·00	26	46	24–25	24–25	32–58
BLAST FURNACES	1·00	34	41	27–35	28–37	36–45
Tin	1·00	16	83	8–16	10–17	71–79
Zinc	1·21	87	86†	57–62	63–85	65–75
Lead	1·02	35	69	21–42	21–44	49–67
Copper and Copper Alloys	0·86	35	29	20–39	25–49	15–29
Aluminium and Magnesium	1·14	57	43	43·50	44·62	36–46
IRON AND STEEL (MELTING AND ROLLING)	0·84	22	22	16–22	4–26	13–23
IRON FOUNDRIES	1·05	23	18	14–24	15–30	9–18
Solid Fuel Cast-Iron Stoves and Grates	1·00	41	57	23–45	23–45	33–54
Other Cast-Iron Stoves and Grates	0·93	78	70	66–77	63–83	56–65
Iron Engineering Castings	1·24	13	17	7–13	5–25	9–17
SMALL ARMS	1·88	35	82	24–48	8–43	54–63
TEXTILE MACHINERY	1·02	27	35	18–27	18–28	27–35
PRINTING MACHINERY	1·16	41	29	34–40	29–51	16–27
MARINE ENGINEERING	1·08	30	26	16–32	15–36	14–25
SHIPBUILDING	1·22	30	19	29–30	23–42	16–19
CONSTRUCTIONAL ENGINEERING	1·11	21	18	10–20	10–28	9–17
MACHINE TOOLS	1·44	30	14	14–27	12–50	7–14
Scales and Weighing Machinery	1·00	71	80‡	61–80	56–76	49–65
Gas Meters	1·00	63	60	50–73	50–73	46–69
Refrigerating Machinery	1·28	71	48	44–56	44–74	35–49
Pumps and Pumping Machinery	0·93	34	36	14–28	0–27	16–32
Mining Machinery	0·93	31	30	14–27	0–27	15–30
Agricultural Machinery	0·70	39	48	21–42	0–59	23–45
Heating Apparatus, etc.	0·72	29	33	17–33	0–35	19–38
Electrical Machinery	0·83	48	44	33–58	8–35	30–50
Electric Cookers and Heaters	0·95	56	52	31–53	26–53	29–51
ELECTRIC WIRES AND CABLES	1·06	49	48	38–50	28–60	30–58
Telegraph and Telephone Apparatus	0·81	79	75	56–64	30–63	53–71
Radio Apparatus (excl. valves) and Gramophones	0·94	31	21	25–34	20–34	14–27
BATTERIES AND ACCUMULATORS	1·00	80	74	70–77	69–76	59–71
ELECTRIC LIGHTING ACCESSORIES AND FITTINGS	1·00	37	26	14–26	14–25	10–20
AIRCRAFT	0·93	57	52	55	51–59	39–59
RAILWAY CARRIAGES, WAGONS, ETC.	0·85	39	21	22–24	15–42	12–23
CARTS, PERAMBULATORS, ETC.	1·00	18	29	9–18	8–16	11–22
MOTOR VEHICLES AND CYCLES (Mfg.)	0·97	28	27	21–29	19–30	18–29
Motor Cycles	0·94	63	82*	39–42	12–43	62–82
Cars and Taxis	1·00	47	82	31–60	30–64	47–55
Bicycles, etc.	1·64	62	68	44–65	25–75	54–64
Commercial Vehicles, etc.	1·08	48	46	20–35	18–40	24–42
Motor Bodies, etc.	1·21	38	51	20–39	22–59	26–50

* Four largest units. † Five largest units. ‡ Six largest units.

	Degree of comparability	Gross output concentration-ratio		Estimated principal products concentration-ratio		
		1935	1951	1935 original	1935 revised	1951
PRECIOUS METALS REFINING	1·01	92	80	91–92	90–92	74–86
WATCH AND CLOCK	1·00	36	60	27–33	27–32	50–61
CUTLERY	1·07	26	54*	14–28	13–32	36–59
Razors (excl. Electric)	1·00	59	98*	45–63	45–59	87–97
Knives and Scissors	1·16	18	18	12–23	10–32	8–15
MUSICAL INSTRUMENTS	0·85	33	46	29–35	17–41	41–51
WIRE	1·03	32	28	18–27	19–30	14–25
NEEDLES, PINS, ETC.	1·11	27	23	17–28	16–33	12–24
Needles, pins, fish hooks	1·10	46	37	32–50	25–56	19–38
CHAIN, NAIL, SCREW, ETC.	1·00	20	23*	11–22	10–20	11–23
Anchors and Chains	0·56	16	40	8–15	14–32	22–44
Bolts, Nuts, Screws, Nails, etc.	1·33	28	27	15–28	9–41	17–28
Springs, other than laminated	0·73	30	23	16–28	25–43	10–19
SCIENTIFIC, SURGICAL, ETC. INSTRUMENTS	0·92	29	25	21–27	17–31	16–26
Photographic Plates and Films	0·91	79	90*	73–81	74–94	81–93
HARDWARE, HOLLOW-WARE, ETC.	1·09	13	15	6–12	6–18	8–15
Metal Door and Window Frames	0·96	70	67	50–66	49–70	35–41
Metal Boxes and Containers	1·00	46	68	38–50	39–51	52–74
Safes, Locks, Latches, Keys, etc.	1·07	34	41	23–34	21–38	24–44
Domestic Hollow-ware	1·29	24	25	13–26	10–42	14–27
TOOL AND IMPLEMENT	0·73	9	11	4–7	0–12	5–10
Edge and Similar Tools	1·59	45	30	20–31	15–61	18–28
JEWELLERY AND PLATE	1·02	8	8	4–8	4–10	4–7
COTTON SPINNING AND DOUBLING	1·01	21	22	19–22	19–22	17–23
COTTON WEAVING	0·89	3	3	2–3	0–4	2–3
Woven Cotton Cloth	0·97	4	4	2–4	0–5	2–4
WOOLLEN AND WORSTED	0·91	6	6	3–6	0–7	4–6
Blankets, Shawls, etc.	0·98	31	41†	24–32	20–30	25–39
ASBESTOS	0·64	68	59	62–64	43–93	47–63
TEXTILE PACKING	1·00	29	47	27–29	28–29	36
JUTE	1·00	30	38	25–31	24–31	29–42
RAYON, NYLON, ETC. AND SILK	1·02	44	43	28–41	31–45	26–39
Rayon, Nylon, etc. Cloth	0·70	20	13	8–15	21–33	5–10
LINEN AND SOFT HEMP (G.B.)	1·00	29	26	17–31	17–31	13–26
Carpets, Rugs of Wool	1·01	30	20	29–31	21–32	14–21
ROPE, TWINE AND NET	1·04	30	34	20–31	20–33	27–35
Cordage, Cables, Ropes, etc.	1·47	35	37	21–41	14–57	27–40
TEXTILE FINISHING	0·99	25	24	24–25	24–26	22–24
Woven Cotton Rayon, etc. Cloth—						
Bleaching	1·06	59	77*	38–55	37–59	38–51
Dyeing	1·53	32	30	17–34	11–57	16–31
Printing	1·26	56	51	38–66	31–73	40–57
Cotton Yarn—Finishing	1·03	36	38	25–39	24–40	23–40
Woven Woollen and Worsted Fabrics—Finishing	0·98	30	32	11–20	17–54	21–30
Hosiery and Knitted Fabrics—Finishing	1·00	22	20	12–23	12–23	10–20

* Four largest units. † Five largest units.

	Degree of comparability	Gross output concentration-ratio		Estimated principal products concentration-ratio		
		1935	1951	1935 original	1935 revised	1951
HAIR, FIBRE AND KINDRED TRADES	0·91	21	16	15–21	7–13	8–15
Elastic Goods	1·13	34	51	25–50	22–43	34–49
LACE	1·14	10	8	6–11	5–21	5–8
FLOCK AND RAG	1·03	14	13	12–14	12–17	7–13
CANVAS GOODS AND SACK	0·93	19	12	14–18	10–19	6–11
HOSIERY	1·00	10	13	8–9	9–10	7–14
UMBRELLA AND WALKING STICK	1·00	12	19	10–12	10–12	13–19
HATS, CAPS AND MILLINERY	1·23	9	15	7–9	5–25	11–15
Hats, etc. of Wool Felt	1·00	23	36	14–27	14–27	19–38
Hats, etc. of Fur Felt	1·00	24	31	12–23	12–23	19–30
GLOVE	1·00	15	10	13–15	12–14	6–10
Boots, Shoes, Sandals, etc.	0·99	10	7	9–10	9–11	4–7
TAILORING AND DRESSMAKING	0·98	6	6	5–6	3–6	4–6
SUGAR AND GLUCOSE	1·02	73	88	73–74	74–77	87–90
MARGARINE	1·34	82	79*	45–89	47–74	64–80
ICE	1·00	28	53	26–29	27–29	53
CATTLE, DOG AND POULTRY FOOD	1·02	38	53	33–35	34–35	47–53
GRAIN MILLING	1·02	42	35	41–42	40–43	33–35
COCOA, CHOCOLATE AND SUGAR CONFECTIONERY	1·01	39	39	34–40	33–41	33–42
Cocoa and Chocolate	1·00	64	59	52–67	52–67	48–63
Sugar Confectionery	1·01	12	11	6–12	6–13	6–11
BISCUIT	1·01	34	26	29–34	27–35	19–27
FISH CURING	1·00	9	25*	5–10	8–9	17–26
BACON CURING AND SAUSAGE	1·07	25	17	19–22	19–29	10–18
Sausages	1·00	56	23	22–33	23–32	7–13
Pickles, Sauces, Relishes	0·75	53	52	34–44	11–58	20–34
Jam, Marmalade, Mincemeat	1·08	33	35	22–44	21–48	20–40
BREAD AND FLOUR CONFECTIONERY	0·93	8	18	4–8	3–9	15–18
SPIRIT DISTILLING	1·00	76	85†	73–80	74–81	75–91
SPIRIT RECTIFYING, ETC.	0·93	65	85	62–63	61–70	83–91
WHOLESALE BOTTLING	1·01	33	42*	29	29–31	29–35
SOFT DRINKS, BRITISH WINES AND CIDER	0·93	13	18	7–13	1–14	12–17
Soft Drinks	1·14	21	24	12–24	10–31	16–22
BREWING AND MALTING	1·00	15	14	10–16	11–16	8–15
TOBACCO	1·00	82	79	82	82	79
WALLPAPER	1·00	96	86	95–96	95–96	77–88
NEWSPAPER AND PERIODICALS	0·92	30	25	23–29	23–29	17–25
PAPER AND BOARD	0·99	20	22	16–21	15–22	17–23
Writing Paper	1·00	61	80	33–53	34–55	40–48
Uncoated Board	0·81	66	57	41–58	29–71	27–45
Other Uncoated Printing Paper	1·00	21	47	12–23	6–23	20–38
MANUFACTURED STATIONERY	0·87	19	24	8–15	4–19	13–23
Notepaper, Pads, Envelopes	1·00	63	71	42–63	43–64	46–62
CARDBOARD BOX, CARTONS, ETC.	1·00	16	18	9–14	9–14	9–18
PRINTING AND PUBLISHING, ETC.	1·09	7	9	4–8	4–15	5–9

* Four largest units. † Five largest units.

	Degree of comparability	Gross output concentration-ratio 1935	Gross output concentration-ratio 1951	Estimated principal products concentration-ratio 1935 original	1935 revised	1951
Christmas Cards—Printers	1·60	35	40	16–28	12–60	17–30
Stereotyping, etc.	1·32	16	19	9–17	6–36	12–19
INCANDESCENT MANTLES	1·00	68	100*	68	68	91–100
LINOLEUM AND LEATHERCLOTH	0·99	58	48	55	55–56	40–55
TOYS AND GAMES	1·05	44	40	30–42	28–43	24–40
RUBBER	1·00	49	41	44–51	43–50	36–42
Rubber Tyres and Tubes	1·00	70	76	58–77	58–78	67–81
SPORTS REQUISITES	0·94	23	29	15–17	12–19	19–26
FELLMONGERY	1·04	19	40	15–18	15–23	33–40
Pens, Pencils, etc.	0·62	18	32	10–20	15–28	27–33
FUR	1·06	9	9	9	9–15	5–9
BRUSHES AND BROOMS	1·06	18	16	15–18	15–22	8–16
LEATHER (TANNING AND DRESSING)	1·01	9	12	6–9	6–10	9–12
LEATHER GOODS	1·00	9	10	5–9	4–9	5–10
Furniture, mainly of Wood, Wooden Boxes, etc.	1·19	9	5	5–9	4–8	3–5
TIMBER	0·99	3	3	1–3	2–3	2–3
Saw Mill Products	1·07	8	6	4–8	2–10	4–7
CINEMATOGRAPH FILM PRINTING	1·00	50	66	50	51	65–67

* Five largest units.

APPENDIX K

Changes in the number and average sizes of establishments and business units, 1935–51

	Number of establishments		Number of business units		Average numbers per establishment		Average numbers per business unit	
	1935	1951	1935	1951	1935	1951	1935	1951
Trades with increased concentration								
Coke Ovens and By-Products	113	85	81	24	124	220	174	780
Razors (excl. Electric)	29	13	25	11	101	297	117	351
Incandescent Mantles	10	6	8	5	127	128	159	154
Mineral Oil Refining	25	15	..	8	166	808	..	1,515
Watch and Clock	66	82	..	61	61	136	..	182
Ice	75	16	36	14	25	38	51	43
Glass Containers	64	64	51	48	275	389	345	518
Spirit Rectifying and Compounding	19	14	10	10	49	115	93	161
Metalliferous Mines and Quarries	85	64	44	33	128	125	247	242
Lead	73	48	46	40	53	67	85	80
Building Bricks	1,022	644	672	397	53	61	81	99
Metal Boxes and Containers	113	113	73	83	182	231	282	315
Tinplate	66	44	34	18	333	385	647	941
China and Porcelain	48	52	40	44	160	256	193	303
Cattle, Dog and Poultry Food	143	209	96	160	63	78	94	102
Cine-Film Printing	15	19	10	18	57	126	85	133
Toilet Preparations and Perfumery	82	81	76	77	83	126	90	133
Sugar and Glucose	43	50	22	25	384	376	750	752
Fish Curing	237	166	89	129	23	34	62	44
Wrought Iron and Steel Tubes	94	156	62	81	302	272	458	524
Bread and Flour Confectionery	2,644	1,914	1,430	1,512	42	69	77	87
Cement	65	48	25	12	158	257	409	1,027
Soap and Glycerine	65	88	39	74	274	214	457	254
Drugs and Pharmaceuticals	199	286	161	232	109	177	135	219
Textile Packing	123	64	54	42	41	42	92	65
Sports Requisites	133	124	94	104	62	61	88	72
Slate Mines and Quarries	45	27	38	21	213	177	253	227
Trades with decreased concentration								
Polishes and Canvas Dressings	44	41	38	38	144	113	167	122
Wallpaper	37	32	17	16	165	173	359	345
Clay Sanitary Ware	111	94	64	83	115	118	199	133
Bacon Curing and Sausage	384	404	..	320	51	58	..	73
Carpets, Rugs of Wool	98	97	..	59	303	277	..	454
Biscuit	98	131	71	92	449	319	620	454
Linoleum, Leathercloth and Allied Trades	38	33	33	25	356	441	378	582
Rubber	180	328	..	252	309	304	..	395
Grain Milling	502	355	308	240	60	90	98	133
Match	30	34	19	27	126	119	199	145
Glove	157	206	..	153	65	53	..	71
Fur	209	196	144	187	37	38	53	40
Boots, Shoes, Sandals, etc.	750	862	626	649	155	132	186	175
Textile Finishing	857	759	446	538	117	116	224	163

APPENDIX L

REGRESSION AND CORRELATION COEFFICIENTS FOR VARIABLES IN ANALYSIS OF CHAPTER XI

(1) *Changes in concentration and in other variables*

$r_{c'u'} = -0{\cdot}27$	$b_{c'u'} = -0{\cdot}29(\pm0{\cdot}17)$	$b_{u'c'} = -0{\cdot}26(\pm0{\cdot}16)$
$r_{c'x'} = 0{\cdot}63$	$b_{c'x'} = 0{\cdot}54(\pm0{\cdot}11)$	$b_{x'c'} = 0{\cdot}74(\pm0{\cdot}16)$
$r_{c'v'} = 0{\cdot}44$	$b_{c'v'} = 0{\cdot}46(\pm0{\cdot}16)$	$b_{v'c'} = 0{\cdot}42(\pm0{\cdot}15)$
$r_{c'e'} = 0{\cdot}17$	$b_{c'e'} = 0{\cdot}19(\pm0{\cdot}19)$	$b_{e'c'} = 0{\cdot}15(\pm0{\cdot}16)$
$r_{c'q'} = 0{\cdot}52$	$b_{c'q'} = 0{\cdot}74(\pm0{\cdot}10)$	$b_{q'c'} = 0{\cdot}37(\pm0{\cdot}11)$
$r_{c'm'} = 0{\cdot}09$	$b_{c'm'} = 0{\cdot}13(\pm0{\cdot}27)$	$b_{m'c'} = 0{\cdot}05(\pm0{\cdot}13)$

(2) *Relation between changes in variables other than concentration*

$r_{u'x'} = 0{\cdot}57$	$b_{u'x'} = 0{\cdot}46(\pm0{\cdot}11)$	$b_{x'u'} = 0{\cdot}71(\pm0{\cdot}18)$
$r_{u'e'} = 0{\cdot}47$	$b_{u'e'} = 0{\cdot}49(\pm0{\cdot}16)$	$b_{e'u'} = 0{\cdot}45(\pm0{\cdot}15)$
$r_{v'x'} = -0{\cdot}06$	$b_{v'x'} = -0{\cdot}05(\pm0{\cdot}14)$	$b_{x'v'} = -0{\cdot}07(\pm0{\cdot}21)$
$r_{v'u'} = -0{\cdot}53$	$b_{v'u'} = -0{\cdot}55(\pm0{\cdot}15)$	$b_{u'v'} = -0{\cdot}53(\pm0{\cdot}14)$
$r_{v'e'} = 0{\cdot}49$	$b_{v'e'} = 0{\cdot}52(\pm0{\cdot}16)$	$b_{e'v'} = 0{\cdot}47(\pm0{\cdot}14)$
$r_{u'q'} = -0{\cdot}26$	$b_{u'q'} = -0{\cdot}35(\pm0{\cdot}22)$	$b_{q'u'} = -0{\cdot}20(\pm0{\cdot}13)$
$r_{q'v'} = 0{\cdot}74$	$b_{q'v'} = 0{\cdot}55(\pm0{\cdot}09)$	$b_{v'q'} = 1{\cdot}00(\pm0{\cdot}15)$
$r_{u'm'} = -0{\cdot}50$	$b_{u'm'} = -0{\cdot}74(\pm0{\cdot}22)$	$b_{m'u'} = -0{\cdot}34(\pm0{\cdot}10)$

(3) *Multiple regression equations*

$$c' = -0{\cdot}07(\pm0{\cdot}20)e' + 0{\cdot}49(\pm0{\cdot}19)v' + 1{\cdot}25(\pm0{\cdot}40);\ R^2 = 0{\cdot}20$$

$$c' = 0{\cdot}74(\pm0{\cdot}21)q' + 0{\cdot}13(\pm0{\cdot}23)m' + 0{\cdot}32(\pm0{\cdot}64);\ R^2 = 0{\cdot}28$$

$$c' = 0{\cdot}82(\pm0{\cdot}24)q' - 0{\cdot}14(\pm0{\cdot}19)e' + 0{\cdot}67(\pm0{\cdot}45);\ R^2 = 0{\cdot}28$$

APPENDIX M

METHOD OF ESTIMATING AVERAGE SIZE OF BUSINESS UNIT FOR FACTORY TRADES, 1935

A lower limit to the size of the average business unit in 1935 is given by the average firm's size which, according to the Census of Production *Final Summary Tables*, can be estimated at 125 persons.

Confining attention for the moment to large units and firms—that is, those employing over 500 persons in 1935—the information given by Leak and Maizels for all trades suggests that such units on the average employ 22 per cent more persons than such firms. There is, however, no information for units employing less than 500 persons, and it is necessary, therefore, to make some assumption about them.

It would appear reasonable to assume that units employing less than 500 persons are less likely to be trading under different firm-names than units employing over 500, so that it is improbable that the average size of all business units is more than 22 per cent greater than the average firm size. Thus, the upper limit for the average size of units in factory trades is $1 \cdot 22 \times 125 = 150$–155 persons.

On the other hand, the average size of units is not likely to be much lower than this upper limit since the large units account for such a large part of total employment and must therefore always heavily influence the result. The lower limit, therefore, may be put at around 140 persons (that is, the average unit is larger than the average firm by half the difference between the average firm and the upper limit for the average unit). Thus, the average size of the business unit in 1935 is estimated to be 140–155 persons.

GENERAL INDEX

Titles of articles, Acts of Parliament and works in italics
t. = *tabular statement*

Acquisitions
as factor in concentration changes, 186–90
as method of growth, 121–4
in biscuit trade, 276
in bread and flour confectionery trade, 257
in polishes trade, 268
Advertising, 23, 140, 191
in razors trade, 202–3
in soap trade, 264
Advertising Expenditure and the Revenue of the Press, A Statistical Analysis of, 140 n.
Advertising, Statistical Review of Press, 203 n.
Ady, P. H., 176 n.
Aitchison, J. and Brown, J. A. C., 103 n.
Amalgamations, *see* Mergers
American Capitalism, 46 n.
American Investment in British Manufacturing Industry, 184 n.
Andrews, P. W. S. and Brunner, E., 216 n., 217 n.
Artificial Textile Industry, The, 126 n.

Baking Industry Changes, 256 n., 257 n.
Barna, T., 135 n.
Big Business in a Competitive Society, 47 n.
Board of Trade concentration data
provided, 27, 39, 49, 145
responsibility for, 3
Brick Industry, Committee on
First Report, 225 n.
Second Report, 225 n.
British Economy, The, 1945–50, 176 n.
Brown, J. A. C., 103 n.
Brown, W. R., 235 n.
Brunner, E., 216 n., 217 n.
Building Materials and Components, Report of the Committee of Inquiry on Distribution of, 127 n., 141 n., 228 n.
Burn, D. L., 237 n.
Business units
average size of
categories defined, 66, 295
estimated, all factory trades in 1935, 342
for selected trades in 1951, 329–33 t.
definition, 1, 26, 294
and joint subsidiaries, 42
number of
categories defined, 66, 295
for Census trades in 1951, 296–312 t.
for certain Census trades in 1935, 145, 153
changes in certain trades between 1935 and 1951, 155, 340 t.
ranking of, by employment, 26
size-ratio of
categories defined, 295
for Census trades in 1951, 329–33 t.
definition, 37–8
and alternative, 102, 294
Butts, A., 221 n.

Capacity, destruction of, 178, 287–8, 291
Capital requirements, 134–5
Cement Costs, 139 n., 142 n.
Census trade
construction and definition of, 4, 27–8, 273
definition, changes in, 146
degree of comparability, 146, 294
degree of exclusiveness
changes in, 146–8
definition of, 31, 294
trades classified by, in 1951, 313 t.
degree of specialisation
changes in, 146–8
definition of, 31, 294
trades classified by, in 1951, 313 t.

Census trade (*continued*)
establishments, classification of, 29
significance of concentration, data for, 4–6, 29–30
Censuses of Production and Distribution, Report of the Committee on, 2 n.
Civil Industry and Trade, 179 n.
Clockmaking: an Industry Revives, 211 n.
Collective Discrimination, 142 n., 272 n.
Collusion, 10, 44–5, 73, 77
Competition, 10, 75, 81
Concentration
comparisons of
international, 6–7
over time, 7, 145–8
data for 1951, 3, 8, 49, 296–312 t.
categories defined, 8, 51, 295
classification of trades by category, 8, 50–60
selection of trades for analysis, 8, 49–50, 337, 338 t.
statistical analysis of, 14–15, 100–14
use of logarithms, 102–3
correlation and regression coefficients, 104–14, 334 t.
definitional relationships between variables, 103–4
data for 1935 and 1951 overall comparison, 63–5
and industry structure, 2, 25, 36–8, 40, 66–82
and monopoly power, 2, 5, 25, 41–8
Concentration, changes in
as indicated by concentration-ratios, 144–5
as measured by principal products concentration-ratio, 18, 33
between 1935 and 1951
analysis of trades with increases and decreases in principal product concentration, 18–22
selection of trades for, 18, 148–50
association analysis, 19, 154–9
measurement of changes in trade size for, 153
and for unit size and plant size, 153
case-studies of trades, 193–292
selection of trades, 193–4
data for 185 trades, 335–9 t.
data for 41 selected trades, 152 t.
plants and units, 340 t.
factors contributing to, 22–3, 176–92
regression analysis, 160–6
coefficients of, 341 t.
results summarised, 173–5
and comparability of Census trades, 7
Concentration-ratios
as indicators of concentration changes, 144–5
definition of, 1, 3 n., 26, 294
employment, 33
establishments, 33
for industry groups, 1951, 9, 60, 62
gross output, 32
meaning of, 48
net output, 33
overall employment and net output, 1951, 9, 61–3
principal product, 33
types of, 1
uses of, 5–7
Concentration in American Industry, 51 n.
Concentration in Canadian Manufacturing Industries, 1 n., 105 n., 106 n., 107 n., 109 n.
Concentration of Industry Report, 2 n.
Concentration in Manufacturing, Changes in, 1935 to 1947 and 1950, 2 n., 7 n., 32 n.
Concentration, Measures of, 2 n., 7 n.
Concentration and Price Policy, Business, 2 n., 28 n., 30 n., 33 n., 44 n., 47 n.
Concentration of Production in Manufacturing, 1 n., 105 n.
Concentration of Productive Facilities, 1947, 26 n.
Conklin, M. R. and Goldstein, H. T., 28 n.
Corlett, W. J., 263 n.
Coster, I., 201 n.
Cotton, Working Party Report on, 179 n.
Countervailing buying power, 46
Crowder, W. F., 1 n., 105 n.

Demand, changes in trade, 190–1, 272
Detergents, The Battle of the, 262 n.
Detergents, The Economic Development of, 263 n.
Development Councils, 177
Distribution of Consumer Goods, 141 n.
Distributive methods, 140–1, 272
Duesenberry, J. S., 100 n.
Dunning, J. H., 184 n.

Economies of large-scale operation, 133–4
Edmondson, J. L., 270 n.
Edwards, C. D., 43 n., 44 n.
Edwards, H. V., 286 n., 287 n.
Employment
  by concentration category, 1951, 51
  for trades with
    high concentration, 52–3 t.
    medium concentration, 54–6 t.
    low concentration, 57–60 t.
Entwisle, E. A., 271 n.
Evely, R. W., 51 n., 262 n.
Exports, as factor affecting concentration, 45–6

Federation of British Industries, 177 n.
Film Industry, The British, 241 n.
Firms, relative sizes of, 6
Firms, small
  definition, 293
  importance of, 34–5
  inclusion of, effect on employment concentration, 324 t.
  numbers employed by, frequency distribution of trades, 324 t.
  relative to total number of units, frequency distribution of trades, 324 t.
Fitzgerald, P., 117 n.
Florence, P. Sargant, 31 n., 38 n., 83 n., 133 n.
Flour-Milling, 286 n., 287 n.
Fogarty, M. P., 235 n., 286 n.
Food Council
  Report for 1936, 255 n.
  Report for 1938, 255 n.
Food Prices, Royal Commission on, *First Report*, 254 n., 283 n.

Frankel, P. H., 141 n.

Galbraith, J. K., 46 n.
Garner, F., 256 n., 257 n.
Giant concerns
  definition, 10, 71, 294
  growth of, 25
  presence in trades, 11, 71, 77, 82
Goldstein, H. T., 28 n.
Gowing, M. M., 179 n.
Gross output
  Census definition, 293
  concentration-ratio, 32

Hacking, R. A., 235 n.
Hale, L., 263 n.
Hargreaves, E. L. and Gowing, M. M., 179 n.
Hart, P. E., xv, 246 n.
Hedley of Newcastle, 263 n.
High-concentration trades
  definition, 8, 51
  ease of entry into, 18, 133–9
  in 1951
    employment, by trade, 52–3 t.
    employment and net output concentration-ratios, by trade, 52–3 t.
    number of trades, 8, 51
    number of units, by trade, 52–3 t.
  industry structure among, 68–73
  leading firms, growth of, 16–17, 115–30
    by acquisition, 121–3
    by amalgamations, 116–21
    by combination of different methods, 127–8
    by internal expansion, 124–7
  level of activity in, 17, 132
  monopoly power, in relation to, 42, 48, 68–73, 115
  obstacles to growth of firms in, 18, 133–9

Import Duties Act, 1932, 176
Import quotas, 183, 209
Imports, 45–6
Income, Saving and the Theory of Consumer Behavior, 100 n.
Industrial Areas of Great Britain, Prospects of the, 235 n.

Industrial Combination in England, 117 n.
Industrial Reconstruction and the Control of Competition, 283 n.
Industry structure
  classification of trades by type of, 10, 67 t.
  types of, for trades with
    high concentration, 68–73
    medium concentration, 73–77
    low concentration, 77–81
Investment, Location and Size of Plant, 31 n., 38 n., 133 n.
Iron Ore Supplies, Britain's, 219 n.

Jefferys, J. B., xv, 141 n.

Kahn, A. E., 47 n.
Kaldor, N. and Silverman, R., 140 n.
Kaplan, A. D. H. and Kahn, A. E., 47 n.
Kavanagh, C. J. and Hacking, R. A., 235 n.

Lead, 221 n.
Lead and Its Manifold Uses, 222 n.
Leak, H. and Maizels, A., xv, 1 n., 9, 26, 32 n., 33 n., 44 n., 51 n., 215 n., 267 n.
Linoleum and Felt Base, Working Party Report on, 277 n., 280 n.
Lognormal Distribution, The, 103 n.
Low-concentration trades
  definition, 8, 51
  in 1951
    employment, by trade, 56–60 t.
    employment and net output concentration-ratios, by trade, 56–60 t.
    number of trades, 9, 51
    number of units, by trade, 56–60 t.
  industry structure among, 77–81
Lucas, A. F., 283 n.

Machlup, F., 44 n.
Maintaining Competition, 43 n.
Maizels, A., xv, 1 n., 9, 26, 32 n., 33 n., 44 n., 51 n., 215 n., 267 n.
Market, size of, 45, 86
Medium-concentration trades
  definition, 8, 51
  in 1951
    employment, by trade, 54–6 t.
    employment and net output concentration-ratios, by trade, 54–6 t.
    number of trades, 9, 51
    number of units, by trade, 54–6 t.
  industry structure among, 73–7
Mergers, 23, 87, 116–21, 129, 167, 186
  in biscuits trade, 276
  in bread and flour confectionery trade, 255–7
  in building bricks trade, 226–7
  in grain milling trade, 285–8
  in match trade, 290–1
  in metal boxes trade, 230–1
  in polishes trade, 267
  in soap trade, 261
  in wallpaper trade, 270–1
  in wrought iron and steel tubes trade, 249–52
Metal Industries, Survey of, 195 n., 236 n.
Miller, J. P., 47 n.
Minchinton, W. E., 238 n.
Mineral Development, Report of the Committee on, 215 n.
Monopolies Commission, 25
  reports on
    cast iron rainwater goods, 139 n.
    electric lamps, 45 n.
    insulated electric wires and cables, 47 n.
    linoleum, 279 n.
    matches, 43 n., 46 n., 136 n., 290 n., 291 n.
Monopolies and Restrictive Practices Act, 1948, 2, 25, 177
Monopoly power
  and concentration, 2, 25, 41, 81–2
  and high-concentration trades, 42, 48, 68–73, 115
Monopoly, The Political Economy of, 44 n.
Multi-plant operations, 11–13, 39, 86–96
Multi-product firms, 44

Nationalisation, 22–3, 177, 185
  effect on concentration in
    building bricks trade, 227

coke ovens and by-products trade, 197
Net output
Census definition, 293
concentration-ratio, 33
Night Baking, Report of the Departmental Committee on, 255 n.
Night Baking, Report of the Committee on, 256 n.
Nobel's Explosives Company Ltd and Nobel Industries Ltd, The History of, 1871–1926, 280 n.

Oil Industry, Integration in the, 141 n.
Oil refineries, capacity of, 206 t.
Oil Refining in Britain, 205 n.
Oil in Western Europe, The Price of, 138 n., 208 n.
Oligopoly Power, Ignorance as a Source of, 140 n.

Patents and know-how, 135–7
Plant (or establishment), Census definition, 293
Plant number-ratios, 39, 83
categories of, 295
definition, 294
for selected trades, 1951, 329–33 t.
Plant size
average, 83, 166
categories of, 295
compared with all factory trades, 1935, 171–3
definition, 294
prevalent, 38, 133–4
for selected trades, 1951, 329–33 t.
and unit size, changes in, 166–70
Plant size-ratios, 39, 83
categories of, 295
definition, 294
for selected trades, 1951, 329–33 t.
Plant structure
definition, 36
and ease of entry, 11–13, 38–9, 83–96
and locational factors, 11–13, 38–9, 83–96
for selected trades in 1951, 11, 83–99
in trades with large unit size-ratios, 84–91
in trades with small unit size-ratios, 91–6
summarised, 96–9
and technological economies, 11–13, 39, 83–96
Political and Economic Planning (PEP), 177 n., 219 n., 241 n.
Potters of Darwen, 1839–1939, 271 n.
Prais, S. J., xv–xvi
Price leadership, 10, 73, 77
Principal product concentration
changes in, 1935–51, 18, 147–8
definition, 33–4
estimated for 185 trades, 1935–51, 335–9 t.
formulae for estimating
in Census trades, 1951, 314–18
for Census trades where definitions changed, 318–23
trades with changes in, 1935–51, 152 t.
Principal products, Census definition, 293
Product differentiation, 85
Productivity, Prices and Distribution in Selected British Industries, 234 n., 274 n.

Quotas, 23, 138–9, 188–9

Race against Time, 208 n., 209 n.
Rank, *The Master Millers*, 285 n.
Rationalisation, 184–5, 284
Raw materials
access to, 85, 137–8
and mergers, 188–9
war-time restrictions, 179, 275
Razor Blades, 202 n.
Reckitt, B. N., 267 n., 268 n.
Reckitt and Sons Ltd, The History of, 267 n., 268 n.
Replacement Cost of Fixed Assets in British Manufacturing Industry in 1955, 135 n.
Restrictive arrangements
in distribution, 142–3
in production, 138–9
Restrictive Trade Practices Act, 1956, 25
Rosenbluth, G., 1 n., 2 n., 7 n., 105 n., 106 n., 107 n., 109 n.
Rostas, L., 234 n., 274 n.

Ryan, J., 229 n., 231 n., 232 n.

Scitovsky, T., 33 n., 140 n.
Service trades, 86, 141
Sharpest Edge in the World, The, 201 n.
Shortages and restrictions, 179–80
Silverman, H. A., 126 n.
Silverman, R., 140 n.
Soap Industry, Report on the, 261 n.
Spillers: a Giant of the Milling Trade, 286 n.
State action, 23, 139, 183–6, 208–9, 212
  in sugar-refining trade, 244–6
Statistical Gaps, 7 n.
Steel, Capital Development in: a Study of the United Steel Companies Ltd, 216 n., 217 n.
Steel and the Consuming Industries, 235 n.
Steelmaking, The Economic History of, 1867–1939, 237 n.
Stigler, G. J., 30 n.
Structure of British Industry, The, xv, 1 n., 9, 26, 32 n., 33 n., 44 n., 51 n., 215 n., 267 n.
Subsidies, 184, 255
Sugar Corporation, The British—Private or Public Monopoly, 246 n.
Sugar Industry, Competition and Control in the British, 246 n.
Sugar Industry, Report of the U.K. Inquiry Committee on, 245 n., 246 n.
Sugden, A. V. and Edmonson, J. L., 270 n.
Sugden, A. V. and Entwisle, E. A., 271 n.
Surplus capacity, 23, 116–19, 123, 129, 186–7
  in grain milling, 283–4
  in tinplate, 233–4

Tariffs, 183
  on cutlery, 199
  on watches and clocks, 208
Technological change, 22
  effect on concentration, 181–3
  and mergers, 187–8
  in biscuits trade, 274
  in bread and flour confectionery trade, 254
  in cinematograph film printing trade, 241–3
  in tinplate trade, 234–7
  in wrought iron and steel tubes trade, 249
Tinplate Industry, The British, 238 n.
Tinplate Industry: its Present and Future Prospects, 238 n.
Tinplate Trade in 1935, 235 n.
Tins and Cans, Statistics of, 229 n., 231 n., 232 n.
Trade activity, changes in, 155–8, 169
Trade associations, 177 n., 191, 279, 284
Trade Associations, Industrial, 177 n.
Trusts, Report of the Committee on, 25 n.

Unilever, The History of, 260 n., 261 n.
Units, *see* Business Units

Vertical integration, 43, 137–8
  in coal and steel, 196–7

Wallpaper, A History of English, 1509–1914, 270 n.
Wallpaper Regains Its Popularity, 270 n.
Welsh Reconstruction Advisory Council, *First Interim Report*, 233 n., 234 n.
Wiles, P. J. D., 176 n., 177 n., 179 n.
Wilson, C., 260 n., 261 n.
World War II, effects on concentration, 178–80
  statutory concentration schemes, 178–9
    in building bricks trade, 225
    in linoleum trade, 278–9
    in razors trade, 201
    in tinplate trade, 237–8
Worswick, G. D. N. and Ady, P. H., 176 n.

INDEX OF COMPANIES

Alfred Appleby Chain, 119–20
Allied Bakeries, 189, 257–9, 276, 288
Allied Brick and Tile Works, 226
Allied Cement Manufacturers, 118
Allied Ironfounders, 119
Alma and Cranmore Tube, 251–2
Alpha Cement, 118
Anglo-Celtic Watch, 212–13
Appleby-Frodingham Steel, 216–17
Ashley United Industries, 272
Associated Biscuit Manufacturers, 275–6
Associated Electrical Industries, 128
Associated Lead Manufacturers, 119
Associated Motor Cycles, 123
Associated Portland Cement Manufacturers, 117–18, 188
Atlas Stone, 127
Auto-Strop Safety Razor, 201
Avery, W. and T., 122

Baldwins, 123, 236–7
Barringer, Wallis and Manners, 231
Barry and Staines Linoleum, 124, 279
Beckermet Mining, 216
Beecham Group, 189
Berry Wiggins, 206–7
Bibby, J. and Son, 128, 137, 261, 264
Bigrigg Mining, 216
Birmingham Small Arms, 123, 128
Blyth and Platt, 189, 267, 269
Boord and Sons, 122
Booth's Distilleries, 122
Bowne and Shaw, 218
Brampton Brothers, 119
Briggs, Wm and Sons, 206
Britannia Lead, 221–3
British American Tobacco, 118
British Can, 230–1
British Celanese, 126
British Electricity Authority, 47
British Enka, 126
British Ironfounders' Association, 138
British Lead Mills, 222–3
British Mannesman Tube, 250–1
British Match Corporation, 43, 46, 119, 136, 138, 190, 290–2
British Motor Corporation, 147 n.
British Nylon Spinners, 136
British Oil and Cake Mills, 128, 261
British Petroleum, 126, 205–8
British Portland Cement Manufacturers, 117
British Sugar Corporation, 119, 139, 185, 246–7
British Thomson-Houston, 128
Briton Ferry, 123, 236–8
Bromford Tube, 250–1
Brown and Polson, 127
Brunner Mond, 117, 122
Bryant and May, 119, 178, 290–1
Buchanan-Dewar, 121
Burnett, Sir Robert, 122
Burton's Gold Medal Biscuits, 189, 276
BX Plastics, 127

Cable and Wireless, 47
Capper Pass, 221–2
Carr, 275
Cement Makers' Federation, 142, 188
Cerebos, 117
Chesterfield Tube, 250
Chiswick Products, 266–9
Coats, J. & P., 118
Colgate Palmolive-Peet, 264
Colman, J. and J., 127
Consett Iron, 197
Consolidated Tin Smelters, 120
Co-operative Wholesale Society, 122, 260–4, 284–8, 291
Courtaulds, 126
Coventry Chain, 119
Curtis's and Harvey, 120, 137

Darwins, 199, 201
Denham Laboratories, 242
Distillers, 121–2
Dorman Long, 197–8, 215–16, 218
Dunlop Rubber, 125, 137

Eastman Kodak, 127
Eastwoods, 226
Elliott, F. W., 211

Enfield Clock, 211
English Sewing Cotton, 118
Enthoven, H. J., 221–3
Esso Petroleum, 126, 205–8
Ever-Ready Razor Products, 201–2
Explosives Trades, 120

Fairrie, 121, 245
Federated Foundries, 119
Ferranti, 211
Firestone Tyre and Rubber, 125–6
Fisons, 122
Francis, John D., 211, 213
Frodingham Ironstone, 216–17

Garrard Clocks, 211
Gaumont-British Picture Corporation, 241–2
General Electric, 211, 250, 252
Gillette Industries, 124, 182, 201–3
Glamorgan Hematite Iron Ore, 216–17
Glebe Sugar Refining, 189, 245–6
Glynwed Tubes, 252
Goodlass Wall, 119, 221
Goodlass Wall and Lead Industries, 215, 221–4
Goodyear Tyre and Rubber, 125
Guest, Keen and Nettlefolds, 215

Halkyn District United Mines, 215
Hedley, Thomas, 122, 143, 184, 260–4
Hodbarrow Mining, 216
Howell, 250–1
Hovis, 286–7
Humphries, George, 128, 241–2
Huntley and Palmer, 275–6

Ilford, 127
Imperial Chemical Industries, 117, 120, 122, 136, 186, 222, 280–1
Imperial Smelting, 120
Imperial Tobacco, 118, 142, 186
Incledon and Lamberts, 250
India Tyre and Rubber, 126
Ingersoll, 188, 211–13

Jarrow Tube Works, 251
Johnson, S. C. and Son, 266, 268–9
Jurgens, Anton, 120–1, 128

Kay Film Printing, 241–2
Keen, Robinson, 127
Kemp, George, 275
Kettering Iron and Coal, 216
Kiwi Polish, 267, 269
Kodak, 127, 242

Lever Bros., 121–2, 125, 128, 260–3
Lighting Trades, 120
Linoleum Manufacturers' Association, 279
Llanelly Associated Tinplate Companies, 123, 237–8
Lobitos Oilfields, 206–7
London Brick, 187, 226–7
Lyle, Abram, and Sons, 121, 245
Lyons, J., 125, 257

Macfarlane, Lang, 189, 275–6
Macfie and Sons, 121, 189, 245–6
McVitie and Price, 189, 275–6
Maguire and Paterson, 119, 291
Manbré and Garton, 189, 245–6
Manchester Oil Refinery, 206–7
Margarine Union, 121
Masters, J. John, 119, 290
Maypole Dairy, 120–1
Metal Box, 183, 230–3, 236
Midland Ironstone, 216
Mill Close Mines, 212–13, 215, 221–2
Millers' Mutal Association, 187, 189, 283–4
Millom and Askam Hematite Iron, 216
Mobil Oil, 206–7
Monsted, Otto, 120
Mullard, 128

Nairn, Michael, and Greenwich, 124, 279
National Coal Board, 185, 197–8, 227
Neill, James, 201
Newmark, Louis, 212–13
Nobel Dynamite Trust, 120
Nobel Industries, 120, 137, 280

Olympic Kinematograph Laboratories, 241–2

Pal Personna Products, 202
Peek, Frean, 275–6

Perivale Clock, 211
Perry, 119
Pooley, Henry, and Son, 122

Quirk, Barton and Burns (St Helens), 221

Raleigh Industries, 127
Rank Organisation, 128, 188, 242
Ranks, 187, 258–9, 283–9
Reads, 231–2
Reckitt and Sons, 127, 267–9
Reckitts and Colman, 127
Renold, Hans, 119–20
Renold and Coventry Chain, 120
Robertson, W. H. A., 252
Robinson, F., 231
Ronuk, 266
Rotherham and Sons, 211, 212
Round Oak Steel Works, 252
Rugby Portland Cement, 188

St Helens' Smelting, 221–2
Salt Manufacturers' Association, 117
Salt Union, 117
Salter, George, 122
Sankey Sugar, 189, 245–6
Santon Mining, 218
Scottish Agricultural Industries, 122
Scottish Co-operative Wholesale Society, 261, 286
Shell Petroleum, 126, 205–8
Smith, S., and Sons (England), 188, 210–13
Spillers, 187, 258–9, 283–9
Stanton Ironworks, 198, 218
Steel Company of Wales, 123, 181, 198, 238–40
Stewarts and Lloyds, 123, 188, 198, 215–18, 249–53
Sussex Brick Company (1927), 226–7
Swansea Vale Smelter, 120
Swedish Match Corporation, 119, 136

Tanqueray Gordon, 122
Tate, Henry, and Sons, 121, 245
Tate and Lyle, 121, 189, 245–7
Tayside Floorcloth, 279
Technicolor, 128, 182
Telephone Manufacturing, 211
Thomas, Richard, and Baldwins (*also* Thomas, Richard), 123, 198, 215, 236–40, 252
Timex, 212–13
Tube Investments, 123, 128, 188, 249–53
Tunnel Asbestos Cement, 126
Turner and Newall, 126, 137
Turners Asbestos Cement, 126

Unilever, 121, 128, 137, 143
United Alkali, 117
United Biscuits, 276
United Co-operative Baking Society, 257
United Match Industries, 190, 291
United Steel Companies, 197–8, 215–18
Universal Asbestos Manufacturing, 126

Van den Berghs, 120
Vickers-Armstrong, 211

Walker, John, and Sons, 121, 245
Walkers, Parker, 119
Wall, T., and Sons, 125
Wall Paper Manufacturers, 117, 270–3
Welsbach Incandescent Gas Light, 120
Westburn Sugar Refineries, 189, 245–7
Westclox, 211, 213
Weston, 189
Weston Foods, 276
Wilkinson Sword, 201
Williams, Harvey, 120
Williamson, Jas., 281
Wills, W. D. and H. O., 118

Yorkshire Brick, 226–7

INDEX OF TRADES

Page numbers in italics refer to tabulated material in the text; page numbers in bold to Appendix Tables

Abrasives, **296, 335**
Abrasive wheels, *53*, *69*, *90*, 134, **297, 329**
Accumulators and parts, *52*, *69*, *90*, 134, 136, 140–3, **301, 329**
Agricultural machinery, *56*, *72*, *90*, **299, 331, 336**
Aircraft manufacture and repair, 54, *55*, *72*, 73, 82, *88*, **301, 331, 336**
Aluminium and magnesium, *55*, *72*, 82, *90*, **299, 331, 336**
Anchors and chains, *56*, 75, *76*, *93*, **302, 330, 337**
Animal feedingstuffs, *55*, *72*, *90*, **308, 331**
Asbestos, **306, 337**
Asbestos cement goods, *52*, *70*, 71, *93*, 126, 133, 138, 141–2, **296, 329**
Asbestos manufacture, *53*, *70*, 71, *90*, 134, 138, **306, 329**

Bacon curing and sausage, *58*, *78*, *90*, *152*, 153 n., *159*, **308, 333, 338, 340**
Ball and roller bearings, *53*, *70*, 71, 82, *93*, 133–4, 136, **300, 329**
Batteries and accumulators, **301, 336**
Bedding, *58*, *80*, *93*, **311, 332**
Beer, wholesale bottling of, *56*, *72*, *85*, 86, **309, 331**
Bicycles and tricycles, *53*, *70*, 71, 82, *90*, 127, 134, 140–3, **301, 330, 336**
Biscuit, *56*, 75, *76*, *95*, *152*, *155–9*, *168*, 170, 180, 183, 189, *265*, 273–7, **307, 331, 338, 340**
Blankets, shawls, travelling rugs, *54*, *76*, *93*, **304, 330, 337**
Blast furnaces, *55*, 75, *76*, *93*, **298, 330, 336**
Board, other than coated, **309, 338**
Boilers and boiler-house plant, *53*, *70*, 71, 82, *90*, 134, **299, 329**
Bolts, nuts, screws, rivets, *57*, *78*, 79, *90*, **302, 333, 337**
Boot and shoe, repairs for trade, *58*, *80*, *92*, **307, 332**
Boots, shoes, sandals, *59*, *78*, 79, *85*, *152*, *155–9*, *168*, 170, 179, **307, 333, 338, 340**
Brass manufacture, *59*, *80*, *95*, **303, 332**
Bread and flour confectionery, *59*, 77, *78*, 82, *85*, 86, *152*, *155–9*, *168*, 180, 183, 189, *196*, 253–9, **307, 333, 338, 340**
Brewing and malting, *59*, *79*, 81, *92*, **309, 332, 338**
Brick and fireclay, 149 n., **296, 335**
Brushes and brooms, *59*, *80*, *95*, **311, 332, 339**
Building bricks, *57*, *78*, *85*, *152*, *155–9*, 167, *168*, 185, 187, *196*, 224–8, **296, 333, 335, 340**
Building materials, **296, 335**

Canal, dock and harbour undertakings (civil engineering), *55*, *72*, *85*, 86, **312, 331**
Canvas goods and sack, *59*, *79*, *93*, **305, 332, 338**
Cardboard box, carton and fibreboard packing case, **309, 338**
Carpets, rugs of wool, *57*, *79*, 81, *93*, *152*, 153 n., *159*, 179, **305, 332, 337, 340**
Cars and taxis, 147, **301, 336**
Cartons, *55*, *76*, *95*, **309, 331**
Carts, perambulators, etc., **302, 336**
Cast iron pipes and fittings, *53*, *70*, *87*, 119, 133, **299, 329**
Cast iron stoves: other, *53*, *70*, *93*, 132–3, **329, 336**
Cast iron stoves: solid fuel, *55*, *76*, *93*, **298, 330, 336**
Cattle, dog and poultry food, *152*, *155–9*, *168*, **299, 338, 340**
Cement, *52*, *70*, *92*, 117, 133–5, 138–9, 142–3, *152*, *155–9*, 167,

168, 183, 188, 191, **296, 329, 335, 340**
Chain, nail, screw, **302, 337**
Chemicals (general), *54*, *72*, 73, 82, *88*, **297, 311**
China and earthenware, **297, 335**
China and porcelain, *56*, *76*, *93*, *152*, 179, 183, 188, **297, 330, 335, 340**
Christmas cards—printers, **310, 339**
Cinematograph film printing, *53*, *70*, *95*, 128, 136, *152*, *155–9*, *168*, 182, 188, *196*, 240–3, **311, 329, 339, 340**
Cinematograph film production, *55*, *76*, *93*, **311, 330**
Clay, sand, gravel, chalk, *57*, *78*, 84, *85*, **296, 333**
Coal tar products, **297, 335**
Cocoa and chocolate, *55*, *72*, 82, *90*, **307, 331, 338**
Cocoa, chocolate and sugar confectionery, **307, 338**
Coke ovens and by-products, *54*, *74*, 75, *92*, *152*, *155–9*, 167, *168*, 185, 195–8, **297, 330, 335, 340**
Commercial vehicles, *55*, *72*, 73, 82, *90*, **301, 331, 336**
Constructional engineering, *58*, *78*, 79, *90*, **299, 333, 336**
Copper and copper alloys, *55*, *72*, 82, *90*, **299, 331, 336**
Cordage, cables, ropes, etc., *56*, 75, *76*, *93*, **305, 330, 337**
Corsets and brassières, *57*, *80*, *93*, **306, 332**
Cotton spinners and doublers, *57*, 77, *78*, 82, *88*, **304, 333, 337**
Cotton thread, *52*, 68, *69*, *90*, 118, 132, 135, **304, 330**
Cotton weaving, **304, 337**
Cotton yarn finishing, *56*, *76*, *93*, **305, 330, 337**
Cutlery, 149 n., **302, 337**

Dressmade garments—work done, *59*, *80*, *95*, **307, 332**
Drugs and pharmaceutical preparations, *57*, *78*, 79, *90*, *152*, *155–9*, 167, *168*, 189, 191, **297, 333, 335, 340**
Dry cleaning, valeting, etc., 54, *56*, *72*, 73, *90*, **312, 331**
Dyes and dyestuffs, **297, 335**

Earthenware and stoneware, other, *59*, *79*, *93*, **297, 332, 335**
Edge and similar tools, *57*, *80*, *93*, **302, 332, 337**
Elastic goods, **306, 338**
Electric cookers and heaters, *55*, *72*, *90*, **300, 331, 336**
Electric lamps, *55*, *76*, *93*, **301, 331**
Electric lighting accessories, **301, 336**
Electric wires and cables, *55*, 75, *76*, 82, *93*, **300, 331, 336**
Electrical machinery, *55*, *72*, 73, 82, *88*, **300, 331, 336**
Electrical ware, *55*, *74*, *93*, **297, 330, 335**
Explosives and fireworks, *52*, 68, *69*, 82, *88*, 120, 134, 136–8, 143, **298, 330, 335**

Fellmongery, 56, *57*, *79*, *93*, 150 n., **311, 331, 339**
Fertilisers, *53*, *70*, 71, *85*, 86, 122, 135, 138, 141, 149 n., **297, 330, 335**
Fertilisers, disinfectants, etc., 149 n., **297, 335**
Fibreboard packing cases, *56*, *74*, 75, *93*, **309, 330**
Fish curing, *57*, *78*, *85*, *152*, *155–9*, *168*, 169, 191, **308, 333, 338, 340**
Flock and rag, *59*, *79*, *93*, **306, 331, 338**
Floor coverings, *53*, *70*, *95*, 124, 134–5, 141–3, **311, 329**
Fur, *59*, *80*, *95*, *152*, *155–9*, *168*, 169, **311, 332, 339, 340**
Furniture, upholstered, *59*, *80*, *93*, **310, 332**
Furniture, wooden, *59*, *78*, *90*, **310, 333, 339**

Gas meters, *55*, *74*, *92*, **300, 330, 336**
Glass containers, *55*, 75, *76*, *95*, *152*, *155–9*, 167, *168*, **297, 331, 335, 340**
Glass, other than containers, *55*, *72*, 73, 82, *90*, **297, 331**

Glassware, domestic and fancy, **297, 335**
Glazed tiles, *56*, *76*, *93*, **297, 330, 335**
Glove, *152*, 153 n., *159*, **307, 338, 340**
Gloves and mittens, leather, *59*, *79*, *92*, **307, 332**
Glue, gum, paste and allied, *56*, *76*, *93*, 139, **298, 330**
Grain milling, *152*, *155–9*, *168*, 169, 178, 187–8, 191, *265*, 281–9, **307, 338, 340**

Hair, fibre and kindred, *58*, *80*, *93*, **306, 332, 338**
Hardware, hollow-ware, metal furniture, **302, 337**
Hats, caps and millinery, **307, 338**
Hats, hoods, etc. of fur felt, *57*, *80*, *95*, **307, 332, 338**
of wool felt, *57*, *80*, *95*, **307, 332, 338**
Heating and ventilating apparatus, *57*, *78*, *90*, **300, 333, 336**
Heavy overalls and aprons, *59*, *79*, *95*, **306, 331**
Hollow-ware, domestic, *58*, *80*, *95*, **302, 332, 337**
Hollow-ware, other, *58*, *79*, *93*, **302, 331**
Hosiery and knitted fabrics—finishing, *58*, *79*, *93*, **305, 331, 337**
Hosiery and knitted goods, *59*, *78*, 79, *90*, **304, 333, 337**

Ice, 54, *55*, *74*, *93*, *152*, *155–9*, *168*, 169, **308, 330, 338, 340**
Ice cream, *53*, *70*, *90*, 125, 134–5, 141, 143, **308, 330**
Incandescent mantles, *52*, 68, *69*, *90*, 120, 132, 136, *152*, *155–9*, *168*, 169, **311, 329, 339–40**
Ink, *56*, *76*, *93*, **298, 330**
Iron and steel (melting and rolling), *58*, 77, *78*, 82, *88*, **298, 333, 336**
Iron engineering castings, *58*, *78*, 79, *90*, **299, 333, 336**
Iron foundries, **298, 336**
Iron ore and ironstone, *55*, *74*, *92*, 180, **299, 330**

Jams, marmalade and mincemeat, **308, 338**
Jewellery and plate, *59*, *80*, *95*, **303, 332, 337**
Jute, *56*, *76*, *93*, **305, 330, 337**

Knives and scissors, *58*, *80*, *95*, **302, 332, 337**

Lace, *59*, *80*, *93*, **305, 332, 338**
Laundry work, *59*, *78*, 79, *85*, 86, **312, 333**
Lead, *53*, *70*, 71, *80*, 119, *152*, *155–9*, *168*, 169, 179, *196*, 219–24, **299, 329, 336, 340**
Leather goods, *57*, *80*, *93*, **311, 332, 339**
Leather, tanning and dressing, *59*, *80*, *92*, **311, 332, 339**
Lime and whiting, *58*, *79*, *93*, **296, 331**
Linen and soft hemp, *57*, *79*, *93*, **305, 332, 337**
Linoleum, leathercloth, *152*, *155–9*, *168*, 169, 179, 192, *265*, 277–81, **311, 339–40**
Locomotive manufacturing, *55*, *74*, 75, *93*, **302, 330**

Machine tools, *59*, *78*, 79, *88*, **299, 333, 336**
Magazines and periodicals, *55*, *72*, 73, *88*, **310, 331**
Manufactured stationery, paper bags, **309, 338**
Margarine, *52*, 68, *69*, *90*, 120, 134–5, 137–8, 140–1, **308, 329, 338**
Marine engineering, *57*, *79*, 81–2, *93*, **299, 332, 336**
Match, *52*, 68, *69*, *90*, 119, 134–6, 138, 143, *152*, *155–9*, *168*, 170, 178, 190, 192, *265*, 289–92, **298, 329, 335, 340**
Mechanical cloth and wool felt, *55*, *74*, *93*, **304, 330**
Mechanical engineering (repairing), *59*, *78*, *85*, 86, **300, 333**
Mechanical handling equipment, *58*, *80*, *92*, **300, 332**
Medical, surgical, veterinary instruments, *57*, *78*, *85*, 86 n., **303, 333**
Metal boxes and containers, *54*, *72*, *88*, *152*, *155–9*, *168*, 183, *196*, 228–33, **302, 331, 337, 340**

Metal doors and window frames, 149 n., **302, 337**
Metal furniture, *58*, *80*, *95*, **302, 332**
Metal goods, specialist finishers, *59*, *79*, *95*, **302, 332**
Metalliferous mines and quarries, *152*, *155–9*, *168*, 170, *196*, 213–19, **299, 336, 340**
Milk, whole bottled or processed, *58*, *78*, 79, *85*, **308, 333**
Milled wheat, *56*, *72*, 73, *85*, 86, **307, 331**
Mineral oil refining, *52*, *70*, *93*, 126, 133–6, 138, 140–3, *152*, 153 n., *159*, 182, *196*, 203–8, **298, 329, 335, 340**
Mining machinery, *57*, *79*, *93*, **300, 331, 336**
Motor-bodies, sidecars, trailers, *55*, *72*, 73, 82, *90*, **301, 331, 336**
Motor-cycles (complete), *52*, *69*, *90*, 123, 134, 141–2, 149 n., **301, 329, 336**
Motor vehicles and cycles (manufacturing), 147, **301, 336**
(repairing), *60*, *80*, *93*, **301, 332**
Musical instruments, *57*, *80*, *95*, 149 n., **303, 332, 337**

Narrow fabrics, *59*, *80*, *93*, **306, 332**
Needles, pins, **303, 337**
Needles, pins, fish hooks and metal smallwares, *58*, *80*, *93*, **303, 332, 337**
New building construction, 56, *59*, **312**
Newspaper and periodical printing and publishing, **309, 338**
Newspapers, *57*, 77, *78*, 82, *88*, **310, 333**
Nightwear and underwear, women's and girls', *58*, *78*, *90*, **306, 333**
Non-metalliferous mines and quarries, **296, 335**
Notepaper, pads, envelopes, *53*, *69*, *90*, 141, **309, 329, 338**

Office machinery, *56*, *76*, *93*, **300, 330**
Office machinery requisites, *55*, *74*, *93*, **311, 330**

Oils and greases, lubricating, *56*, *76*, *93*, **298, 331**
Ophthalmic instruments and appliances, *57*, *78*, *85*, **303, 333**
Optical instruments and appliances, other, *55*, *74*, *95*, **303, 330**

Paint and varnish, *58*, *78*, *85*, 86 n., **298, 333, 335**
Paper and board, *58*, 77, *78*, 82, *88*, **309, 333, 338**
Paper bags, *56*, 75, *76*, *95*, **309, 331**
Pens, pencils, crayons, *56*, *76*, *93*, **311, 330, 339**
Photographic and cinematograph apparatus, *55*, *76*, 77, *95*, **303, 330**
Photographic plates and films, *52*, 68, *69*, *90*, 127, 136, 140–1, 143, **303, 329, 337**
Pickles, sauces, relishes, **308, 338**
Plastic goods, *58*, *80*, *95*, **311, 332**
Plastics materials, *55*, *72*, *88*, **297, 331**
Polishes and canvas dressings, *55*, *76*, *95*, *152*, *155–9*, *168*, 170, 180, 189, 265–9, **298, 331, 335, 340**
Pre-cast concrete goods, *59*, *80*, *93*, **296, 332**
Precious metals refining, *52*, *69*, *85*, 86 n., 134–6, 150 n., **303, 329, 337**
Preserved fruit and vegetables, *58*, *78*, 79, *90*, **308, 333**
Preserved meat, *55*, *74*, 75, *93*, **308, 330**
Primary batteries, *52*, *69*, *88*, 134, 136, 140–3, **301, 330**
Prime movers, stationary: internal combustion, *53*, *69*, 82, *88*, 133–4, **299, 329**
Printing and bookbinding machinery, *57*, *80*, *95*, 149 n., **300, 332, 336**
Printing and publishing, bookbinding, engraving, etc., *59*, *78*, 79, *88*, **310, 333, 338**
Proofed garments, *59*, *80*, *93*, **306, 332**
Pumps and pumping machinery, **300, 336**

Radio apparatus and gramophone, *57*, 77, *78*, 82, *88*, **300, 333, 336**

Railway carriages and wagons, *58*, *79*, 81, *92*, **301**, **332**, **336**
Rayon, nylon, etc. and silk, C.F. yarn and staple fibre, *53*, *70*, 71, 82, *93*, 126, 133–6, **305**, **329**, **337**
Razors (excl. electric), *52*, *69*, *90*, 125, 136, 140, *152*, *155–9*, 167, *168*, 179, 182, 184, 191, *196*, 198–203, **302**, **329**, **337**, **340**
Refractory goods, *57*, *80*, *92*, **296**, **332**, **335**
Refrigerating machinery, *55*, *76*, *95*, **300**, **330**, **336**
Retail tailoring and dressmaking, *59*, *80*, *93*, **306**, **332**
Rigid boxes, *59*, *80*, *95*, **309**, **332**
Roofing felts, *55*, *74*, *93*, **296**, **330**, **335**
Roofing tiles of clay, *56*, 75, *76*, *93*, **296**, **330**
Rope, twine and net, **305**, **337**
Rubber, *152*, 153 n., *159*, **310**, **339–40**
Rubber tyres and tubes, *53*, *70*, 71, 82, *95*, 125, 134, 136, 138, 140, 143, **310**, **329**, **339**

Safes, locks, latches, *56*, 75, *76*, *95*, **302**, **330**, **337**
Salt mines, etc., *52*, *70*, *93*, 117, 134, 141, 149 n., **296**, **329**, **335**
Sanitary earthenware, *56*, *74*, *93*, **297**, **330**, **335**
Sanitary ware, clay, *58*, *79*, *93*, *152*, *155–9*, *168*, 169, **296**, **331**, **335**, **340**
Sausages, 149 n., **308**, **338**
Saw mill products, *60*, *78*, *85*, **310**, **333**, **339**
Scales and weighing machinery, *52*, *69*, *85*, 86, 122, 136, 141, **300**, **329**, **336**
Scientific, engineering, industrial instruments, *57*, *78*, 79, *90*, **303**, **333**
Scientific, surgical and photographic instruments, **303**, **337**
Scrap metal processing, *56*, *72*, *85*, **303**, **331**
Seed crushing and oil refining, *53*, *69*, *88*, 128, 134–5, 137–8, **298**, **329**, **335**
Shipbuilding and ship repairing, *58*, 77, *78*, 82, *88*, 149 n., **299**, **333**, **336**
Shirts and underwear, men's and boys', *59*, *79*, *93*, **306**, **331**
Shop and office fittings, *58*, *78*, *85*, 86 n., **310**, **333**
Slate quarries and mines, *54*, *74*, 75, *95*, *152*, *155–9*, *168*, 170, **296**, **330**, **335**, **340**
Small arms, *53*, *69*, *90*, 134, 149 n., **300**, **329**, **336**
Soap and glycerine, *53*, *70*, *90*, 122, 134–5, 137–8, 140–1, 143, *152*, *155–9*, *168*, 170, 184, 191, *196*, 259–64, **298**, **330**, **335**, **340**
Soap, candles and glycerine, 149 n., **298**, **335**
Soft drinks, British wines and cider, **309**, **338**
Soft drinks, including fruit juices, *58*, *78*, *85*, 86, **309**, **333**, **338**
Spirit distilling, *52*, *70*, *85*, 86, 121, 135, 137, 139–40, **309**, **330**, **338**
Spirit rectifying and compounding, *53*, *70*, *93*, 122, 137, 139, 140, *152*, *155–9*, *168*, **309**, **329**, **338**, **340**
Sports requisites, *57*, *80*, *95*, *152*, *155–9*, *168*, 170, 179, 191, **311**, **332**, **339**, **340**
Springs, other than laminated, *58*, *80*, *95*, 149 n., **302**, **332**, **337**
Starch, *53*, *70*, *95*, 127, 134–6, **308**, **329**
Steel drop forgings, *56*, 75, *76*, *95*, **302**, **330**
Steel sheets, *55*, *74*, 75, *93*, **299**, **390**
Stereotyping, electrotyping, engraving, etc., **310**, **339**
Stone, *59*, *78*, 84, *85*, **296**, **333**
Sugar and glucose, *52*, *69*, 82, *88*, 121, 133–6, 139, 143, *152*, *155–9*, *168*, 170, 183–4, 189, *196*, 243–7, **307**, **330**, **338**, **340**
Sugar confectionery, *59*, *80*, *95*, **308**, **332**, **338**

Tailored garments, making-up, *59*, *78*, *88*, **307**, **333**
Tailoring, dressmaking, etc., **306**, **338**
Tea blending, *55*, *72*, *90*, **308**, **331**
Telegraph and telephone apparatus, **301**, **336**

Textile finishing, *152*, *155–9*, *168*, 170, 179, **305**, **337**, **340**
Textile machinery and accessories, 54, *56*, *72*, 73, 82, *88*, **299**, **331**, **336**
Textile packing, *55*, 75, *76*, *93*, *152*, *155–9*, *168*, 169, **305**, **330**, **337**, **340**
Timber, **310**, **339**
Tin, *53*, *70*, *95*, 120, 132, **299**, **329**, **336**
Tinplate, *53*, *70*, *92*, 123, 133–4, 136, 138–9, 143, *152*, *155–9*, 167, *168*, 179, 181, 187, 191, 196, 233–40, **299**, **329**, **335**, **340**
Tobacco, *53*, *70*, 71, 82, *88*, 118, 134, 139–40, 142–3, 150 n., **309**, **330**, **338**
Toilet preparations and perfumery, *56*, 75, *76*, *95*, *152*, *155–9*, *168*, 179–80, 184, 191, **298**, **331**, **335**, **340**
Tool and implement, **302**, **337**
Toys and games, *56*, *72*, 73, *90*, **311**, **331**, **339**
Tramway, trolley-bus and omnibus undertakings (civil engineering), *53*, *70*, *95*, 134, 139, **312**, **329**
Transmission chains, *52*, 68, *69*, *90*, 119, 134, 136, **300**, **329**

Umbrella and walking stick, *59*, *79*, *93*, 150 n., **307**, **331**, **338**

Valves and cathode ray tubes, *52*, *70*, *93*, 128, 133–4, 136, 142, **301**, **329**
Vinegar and other condiments, *52*, *70*, *95*, 132, **308**, **329**

Wallpaper, *52*, 68, *69*, *85*, 86, 117, 132, 134–5, 141–3, *152*, *155–9*, *168*, 169, 191, *265*, 269–73, **309**, **329**, **338**, **340**
Watch and clock, *55*, *72*, *90*, *152*, 153 n., *159*, 180–1, 184–5, 188, 191, *196*, 208–13, **303**, **331**, **337**, **340**
Wholesale bottling, **309**, **338**
Wholesale dressmade garments tailoring, *59*, *80*, *93*, **306**, **332**
men's and boys', *58*, 77, *78*, 82, *88*, **306**, **333**
women's and girls', *59*, *78*, *90*, **306**, **333**
Wines and spirits, wholesale bottling, *52*, *70*, *88*, 137, **309**, **330**
Wire and wire manufactures, *58*, *78*, 79, *85*, **303**, **333**, **337**
Wooden boxes, packing cases, *60*, *79*, *93*, **310**, **331**
Woollen and worsted, **304**, **337**
Woollen yarns, *58*, *79*, *93*, **304**, **331**
Worsted yarns, *58*, 77, *78*, *85*, **304**, **333**
Woven cloth, rayon, nylon, etc., 149 n., **305**, **337**
Woven cotton cloth, *60*, *80*, *92*, **304**, **332**, **337**
Woven cotton, rayon, nylon fabrics
bleaching, **305**, **337**
dyeing, *57*, *80*, *92*, **305**, **332**, **337**
printing, *55*, *72*, *85*, 86, 86 n., **305**, **331**, **337**
Woven woollen fabrics, *59*, *80*, *93*, **304**, **332**
Woven woollen and worsted fabrics—finishing, *57*, *80*, *95*, **305**, **332**, **337**
Woven worsted fabrics, *58*, *78*, *85*, **304**, **333**
Writing paper, **309**, **338**
Wrought iron and steel tubes, *52*, *70*, 71, 82, *88*, 123, 134, 138, *152*, *155–9*, *168*, 170, 182, 188, *196*, 247–53, **299**, **330**, **335**, **340**

Zinc, *52*, *70*, *90*, 120, **299**, **329**, **336**

For EU product safety concerns, contact us at Calle de José Abascal, 56–1°,
28003 Madrid, Spain or eugpsr@cambridge.org.

www.ingramcontent.com/pod-product-compliance
Ingram Content Group UK Ltd.
Pitfield, Milton Keynes, MK11 3LW, UK
UKHW012159180425
457623UK00018B/278

* 9 7 8 1 1 0 7 6 0 1 3 4 5 *